THE ROUGH GUIDE TO

Mallorca & Menorca

written and researched by

Phil Lee
DRECERA

with additional contributions by

Patrick Alexander and Roger Norum

ROUGH GUIDES

roughguides.com

Contents

INTRODUCTION   4

Where to go	6	Itineraries	18
Things not to miss	12		

BASICS   20

Getting there	21	Festivals	32
Getting around	23	Sports and outdoor activities	33
Accommodation	25	Shopping	35
Food and drink	28	Travel essentials	36
The media	31		

THE GUIDE   42

1 Palma and around	42	4 Southern Mallorca	154
2 Western Mallorca	86	5 Menorca	190
3 Northern Mallorca	122		

CONTEXTS   240

History	241	Language	271
Flora and fauna	259	Glossary	280
Books	267		

SMALL PRINT & INDEX   282

OPPOSITE CIUTADELLA, MENORCA **PREVIOUS PAGE** FORNALUTX, MALLORCA

Introduction to
Mallorca & Menorca

Mallorca "presents to the delighted eye a charming blend of savage wilderness and fertile cultivation. In no part of the world can one behold a more complete picture gallery of all the varieties of natural scenery", wrote Captain Clayton as he explored the island in the 1860s. Very few English-speaking travellers ventured to Mallorca and Menorca in the nineteenth century, but those who did were suitably impressed by the beauty of the landscape if not by the islanders themselves, who were generally disparaged as disagreeable and unruly. The same conflicting attitudes survive today: millions of tourists count Menorca and Mallorca as a favourite holiday destination, though surprisingly few know much about the islanders. In fact, this easterly section of the Balearic archipelago, which also includes Ibiza and Formentera, has a rich cultural history and many of its inhabitants still live in the most charming of country towns – Petra, Sineu and Ciutadella to name but three – well away from the teeming resorts of the coast.

The islands' image embraces extreme ends of the spectrum: on one level, **Mallorca** is a popular haunt of the rich and famous; on the other it has an unenviable reputation for tacky tourism built on sun, sex, booze and high-rise hotels. The truth is that Mallorca manages to be both at the same time: at 5pm you can be carousing with the Brits in Magaluf and half an hour later you can be sipping a coffee in a quiet mountain village. The good news is that the ugly development of the 1960s, which submerged tracts of coastline beneath hotels, villas and apartment blocks, is constrained to the Bay of Palma and a handful of mega-resorts notching the east coast, and for the most part Mallorca remains handsome and frequently fascinating, from the craggy mountains and medieval monasteries of its north coast to the antique towns of the central plain.

ABOVE OLIVE GROVE NEAR VALLDEMOSSA; BOUGAINVILLEA, DEIÀ; TAPAS

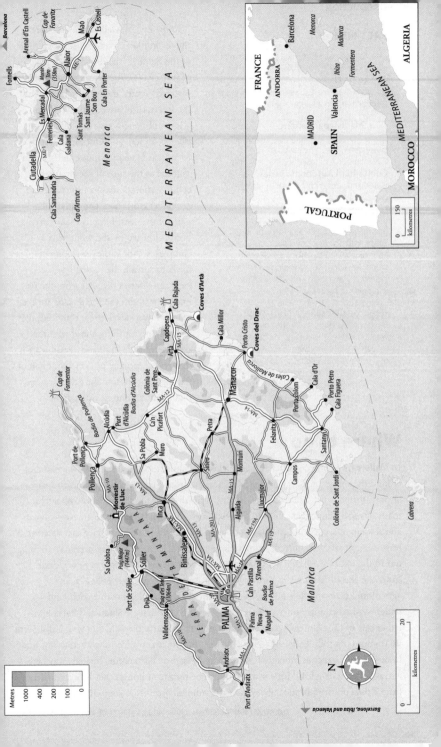

FACT FILE

• The Balearic islands have a **population** of just under 1,200,000, of which about a fifth are ex-pats. Of these 24,000 are British, with an average age of 46.6 years, and 37,000 are German with an average age of 48.

• The **Spanish parliament** – the Cortes Generales – sits in Madrid, but many of its powers have been devolved to 17 autonomous regions, one of which – the **Comunidad Autónoma de las Islas Baleares** – covers the Balearics, whose capital is Palma.

• The mountains of Mallorca are home to the islands' ornithological star turn, the rare **black vulture** (Aegypius monachus), a dark and solitary bird of striking proportions, standing 130cm tall, weighing anywhere between 7 and 14kg and with an adult wingspan of nearly 3m.

• Spain is a **Catholic** country, though only 15 percent of its population attends Mass every week. The decline in religious observance is reflected in the shortage of monks and nuns, and the fact that several of Mallorca's monasteries have been deconsecrated and turned into inexpensive lodgings (see p.26).

To the east of Mallorca lies **Menorca**, the second-largest and most agricultural of the Balearic islands, with a population of just 70,000. Menorca's rolling fields, wooded ravines and humpy hills fill out the interior in between its two main – but still small – towns of **Maó**, the island's capital, and **Ciutadella**. Much of Menorca's landscape looks pretty much as it did at the turn of the twentieth century, though many of the fields are no longer cultivated, and only along parts of the coast have its rocky coves been colonized by sprawling villa complexes. Nor is the development likely to spread: the resorts have been kept at a discreet distance from the two main towns and the Menorcans are keen to avoid over-development. Indeed, they are currently pushing ahead with the creation of a chain of conservation areas that will eventually protect about half of the island, including the pristine coves that count among its real delights.

Where to go

In **Mallorca**, the obvious place to begin a visit is **Palma**, the island capital, which arches around the shores of its bay just a few kilometres from Mallorca's busy international airport. Palma is the Balearics' one real city, a bustling, historic place whose oligarchic mansions and magnificent Gothic cathedral serve as a fine backdrop to an excellent café and restaurant scene. Add to this lots of good hotels and you've got a city that deserves at least a couple of days. Indeed, many visitors spend their entire holiday here, day-tripping out to the rest of the island – an easy proposition as it's only a couple of hours' drive from one end of Mallorca to the other. To the east of Palma stretches **Es Pla**, an agricultural plain that fills out the centre of the island, sprinkled with ancient and seldom-visited country towns, the most interesting of which are **Sineu** and **Petra**. On either side of the plain are coastal mountains. To the north, the wild and wonderful **Serra de Tramuntana** rolls along the entire coastline, punctuated by deep sheltered valleys and beautiful cove **beaches**, notably Cala Deià and Platja de Formentor. Tucked away here also is **Sóller**, a delightful little town of old stone merchant houses that is best reached from Palma on the antique **railway**, an extraordinarily scenic journey. The mountains

also hide a string of picturesque villages, most memorably **Estellencs**, **Banyalbufar**, **Deià**, the long-time haunt of Robert Graves, and **Fornalutx**, as well as a pair of intriguing monasteries at **Valldemossa**, where Chopin and George Sand famously wintered, and **Lluc**, home to a much-venerated statue of the Madonna. The range is also crisscrossed with footpaths and makes for ideal **hiking**, particularly in the cooler spring and autumn. Beyond Lluc, the mountains roll down to a coastal plain that holds the lovely little town of **Pollença** and one of the island's most appealing medium-sized resorts, **Port de Pollença**, which is itself just along the bay from the sprawling but well-kept resort of **Port d'Alcúdia**. In the north, Mallorca finishes with a final scenic flourish in the rearing cliffs of the **Península de Formentor**.

Mallorca's second mountain range, the gentler, greener **Serres de Llevant** shadows the coves of the east coast and culminates in the pine-clad headlands and medieval hill towns of the island's northeast corner. Many of the east coast resorts are overblown, but the pick are **Cala Rajada**, close to several fine beaches, and **Porto Petro**. There are also a couple of easily visited cave systems – the most diverting is the **Coves del Drac** – and the comely hilltop town of **Artà**, close to the substantial prehistoric remains of **Ses Paisses**.

Smaller, flatter **Menorca**, the most easterly of the Balearics, boasts two attractive towns, the island capital of **Maó**, just 5km from the airport, and **Ciutadella**, 45km to the west. Both towns have preserved much of their eighteenth- and early nineteenth-century appearance, though Ciutadella has the aesthetic edge, the many lanes and alleys of its ancient centre shadowed by fine old mansions and monasteries. Linking the two, the island's only main road, the **Me-1**, slips across the rural interior, passing the pleasant

BINIARAIX

Author picks

Our authors have made countless trips to Mallorca and Menorca over the years, but there are some things they like to do, or places they just have to visit, every time they return. Here's a selection of their favourites.

Prettiest villages Both Menorca and Mallorca are threaded with pretty villages, but three of the best are Estellencs (see p.117), where the tourist presence is noticeably thin, Biniaraix (see p.98), the trailhead for some dramatic mountain walks, and Orient (see p.100), a place so quiet that you can hear the softest of bird calls.

Mallorcan Primitives Not Primitive Mallorcans, but rather a school of medieval artists, who produced many exquisite devotional paintings on display in Palma at the cathedral (see p.50) and at the Museu Diocesà (see p.55).

Mountain roads Not for the faint-hearted, or the poor-of-steering, some of Mallorca's mountain roads offer superb views: try the hairpins of the Castell d'Alaró (see p.102) and the lane up to the Ermita de Nostra Senyora del Puig (see p.135) for starters.

Great hikes Both Mallorca and Menorca offer the adventurous hiker some wonderful experiences: the circular hike from Valldemossa on the Archduke's Path is a particular favourite (see p.114) as is the hike from Es Grau to Sa Torreta on Menorca (see p.216).

Our author recommendations don't end here. We've flagged up our favourite places – a perfectly sited hotel, an atmospheric café, a special restaurant – throughout the guide, highlighted with the ★ symbol.

FABULOUS FINCAS

The Balearics are dotted with old stone **fincas** (or farmhouses), many of which have been turned into holiday homes and hotels. The largest – for example *La Granja* (see p.112) and *Raixa* (see p.100) – are effectively rural palaces that have become tourist attractions in their own right, but the bulk offer lodgings, mostly at the top end of the market. Prime examples include *Ca's Xorc* (see p.94) in the mountains near Sóller; *Can Llenaire* (see p.140) still part of a working farm and with panoramic coastal views; *Es Castell* (see p.132), a wonderful hotel in the foothills of the Serra de Tramuntana; and the *Biniarroca Hotel*, near Sant Lluís in Menorca (see p.213). The charm of staying in a *finca* lies at least in part in the solidity and simplicity of its architectural form: a stone or stone-and-rubble exterior, a flagged exterior courtyard, shuttered and grilled rectangular windows, and high, wood-beamed ceilings. It's also usual to find *fincas* surrounded by a raft of specialist agricultural buildings, from olive presses and workshops through to barns and store houses.

ABOVE *BINIAROCCA HOTEL*, MENORCA **OPPOSITE** CALA TURQUETA

market towns of **Es Migjorn Gran**, **Es Mercadal** and **Ferreries**. A series of side roads branch off to the island's **resorts**, the best appointed of which are **Cala Galdana** and the one-time fishing village of **Fornells**, as well as a string of wind-battered headlands and remote **cove beaches**. The highway also squeezes past **Monte Toro**, Menorca's highest peak and the site of a quaint little convent, with superlative island-wide views. Menorca's other claim to fame is its smattering of prehistoric remains – two of the most important being **Talatí de Dalt**, outside Maó, and the **Naveta d'es Tudons**, near Ciutadella.

BEST BALEARIC BEACHES

MALLORCA

Cala Deià Crystal-clear waters and a narrow pebbly beach in a hoop-shaped cove at the end of a lovely wooded gulch. Great setting; great beach bar-restaurant. See p.105

Cala Tuent Not much sand here – it's all shingle and pebble – but the mountain setting is a delight and the beach is rarely crowded. See p.128

Es Trenc Whichever way you cut it, most of Mallorca's beaches are crowded, but not this one – a long sandy strand on the south coast. See p.188

Platja de Palma Roast and pose amongst the muscle-flexing, oiled pecs and abs. See p.84

Port d'Alcúdia A long and immaculately maintained stretch of golden sand on the north coast. See p.149

Port de Pollença A bucket-and-spade family affair, with safe bathing and sandcastle building. See p.138

MENORCA

Cala Macarella A real treat, the cove's band of white sand is flanked and framed by handsome limestone cliffs. See p.227

Cala Pregonda It takes a good deal of effort to get here, but the reward is a wide slice of sand in a beguiling setting. See p.219

Cala Turqueta Exquisite and beautiful beach, comprising a handsome horseshoe of white sand set beneath limestone cliffs. See p.238

Platja de Cavalleria A slender arc of pristine sand is framed by grassy dunes at this delightful north coast beach. See p.219

things not to miss

It's not possible to see everything that Mallorca and Menorca have to offer in one trip – and we don't suggest you try. What follows is a selective taste of the islands' highlights: gorgeous beaches and magnificent scenery, quaint towns and great places to eat and drink. Each entry has a page reference to take you straight into the Guide, where you can find out more. Coloured numbers refer to chapters in the Guide.

1 PALMA–SÓLLER TRAIN

Page 91

Take a trip on the vintage train that wends its way over the mountains from Palma to Sóller providing wonderful views and serving as a fine introduction to Mallorca's dramatic landscapes.

2 HIKING IN THE SERRA DE TRAMUNTANA

Page 90

Rolling along the west coast, this rugged mountain range holds scores of exhilarating hiking trails.

3 MONESTIR DE LLUC

Page 129

This rambling monastery holds the Balearics' most venerated icon, La Moreneta, and is also a great base for mountain hikes.

4 VALLDEMOSSA

Pages 108–112

Sitting pretty in the hills, the ancient town of Valldemossa is home to a fascinating monastery whose echoing cloisters and shadowy cells once accommodated Chopin and George Sand.

5 PENÍNSULA DE FORMENTOR

Page 142

The knobbly peaks and sheer cliffs of this spectacular peninsula backdrop one of Mallorca's best beaches and ritziest hotels.

6 TALATÍ DE DALT
Page 202

In an attractive rural setting close to Maó, this extensive site is one of the most satisfying of Menorca's many prehistoric remains.

7 SANTUARI DE SANT SALVADOR, ARTÀ
Page 167

The sun-bleached roofs of small-town Artà clamber up the steepest of hills to this shrine, one of Mallorca's most important, with the prehistoric village of Ses Païsses close at hand.

8 THE MALLORCAN PRIMITIVES
Pages 50, 55 & 59

A medieval school of painters who produced strikingly naive devotional works – Joan Desi being one of its most talented practitioners.

9 DEIÀ
Pages 103–107

No wonder Robert Graves made his home in the coastal village of Deià – an enchanting huddle of old stone buildings set against a handsome mountain backdrop.

10 CABRERA
Page 188

Now a national park, this austere, scrub-covered islet is home to a battered hilltop castle, a wealth of birdlife – and the rare Lilford's wall lizard.

11 CIUTADELLA
Pages 228–237

The prettiest town on Menorca, the island's former capital sits alongside a narrow inlet, its network of cobbled lanes flanked by handsome mansions.

12 SÓLLER
Pages 91–95

In a handsome mountain setting, Sóller is an appealing country town of old stone mansions surrounded by orange and lemon groves.

13 PALMA CATHEDRAL
Pages 47–51

Dominating the waterfront, the monumental bulk of Palma's magnificent cathedral offers one of Spain's finest examples of the Gothic style, its interior flooded with kaleidoscopic shafts of light.

14 CAP DE FAVÀRITX
Page 216

This windswept cape, with its bare, lunar-like rocks, is a scenic highlight of Menorca's north coast.

15 MAÓ
Pages 196–205

Menorca's modest capital has an amiable small-town feel, its tiny centre graced by old stone houses occupied by laid-back cafés and old-fashioned shops.

16 EATING IN PALMA
Pages 73–75

Try the islanders' favourite nibble – a spiralled flaky pastry known as an *ensaimada* – at one of Palma's string of delightful cafés and patisseries.

17 JARDINS D'ALFÀBIA
Page 99

The lush, oasis-like Jardins d'Alfàbia are the finest gardens on Mallorca, their watered trellises and terraces dating back to the Moors.

Itineraries

Mallorca and Menorca's attractions are myriad – our itineraries guide you round Mallorca's must-see sights and Menorca's unique prehistoric remains.

GRAND TOUR OF MALLORCA

Spend a few days in Palma before threading your way along the island's invigorating, surf-battered coast, via quiet villages and wondrous scenery.

❶ **Palma** Allow three days to explore the capital's ancient nooks and crannies and enjoy its first-rate cafés and restaurants. **See pp.44–78**

❷ **Estellencs** Some people say this is the island's prettiest village, a huddle of ancient

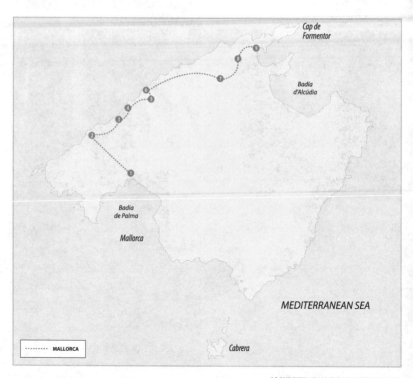

ABOVE ESTELLENCS; THE MONASTERY AT LLUC

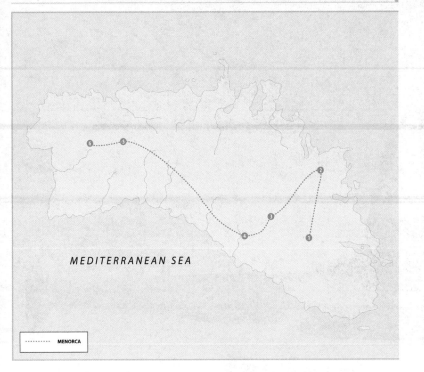

houses clinging gingerly to steep, sea-facing slopes. **See p.117**

❸ **Valldemossa** A hilltop town with the island's most fascinating monastery, where Chopin spent an unforgiving winter. **See p.108**

❹ **Deià** Between mountain and sea, chi-chi Deià has a scattering of old stone houses perched high above the ocean. **See p.103**

❺ **Sóller** Wandering the narrow cobbled streets of this beguiling town gives you the full flavour of traditional island life. **See p.91**

❻ **Port de Sóller** Arced around a horseshoe-shaped bay, this recently upgraded resort has a superb selection of restaurants. **See p.95**

❼ **Lluc** The monks may have gone, but the monastery and its shrine remains, making it one of the island's key sights . **See p.129**

❽ **Pollença** A cosy town with a low-key feel in the prettiest of settings. **See p.132**

❾ **Port de Pollença** Safe bathing and a long sandy beach are the key to this resort's popularity with families. **See p.138**

TAULAS AND TALAYOTS: A TOUR OF MENORCA'S PREHISTORY

Menorca is strewn with prehistoric remains from the Talayotic period, which is named after the distinctive conical rock mounds – *talayots*. They are often found next to T-shaped *taulas* of around 4m high.

❶ **Talatí de Dalt** This delightful prehistoric site features a *taula*, a large *talayot* – and a tribe of free-range hogs. **See p.202**

❷ **Sa Torreta** A remote prehistoric settlement in a fine location. **See p.217**

❸ **Torralba d'en Salord** A rural setting and one of the best-preserved *taulas* on the island makes this a worthwhile diversion. **See p.221**

❹ **Torre d'en Gaumés** One of the largest prehistoric settlements on the island, with three *talayots*, a *taula* and the remains of a water collection system. **See p.221**

❺ **Torrellafuda** A well-preserved *talayot* in a lovely, rustic setting. **See p.227**

❻ **Naveta d'es Tudons** The island's most intact *naveta*, or stone ossuary. **See p.227**

HIKING IN THE SERRA DE TRAMUNTANA

Basics

21 Getting there
23 Getting around
25 Accommodation
28 Food and drink
31 The media
32 Festivals
33 Sports and outdoor activities
35 Shopping
36 Travel essentials

Getting there

Literally hundreds of flights shuttle back and forth between Britain and Ireland and Mallorca and Menorca during the summer season, and although the pace slackens in winter, there is still a wide choice of flights to Mallorca, if somewhat fewer to Menorca. Visitors from North America, Australasia and South Africa, on the other hand, will need to fly to a European hub airport, such as London, Madrid or Barcelona, before catching an onward flight to the islands. It's also possible to reach Mallorca and Menorca by ferry and catamaran from Spain's east coast, but obviously this takes much longer.

Flights from the UK

Mallorca and Menorca are readily reached from London and a veritable raft of regional airports **in the UK**. **Flying times** are a little over 2hr (2hr 45min from Manchester). Fierce competition tends to keep **fares** way down on flights from London to Palma, but from regional airports fares are more variable. If you strike lucky, a return fare can cost as little as £100, though £220 is more normal, whereas a standard, fully flexible return can cost up to £500.

Flights from Ireland

There is a good range of flights **from Ireland** to both islands during the summer, but out of season you may have to travel via London, Madrid or Barcelona. The **flying time** from Dublin direct to either island is just under 3hr. **Prices** are highest in August – reckon on around £200 return from Belfast, €400 from Dublin – but drop a little in the months either side.

Flights from the USA

There are no direct nonstop flights **from the USA** to

Mallorca or Menorca, but there are direct nonstop flights from several US cities to Madrid and Barcelona, from where it's a short and easy hop to either island. Often, it's cheaper to travel to London (or an alternative hub city) and pick up an onward flight from there. As sample **fares**, a return, nonstop flight from New York to Barcelona with Delta (ⓦdelta.com) costs upwards of US$1200, US$1400 from Atlanta to Madrid; from here there are regular flights on to the islands (see p.22). The **flying time** on a direct, nonstop service from New York to Madrid is just over 7hr.

Flights from Canada

There are no nonstop/direct flights **from Canada** to Mallorca and Menorca. However, you can fly from several of Canada's major cities using a combination of airlines and travelling via another European capital, from where you can pick up an onward flight to the islands. **Fares** from Toronto to a European hub city go for around Can$1100, Can$1400 from Vancouver. The **flying time** from Toronto to Madrid is 7hr 30min.

Flights from Australia and New Zealand

There are no nonstop/direct flights to Spain **from Australia and New Zealand**, and you'll need to change planes once or twice to reach Madrid or Barcelona, from where there are regular flights on to Mallorca and Menorca. For **flying times**, count on 24hr via Asia or 30hr via the USA, not including time spent on stopovers. **Fares** from Sydney or Melbourne to Madrid or Barcelona are around A$1800–2500, NZ$2500–3000 from Christchurch or Wellington. Another option is to pick up a cheap ticket to London, and then continue your journey to Mallorca or Menorca with a no-frills budget airline.

Flights from South Africa

There are no direct/nonstop flights to Spain **from South Africa** – you have to fly to a European hub

---

A BETTER KIND OF TRAVEL

At Rough Guides we are passionately committed to travel. We believe it helps us understand the world we live in and the people we share it with – and of course tourism is vital to many developing economies. But the scale of modern tourism has also damaged some places irreparably, and climate change is accelerated by most forms of transport, especially flying. All Rough Guides' flights are carbon-offset, and every year we donate money to a variety of environmental charities.

to catch an onward plane to Mallorca or Menorca. As for **fares**, flights from Cape Town to a European hub cost around ZAR8600; from Johannesburg, ZAR7300. The **flying time** on a direct, nonstop flight from South Africa to London is just over 11hr.

Flights from mainland Spain

Menorca and more especially Mallorca are easily reached **by plane from mainland Spain** with regular scheduled flights departing for the islands from a number of Spanish cities, including Valencia, Barcelona and Madrid. Journey times are minimal (Barcelona to Palma takes just 40min) and **ticket prices** modest, starting out at just €130 for the one-way flight from either Barcelona or Madrid to Palma: the principal carrier is Iberia (ⓦ iberia.com).

Flights between the Balearic islands

Three of the **Balearic islands** have international airports – Ibiza, Mallorca and Menorca – and there are frequent inter-island **flights**, though flights linking Ibiza and Menorca are often routed via Mallorca. There's usually no problem with seat availability, but you need to book ahead during the height of the season and on public holidays. The main carrier is **Iberia** (ⓦ iberia.com), which operates between six and eight inter-island flights daily: one-way **fares** between any of the islands start at €90. The **flying time** between Ibiza and Mallorca as well as Mallorca and Menorca is 40min.

By train from the UK

It takes between 13hr and 18hr **by train from London** to reach Barcelona, from where there are regular ferries to Palma and Maó (see below). A standard London-to-Barcelona return costs from £300. For through ticketing, contact **Rail Europe** (ⓦ raileurope.co.uk).

By car and ferry from the UK

If you intend to travel to either Mallorca or Menorca **by car and ferry from the UK**, you'll need lots of time – a couple of days, maybe more. The quickest route is across the Channel via **Eurotunnel** (ⓦ eurotunnel.com), followed by the long drive across France and Spain to one of the ferry ports that serve the Balearics (see below). To save driving time – if not overall journey time – you could also take a car ferry direct from the UK to Spain. There are three main options: Plymouth or Portsmouth to Santander, and Portsmouth to Bilbao. All are operated by **Brittany Ferries** (ⓦ brittany-ferries.co.uk).

Ferries and catamarans from mainland Spain

Three companies – Acciona Trasmediterranea, Iscomar and Balearia (see below) – operate a network of **car ferry and catamaran services from three main ports** on the Spanish mainland (Valencia, Denia and Barcelona) to two ports on Mallorca (Palma and Port d'Alcúdia) and two ports on Menorca (Maó and Ciutadella). All three ferry companies apply a complex fare structure depending on the time of year, length of stay, accommodation on board and any accompanying vehicle. That said, fares are roughly the same no matter which mainland port you depart from and which island you sail to: for example, a Balearia passenger **ticket** (without a cabin) from Barcelona to Maó or Palma starts at €40 on a car ferry and €50 on a catamaran; cars up to 2m cost from €140; and return tickets cost about twice as much as a single.

As regards **sailing times**, a regular car ferry takes 8hr to get from Barcelona to Palma, just over half that on a catamaran; and 30min or so less for Maó. Most services run all year, others have a winter break (usually Jan–March).

In all cases, **advance booking** is recommended and is well-nigh essential if you're taking a vehicle or need a cabin. **Tickets** can be purchased at the port of embarkation or in advance by phone and online.

FERRY AND CATAMARAN CONTACTS

Acciona Trasmediterranea ☏ 902 45 46 45, ⓦ trasmediterranea.es
Balearia ☏ 902 16 01 80, ⓦ balearia.com
Iscomar ☏ 902 11 91 28, ⓦ iscomar.com

Ferries and catamarans between the Balearic islands

The same three companies – Acciona Trasmediterranea, Iscomar and Balearia (see above) – also operate **inter-island car ferries and catamarans**. There are frequent sailings between Mallorca and Menorca and Mallorca and Ibiza, but vessels linking Menorca and Ibiza are usually routed via Mallorca. Once again, **fares** are complicated, with a one-way passenger ticket on a car ferry from Port d'Alcúdia to Ciutadella with Iscomar costing from around €50: cars up to 2m in length cost a further €80. **Journey times** are manageable: Ibiza to Palma is 4hr by car ferry, half that by catamaran; Maó to Palma 6hr, 3hr 30min by catamaran; and Port d'Alcúdia to Ciutadella just 1hr by catamaran. Most services run all year, others have a winter break (usually Jan–March).

BALEARIC AGENTS AND TOUR OPERATORS

Balearic Discovery ☎ 971 87 53 95, ⓦ balearicdiscovery.com.
Friendly and efficient, this Mallorca-based company offers tailor-made trips and holidays both on and off the usual tourist trail. The owners know the island like the back of their hands and have some superb *fincas* to rent.

Mallorcan Walking Tours (MWT) Port de Pollença, Mallorca ☎ 609 70 08 26, ⓦ mallorcanwalkingtours.puertopollensa.com.
Small, excellent, island-based company operating an outstanding range of hikes (see p.138).

Nature Trek UK ☎ 01962 733 051, ⓦ naturetrek.co.uk.
Wildlife/natural world specialist offering 8-day birdwatching tours of both islands.

North South Travel UK ☎ 01245 608 291, ⓦ northsouthtravel.co.uk. Friendly, competitive travel agency, offering discounted fares worldwide. Profits are used to support projects in the developing world, especially the promotion of sustainable tourism.

Tramuntana Tours c/Sa Lluna 72, Sóller ☎ 971 63 24 23, ⓦ tramuntanatours.com. Small but highly recommended company offering guided walks and an extensive programme of adventurous activities (see p.94).

Getting around

On both Mallorca and Menorca public transport is good. There's a reliable bus network between all the major settlements, a multitude of taxis, a plethora of car rental firms, plenty of bicycles to rent, plus a couple of useful train lines on Mallorca. Distances are small and consequently the costs of petrol and fares are low: on Mallorca, for example, it's only 60km from Palma on the south coast to Alcúdia on the north shore, while Menorca has only one major road across the island, a distance of just 45km. Hopping from one island to the other is easy and economical too, as there are regular and inexpensive inter-island flights and ferries (see p.22) – though it's advisable to book ahead in July and August.

By bus

Both Menorca and Mallorca have an extensive network of reliable **bus services** linking the main towns – Palma, Maó and Ciutadella – with most of the villages and resorts of the coast and interior, though in winter (Nov–April) and on Sundays and holidays buses to most resorts are scaled back, and in Menorca some resorts have no services at all. These main bus routes are supplemented by more intermittent local services. **Ticket prices** are very reasonable: the one-way fare from Palma to Port de Sóller, for instance, is just €3, from Maó to Ciutadella €5. In addition, Palma has its own public transport system, with buses linking the centre with the suburbs and surrounding beach resorts (see p.71) – as do most of the larger resorts, with either bus or electric mini-train.

On all island bus services, **destinations** are marked on the front of the bus. Passengers enter at the front and buy tickets from the driver, though you can also buy tickets in advance at a bus station. **Bus stops** are clearly marked in bright yellow and red colours. A confusing variety of **bus companies** operate the various routes on Mallorca, but their efforts are coordinated by **Transports de les Illes Balears**; on Menorca, the co-ordinating authority is **Transportes Menorca** (TMSA). Island-wide **timetables** are available at major bus stations and most tourist offices carry local timetables.

BUS CONTACTS

Palma EMT buses ☎ 971 21 44 44, ⓦ emtpalma.es
Mallorca buses ☎ 971 17 77 77, ⓦ tib.org
Menorca buses ☎ 971 36 04 75, ⓦ tmsa.es

By train

Mallorca has its own, narrow-gauge **train network**. One line, which has vintage rolling stock and is especially popular with tourists, travels through magnificent mountain scenery from Palma to Sóller (see p.91); the second, a modern line geared up for local use, shuttles across the flatlands of the interior, travelling from Palma to Binissalem and Inca, where the line forks, with one branch nudging south to Sineu, Petra and Manacor, the other pushing on to Muro and Sa Pobla. At the time of writing, work is also underway to extend the line from Sa Pobla to Alcúdia. Both lines have their terminus train stations adjoining Plaça Espanya in Palma (see p.70). The **return fare** from Palma to Sóller on the vintage line is €19.50, €12.50 one-way, whereas fares on the more modern line are trifling – it's just €4, for instance, from Palma to Inca. The stations on the modern line also serve as starting points for buses to the surrounding towns and villages.

RAIL CONTACTS

Mallorcan trains (Inca line) ☎ 971 17 77 77, ⊛ tib.org
Mallorcan trains (Sóller line) ☎ 902 36 47 11, ⊛ trendesoller .com

By car

Getting around by public transport is easy enough, but you'll obviously have more freedom if you have **your own vehicle** – most of the more secluded beaches are, for example, only accessible under your own steam. Major and minor roads are very good on both islands, but country byroads are variable, ranging from middling dirt-and-gravel tracks to the most precarious of dirt trails, which are particularly lethal after rain. Traffic is generally well behaved, but noisy, especially in Palma, where the horn is used as a recreational tool as well as an instrument of warning. **Fuel** (*gasolina*) comes in three main grades. Different companies use different brand names, but generally *Super Plus* is 98-octane fuel, selling at about €1.60 per litre, and *Super* is 95-octane, selling at about €1.50 per litre; both are without lead (*sense plom/sin plomo*). Diesel (*gasoleo* or *gasoil*) costs about €1.40 per litre. Both Menorca and Mallorca are well supplied with petrol stations; a few are open 24 hours a day, seven days a week, though most close around 9pm or 10pm and on public holidays.

Most foreign **driving licences** are honoured in Spain, including all EU, US, Australasian and Canadian ones. If you're bringing **your own car**, you must have adequate insurance, preferably including coverage for legal costs, and it's advisable to have an appropriate **breakdown policy** from your home motoring organization too.

Some rules of the road

Speed limits are posted throughout the Balearics: the maximum on main urban roads is 50kph, on other roads 90kph or 100kph, on motorways 120kph. Speed traps are fairly frequent and if you're stopped for any violation, the Spanish police can (and usually will) levy a stiff on-the-spot fine of up to €1500 before letting you go on your way. Most **driving rules and regulations** are pretty standard: seat belts are compulsory; "Stop" signs mean exactly that; drink-driving will land you in big trouble; and you yield to traffic coming from the right at all junctions, whether or not there's a "give way" sign. A

Addresses are usually abbreviated to a standard format. For example, "c/Bellver 7" translates as Bellver Street (*carrer*) no. 7; and "Plaça Rosari 5, 2è" means the second floor at Plaça Rosari no. 5 (Plaça means square). "Passeig d'es Born 15, 1–C" means suite C, first floor, at no. 15; and "s/n" (*sense número*) indicates a building without a street number. In Franco's day, most avenues and boulevards were named after Fascist heroes and, although nearly all were relabelled years ago, there's still some confusion in remoter spots. Another source of bafflement can be house numbers: some houses carry more than one number (the by-product of half-hearted reorganizations), and on many streets the sequence is impossible to fathom.

single, unbroken white line in the middle of the road means no overtaking, even if the rule is frequently ignored, and note that drivers often sound their horns when overtaking. On major trunk roads, turnings that take vehicles across oncoming traffic are being phased out and replaced by semicircular minor exits that lead round to traffic lights on the near side of the major road.

Finally, drivers do not have to stop (and often don't) at **zebra crossings** unless they are attached to traffic lights. On their own, zebra crossings merely indicate a suitable pedestrian crossing place; if you stop at a crossing, as you might do in Britain, the pedestrians will be amazed and someone may well crash into your rear end.

Car rental

On both islands, there are scores of companies offering **car rental** (still rendered in Castilian as *coches de alquiler*) and their offices throng the islands' resorts, larger towns and airports. All the major international players have outlets, and there are also dozens of small companies. Comprehensive lists of car rental companies are normally available from the islands' tourist offices.

To **rent a car**, you must be 21 or over (and have been driving for at least a year), and you'll probably need a credit card – though some places will accept a hefty deposit in cash and some smaller companies simply ignore all the normal regulations altogether. However, no car rental firm will allow you to transport their vehicles **from one Balearic island to another**. If you're planning to spend much time driving on rougher tracks, you'll be better off with a **four-wheel drive** (about thirty percent more expensive than the average car and available from larger rental agencies).

Rental charges vary enormously: out-of-season costs for a standard car can fall to as little as €20 per day with unlimited mileage; in July and August, by comparison, the same basic vehicle could set you back €80 a day if not more – though weekly prices are usually less expensive. Shopping around is really worthwhile – Affordable Car Hire (ⓦaffordable carhire.com) is a good place to start, with reasonable rates. That said, **local rental firms** often give the best deals, though you should always check the policy for the excess applied to claims, and ensure that it includes CDW (collision damage waiver) and adequate levels of financial cover. Finally – and this is really annoying – many car rental companies charge you for the full tank of petrol that is in your car when you collect it (€90 or so) – whether it is used or not: legend has it that disgruntled tourists now drive round and round the airport until all the fuel is consumed.

Taxis

The excellence of the islands' bus and train services means it's rarely necessary to take a **taxi**, though they are a convenient way of getting back to your hotel after a day's hiking, in which case you should fix a collection point before you set out – there's no point wandering round a tiny village hoping a taxi will show up. Throughout the Balearics, the taxis of each town and resort area have their own livery: Palma taxis, for example, are black with a cream-coloured roof and bonnet. Local journeys are metered, though there are supplementary charges for each piece of luggage and for travel at night and on Sundays. For **longer journeys** there are official prices, which should be displayed at the airport and at some taxi stands. Naturally, you're well advised to check the price with the driver *before* you get going. **Fares** are reasonable, but not inexpensive: the journey from the airport to downtown Palma, a distance of around 11km, will cost you in the region of €20, while the fare from Sóller to Pollença is €80.

Cycling

Cycling can be an enjoyable way of exploring the islands, though the quiet(er) roads of Menorca are more suitable for easy family outings than the busier roads of Mallorca. Menorca is also a good deal flatter, which means the going is much easier – though ardent cyclists may prefer the mountain challenges of Mallorca. The Spanish are keen cycling fans, and many of the roads are signed for cyclists, even though bicycle lanes per se are rare. However, drivers are not necessarily obliging on the roads and neither is information readily forthcoming – local tourist offices rarely have much in the way of route information.

For **route planning**, check ⓦbikemap.net, while for Mallorca the best **bike map** is *Bike Mallorca*, which is clearly marked with colour-coded cycle routes and inclueds a list of major bike shops too: you can order it from Amazon. Bear in mind that cyclists are not permitted into the Sóller tunnel at the end of the Palma–Sóller road. Bicycles are transported free on the Palma–Inca train line and either free or at minimal cost on ferries from the mainland (and between the Balearic islands); you can't, however, take bikes on the Palma–Sóller train and, although some buses allow cycles, most do not.

Renting a bike costs from about €8 to €14 a day for an ordinary bike, about thirty percent more for a mountain bike. Renting is straightforward: there are dozens of suppliers (usually several at every resort) and tourist offices can provide a list or advise you of the nearest outlet.

Accommodation

Package-tour operators have a virtual stranglehold on thousands of hotel and hostal rooms, villas and apartments in both Mallorca and Menorca. Nevertheless, there is sufficient slack in the system to allow independent travellers a good selection of accommodation for most of the year, though things can get tight from June to September – when advance reservations are strongly advised. Outside peak season, it's often worth bargaining over room prices – though note that closure in winter is commonplace in Menorca and frequent in Mallorca. Most hoteliers speak or read at least a modicum of English, so you can usually book over the internet or by phone, but in either case a confirmatory email is always a good idea.

Many hotels and *hostales* have rooms at different **prices**, and tend to offer the more expensive ones first. Some places also have rooms with three or four beds at not much more than the price of a double room, though people travelling alone invariably end up paying over the odds.

TOP 5 HOSTALES – CHARMING AND INEXPENSIVE

Bellavista Port de Pollença. See p.140
Catalina Vera Port d'Andratx. See p.120
Miramar Deià. See p.106
Playa Colònia de Sant Jordi. See p.187
S'Engolidor Menorca. See p.223

In **Mallorca** the easiest place to get a last-minute room is Palma, with Sóller and Pollença not far behind, though you might also consider staying at one of the island's former monasteries (see below), where there's nearly always a vacancy and prices are very low. In **Menorca**, accommodation is thinner on the ground, with only Maó, Ciutadella and maybe Fornells likely to have high-season vacancies.

Hostales and hotels

Traditionally, Balearic accommodation has been divided into five categories – **fondas**, **casas de huéspedes**, **pensions**, **hostales and hotels**. Today, however, the first three categories, which were the least expensive, have almost completely disappeared and you are left with *hostales* and hotels. **Hostales** are categorized with one to three stars, and many offer good, functional, en-suite rooms, mostly with showers and not baths. Some *hostales* are designated **hostal-residencias**, again categorized from one- to three- star. The *residencia* designation means that no meals other than breakfast are served, but that does not mean that all *hostales* without the *residencia* tag serve anything more than breakfast. No matter the star classification, **prices** at this end of the market start at around €80 for a double room.

Hotels are also graded by stars, ranging from no stars to five stars, though the distinction between hotels and *hostales* is often rather blurred. One- and no-star hotels cost no more than three-star *hostales*

(sometimes less), but three-star hotels cost a lot more, and at four or five stars you're in the luxury class with prices to match. There are also a handful of **hotel-residencias**, where the only meal provided is breakfast, and an increasing number of (un-starred) **hotels d'interior**, mostly bijou family-run hotels away from the coast (hence "interior"). On average, a double room in a two-star hotel should cost in the region of €80–100.

It's safe to assume that bedrooms will be of a decent standard in all the higher categories, but amongst the budget rooms you'd be advised to ask to see the room before you part with any money: standards vary greatly (even between rooms in the same place) and it does no harm to check that there's hot water if there's supposed to be, or that you're not stuck at the back in an airless box.

By law, each establishment must **display its room rates**, and there should be a card on the room door showing the prices for the various seasons. If you think you're being overcharged, complain there and then.

Monasteries

Mallorca's monasteries have run out of monks, so five of them now let out empty cells to visitors of both sexes (see box below). All occupy delightful settings in the hills or on hilltops, and the majority are dotted across the interior of the island. At all five, you can just turn up and ask for a room, but it's

ACCOMMODATION SIGNAGE

In theory at least, every place offering accommodation in the Balearics has to carry a **square blue sign** on the outside, inscribed with its category and number of stars. These are as follows:

F	*fonda*
CH	*casa de huéspedes*
P	*pensió*
H̩	*hostal*
H̩R	*hostal-residencia*
H	*hotel*

MALLORCA'S MONASTERY ACCOMMODATION

Ermita de la Victòria near Alcúdia. See p.147
Ermita de Nostra Senyora de Bonany near Petra. See p.163
Ermita de Nostra Senyora del Puig outside Pollença. See p.136
Monestir de Lluc. See p.131
Santuari de Nostra Senyora de Cura on Puig Randa. See p.165
Santuari de Sant Salvador near Felanitx. See p.180

ACCOMMODATION PRICES

Throughout the Guide, the price quoted in each accommodation review is the lowest **rate** you're likely to pay for a double or twin room in high season (usually June to Sept). Single rooms, where available, usually cost between 60 and 80 percent of a double or twin. At Mallorca's hikers' hostels, we give the price of a dormitory bed (few have doubles) and at campsites, the cost of a tent pitch including two people plus a car, unless otherwise stated.

a better idea to phone ahead or get the local tourist office to make a reservation on your behalf. A double room at the more rough-and-ready monasteries costs around €20 per night, rising to €60–70 at Sant Salvador and Cura; easily the most popular monastery is Lluc. Reasonably priced **food** is usually available, but check arrangements when you book. In the same vein, the *Hostatgeria Castell d'Alaró* provides simple accommodation within the walls of a **hilltop fortress** near Alaró (see box below), while the former **monastic lodgings** above the Ermita de la Victòria (see box opposite) have been turned into a small budget hotel.

Mallorca's mountain refuges

Mallorca's principal long-distance hiking route is the **Ruta de Pedra en Sec** (Dry-stone Route), the **GR221** (see p.34), which threads its way across the Serra de Tramuntana mountains. It begins in Sant Elm and passes through Sóller before continuing onto Pollença. To assist hikers, Mallorca's governing council is in the process of constructing **six refugis** (hikers' hostels) on the GR221. Four are finished and in use (see box below), one, the *Pont Roma* in Pollença (see p.135), is closed for repairs until 2013, and one is still being built at La Trapa, near Sant Elm (see p.119). Each of these hikers' hostels offers simple but adequate lodgings in dormitory-style rooms with bunk beds and shared bathrooms. The **charge** is just €11 per person per night, with breakfast €4.50, a two-course lunch €10.50, and a main meal at dinner €8; picnic lunches are also available (€6.50). Advance reservations are required a minimum of five days and a maximum of two months beforehand either direct with the hostel

concerned or on the website ⓦwww.consellde mallorca.net. The private sector, however, are unhappy about these government-subsidized hostels and their future ownership has become a political hot potato.

Agrotourism and fincas

Old stone **fincas** (farmhouses) are a prominent part of the Balearic landscape. Some have been converted into holiday homes and are leased out to package-tour operators, while others can be booked direct or through the government agency responsible for developing rural tourism, the **Associació Agroturisme Balear** (ⓣ971 72 15 08, ⓦagroturismo-balear.com). They are not, however, cheap: prices range from €80 to €200 per person per night, and a minimum length of stay of anything between two nights and two weeks is often stipulated (see box, p.10).

Camping

Menorca has two **official campsites**: the well-appointed *Son Bou* (see p.222) and the plainer but very pleasant *S'Atalaia* (see p.227), near the resort of Cala Galdana. The *Son Bou* can accommodate about four hundred campers, the *S'Atalaia* just one hundred – and both take tents, trailer caravans and motor caravans. Although neither has a seashore

MALLORCA'S MOUNTAIN REFUGES

Can Boi Deià. See p.106
Hostatgeria Castell d'Alaró. See p.102
Muleta Port de Sóller. See p.97
Son Amer near Lluc. See p.131
Tossals Verds east of the Embassament de Cúber. See p.128

TOP 10 PLACES TO STAY

Biniarroca Hotel Menorca. See p.213
Hotel Born Palma. See p.72
Hotel Ca's Xorc near Sóller. See p.94
Hotel Dalt Murada Palma. See p.72
Es Castell Binibona. See p.132
Fornalutx Petit Hotel. See p.99
Hotel Nord Estellencs. See p.118
Hotel Rural Binigaus Vell Menorca. See p.225
Hotel Rural Morvedrà Nou Menorca. See p.236
Hotel Rural Son Palou Orient. See p.100

location, they're both very popular, and in the summer it's best to make a reservation well ahead of time. Prices and specific details of each site are given in the relevant chapters. There are currently no recommendable campsites on **Mallorca**.

Camping rough is legal, but not encouraged, and has various restrictions attached: you're not allowed to camp in urban areas, military zones, parks and tourist resorts. Neither are you allowed to camp on beaches – though there is some latitude if you're discreet – and if you want to camp out in the countryside you'll need to ask locally and/or get permission from the landowner.

Food and drink

Traditional Balearic food, which has much in common with Catalan food, is far from delicate, but its hearty soups and stews, seafood dishes and spiced meats can be delicious. In common with other areas of Spain, this regional cuisine has, after many years of neglect, experienced something of a renaissance, and nowadays restaurants offering Cuina Mallorquína (and to a lesser extent Cuina Menorquína) are comparatively commonplace and should not be missed. Neither should a visit to one of the islands' many pastry shops (pastisserias or pastelerias), where you'll find the tastiest of confections and the Balearics' gastronomic pride and joy – the ensaimada (a spiralled flaky pastry).

While scores of touristy restaurants dish up bland and overpriced pizza, burgers and pasta, or sanitized versions of local favourites, there are still plenty of places where the food is more distinctive and flavoursome. **Fresh fish and seafood** can be excellent, though it's almost always expensive, partly because much of it is imported – despite the best efforts of the local fishing industry. Nevertheless, you're able to get hake, cod (often salted) and squid at very reasonable prices, while fish stews and soups are often truly memorable, as is the *caldereta de llagosta*, a Menorcan lobster stew. **Meat** can be outstanding too, usually either grilled and served with a few fried potatoes or salad, or – like ham – cured or dried and served as a starter or in sandwiches. Veal is common, served in large stews, while poultry is often mixed with seafood (chicken and prawns) or fruit (chicken/duck with prunes/pears).

Vegetables rarely amount to more than a few chips or boiled potatoes with the main dish, though there are some splendid vegetable concoctions to watch out for, such as *tumbet*, a pepper, potato, pumpkin and aubergine stew with tomato purée. It's usual to start a full lunch or evening meal with a salad, either a standard green or mixed affair, or one of the islands' own salad mixtures, which come garnished with various vegetables, meats and cheeses. **Dessert** is often fruit, ice cream or *flam*, the local version of *crème caramel*, though the pricier places have all sorts of fancier concoctions.

Opening hours vary considerably. As a general rule cafés open from around 9am until at least early in the evening, and many remain open till late at night. Restaurants open from around noon until sometime between 2pm and 4pm, before reopening in the evening from around 7/8pm until 10/11pm. Those restaurants with their eye on the tourist trade often stay open all day and can be relied upon on Sundays, when many local spots close.

There are lots of **websites** recommending island restaurants, but the pick of the lot (for Mallorca) is ⓦmallorca-restaurants-121.com. There is a **menu reader** and a list of popular **Balearic dishes** in Contexts (see p.278).

Breakfast and snacks

The less expensive hotels and *hostales* usually serve a basic **continental breakfast** and only at the pricier places is there much more on offer. Consequently, it's often less expensive and more enjoyable to eat out at a local café or café-bar. A traditional Balearic breakfast (or lunch) dish is *pa amb tomàquet* (*pan con tomate* in Castilian) – a massive slice of bread rubbed with tomato, olive oil and garlic, which you can also have topped with ham – washed down with a flagon of wine. *Pa amb oli* (bread rubbed with olive oil) arrives in similar style, but dispenses with the tomato. If that sounds like gastronomic madness, other breakfast standbys include *torradas* (*tostadas*; toasted rolls) with oil or butter and jam, and *xocolata amb xurros* (*chocolate con churros*) – long, fried tubular doughnuts that you dip into thick drinking chocolate. Most places also serve *ou ferrat* (*huevo frito*; fried egg) and cold *truita* (*tortilla*; omelette).

Coffee, bread rolls and **pastries** (*pastas*), particularly croissants and doughnuts, are available at some bars and cafés, but for a wider selection, head for a *pastisseria* (pastry shop) or *forn* (bakery). Some bars specialize in **sandwiches** (*bocadillos*), usually outsize affairs in French bread served either hot or cold, or you can get them prepared – or buy the materials to do so – at grocery shops. Menorcan cheese (*formatge*), commonly known as *queso Mahón*, is a popular filling – the best is hard and has a rind.

Tapas and racions

Traditionally, **tapas** are small snacks of three or four chunks of fish, meat or vegetables, cooked in a sauce or served with a dollop of salad. In many cafés and café-bars, tapas are lined up along the counter, so you can see what's available and order by pointing without necessarily knowing the names; other places have blackboards. The confusion is that many places (including restaurants) sell tapas that are in effect full (regular) meals with prices to match. "Proper" tapas should cost about €5, €10 at the most. Other variations of tapas are **racions** (*raciones* in Castilian), which are bigger portions of the same, and **pinxtos**, which are smaller versions.

Full meals

Full meals are usually eaten in a **café or restaurant**, though the distinction between the two is often blurred, the main difference being the price: a main course at a restaurant costs in the region of €20–25, a third less in the average café. Many restaurants and cafés have a daily set menu for about €20 – the lunchtime **menú del día** is often a really good deal, comprising two, three or four courses, including bread and a third- to a half-litre of wine per person. The other thing to take account of is **IVA**, a sales tax of ten percent, which is either included in the prices (in which case it should say so on the menu) or added to your bill at the end.

Vegetarians and vegans

Palma has a couple of **vegetarian** restaurants and most of the resorts are accustomed to having vegetarian guests, but elsewhere the choice isn't so great and is essentially confined to large salads, fried eggs and chips or omelettes. If you eat fish, however, you'll find seafood almost everywhere.

If you're a **vegan**, you'll no doubt come prepared to cook your own food at least some of the time. That said, some restaurant salads and vegetable dishes are vegan – like *espinacs a la Catalana* (spinach, pine nuts and raisins) and *escalivada* (aubergine/eggplant and peppers) – but they're

---

I'M A VEGETARIAN

If you're a **vegetarian**, try in Catalan "Sóc vegetarià/ana – es pot menjar alguna cosa sense carn?" (I'm a vegetarian – is there anything without meat?). In Castilian, that's "Soy vegetariano/a – hay algo sin carne?" Alternatively, you may be better understood if you simply resort to the Catalan "No puc menjar carn" (I can't eat meat).

---

few and far between. Fruit and nuts are widely available, and most pizza restaurants will serve you a vegetarian pizza without cheese: ask for *vegetal sense formatge* (in Castilian, *vegetal sin queso*).

Drinking and drinks

As you might expect, **bars** and **café-bars** are legion in both Mallorca and Menorca. Bars situated in old wine cellars are sometimes called *cellers* or *tavernas*, while a *bodega* traditionally specializes in wine. **Opening hours** vary, but you should have little trouble getting a drink in Palma between noon and 2am or even 3am, and until at least 11pm, sometimes midnight, elsewhere. Nightclubs tend to close by 3am or 4am, while some bars close on Sundays; don't expect much to be open in the resorts out of season.

Wine

Wine (*vi* in Catalan, *vino* in Castilian) is the invariable accompaniment to every meal and remains, as a general rule, inexpensive whether it be red (*negre/ tinto*), white (*blanc/blanco*) or rosé (*rosada/rosado*). The thing to check for on a bottle of Spanish wine is either of the top two appellations, **Denominació d'Origen** or **Denominació d'Origen Qualificada**, as this indicates it has passed muster with the industry's national watchdog. More than seventy regions of Spain currently carry DO status, including two on Mallorca – Pla i Llevant and Binissalem. Overall, Mallorca has 35 vineyards, producing around two million bottles annually, and a selection is available at most good cafés and restaurants on Mallorca and to a lesser extent on Menorca.

Spain's **sparkling wines** are big sellers too, their popularity built on the performance of two producers, Freixenet and Codorniú, which hail from a small area west of Barcelona. Local grape varieties are used and the best examples, known as **cava**, are made by the same double-fermentation process as is used in the production of champagne. For a comprehensive introduction to the wines of Spain, consult ⓦwinesfromspain.com.

Mallorcan wine

The Balearics became a major **wine producer** in classical times, but it was the Moors who finessed the sweet "Malvasia" wine – akin to Madeira – that was long one of the islands' main exports. This all ended in the late nineteenth century when the islands' vineyards were devastated by **phylloxera**, which arrived in Spain from North America in 1878, and within twenty years had destroyed Spain's existing vine stock and made thousands bankrupt. Indeed, vine cultivation has never re-established itself on Ibiza or Menorca, and Mallorcan wines, produced from newly imported vines, were long regarded as being of only average quality.

During the late 1980s, however, a concerted effort was made to raise the standard of Mallorcan wine-making, with new methods, new equipment and investment, especially in and around **Binissalem** (see p.159). The results were encouraging and in 1991 Binissalem was awarded its Denominació d'Origen. It remains Mallorca's leading wine, but its success has inspired others and in 2000 a second Denominació d'Origen was granted, **Pla i Llevant**, covering the central and eastern part of the island from Algaida to Felanitx.

Widely available throughout Mallorca, **red Binissalem** is a robust and aromatic wine made predominantly of the local mantonegro grape. It is not unlike Rioja, but it has a distinctly local character, suggesting cocoa and strawberries. The biggest producer of the wine is **Franja Roja**, who make the **José Ferrer** brand, with prices starting at

---

TOP 10 MALLORCAN WINES

James Hiscock, of the *Es Castell* hotel (see p.132, has selected his ten top tipples.

RED WINES

Aia Miquel Oliver, Petra. Merlot. Full and fruity, complex, potent aroma with hints of toast from fine woods and fruity, earthy tones. Guide price €15.

Son Negre Anima Negre, Felanitx. In the late 1990s this special wine was given 94/100 by the Parker Wine Guide and achieved international recognition. Made with 95 percent Callet grapes, it's described by Parker as having "a compelling nose of oak, minerals, Asian spices, lavender, black cherry and black raspberry." It's very expensive, at a guide price of €150.

Pedra José Luis Ferrer, Binissalem (Organic). Ferrer is the biggest wine producer on the island and Pedra is its first foray into organic wines. A mixture of Mantonegro and Cabernet Sauvignon, it's a deep violet red, with balsamic and ripe fruit notes, plus smooth, long and lingering fragrances. Guide price €8.50.

Añada Macia Batle, Santa Maria. A young wine, like a Beaujolais. With some tannins, it has a freshness on the palate, with gentle tones to keep drinking till the small hours. Works well chilled, and eaten with barbecued meat. Guide price €5.

L'Ú, Mortix. From the heights of the Serra Nord mountains comes the treasure that is L'Ú. This is a wine with a deep first taste, friendly, smooth, but strong on the palate. Drink it with roast meats, game, fish or chicken. Guide price €28.

WHITES AND ROSÉ

Novell Pere Seda, Manacor. A great value-for-money white wine: crisp, medium dry, clean citrus fruit aromas, with floral hints. Deceptively drinkable when chilled, and well priced. Guide price €3.50.

Moli de Vent Blanc Jaume Mesquida, Porreres. A very dry, light "Sauvignon-blanc-y" white, with Doradillo, Martorell and Chardonnay grapes, perfect for white fish. Guide price €7.50.

Son Prim Merlot Blanc Peach in colour, with real "body", the white wine for those who normally drink red. Good with veal and seafood. Guide price €11.

Ecologic Rosé Binigrau (Organic). Made with organically grown Mantonegro and Merlot grapes from some of the region's oldest vines. Perhaps in common with many organic wines from Mallorca, "when it's good, it's very very good…". A bright, cherry-coloured wine with fruit aromas, full and ripe. Drink with suckling pig. Guide price €10.

Butibalausi Rosado Can Majoral, Algaida (Organic). Named after the Christianization of a Moorish hamlet near Algaida, this rosé has intense red fruit aromas and is crisp on the palate, with a rich and persistent ending. Great for paellas Guide price €7.50.

around €8 per bottle, or €15 for the superior varieties; you can also visit their Binissalem winery (see p.160). Names to look out for with the white wines of the Pla i Llevant designation lead off with the white wines of **Miquel Oliver** from around Petra. Also around the island are various country wineries making inexpensive and unpretentious wine predominantly for local consumption. The best places to sample these local, coarser wines is in the **cellers** and bars of the country towns of the interior – and the best of them carry the label **Vin de la Terra**.

Spirits and sherry

When ordering **spirits** in the Balearics, you'll usually get an international brand unless you specify otherwise – ask for *nacional* if you want the cheaper Spanish varieties: Larios **gin** from Málaga, for instance, is about half the price of Gordons, but around two-thirds the strength and a good deal rougher. Gin is also made in Menorca: the Menorcans learnt the art of gin-making from the British and still produce their own versions, in particular the waspish **Xoriguer**. **Sherry** – *vino de Jerez* – is the classic Andalucian fortified wine, served chilled or at room temperature. The main distinctions are between *fino* or *jerez seco* (dry sherry), *amontillado* (medium), and *oloroso* or *jerez dulce* (sweet).

In mid-afternoon – or even at breakfast – many islanders take a *copa* of **liqueur** with their coffee. The best – certainly to put *in* your coffee – is **coñac**, excellent Spanish brandy, mostly from the south and often deceptively smooth. If you want a brandy from Mallorca, try the mellow but hard-hitting Suau.

Almost any **mixed drink** seems to be known as a *Cuba libre* or *cubata*, though strictly speaking this only refers to rum and Coke. For mixers, ask for orange juice (*suc de taronja* in Catalan), lemon (*llimona*) or tonic (*tònica*).

Beer

Pilsner-type beer, **cervesa** (more usually seen in Castilian as *cerveza*), is generally pretty good, though more expensive than wine. The two main brands you'll see everywhere are San Miguel and Estrella. Beer generally comes in 300ml bottles or, slightly cheaper, on tap: a small glass of draught beer is a *cana*, a larger glass a *cana gran*. Equally refreshing, though often deceptively strong, is **sangría**, a wine-and-fruit punch, which you'll come across at *festas* and in tourist resorts.

Soft drinks

Soft drinks are much the same as anywhere in the world, but one local favourite to try is *orxata*

(*horchata* in Castilian) – a cold milky drink made from tiger nuts. Also, be sure to try a *granissat*, or iced fruit-squash; popular flavours are *granissat de llimona* or *granissat de café*. You can get these from **orxaterias and gelaterias** (ice cream parlours; *heladerías* in Castilian).

Although you can drink the **water** almost everywhere, bottled water – *aigua mineral* – is ubiquitous, either sparkling (*amb gas*) or still (*sense gas*).

Coffee and tea

Coffee is invariably espresso, slightly bitter and, unless you specify otherwise, served black (*café sol*). A slightly weaker large black coffee is called a *café americano*. If you want it white ask for *café cortado* (small cup with a drop of milk) or *café amb llet* (*café con leche* in Castilian) made with hot milk. For a large cup ask for a *gran*. Black coffee is also frequently mixed with brandy, cognac or whisky, all such concoctions termed *carajillo*; a liqueur mixed with white coffee is a *trifásico*. **Decaffeinated coffee** (*descafeinat*) is increasingly available, though in fairly undistinguished sachet form.

Tea (*te*) comes without milk unless you ask for it, and is often weak and insipid. If you do ask for milk, chances are it'll be hot and UHT, so your tea isn't going to taste much like the real thing. Better are the infusions that you can get in some bars, such as mint (*menta*), camomile (*camamilla*) and lime (*tiller*).

The media

English-language newspapers and magazines are widely available in both Mallorca and Menorca, and most hotel (if not hostal) rooms have satellite TV.

Newspapers and magazines

British and other European **newspapers**, as well as the *International Herald Tribune*, are widely available in the resort areas and larger towns of Mallorca and Menorca. These are supplemented by a hotchpotch of locally produced English papers and journals, easily the most informative of which is the enjoyably chatty **Majorca Daily Bulletin**. The online edition is available at ⓦ majorcadailybulletin.es.

Spain is awash with glossy **magazines**, both native to the country and Spanish versions of international periodicals. And, of course, Spain is the home of *Hola* – the original of the UK's glossy gossip mag, *Hello*.

Television and radio

Spaniards love their **television**, and consequently you'll catch more of it than you might expect sitting in bars and cafés. On the whole it's hardly riveting, the bulk being a mildly entertaining mixture of kitsch game shows and foreign-language films and TV series dubbed into Spanish. **Soaps** are a particular speciality, either South American *culebrones* ("serpents" – they go on and on) or well-travelled British or Australian exports, like *EastEnders* (*Gent del Barri*). **Sports fans** are well catered for, with regular live coverage of football (soccer) matches. The number of TV stations is increasing all the time, but the main national channels are operated by TVE. Most Balearic hotel rooms have satellite TV, which gives access to some or all of the international channels – CNN and so forth.

Frequencies and schedules for the BBC World Service (**W** bbc.co.uk/worldservice), Radio Canada (**W** rcinet.ca) and Voice of America (**W** voanews.com) are listed on their respective websites.

Festivals

Every town and village in Mallorca and Menorca takes at least one day off a year to devote to a festival. Usually it's the local saint's day, but there are also celebrations for the harvest, deliverance from the Moors, of safe return from the sea – any excuse will do. Each festival is different, with a particular local emphasis, but there is always music, dancing, traditional costume and an immense spirit of enjoyment. The main event of most festas is a parade, either behind a revered holy image or a more celebratory affair with fancy costumes and gigantones, giant carnival figures that rumble down the streets to the delight, or terror, of children. Whilst festas take place throughout the year, Easter Holy Week (Setmana Santa) stands out, its passing celebrated in many places with elaborate processions.

JANUARY

Revetla de Sant Antoni Abat (Eve of St Antony's Day) 16 Jan. Celebrated by the lighting of bonfires (*foguerons*) in Palma and several of Mallorca's villages, especially Sa Pobla and Muro. In these two villages, the inhabitants move from fire to fire, dancing around in fancy dress and

eating *espinagades*, traditional eel-and-vegetable patties. Also takes place in Sant Lluís on Menorca.

Beneides de Sant Antoni (Blessing of St Antony) 17 Jan. St Antony's feast day is marked by processions in many of Mallorca's country towns, notably Sa Pobla and Artà, with farmyard animals herded through the streets to receive the saint's blessing.

Processó d'els Tres Tocs (Procession of the Three Knocks) 17 Jan. Held in Ciutadella, Menorca, this procession commemorates the victory of Alfonso III over the Muslims here on January 17, 1287. There's a mass in the cathedral first and then three horsemen lead the way to the old city walls, where the eldest of the trio knocks three times with his flagstaff at the exact spot the Catalans first breached the walls.

Revetla de Sant Sebastià (Eve of St Sebastian's Day) 19 Jan. Palma has bonfires, singing and dancing for St Sebastian.

Festa de Sant Sebastià 20 Jan. This feast day of medieval origin is celebrated in Pollença with a procession led by a holy banner (*estenard*) picturing the saint. It's accompanied by *cavallets* (literally "merry-go-rounds"), two young dancers each wearing a cardboard horse and imitating the animal's walk. You'll see *cavallets* at many of the island's festivals.

FEBRUARY

Carnaval Towns and villages throughout the islands live it up during the week before Lent with marches and fancy dress parades. The biggest and liveliest is in Palma, where the shindig is known as *Sa Rua* (the Cavalcade).

MARCH/APRIL

Setmana Santa (Holy Week). On **Maundy Thursday**, a much-venerated icon of the crucified Christ, *La Sang*, is taken from the eponymous church on the Plaça del Hospital (off Passeig de la Rambla) in Palma and paraded through the city streets. There are also solemn **Good Friday** (*Divendres Sant*) processions in many towns and villages, with the more important taking place in Palma and Sineu. Most holy of all, however, is the Good Friday **Davallament** (The Lowering), the culmination of Holy Week in Pollença. Here, in total silence and by torchlight, the inhabitants lower a figure of Christ down from the hilltop Oratori to the church of Nostra Senyora dels Àngels.

During Holy Week there are also many **romerias** (pilgrimages) to the island's holy places, with one of the most popular being the climb up to the Ermita Santa Magdalena, near Inca. The Monestir de Lluc, home to Mallorca's most venerated shrine, is another focus, with the penitential trudging round its Camí dels Misteris del Rosari (The Way of the Mysteries of the Rosary).

In Menorca's Ciutadella, there's also the **Matança dels bruixots** (the Slaughter of the Wizards), in which puppets representing well-known personalities are hung in the streets.

MAY

Festa de la Verge del Toro (The Festival of the Virgin of the Bull) 8 May. The day of the patron saint of Menorca begins with a special mass at the hilltop shrine of Monte Toro and continues with a shindig down in the little town of Es Mercadal.

Sa Fira i Es Firó Mid-May. In Port de Sóller and Sóller. This knees-up features mock battles between Christians and infidels in commemoration of the thrashing of a band of Arab pirates in 1561. Lots of booze and firing of antique rifles into the air.

JUNE

Corpus Christi Early to mid-June. At noon in the main square of Pollença an ancient and curious dance of uncertain provenance takes place – the *Ball de les Àguiles* (Dance of the Eagles) – followed by a religious procession.

Festa de Sant Joan 23–25 June. This midsummer festival has been celebrated in Ciutadella since the fourteenth century. There are jousting competitions, folk music, dancing and processions following a special mass held in the cathedral on the 24th. Another highlight is on the Sunday before the 24th, when the *S'Homo d'es Bé* (the Man of the Lamb) leads a party of horsemen through the town. Clad in animal skins and carrying a lamb in honour of St John the Baptist, he invites everyone to the forthcoming celebration.

JULY

Día de Virgen de Carmen 15–16 July. The day of the patron saint of seafarers and fishermen is celebrated in many coastal settlements – principally Palma, Maó, Port de Sóller, Colònia de Sant Pere, Porto Colom and Cala Rajada – with parades and the blessing of boats.

Festa de Sant Martí Third Sun. The feast day of St Martin is celebrated in Es Mercadal, Menorca, with a popular religious procession followed by dancing and all sorts of fun and games.

Festa de Sant Jaume Last Sunday. This festival in Alcúdia and Menorca's Es Castell celebrates the feast day of St James with a popular religious procession followed by folk dances, fireworks and the like.

AUGUST

Mare de Déu dels Àngels 2 Aug. Moors and Christians battle it out again, this time in Pollença.

Festa de Sant Llorenç Second weekend. High jinks on horseback through the streets of Alaior, Menorca.

Cavallet 20 Aug. Dances in Felanitx (see p.179).

Festa de Sant Bartomeu Last week. Three days of festivities in Ferreries, Menorca.

SEPTEMBER

Festa de la Mare de Déu de Gràcia 7–9 Sept. This three-day festival in Maó celebrates the Virgin of Grace, the city's patron saint, and begins with a pilgrimage to the chapel of the Virgin. Thereafter, there are processions and parades along with horseback games.

Nativitat de Nostra Senyora (Nativity of the Virgin) Second week. In Alaró, honouring the Virgin with a pilgrimage to a hilltop shrine near the Castell d'Alaró.

OCTOBER

Festa d'es Butifarra (Sausage Festival) Third Sun. Of recent origin, this festival follows on from tractor and automobile contests held in the village of Sant Joan. It features folk dancing and traditional music as well as the eating of specially prepared vegetable pies (*coca amb trampó*) and sausages (*berenada de butifarra*).

DECEMBER

Nadal (Christmas). Christmas is especially picturesque in Palma and Ciutadella, where there are Nativity plays in the days leading up to the 25th.

Sports and outdoor activities

During the day at least, tourist life on Mallorca and Menorca is centred on the beach. There are long and generous strands at several of the major resorts – for instance Port d'Alcúdia, Port de Pollença, S'Arenal and Son Bou – and several dozen smaller cove beaches. At all the larger resorts, a veritable army of companies offer equipment for hire for a wide range of beach sports and activities, from sailing and pedalo pedalling through to jet skiing, water boarding, windsurfing and scuba diving, not to mention sandcastle-building competitions. For best beaches see box, p.11.

Away from the coast, **cycling** (see p.25) is a popular pastime as is **horseriding**, with a clutch of stables and many kilometres of bridle path. The most popular riding areas on Mallorca are the low hills of the Serres de Llevant in the east and the foothills of the Serra de Tramuntana, whilst Menorca's stables are mostly inland close to the (one) main road. For a list of outlets in Mallorca, see Ⓦ mallorcaonline.com/sport/equitau.htm; for Menorca, begin with Ⓦ menorcaacavall.com. A wide range of **adventure sports** are offered by Mallorca's Tramuntana Tours (see p.94), including **canyoning**, which has recently experienced a dramatic increase in popularity.

Hiking

Hiking is a popular activity on both islands, with hundreds of hikers arriving here every year. On both Mallorca and Menorca, the prime **hiking seasons** are spring – March, April and May – and autumn, from early October to mid-November. The islands are also warm enough to allow for pleasant hiking in the depths of winter, though there's more rain at this time of year, temperatures can drop dramatically, snow is fairly common on the high peaks of Mallorca, and the number of daylight hours is restricted. In summer, by comparison, the heat makes all but the shorter hikes unpleasant and very tiring plus you'll have to haul a large quantity of water around with you. Bear in mind also that the mountains are prone to mists, though they usually lift at some point in the day and for obvious safety reasons, lone mountain walking is not recommended.

On **Mallorca**, the prime hiking area is the Serra de Tramuntana mountain range that bands the northern coast. Until the early 1990s, the assorted foot, mule and cart tracks that lattice the range were poorly signed and difficult to navigate. Things aren't perfect yet – far from it – but today the mountains boast a dense network of clearly signposted **hiking trails**, including a well-marked long-distance trail, the Ruta de Pedra en Sec (Dry-stone Route), or **GR221**, which runs right across the mountains from Sant Elm in the west to Sóller and then Pollença. The GR221 is equipped with several strategically placed **hikers' hostels** or *refugis* (see p.27). In addition, we have described a number of **day-long hikes** on Mallorca (see p.114, p.141, & p.148) and recommended two Mallorcan companies that organize **guided hikes** – Mallorcan Walking Tours (see p.138) and Tramuntana Tours (see p.94).

Menorca is sufficiently rural to offer pleasing walks almost everywhere, though it's the island's wild and windswept northern coast that offers the most dramatic scenery, its craggy capes and headlands sheltering a clutch of beautiful cove beaches. Although Menorca has no high mountains, it does possess deep wooded gorges that attract hikers too. As for **hiking trails**, the island's pride and joy is the **Camí de Cavalls**, a long-distance footpath that circumnavigates the whole island, bringing together a network of old mule and military trails. We have also described four **day-long hikes** on Menorca (see p.208, p.216, p.224 & p.227).

Hiking guides and maps

The best **hiking guides and maps** to Mallorca and Menorca are not available on the islands. These are *Walk! Mallorca (North & Mountains)* and *Walk! Menorca*, published by Discovery Walking Guides (Ⓦ www.walking.demon.co.uk). Both come with a complete set of GPS waypoints (available as downloadable gpx files from the website), which allows for route inputting into a navigation device – a useful bonus when walking in an area where signposting can be sporadic and inconsistent. The guides are supplemented by clear 1:40,000 maps and in the same series there are separate guides to West Mallorca and the island's principal long-distance hiking route, the GR221, the Ruta de Pedra en Sec (Dry-stone Route). Alternatively, the long-established Cicerone *Walking in Mallorca* guide (4th ed. 2006) covers all the island's classic walks and has a GR221-specific companion guide, *Trekking through Mallorca* (1st ed. 2009).

On Mallorca, Sóller tourist office (see p.94) and Tramuntana Tours (see p.94) sell a good range of hiking guides with maps, including those produced by Triangle Postals (Ⓦ triangle.cat), whose *GR221 Serra de Tramuntana* provides a detailed route description. Alternatively, Editorial Alpina (Ⓦ editorialalpina.com) publishes five Mallorca walking guides (€10–15), three of which combine to cover the northwest coast – *Mallorca Tramuntana Sud*, *Mallorca Tramuntana Central* and *Mallorca Tramuntana Norte*. The English-language editions of these three are clearly written and the **maps** (at 1:25,000) are detailed and well presented. The company also publishes a walking guide and map (1:50,000) to the whole island and a (Spanish only) guide and map (1:50,000) to 26 selected hikes.

Windsurfing

Windsurfing is common in lots of resorts on both islands, but one of the prime spots is the windswept coast and wide, wave-less bay of Fornells, on Menorca (see pp.216–218). Fornells is home to one of the best windsurfing companies in the Balearics, **Wind Fornells** (Ⓦ windfornells.com).

Scuba diving

By and large, **scuba diving** off Mallorca is something of an anticlimax: there may be lots of

---

PARKS AND PROTECTED AREAS

There are more than thirty protected areas in Mallorca, mainly concentrated in the north of the island, and four **Parcs Natural** (Natural Parks) – Mondragó on the east coast (see p.182); Sa Dragonera (see p.119); S'Albufera (see p.152); and the Península de Llevant just north of Artà and including the Ermita de Betlem (see p.170). Menorca has one, S'Albufera des Grau (see p.215), but most of the rest of the island is protected to some extent or another, hence its UNESCO designation as a "Reserva de la Biosfera" (Biosphere Reserve). Finally, Cabrera island (see p.188) and its surrounding waters are a Parc Nacional.

companies offering this service, but the island's underwater world lacks colour and clarity with the exception of the clear and reefy waters around the island of Sa Dragonera. Menorca, on the other hand, offers first-rate diving with visibility averaging around 30m, lots of reefs and a scattering of shipwrecks. Some divers swear by Menorca's north coast, but others prefer the west.

DIVING CONTACTS

Diving Center Fornells Fornells, Menorca ☎ 971 37 64 31, Ⓦ divingfornells.com

Diving Centre Poseidon Ciutadella, Menorca ☎ 971 38 26 44, Ⓦ bahia-poseidon.de

Scuba Activa Sant Elm, Mallorca ☎ 971 23 91 02, Ⓦ scuba-activa.com

Shopping

Big-city Palma has its share of chain and department stores as well as a scattering of specialist outlets (pp.76–78), but everywhere else – on both Mallorca and Menorca – is too small to offer much of a shopping "scene". That said, open-air markets (see p.36), mostly selling fresh fruit and vegetables as well as tourist trinkets, are extremely popular and lots of towns have one, either once or twice weekly; go early – at about 8am – to get the best deals.

As for **island specialities**, look out for artificial pearls from Manacor; Camper shoes; fancy green-tinted glass chandeliers; and *siurells*, white clay whistles flecked with red and green paint and shaped to depict a figure, an animal or rural scene – they are almost always mass-produced today, but have a long island pedigree as tokens of friendship. In addition, Mallorcan wine (see p.30) and Menorcan cheese, gin and honey come highly recommended, and you shouldn't leave the Balearics without sampling an *ensaimada* (spiralled flaky pastry).

Shopping hours are normally Monday to Friday 9.30/10am to 1.30/2pm and 5 to 7/8pm, plus Saturday morning 9.30/10am to 1.30/2pm, though big department stores operate longer hours,

CLOTHING AND SHOE SIZES

WOMEN'S DRESSES AND SKIRTS

American	4	6	8	10	12	14	16	18
British	8	10	12	14	16	18	20	22
Continental	38	40	42	44	46	48	50	52

WOMEN'S BLOUSES AND SWEATERS

American	6	8	10	12	14	16	18
British	30	32	34	36	38	40	42
Continental	40	42	44	46	48	50	52

WOMEN'S SHOES

American	5	6	7	8	9	10	11
British	3	4	5	6	7	8	9
Continental	36	37	38	39	41	42	43

MEN'S SUITS

American	34	36	38	40	42	44	46	48
British	34	36	38	40	42	44	46	48
Continental	44	46	48	50	52	54	56	58

MEN'S SHIRTS

American	14	15	15.5	16	16.5	17	17.5	18
British	14	15	15.5	16	16.5	17	17.5	18
Continental	36	38	39	41	42	43	44	45

MEN'S SHOES

American	7	7.5	8	8.5	9.5	10	10.5	11	11.5
British	6	7	7.5	8	9	9.5	10	11	12
Continental	39	41	41	42	43	44	44	45	46

typically Monday to Saturday 9.30am to 9.30pm and Sunday 11am to 8pm. In the resorts, many shops and stores are open daily from 9.30am till late.

PRINCIPAL OPEN-AIR MARKETS (MERCATS)

Palma has a wide array of markets (see p.78).

Mondays: Calvià; Manacor.

Tuesdays: Alcúdia; Artà; Maó.

Wednesdays: Andratx; Capdepera; Petra. Port de Pollença; Santanyí; Selva; Sineu.

Thursdays: Alaior; Inca.

Fridays: Algaida; Binissalem; Ciutadella.

Saturdays: Alaró; Bunyola; Cala Rajada; Ciutadella; Maó; Santanyí; Sóller.

Sundays: Alcúdia; Felanitx; Pollença; Porto Cristo; Valldemossa.

Travel essentials

Climate

There's little difference between the **climates** of Mallorca and Menorca. Spring and autumn are the ideal times for a visit, when the weather is comfortably warm, with none of the oven-like temperatures that bake the islands in July and August. It's worth considering a winter break too: even in January it's usually warm enough to sit out at a café in shirtsleeves. Both islands see occasional rain in winter, however, and the Serra de Tramuntana mountains, which protect the rest of Mallorca from inclement weather and the prevailing northerly winds, are often buffeted by storms, while Menorca, where there's no mountain barrier, can be irritatingly windy. Reflecting their agricultural past, the islanders have names for the four main winds that blow across their land – Tramuntana, Ponent, Migjorn and Llevant, respectively northerly, westerly, southerly and easterly.

Costs

In both Mallorca and Menorca, hotel and restaurant prices are on a par with most of the rest of Europe. On **average**, if you buy your own picnic lunch, stay in inexpensive *hostales* and hotels, and stick to cheaper bars and restaurants, you could get by on around €60 per person per day, assuming you're sharing a room. If you stay in three-star hotels and eat at quality restaurants, you'll need more like €120 a day per person, with the main variable being the cost of your room – and bear in mind that room prices rise steeply in peak season. On €180 a day and upwards, you'll be limited only by your energy reserves, unless you're planning to stay in a five-star hotel, in which case this figure won't even cover your bed.

A sales tax, **IVA**, is levied on most goods and services at anywhere between four and twenty-one percent – necessities attract a tax of four percent, and most tourist stuff (meals and hotels for instance) ten percent. Check in advance to see if IVA is included in the price of your bigger purchases, otherwise you may be in for a bit of a shock. As for **tipping**, taxi drivers, restaurant and bar staff anticipate a tip of between ten and fifteen percent.

Crime and personal safety

Other than the ETA bombings of 2009, Mallorca and Menorca have very low **crime rates**. In the islands' villages and small towns petty crime is unusual, and serious offences, from burglary to assault and

AVERAGE DAYTIME TEMPERATURES AND RAINFALL												
	Jan	Feb	Mar	Apr	May	Jun	Jul	Aug	Sep	Oct	Nov	Dec
AVERAGE DAILY MAX/MIN TEMP (°C)												
	15/5	15/5	17/6	19/7	23/10	27/15	31/17	31/18	28/16	24/13	19/8	16/6
AVERAGE DAILY MAX/MIN TEMP (°F)												
	59/41	59/41	63/43	66/45	73/50	81/59	88/63	88/64	82/61	75/55	66/46	61/43
AVERAGE HOURS OF SUNSHINE PER DAY												
	4	6	6	7	9	10	11	11	8	5	4	4
AVERAGE NUMBER OF DAYS WITH RAIN												
	11	8	8	9	7	5	3	4	8	11	12	12

beyond, extremely rare. Of the three larger towns, only Palma presents any problems, and that's mostly low-key stuff such as the occasional fight and minor theft. Taking commonsense precautions and steering clear of the noisy and **aggressive males** that commonly colonize some late-night bars at the seedier resorts – S'Arenal and Magaluf have the worst reputations – should keep you out of trouble. **Theft from parked cars** is also a problem, especially at major tourist attractions, so don't leave anything in view when you park.

If you are a victim of crime, you'll need to report it to the police (see below), not least because your insurance company will require a **police report** or number. Many police officers speak English, especially in the towns and resort areas, but you can't bank on it. Whilst the police are generally polite, they can become unpleasant if you get on the wrong side of them, so keep your cool at all times.

The police

There are three main types of **police** in the Balearics, all of them armed: the Guardia Civil, the Policía Nacional and the Policía Local. The **Guardia Civil**, who are dressed in green, police the highways and the countryside; the brown-uniformed **Policía Nacional**, who are mainly seen in Palma, guard key installations and/or personnel and control crowds and demonstrations; and the **Policía Local**, who wear blue uniforms, operate in the towns. The Policía Local are generally reckoned to be the most sympathetic.

Electricity

Spanish **electricity** runs at 220 volts AC, with standard European-style two-pin plugs. Brits will need a plug adaptor to connect their appliances; North Americans should bring both an adaptor and a transformer.

Entry requirements

Citizens of the EU/EEA, including the UK and Ireland, plus citizens of Australia, New Zealand, Canada and the USA do not need a **visa** to enter Spain if staying for ninety days or less, but they do need a current **passport**. Travellers from South

> ### EMERGENCY PHONE NUMBER
> For medical, fire and police emergencies, call ☎112.

Africa, on the other hand, need a passport and a tourist visa for visits of less than ninety days; visas must be obtained before departure and are available from the Spanish embassy (see below).

For stays of **longer than ninety days**, there are few hindrances for EU/EEA residents, but everyone else needs a mix of **visas and permits**. In all cases, consult your Spanish embassy at home before departure.

SPANISH EMBASSIES ABROAD

All the embassies below are on the Spanish government website ⓦ maec.es.
Australia 15 Arkana St, Yarralumla, Canberra, ACT 2600 ☎ 02 6273 3555.
Canada 74 Stanley Ave, Ottawa, Ontario K1M 1P4 ☎ 1 613 747 2252.
Ireland 17A Merlyn Park, Ballsbridge, Dublin 4 ☎ 01 269 1640.
New Zealand Level 11, BNZ Trust House Bldg, 50 Manners St, Wellington 6142 ☎ 04 802 5665.
South Africa 337 Brooklyn Rd, Menlo Park, Pretoria 0102 ☎ 012 460 01 23.
UK 39 Chesham Place, London SW1X 8SB ☎ 0207 235 5555. Also consulates in London and Edinburgh.
USA 2375 Pennsylvania Ave NW, Washington DC 20037 ☎ 01 202 452 0100. Also consulates in Boston, Chicago, Houston, Los Angeles, Miami, New Orleans, New York, San Francisco and Washington DC.

Gay and lesbian travellers

The **gay and lesbian scene** is fairly low-key in Mallorca and almost invisible in Menorca – in striking contrast to neighbouring Ibiza. Most of the action takes place in Palma on Avinguda Joan Miró, just south of Plaça Gomila. In 2005, Spain became the fourth country (after Canada, the Netherlands and Belgium) to legalize gay marriage and there is now a battery of laws against discrimination on the grounds of sexual preference.

Health

Under reciprocal health care arrangements, all citizens of the EU (European Union) and EEA (European Economic Area) are entitled to **free medical treatment** within Spain's public health care system. Non-EU/EEA nationals are not entitled to free treatment and should, therefore, take out their own medical insurance. EU/EEA citizens may want to consider private health insurance too, to cover the cost of items not within the EU/EEA scheme, such as dental treatment and repatriation on medical grounds. No **inoculations** are currently required for Mallorca or Menorca.

The **public health care system** in the Balearics is of an excellent standard and widely available, with clinics and hospitals in all the larger towns. If you're seeking treatment **under EU/EEA reciprocal health arrangements**, check that the medic you see is seeing you as a patient of the public system, so that you receive free treatment just as the locals do. You may be asked to show your passport and **European Health Insurance Card (EHIC)** to prove that you are eligible for EU/EEA health care – sometimes no one bothers, but always have it with you in case.

If you have an insurance policy covering **medical expenses**, you can seek treatment in either the public or private health sectors, the main issue being whether – at least in major cases – you have to pay the costs upfront and then wait for reimbursement or not. Note that in the larger resorts your hotel will probably be able to arrange an appointment with an **English-speaking doctor**, who will almost certainly see you as a private patient; elsewhere, you'll be lucky if the medic speaks English.

Minor complaints can often be remedied at the ubiquitous **pharmacy** (*farmàcia*): pharmacists are highly trained, willing to give advice (often in English), and able to dispense many drugs which would only be available on prescription in many other countries. **Condoms** are available from most *farmàcias* and from all sorts of outlets in the resorts, such as bars and vending machines. It's a good job: a recent survey of 18- to 30-year-old visitors found that the average time between arrival and first sexual contact was 3hr 42min.

Insurance

Even though EU/EEA health care privileges apply in Spain, it's a good idea to take out an **insurance policy** to cover against theft, loss and illness or injury. For non-EU/EEA citizens, insurance is a must. A typical policy usually provides cover for the loss of baggage, tickets and – up to a certain limit – cash or cheques, as well as cancellation or curtailment of your journey. Private health insurance also covers the cost of items not included by the EU medical scheme, such as dental treatment and repatriation on medical grounds. In the case of major expense, the more worthwhile policies promise to sort matters out before you pay rather than after, but if you do have to pay upfront, make sure you always keep full doctors' reports, signed prescription details and all receipts. In the event that you have anything stolen, you must obtain an official statement from the police (see p.37).

Internet and email

Almost all hotels and *hostales* provide **internet access** for their guests either free or for a small charge. Failing that, head for the nearest library, where internet access is almost always free, if sometimes for a fixed period only – usually about an hour.

Mail

On both islands, there is a **post office** (*correu*) in every town and most larger villages; the majority are handily located on or near the main square. Opening hours are usually Monday to Friday 9am to 2pm, though the post offices in Palma, Maó and Ciutadella are open longer. All post offices close on public holidays. The post is slow but reasonably reliable, with letters or cards taking about a week to reach Britain and Ireland, up to two weeks to North America and Australasia. You can buy **stamps** (*segells*) at tobacconists (look for the brown and yellow *tabac* or *tabacos* sign) and at scores of souvenir shops as well as at post offices. **Post boxes** are yellow; where you have a choice of slots, pick the flap marked *províncies i estranger* or *altres destinos*. **Postal rates** are inexpensive, with postcards and small letters

---

ROUGH GUIDES TRAVEL INSURANCE

Rough Guides has teamed up with WorldNomads.com to offer great **travel insurance** deals. Policies are available to residents of more than 150 countries, with cover for a wide range of adventure sports, 24hr emergency assistance, high levels of medical and evacuation cover and a stream of travel safety information. Roughguides.com users can take advantage of their policies online 24/7, from anywhere in the world – even if you're already travelling. And since plans often change when you're on the road, you can extend your policy and even claim online. Roughguides.com users who buy travel insurance with WorldNomads.com can also leave a positive footprint and donate to a community development project. For more information, go to ⓦ roughguides.com/shop.

attracting two tariffs: one to anywhere in Europe, the other worldwide.

Maps

Detailed **road maps** of Mallorca and/or Menorca are widely available from newsagents, tourist offices, petrol stations, souvenir shops and bookshops; for the most part they cost €4–8. The quality varies enormously and many are out of date, so before you buy a map check the **road numbers**: all Balearic road numbers were changed in 2006, so – for example – the main road along Mallorca's north coast was the C710, but is now the Ma-10, while Menorca's only main road is now the Me-1 (not the C721). You're also better off buying a **Catalan** map rather than a Castilian (Spanish) or even an English or German map. Check the spelling of Port de Pollença on Mallorca's north coast – if it reads "Puerto de Pollensa", you've got a Castilian map; similarly, on Menorca, check the capital is marked Maó, not the Castilian "Mahón".

Currently, the most accurate **road maps** of both Mallorca (1:130,000) and Menorca (1:60,000) are published by **Triangle Postals** (Ⓦtriangle.cat). Both have indexes, mark major hiking routes and have large-scale inset city maps (of Palma, Ciutadella and Maó). Both are widely available on their respective islands and can also be ordered online from the publisher. For hiking maps, see p.34.

Money and exchange

Spain's currency is the **euro** (€), which is made up of 100 cents. The **exchange rate** at time of writing was 0.82 to the British pound; 1.30 to the US dollar; 1.29 to the Canadian dollar; 1.25 to the Australian dollar; 1.65 to the New Zealand dollar; and 11.25 to the South African Rand. Euros come in notes of €500, €200, €100, €50, €20, €10 and €5, and coins of €2, €1, 50c, 20c, 10c, 5c, 2c and 1c, though many retailers will not accept the €500 and €200 notes – you have to break them down into smaller denominations at the bank. All well-known brands of **travellers' cheque** in all the major currencies are widely accepted in Mallorca and Menorca, and you can change them as well as foreign currency into euros at most Balearic banks and savings banks, which are ubiquitous. **Banking hours** are usually Monday to Friday from 9am to 2pm, with many banks opening on Saturday mornings from 9am to 1pm from October to April. **ATMs** are commonplace in Palma, Maó, Ciutadella and all the larger resorts. Almost all ATMs give instructions in a variety of languages, and accept a host of **debit cards** without charging a transaction fee. **Credit cards** can be used in ATMs too, but in this case transactions are treated as loans, with interest accruing daily from the date of withdrawal. All major credit cards, including American Express, Visa and Mastercard, are widely accepted.

Opening hours and public holidays

Although there's been some movement towards a northern European **working day** in Menorca and Mallorca – especially in Palma and the major tourist resorts – most shops and offices still close for a **siesta** of at least two hours in the hottest part of the afternoon. There's a lot of variability, but basic working hours are typically Monday to Friday 9am to 1pm and 4pm to 7pm, Saturday 9am to 1pm; notable exceptions are the extended hours operated by the largest department stores, some major tourist attractions and most tourist and souvenir shops. Government offices are closed on Saturdays. In winter (Nov–March), Menorca's tourist industry pretty much shuts up shop and although things aren't so clear cut in Mallorca most of the resorts scale right down.

Local festivals (see p.32) are a prominent feature of island life and they work in tandem with **public holidays**, whose precise dates and details are fixed annually – so there may be some (minor) variations to the list in our box (see below). The island's resorts

---

PUBLIC HOLIDAYS

January 1 New Year's Day (*Cap d'Any*)
January 6 Epiphany (*Reyes Magos*)
Maundy Thursday (*Dijous Sant*)
Good Friday (*Divendres Sant*)
May 1 Labour Day (*Día del Treball*)
August 15 Assumption of the Virgin (*Assumpció*)
October 12 Spanish National Day (*Día de la Hispanidad*)
November 1 All Saints (*Tots Sants*)
December 6 Constitution Day (*Día de la Constitució*)
December 8 Immaculate Conception (*Inmaculada Concepción*)
December 24 Christmas Eve
December 25 Christmas Day (*Nadal; Navidad in Castilian*)
December 26 Boxing Day/St Stephen's Day (*Dia de Sant Esteban*)

are generally oblivious to public holidays as are hotels and most restaurants, but almost all businesses and shops close and public transport is reduced to a skeleton service.

Phones

The **international phone code** for Spain is 34. Note that most Balearic phone numbers begin with ☎971, but this is an integral part of the number, not an (optional) area code. You'll get **mobile phone** reception in all but the remoter corners of Mallorca and Menorca, with the network fixed at GSM900/1800, the band common to the rest of Europe, Australia and New Zealand. Mobile/cell phones bought in North America will need to be able to adjust to this GSM band. Note that **call charges** in Spain can be excruciating – particularly irritating is the supplementary charge you often have to pay on incoming calls – so check with your supplier before you depart. You may find it cheaper to buy a **Spanish SIM card**, though this can get complicated: many mobiles/cells will not permit you to swap SIM cards and the connection instructions for the replacement SIM card can be in Spanish only. You can buy SIM cards at high-street phone companies for around €5 per card. **Text messages** are normally charged at bearable rates – and with your existing SIM card in place. The **Spanish phone directory** is available (in Spanish) at ⓦpaginas-amarillas.es.

Smoking

On January 1 2006, smoking became **illegal** in Spain inside all theatres, bars and restaurants as well as on public transport, though scores of restaurants

---

INTERNATIONAL CALLS

PHONING HOME FROM SPAIN

To make an **international phone call from Spain**, dial the appropriate international access code as below, then the number you require, omitting the initial zero where there is one.
Australia ☎0061
Canada ☎001
New Zealand ☎0064
Republic of Ireland ☎00353
South Africa ☎0027
UK ☎0044
USA ☎001

---

and bars managed to avoid the ban though local exemptions. Follow-up legislation, passed in 2011, removed most of these exemptions and today, all bars and restaurants are smoke-free inside – though, of course, smoking is still allowed outside on the terrace.

Time zones

Spain is on **Central European Time** (**CET**) – one hour ahead of Greenwich Mean Time, six hours ahead of US Eastern Standard Time, nine hours ahead of US Pacific Standard Time, nine hours behind Australian Eastern Standard Time and eleven hours behind New Zealand. There are, however, minor variations during the changeover periods involved in **daylight saving**. In Spain, the clocks go forward an hour on the last Sunday of March and back an hour on the last Sunday of October.

Tipping

Taxi drivers, restaurant and bar staff anticipate a tip of between ten and fifteen percent.

Tourist information

In **Mallorca**, there's a helpful **provincial tourist office** at the airport (see p.69) and another in the centre of Palma (see p.71). Both will provide free road maps of the island and leaflets detailing all sorts of island-wide practicalities. In addition, most towns and almost every resort has its own **tourist office**. These vary enormously in quality, and while they are generally useful for local information, they cannot be relied on to know anything about what goes on outside their patch. In **Menorca**, there are extremely efficient year-round **tourist offices** in the two main towns, Maó and Ciutadella, and a tourist information desk at the airport.

USEFUL WEBSITES

ⓦ **conselldemallorca.net** Extensive, multilingual government site including details of – and reservations for – Mallorca's hikers' hostels or refugis (see p.27).

ⓦ **mallorcaweb.com** and ⓦ **menorcaweb.com** Compendious websites dedicated to many aspects of island life.

ⓦ **spain.info** The official website of the Spanish National Tourist Office (SNTO) provides an excellent introduction to the country, and its myriad synopses – on everything from national parks to accommodation – are concise, clear and temptingly written.

Ⓦ **visitbalears.com** The Balearic government's official, English-language tourist site with separate sections for all of the islands. It covers a wide range of topics – from shopping to nature – and is clearly laid out; a useful introduction.

Travelling with children

Most Balearic *hostales*, pensions and hotels welcome **children** and many offer rooms with three or four beds. Restaurants and cafés almost always encourage families too. Many package holidays have **child-minding facilities** as part of the deal and many more organize a programme of kids' activities. Younger children will, of course, be quite happy to play around on the beach, but pre- and early teens may want more excitement, which is available on Mallorca at three water/theme parks: Hidropark in Port d'Alcúdia (see p.151); Western Water Park in Magaluf (see p.82); and Aqualand in S'Arenal (see p.85). **Concessionary rates** for children under 14/15 years are commonplace and infants go free. At restaurants, some places will prepare food specially for babies, though you might want to bring powdered milk – babies, like most Spaniards, are pretty contemptuous of the UHT stuff generally available. Disposable nappies and other basic supplies are widely available in the resorts and larger towns.

Travellers with disabilities

Despite their popularity as holiday destinations, facilities for **travellers with disabilities** on both Mallorca and Menorca lag some way behind most of the EU. That said, things are improving. Hotels with wheelchair access and other appropriate facilities are increasingly common and, by law, all new public buildings in Spain are required to be fully accessible. On the other hand, toilet facilities for people with disabilities are rare; car rental firms are very ill-stocked with adapted vehicles, even though there are designated disability parking bays; and few buses outside Palma's EMT services have low-floor access. More positively, **flying** to the islands should pose few problems as almost all the scheduled airlines are more than willing to assist.

Palma and around

47 Palma

69 Arrival and departure

71 Information

71 City tours

71 Getting around

71 Accommodation

73 Eating and drinking

75 Nightlife and entertainment

76 Shopping

78 Directory

78 Around Palma

HARBOURFRONT AND CATHEDRAL

1

Palma and around

A vibrant and urbane place of careful coiffures and well-cut suits, Palma is the Balearic islands' only major city, a lively, busy metropolis of 400,000 people akin to the big cities of the Spanish mainland – and a world away from the heaving tourist enclaves of the surrounding bay. In 1983, Palma became the capital of one of Spain's newly established autonomous regions, the Balearic islands, and since then a long-term programme has restored the architectural delights of the old town and equipped the city centre with a raft of inviting shops, hotels, restaurants, cafés and bars, all enclosed by what remains of the Renaissance city walls and their replacement boulevards.

While the boulevards encourage downtown Palma to look into itself and away from the sea, its **harbour** has always been the city's economic lifeline. The Romans were the first to recognize the site's strategic value, establishing a military post here known as Palmaria, but real development came with the Moors, who made their **Medina Mayurka** a major seaport protected by no fewer than three concentric walls. Jaume I of Aragón captured the Moorish stronghold in 1229 and promptly started work on the **Cathedral**, whose mellow sandstone still towers above the waterfront, presenting from its seaward side – in the sheer beauty of its massive proportions – one of Spain's most stunning sights.

As a major port of call between Europe and North Africa, Palma boomed under both Moorish and medieval Christian control, but its wealth and prominence came to a sudden end with the Spanish exploitation of the New World: from the early sixteenth century, Madrid looked west across the Atlantic and Palma slipped into Mediterranean obscurity. One result of its abrupt decline has been the preservation of much of the **old town**, its beguiling tangle of narrow, labyrinthine streets and high-storeyed houses holding the Gothic **Basílica de Sant Francesc** at its core.

Yet for most visitors, Palma's main appeal is its sheer vitality: at night scores of excellent **restaurants** offer the best of Spanish, Catalan and Mallorcan cuisine, while the city's **cafés** buzz with purposeful chatter. Palma also boasts **accommodation** to match most budgets, making it a splendid base from which to explore the island. In this respect, the city is far preferable, at least for independent travellers, to the string of resorts along the neighbouring **Badía de Palma** (Bay of Palma), where most of the accommodation is block-booked by tour operators. If you are tempted by a cheap package, however, it's as well to bear in mind that the more agreeable of the resorts lie to the west of the city, where a hilly coastline of rocky cliffs and tiny coves is punctuated by small, sandy beaches. Development is ubiquitous, but **Cala Major** is of interest as the site of the former home and studio of Joan Miró; well-to-do **Illetes** has a couple of lovely cove beaches; and pint-sized **Cala Fornells** has a fine seashore setting – and is also within easy reach of the spacious sandy shorelines of family-oriented **Santa**

Orientation p.47
Gaudí's restoration work p.51
Joan March p.57
The aristocracy at home: the mansions of Palma p.60
A Catholic hero: The life and times of Ramon Llull p.62

Palma's top 5 hotels p.73
La Ruta Martiana – the Route of the Martians p.75
Top 5 sandy beaches around Palma p.78

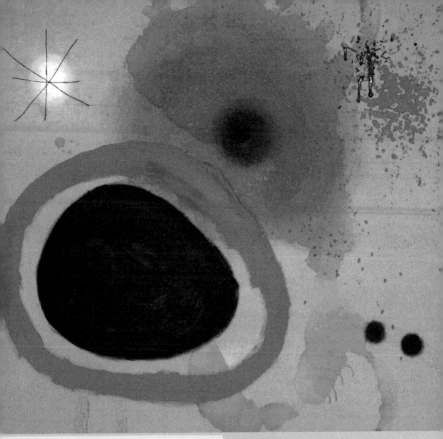

MIRÓ PAINTING

Highlights

❶ Palma Cathedral One of Spain's finest Gothic cathedrals, whose honey-coloured walls dominate the waterfront from the crest of a hill. **See p.47**

❷ Mallorcan Primitives The Museu de la Catedral holds a fascinating selection of works by the Mallorcan Primitives group of medieval painters. **See p.50, p.55 & p.59**

❸ The old town The most intriguing part of the city, the old town's narrow lanes and alleys are flanked by a handsome medley of Gothic churches and Renaissance mansions. **See pp.58–63**

❹ Hotels in Palma Palma has the island's finest selection of hotels, from modernist-chic to fine old townhouses – and the *Dalt Murada* is among the best. **See p.73**

❺ Fundació Pilar i Joan Miró, Cala Major Joan Miró hunkered down in Mallorca to avoid the attentions of General Franco, creating some of his finest paintings here during his long exile. **See p.80**

❻ Platja de Palma, S'Arenal The most self-conscious beach in Mallorca, awash with preening pectorals, this 4km-long band of fine white sand stretches around the Bay of Palma. **See p.84**

HIGHLIGHTS ARE MARKED ON THE MAP ON P.46

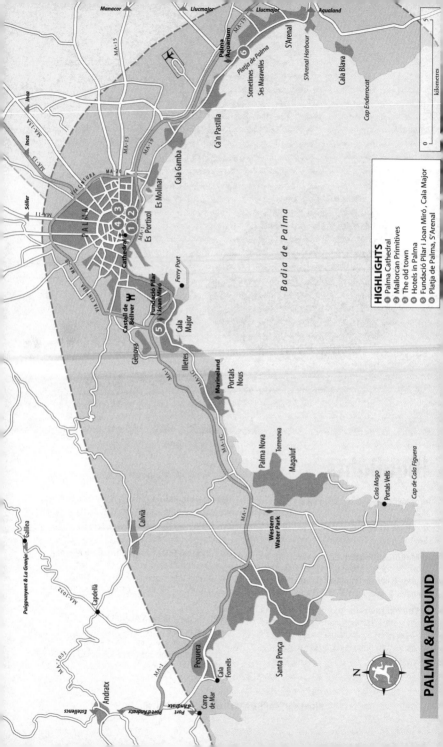

PALMA & AROUND

HIGHLIGHTS
1 Palma Cathedral
2 Mallorcan Primitives
3 The old town
4 Hotels in Palma
5 Fundació Pilar i Joan Miró, Cala Major
6 Platja de Palma, S'Arenal

kilometres

0   5

N

ORIENTATION

Almost everything of interest in **Palma** is located in the **city centre**, a roughly circular affair whose southern perimeter is defined by the Cathedral and the remains of the old city walls, which in turn abut the coastal motorway (the **Ma-1**) and the harbour. The city centre's landward limits are determined by a zigzag of wide **boulevards** built beside or in place of the old town walls. Two of these boulevards, Avinguda de la Argentina and Avinguda Gabriel Alomar i Villalonga, connect with the **Ma-1**, thereby completing the circle. The **Ma-20** ring road around the suburbs loops off from the coastal motorway to create a much larger, outer circle.

The city centre itself is crossed by four interconnected avenues: **Passeig d'es Born**, **Avinguda Jaume III**, **c/Unió** (which becomes **c/Riera** at its eastern end) and **Passeig de la Rambla**. Your best bet is to use these four thoroughfares to guide yourself around the centre – Palma's jigsaw-like side streets and squares can be very confusing. Central Palma is about 2km in diameter, a walk of roughly 30min from one side to the other; taxi fares are reasonable. The closest **beach** to the city centre is the narrow strip of sand next to the *autovia* (motorway) just east of Avgda Gabriel Alomar i Villalonga. However, swimming is not recommended here as the water is too polluted and most locals head east to the **Platja de Palma** instead (see p.84), around a 40min trip by bus (EMT #15).

Ponça and **Peguera**. Places to avoid include lager-swilling **Magaluf** and all the larger resorts to the east of Palma, where the pancake-flat shoreline is burdened by a seamless band of skyscrapers stretching from **Ca'n Pastilla** to **S'Arenal** – behind what is, admittedly, one of the island's longest and most impressive beaches, the **Platja de Palma** (see p.84).

Palma

There's not much argument as to where to start a tour of Palma – it's got to be the **Cathedral**, which dominates the waterfront from the crest of a hill. Central Palma's other landmark is the **Palau de l'Almudaina** next door, an important royal residence from Moorish times and now, much modified, the repository of a mildly engaging assortment of municipal baubles. Spreading northeast behind the cathedral are the narrow lanes and ageing mansions of the most intriguing part of the **old town**. A stroll here is a pleasure in itself, and tucked away among the side streets are three good diversions: the **Museu de Mallorca** – the island's most extensive museum – the ecclesiastical treasures of the **Museu Diocesà**, and the Baroque **Basílica de Sant Francesc**. North of the old town lies the heart of the early twentieth-century city, where the high-sided tenements are graced by a sequence of flamboyant buildings in the *Modernisme* style (the Spanish, and especially Catalan, form of Art Nouveau), particularly on and around **Plaça Weyler** and **Plaça Major**.

The Cathedral

Plaça Seu • April, May & Oct Mon–Fri 10am–5.15pm, Sat 10am–2.15pm; June–Sept Mon–Fri 10am–6.15pm, Sat 10am–2.15pm; Nov–March Mon–Fri 10am–3.15pm, Sat 10am–2.15pm • €6, which includes entrance to the museum • ☎ 902 02 24 45, ⓦ catedraldemallorca.org

Legend has it that when the invasion force of Jaume I of Aragón and Catalunya stood off Mallorca in 1229, a fierce gale threatened to sink the fleet. The desperate king promised to build a church dedicated to the Virgin Mary if the expedition against the Moors was successful. It was, and Jaume fulfilled his promise, starting construction work the following year. The king had a political point to make, too – he built his cathedral, a gigantic affair of golden sandstone, bang on top of the Great Mosque inside the Almudaina, the old Moorish citadel. The Reconquista – the expulsion of the Moors by the Christians – was to be no temporary matter. As it turned out, the

Cathedral ("La Seu" in Catalan) was five hundred years in the making, and whilst there are architectural bits and bobs from several different eras, the church remains essentially Gothic, with massive exterior buttresses – its most distinctive feature – taking the weight off the pillars within. The whole structure derives its effect from its sheer height, impressive from any angle, but startling when viewed from the waterside esplanade.

The exterior

The finest of the cathedral's three doors is the **Portal del Mirador** ("Lookout Door"), which overlooks the Bay of Palma from the south facade. Dating from the late fourteenth century, the recently buffed and scrubbed Mirador features a host of Flemish-style ecclesiastical and biblical figurines set around a tympanum where heavily bearded disciples sit at a Last Supper. In contrast, the west-facing **Portal Major** ("Great Door"), across from the Palau de l'Almudaina, is a neo-Gothic disaster, an ugly reworking – along with the 60m-high flanking turrets – of a far simpler predecessor that was badly damaged by an earthquake in 1851.

On the north side is a third door, the **Portal de l'Almoina**, whose delicately carved Gothic design dates from 1498. Above rises the solid squareness of the **bell tower** (closed to the public), an incongruous, fortress-like structure that clearly did not form

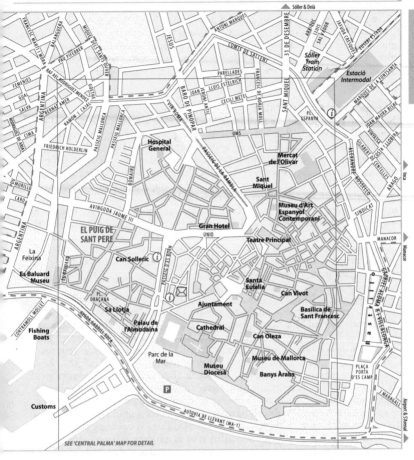

part of the original design. When the largest of the bells, the 5700-kilo N'Eloi, was tolled in 1857, it shattered most of the cathedral's windows.

The nave

You **enter the cathedral** on the north side, from beside the Portal de l'Almoina, and proceed through the museum (see p.50). The majestic proportions of the interior are seen to best advantage from the western end – from the Portal Major. In the central aisle of the **nave**, fourteen beautifully aligned, pencil-thin pillars rise to 21m before their ribs branch out, like fronded palm trees, to support the single-span, vaulted roof. The nave, at 44m high, is one of the tallest Gothic structures in Europe, and its 121m length is of matching grandeur. This open, hangar-like construction, typical of Catalan Gothic architecture, was designed to make the high altar visible to the entire congregation and to express the mystery of the Christian faith, with kaleidoscopic floods of light filtered in through the **stained-glass windows**. Most of the original glass was lost long ago, but recent refurbishment has returned a number of windows to their former glory and, now that some others have been un-bricked, the cathedral has re-emerged from the gloom imposed by Renaissance, Baroque and neo-Gothic architects. There are seven rose windows, the largest of which crowns the triumphal

1

arch of the apse towards the east end and boasts more than 1200 individual pieces of glass; providing the morning sun is out, it showers the nave with a wonderful, dappled light. The cathedral's designers also incorporated a specific, carefully orchestrated artifice: twice a year, at 6.30am on Candlemas and St Martin's Day, the sun shines through the stained glass of the eastern window onto the wall immediately below the rose window on the main, western facade.

The Capella del Corpus Christi

The aisles to either side of the nave are flanked by a long sequence of **chapels**, dull affairs for the most part, dominated by dusty Baroque altars of gargantuan proportions and little artistic merit. The exception, and the cathedral's one outstanding example of the Baroque, is the **Capella del Corpus Christi**, at the head of the aisle to the left of the high altar. Begun in the sixteenth century, the chapel's tiered and columned altarpiece features three religious scenes, cramped and intense sculptural tableaux depicting – from top to bottom – the temptations of St Anthony, the presentation of Jesus in the temple, and the Last Supper. Just in front and across from the chapel is a massive stone **pulpit** that was moved here by Gaudí (see box opposite), a makeshift location for this excellent illustration of the Plateresque style. Dated to 1531, the pulpit's intricate floral patterns and bustling Biblical scenes cover a clumsy structure, the upper portion of which is carried by telamons, male counterparts of the more usual caryatids (supporting columns draped in female clothing).

The Capella de la Trinitat

At the east end of the church, to the right of the high altar, the walls of the **Capella del Santíssim** are covered by a bizarre plaster-and-ceramic dreamscape by the Mallorcan artist Miquel Barceló (b.1957). At the back of this chapel a door leads through to the tiny **Capella de la Trinitat** (Trinity Chapel): although you can't actually go inside it today, there are vague plans to open it up at some point. Completed in 1329, the chapel houses the remains of Jaume II and Jaume III, two notable medieval kings of Mallorca (see p.248). Initially, the bodies were stored in a tomb that operated rather like a filing cabinet, allowing the corpses to be venerated by the devout. They were viewed in 1809 by the first British traveller to write an account of a visit to Mallorca, the unflappable Sir John Carr, who calmly observed that, "considering the monarchs had been dead for five hundred years…they were in a state of extraordinary preservation". This gruesome practice was finally discontinued during the nineteenth century, and alabaster sarcophagi now enclose the royal bones.

The Museu de la Catedral

The ground floor of the bell tower and two adjoining chapterhouses have been turned into the **Museu de la Catedral**, which holds an eclectic assortment of ecclesiastical knick-knacks gathered here by whim and accident, but remarkable all the same.

Room one

The most valuable exhibit in the museum's first room is a gilded silver **monstrance** of extraordinary delicacy: displayed in a glass case in the middle of the room, its fairy-tale decoration dates from the late sixteenth century. On display around the walls is a hotchpotch of chalices and reliquaries and a real curiosity, the portable altar of Jaume I, a wood-and-silver chessboard with each square containing a bag of holy relics.

Room two

The museum's second room is devoted to the Gothic works of the **Mallorcan Primitives**, a school of painters that flourished on the island in the fourteenth and fifteenth centuries, producing strikingly naïve devotional works of bold colours and cartoon-like detail. The work of two of the school's leading fourteenth-century practitioners is

GAUDÍ'S RESTORATION WORK

The first attempt to return Palma's cathedral to something like its original Gothic splendour was made at the beginning of the twentieth century, when an inspired local bishop commissioned the *Modernista* Catalan architect **Antoni Gaudí** (1852–1926) to direct a full-blown restoration. At the time, Gaudí was renowned for his fancifully embellished metalwork, and his functionalist extrapolation of Gothic design was still evolving. This experimentation led ultimately to his most famous and extravagant opus, the church of the Sagrada Familia in Barcelona, but here in Palma his work was relatively restrained – though still deeply controversial. Indeed, certain Catholic dignitaries objected to the revamp and when, in 1926, a Barcelona tram flattened Gaudí they must have thought their prayers had been answered.

Gaudí worked on Palma's cathedral intermittently between 1904 and 1914, during which time he removed the High Baroque altar and shifted the ornate choir stalls from the centre to the side of the cathedral, placing them flat against the walls. The new **high altar**, a medieval alabaster table of plain design, was then located beneath a phantasmagorical **baldachin**, a giant canopy, enhanced by hanging lanterns, which was supposed to symbolize the Crown of Thorns. It's not a great success, though to be fair Gaudí never had time to complete it – he wanted it to be made of wrought iron, but what you see today is in fact a trial piece fashioned from cork, cardboard and brocade. Other examples of Gaudí's distinctive workmanship are dotted around the cathedral. The **railings** in front of the high altar are twisted into shapes inspired by Mallorcan window grilles, while the wall on either side of the **Bishop's Throne**, at the east end of the church, sports ceramic inlays with brightly painted floral designs.

Gaudí's main concern was to revive the Gothic tradition by allowing extra light, and so he introduced **electric lighting**, bathing the apse in bright artificial light and placing lamps and candelabra throughout the church. This was all very innovative: at the time, no Spanish choir had ever opened out in this way and electric lighting was a real novelty. The artistic success of the whole project was undeniable, and it was immediately popular with the congregation. Like the rest of his work, however, it did not bring Gaudí much international acclaim: it was only in the 1960s that his techniques were championed and copied across western Europe, and that his crucial role in the development of modernism was finally acknowledged.

displayed here, beginning with the so-called **Master of the Privileges**, noted for his love of warm colours and minute detail. His work is shown to good advantage in a large (though unlabelled), cartoon-like panel painting of *The Life of St Eulalia*, whose martyrdom fascinated and excited scores of medieval Mallorcan artists. A Catalan girl-saint, Eulalia defied the Roman emperor Diocletian by sticking to her Christian faith despite all sorts of ferocious tortures, which are depicted here in ecstatic detail. She was eventually burned at the stake and at the moment of her death, white doves flew from her mouth. The Master of the Privileges was greatly influenced by Italian painters, but his contemporary, the **Master of Montesión**, looked to his Catalan contemporaries for his sense of movement and tight draughtsmanship as seen in two panels displayed here, one of the *Crucifixion*, the other of the *Virgin Mary*. Later, the work of the Mallorcan Primitives shaded into the new realism of the Flemish style, which was to dominate Mallorcan painting throughout the sixteenth century. **Joan Desi**'s (unlabelled) *Panel of La Almoina* illustrates the transition – it's the large panel showing St Francis, complete with stigmata, at the side of Christ. One of Desi's pupils was **Alonso de Sedano**, who adopted a similar style in his *Martyrdom of St Sebastian*, which has the saint pierced by so many arrows that he looks like a sort of pin cushion.

Room three

The museum's third and final room, the **Baroque chapterhouse**, is entered through a playful Churrigueresque doorway, above which lively cherubic angels entertain a delicate Madonna. Inside, pride of place goes to the High Baroque **altar**, a gaudy, gilded affair surmounted by the Sacred Heart, a gory representation of the heart of

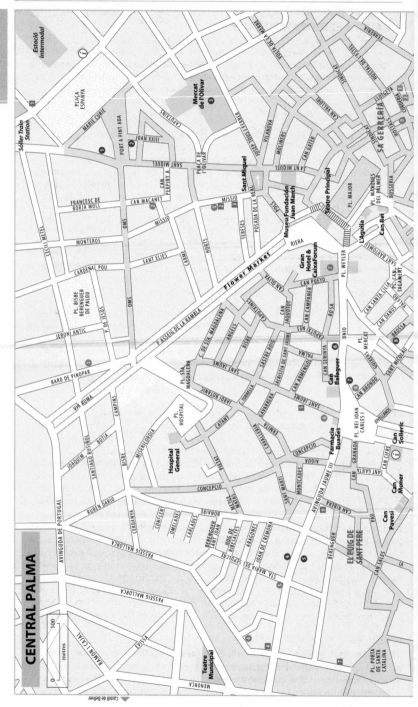

CENTRAL PALMA

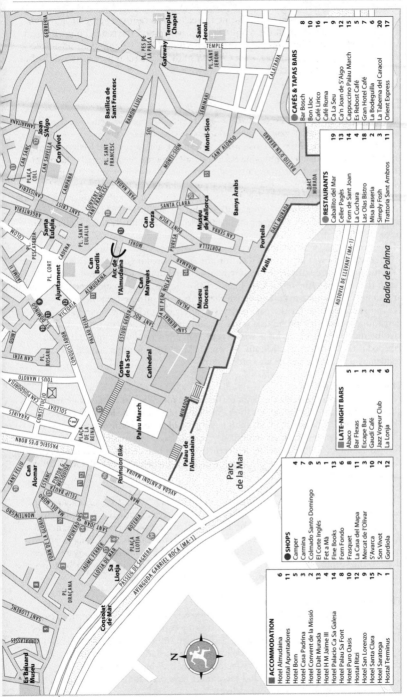

● **CAFÉS & TAPAS BARS**

Bar Bosch	8
Bon Lloc	10
Café Lírico	16
Café Roma	1
Ca La Seu	9
Ca'n Joan de S'Aigo	12
Cappuccino Palau March	15
Es Rebost Café	5
Gran Hotel Café	7
La Bodeguilla	6
La Taberna del Caracol	20
Orient Express	17

● **RESTAURANTS**

Caballito del Mar	19
Celler Pagès	13
Forn de Sant Joan	14
La Cuchara	4
Las Olas Bistro	18
Misa Brasería	2
Simply Fosh	3
Trattoria Sant Ambrós	11

● **LATE-NIGHT BARS**

Abaco	5
Bar Flexas	1
Escape Bar	3
Gaudí Café	10
Jazz Voyeur Club	2
La Lonja	6

● **SHOPS**

Camper	4
Carmina	7
Colmado Santo Domingo	9
El Corte Inglés	5
Fet a Mà	1
Fine Books	13
Forn Fondo	6
Frasquet	8
La Casa del Mapa	11
Mercat de l'Olivar	12
S'Avarca	3
Son Vivot	15
Gordiola	2
	1

■ **ACCOMMODATION**

Hotel Almudaina	6
Hostal Apuntadores	11
Hotel Born	5
Hotel Casa Padrina	3
Hotel Convent de la Missió	13
Hotel Dalt Murada	2
Hotel H M Jaime III	4
Hotel Palacio Ca Sa Galesa	14
Hotel Palau Sa Font	8
Hotel Puro Oasis	10
Hostal Ritzi	12
Hotel San Lorenzo	9
Hotel Santa Clara	15
Hotel Saratoga	7
Hostal Terminus	1

1

Jesus that was very much in vogue during the eighteenth century. Some imagination went into the designation of the reliquaries displayed round the room, comprising an unlikely collection of bits and pieces of various saints. Of more appeal are a pair of finely carved Baroque **crucifixes**, each Christ a study in perfect muscularity swathed in the flowing folds of a loincloth.

The Palau de l'Almudaina

Plaça Seu • Tues–Sun: April–Sept 10am–8pm; Oct–March 10am–6pm • €9, but free to EU citizens showing their passport on Wed & Thurs pm (April–Sept 5–8pm; Oct–March 3–6pm); audioguide €4 • ☎ 971 21 41 34, ⊕ patrimonionacional.es

Originally the palace of the Moorish *walis* (governors), and later of the Mallorcan kings, the **Palau de l'Almudaina** (Almudaina Palace) stands opposite the cathedral. The present structure, built around a central courtyard, owes much of its appearance to Jaume II (1276–1311), who spent the last twelve years of his life in residence here. Jaume converted the old fortress into a lavish palace that incorporated both Gothic and Moorish features, an uneasy mixture of styles conceived by the Mallorcan Pedro Selva, the king's favourite architect. The two most prominent "Moorish" attributes are the fragile-looking outside walls, with their square turrets and dainty crenellations, and the delicate arcades of the main loggia, which can be seen from the waterside esplanade below.

Once Mallorca was incorporated within the Aragonese kingdom, the Palau de l'Almudaina became surplus to requirements, though it did achieve local notoriety when the eccentric Aragonese king Juan I (1387–95) installed an **alchemist** in the royal apartments, hoping he would replenish the treasury by turning base metal into gold. He didn't succeed. Today the palace serves a variety of official functions, has a small garrison to protect it, and holds a series of state apartments kept in readiness for visiting dignitaries and the king, which is presumably why those exhibits that are labelled carry Castilian inscriptions. When the king or some other bigwig is in residence, parts of the palace are cordoned off.

The Salón de Consejos

A visit begins with a series of medieval corridors and rooms whose rough stonework is almost entirely devoid of ornamentation, but things pick up in the **Salón de Consejos** (Hall of Councils), where the walls sport a group of admirable Flemish tapestries, fifteenth- and sixteenth-century imports devoted to classical themes. Amongst them is a Roman Triumph, a blood-curdling war scene, and, best of the lot, the suicide of Cleopatra, showing a particularly wan-looking queen with the guilty asp slithering discreetly away.

Comedor de Oficiales

The **Comedor de Oficiales** (Officers' Mess) possesses a handful of Flemish genre paintings, fine still-life studies including one by the seventeenth-century Antwerp-based artist Frans Snyders – there's no label, but it's the painting with the man, the woman, the cat and several carcasses. Snyders was a contemporary of Rubens and odd-jobbed for him, painting in the flowers and fruit on many of his canvases. Next door to the Comedor, there are charming views out across the city and harbour from the **terraza** (terrace), which holds a small formal garden.

The Sala de Guardia

Inside the **Sala de Guardia** (Guard Room) are several dire eighteenth-century Spanish tapestries. Crude and inexact, these are in striking contrast to the Flemish tapestries exhibited elsewhere, but by then Spain had lost control of the Netherlands and the Spanish court could no longer acquire pieces from its traditional suppliers. In 1725, the Spanish king founded a tapestry factory in Madrid, but its products – as demonstrated here – were poor, and there must have been some aesthetic gnashing of teeth when the Spanish court took delivery.

The Baños Árabes

Better preserved than the Arab baths in Palma's old town (see p.58), the **Baños Árabes** (Arab Baths) here are a rare survivor from Moorish times, comprising three stone-vaulted chambers, one each for cold, tepid and hot baths. Enough remains to see how this sophisticated set-up worked and why the Christian kings who supplanted the Moors adopted them lock, stock and barrel.

The Salón Mayor

From the central **courtyard**, the **Escalera Real** (Royal Staircase), installed by Philip II, leads up to the **state apartments** that fill out the palace's upper level. These apartments are really rather sterile, but there are several splendidly ornate Mudéjar wooden ceilings and one architectural peculiarity: extra floors were inserted into the original structure and the result is most clearly visible on the top floor, where the **Salón Mayor** (Main Hall) is framed by heavy stone arches. In this room also is a magnificent seventeenth-century tapestry, *The Siege of Carthage*, which covers most of the back wall. The adjoining **Despacho de Su Majestad el Rey** (Office of the King), with its attractive Gothic gallery, was where the Moors surrendered to Jaume I in 1229.

The Capella de Santa Ana

In the courtyard, the **Capella de Santa Ana** (Chapel of St Anne) is a largely fourteenth-century Gothic structure that is still used for army officers' masses and weddings. The interior, with its fine vaulted and embossed ceiling, is decidedly intimate, almost cosy, a suitable home for the **Capella de St Praxedis**, which, with its medieval effigy and reliquary, is devoted to a much venerated saint. A fourth-century figure, Praxedis survived the massacre of her Christian companions and had the presence of mind to mop up their blood with a sponge and preserve it for later worship; Jaume III brought the reliquary back with him from Rome. Incidentally, the delicate marble carving above the chapel entrance is carved in the Romanesque style, a deliberate use of what was by then an archaic tradition. The three figures above the door depict the Virgin Mary with saints Anne and Joachim to either side.

The Museu Diocesà

C/Mirador 5 • Mon–Sat 10am–2pm • €3 • ☎ 971 72 38 60

The smartly turned out **Museu Diocesà** (Diocesan Museum) occupies part of the old bishop's palace, a handsome courtyard complex round the back of the cathedral, directly above the old city walls. The museum's highlight is the city's largest collection of **Mallorcan Primitive art**, displayed on the ground floor alongside an assortment of religious statuary and a scattering of reliquaries. Later – and lesser – items are displayed upstairs.

The ground floor

In the first room beyond reception is the striking *Passion of Christ* by an unknown artist dubbed the **Master of the Passion of Mallorca**. Dated to the end of the thirteenth century, the painting consists of a series of small vignettes outlining the story of Christ, but the artistry is in the warm and gentle detail: the Palm Sunday donkey leans forward pushing his nose towards a child; one of the disciples reaches out across the Last Supper table for the fish; and two of Jesus' disciples slip their sandals off in eager anticipation during the Washing of the Feet. Opposite is another fine work, **Pere Niçard**'s large and dramatic, late fifteenth-century *St George and the Dragon*, a panel painting in which the stern fortifications of Palma appear in the background. Below the saint, to either side of Christ emerging from his tomb, are smaller paintings depicting the conquest of Mallorca by Jaume I – the storming of Palma on the right and the administering of (rough) justice to the left.

1

In the next room, the museum displays an intriguing *St Paul* retable by the **Master of Bishop Galiana**, whose tight lines are very much in the Catalan tradition. This particular panel painting is a didactic cartoon-strip illustrating the life of St Paul, who is shown with his Bible open and sword in hand, a view of the Church militant that must have accorded well with the preoccupations of the powerful bishops of Mallorca. Look out also for the way Galiana portrays the Conversion on the road to Damascus, with Saul/Paul struck by a laser-like beam of light. Exhibited elsewhere on the ground floor are several paintings by **Pere Terrencs**, but it is his *Crucifixion* that catches the eye, a sophisticated, early sixteenth-century work of strong, deep colours set within a triangulated structure. Above is the blood-spattered, pale-white body of Christ, while down below – divided by the Cross – are two groups, one of hooded mourners, the other a trio of nonchalant Roman soldiers in contemporary Spanish dress. Terrencs has chosen to ignore the two thieves who were crucified with Christ, showing him suffering alone on a bare and barren hill.

The first floor

Upstairs, the museum's first floor has a few modest paintings from the seventeenth century onwards, a room full of ceramics, and a **graffiti wall** where generations of bored priests doodled and dawdled. Curiously, there are also a few bits of furniture designed by **Gaudí**, who lodged here at the palace when he was working on the cathedral (see p.51).

The Palau March

C/Palau Reial 18 • April–Oct Mon–Fri 10am–6pm, Sat 10am–2pm; Nov–March Mon–Fri 10am–5pm, Sat 10am–2pm • €4.50 • ☎ 971 71 11 22, ⓦ fundacionbmarch.es

Just along the street from the cathedral, the arcaded galleries and imperious Italianate bulk of the **Palau March** fill out the entire block between c/Palau Reial and c/Conquistador. The *palau* was built between 1939 and 1945 in the general style of the city's earlier Renaissance mansions on behalf of **Joan March**, long the island's most powerful citizen (see box opposite). A visit begins with the palace's most enjoyable feature, its splendid **Italianate courtyard**, which offers attractive views over the city centre and displays a potpourri of modern **sculpture** drawn from the March collection. Amongst the twenty or so pieces exhibited, there are two Henry Moores, a Rodin torso and two small marbles by Barbara Hepworth.

Beyond the courtyard, the **interior** of the *palau* is a anticlimax, its cold stone walls displaying an odd and unsatisfying mix of curios. As you enter the building on the right-hand side of the courtyard, beside the Rodin, the first mini-room gives some background information on the kitsch, eighteenth-century **Neapolitan figurines** that are the villa's main exhibit – as displayed in several subsequent rooms and culminating in a **Nativity Scene**, complete with a veritable army of small models packed into a large glass cabinet. It's difficult to know quite what to make of all this – and things get worse on the first floor, where the Spanish painter **Josep Maria Sert** (1874–1945) was responsible for both the brutal muscularity of the ceiling painting at the top of the stairs and the March family's one-time **music room** just beyond. The latter is decorated with racist murals depicting New Orleans jazz scenes of frolicking "Negroes" – Sert did much better elsewhere. The only modest lights in the cultural gloom are the adjoining **map room**, which holds an idiosyncratic collection of old maps, and several coldly opulent ersatz nineteenth-century period rooms.

The city walls and the Parc de la Mar

A wide flight of steps leads down from between the cathedral and the Palau de l'Almudaina to a handsomely restored section of the **Renaissance city walls**, whose

JOAN MARCH

One of the most controversial figures in Mallorca's recent history, **Joan March** (1880–1962) was born a peasant's son in the small town of Santa Margalida on the east side of the island. At school, he showed his entrepreneurial flair by loaning money to his classmates at a high rate of interest and deciding, so the story goes, to start a trade in cigarettes, charging by the puff. March's father was a pig herder and at the age of 20 Joan negotiated the first of his major business deals, supplying meat direct to a sausage factory in Barcelona. In the next few years he allegedly established a dominant position in the **tobacco smuggling** trade with Algeria, displaying a ruthlessness that made him feared and loathed in equal measure.

March made more money in World War I, when both the British and the Germans paid him for his services, and took advantage of the difficulties experienced by the island's landed aristocracy to make yet more. For a variety of reasons, including the phylloxera infestation of the vineyards (see p.30), many of Mallorca's large estates had become uneconomic. March bought them up for a song and then sold them back to the farm hands who had previously worked them. The profit on each transaction was small, but there was the economy of scale: March sold no less than forty thousand land titles, an enormous number for a small island, and by these means transformed the structure of Mallorcan society as an accidental corollary to his greed.

During the Spanish Civil War, it seems likely that March loaned **Franco** money on generous terms and helped the Fascists with military supplies. Whatever the truth, March did become the richest man in Franco's Spain and was much favoured by the regime, though he was not averse to playing it both ways: recently declassified documents have revealed that during World War II the British paid him handsomely for his efforts in keeping Spain neutral.

In 1955, for reasons that remain obscure, he decided to reinvent himself, becoming a **patron of the arts**, buying up dozens of sculptures and paintings and giving millions of pesetas to a new charitable foundation, the **Fundación Juan March**. In Palma, the *fundación* runs a major art gallery (see p.67) and March's old house, the Palau March (see opposite) is open to the public. However, the man is now mainly recalled by the bank he set up in 1926, the **Banca March**, which has branches right across the island.

mighty zigzag of bastions, bridges, gates and dry moats once encased the whole city. These replaced the city's **medieval walls**, portions of which also survive – look back up from the foot of the steps and a large chunk is clearly visible beneath the cathedral. Constructed of sandstone blocks and adobe, the earlier fortifications depended for their efficacy on their height, with a gallery running along the top from which the defenders could fire at the enemy. By the middle of the fifteenth century, however, the development of more effective artillery had shifted the military balance in favour of offence, with cannons now able to breach medieval city walls with comparative ease. The military architects of the day soon evolved a new design in which walls were built much lower and thicker to absorb cannon shot, while four-faced bastions – equipped with artillery platforms – projected from the line of the walls, providing the defenders with a variety of firing lines. The whole caboodle was protected by a water-filled **moat** with deep, sheer sides. The costs of refortifying the major cities of western Europe were astronomical, but every country joined in the rush. In Palma, the Habsburgs ordered work to start on the new (Renaissance) design in the 1560s, though the chain of bastions was only completed in 1801.

The city walls' walkway

A wide and pleasant **walkway** runs from the foot of the steps below the cathedral along the top of the Renaissance walls, providing delightful views of the city and harbour plus an insight into the tremendous strength of the fortifications. Heading **west**, the walkway leads to the **tiered gardens** of a lush Moorish-style park, which tumbles down to – and runs along beside – Avinguda d'Antoni Maura, an extension of the tree-lined Passeig d'es Born (see p.64).

1

Heading **east** from the steps below the cathedral, the walkway along the city walls passes above the planted trees, concrete terraces and ornamental lagoon of the **Parc de la Mar**, an imaginative and popular redevelopment of the disused land that once lay between the walls and the coastal motorway. Indeed, it has proved so popular that the municipality are considering shoving the highway underground so that they can extend the park to the seashore.

Wall and walkway zigzag along the south side of old Palma before eventually fizzling out at Plaça Llorenç Villalonga, but long before that – just a couple of minutes from the cathedral – you reach the double **Portella gateway**, where you go down one of the wide stone ramps to reach the foot of c/Portella near the Banys Àrabs (see below).

The old town

The medina-like maze of streets to the rear of the cathedral constitutes the heart of the **old town**, which extends north to Plaça Cort and east to Avinguda Gabriel Alomar i Villalonga. Long a neglected corner of the city, most of the district has now been refurbished and its antique charm restored. The area's general appearance is its main appeal, and you can spend hours wandering down narrow lanes and alleys, loitering in squares and gazing at Renaissance mansions. It's also worth looking out for the district's two finest churches – the **Església de Santa Eulalia** and the **Basílica de Sant Francesc** – plus the city's most extensive museum, the **Museu de Mallorca**.

The Banys Àrabs

C/Can Serra 7 • Daily: June–Sept 9am–8pm; Oct–May 9am–6pm • €2 • ☎ 971 72 15 49

North of the Portella gate (see above), the first turning on the right leads to the **Banys Àrabs** (Arab Baths), one of the few genuine reminders of the Moorish presence. Dating back to the tenth century, this brick *hammam* (bath house) consists of a small horseshoe-arched and domed chamber that was once heated through the floor. The arches rest on stone pillars, an irregular bunch thought to have been looted from the remains of the island's Roman buildings. The baths are reasonably well preserved, but if you've been to the baths in Girona or Granada, or even the Baños Árabes in the Palau de l'Almudaina (see p.54), these are really rather dull. The lush garden outside, with tables where you can picnic, is perhaps nicer.

The Museu de Mallorca

C/Portella 5 • Currently closed for refurbishment, but scheduled to re-open in 2013 when opening hours are likely to be Tues–Sat 10am–6pm, Sun 10am–2pm • ☎ 971 71 75 40, ⊕ museudemallorca.es

The expansive **Museu de Mallorca** occupies **Can Aiamans**, a rambling Renaissance mansion, whose high-ceilinged rooms make a delightful setting for an enjoyable medley of Mallorcan artefacts. The earliest exhibits date from prehistoric times, but there's also a superb assortment of Gothic paintings and some excellent examples of *Modernista* fittings and furnishings. The labelling is patchy but hopefully the **major revamp**, which is currently underway, will rectify matters; it's also possible that the layout of the museum will change – so the description below should be treated with caution.

Prehistory, the Romans and the Moors

Currently, the collection begins in the **basement**, on the right-hand side of the entrance courtyard, with a series of rooms that track through the island's early history. Here you'll find a ragbag of **archeological finds** and displays on the *navetas* and *talayots* typical of the Balearics' early Talayotic culture (see p.242). The **Late Talayotic Period** (500/400 BC–123 AD) is when the islanders either made – or possibly imported – the finely detailed and extremely **bellicose statuettes** that are some of the museum's most prized artefacts. Of the dozen or so statuettes, most are of nude aggressive men, helmeted and armed, and representative of a warlike culture: indeed, such was the islanders' reputation as warriors that the Carthaginians recruited hundreds of them to fight in their armies during the Punic Wars against Rome in the third century BC. Equally striking is the **Bou de Talapí**, an angular carving of a bull's head that exudes a brutish strength of almost disconcerting proportions.

The museum also possesses a number of finely worked funerary tablets from **Roman Mallorca**, while highlights of the **Moorish** period include some ornate Mudéjar wooden panelling and an exquisite selection of Arab and Moorish jewellery.

The Mallorcan Primitives

On the left-hand side of the entrance courtyard, an old stone stairway leads up to a section devoted to the city's second largest collection of **Mallorcan Primitive painters** after the Museu Diocesà (see p.55). On display are works by the Masters of Montesión and Castellitx and an especially fine panel painting entitled *Santa Quiteria*, whose lifelike, precisely executed figures – right down to the king's wispy beard – are typical of the gifted **Master of the Privileges** (possibly Joan Loert). There's also a curious thirteenth-century work by an unknown artist dedicated to St Bernard of Clairvaux, the founder of the Cistercian order, with the saint on his knees devotedly drinking the milk of the Virgin Mary.

One of the most talented of the Mallorcan Primitives was **Francesc Comes** (1379–1415), whose skill in catching subtle skin textures both matched his Flemish contemporaries and represents a softening of the early Mallorcan Primitives' crudeness. The museum exhibits several of his paintings, including a striking *St George*, in which the saint – girl-like, with typically full lips – impales a lime-green dragon with more horns/hooks than could possibly be useful.

Active around 1500, the **Master of the Predellas** – probably a certain Joan Rosató – was one of the last talented exponents of Mallorcan Gothic. He is well represented by his Bosch-like triptych of the *Life of Santa Margalida*, with each group of onlookers a sea of ugly, deformed faces and cruelly curious eyes. The work outlines the life of **Margaret of Antioch**, the highly venerated patron saint of pregnant women. During the reign of the Roman emperor Diocletian (284–305 AD) she refused to marry a pagan prefect and was consequently executed after being tortured with gusto. As if this weren't enough, Satan, disguised as a dragon, swallowed her, but couldn't digest her holiness, so his stomach opened up and out she popped unharmed.

The Counter-Reformation

The stodgy art of the **Counter-Reformation** was a poor successor to the Mallorcan Primitives, but Palma's own Miquel Bestard (1590–1633) redeems the genre rather with his whopping *Feeding of the Five Thousand*. Miraculously, Jesus feeds the hungry crowd from a meagre supply of loaves and fishes, but the subtext is much more revealing: Bestard's crowds are well behaved and respectful of authority – just what the Catholic hierarchy had in mind.

Modern art and the *Modernista* school

The museum possesses a mildly engaging assortment of nineteenth- and early twentieth-century paintings by both native artists and foreign artists once resident in Mallorca. This includes a neat sample of works by Mallorca's own **Juli Ramis** (1909–90), whose striking style is illustrated by his oil-on-fabric *Tres Cavalls* (Three Horses) and the radiant blues of *Tardor en blau* (Blue Autumn). A native of Sóller, Ramis left the island when he was nineteen to spend the next sixty years abroad, travelling widely and becoming acquainted with some of the leading artistic lights of his day. Ramis mixed his styles, but was essentially an Expressionist with Surrealist leanings. He returned to Mallorca in the last years of his life and died in Palma.

1

THE ARISTOCRACY AT HOME: THE MANSIONS OF PALMA

Most of medieval Palma was destroyed by fire, so the **patrician mansions** that characterize the old town today mostly date from a reconstruction programme that began in the late seventeenth and ended in the early eighteenth century. Consequently they are surprisingly uniform in layout, built in the fashionable **Renaissance style**, with columns and capitals, loggias and arcades tucked away behind outside walls of plain stone three or four storeys high. Entry to almost all of these mansions was through a great arched **gateway**, which gave onto a rectangular courtyard around which the house was built. Originally, the **courtyard** would have been cheered by exotic trees and flowering shrubs, and equipped with a fancy stone and ironwork well-head, where visitors could water their horses. From the courtyard, an **exterior staircase** led up to the main public rooms – with the servants' quarters below and the family's private apartments up above. For the landed gentry, it was a very comfortable life indeed: as one British gentleman stated approvingly in the 1840s, "The higher classes lead a life of perfect inactivity – doing little, but eating occasionally ... It is difficult to imagine a less agitated or more objectless existence."

Very few of these mansions are open to the public, and all you'll see for the most part is the view from the gateway – the municipality actually pays people to leave their big wooden gates open. Several have, however, passed into the public domain, the Can Aimans, now the home of the Museu de Mallorca (see p.58), being the prime example. Others that merit a look are Can Bordils (see below), Can Oleza (see below), Can Vivot (see opposite) and Can Solleric (p.65), but only the last one of these is open to the public.

The museum also possesses a substantial collection of **Modernista** fittings and furnishings, mostly retrieved from shops and houses that have since been demolished. Of particular interest are the charming wall tiles manufactured at the island's **La Roqueta** works. The pottery was in production for just twenty years (1897–1918), but this coincided with the vogue for the *Modernista* pieces in which La Roqueta excelled.

Around Carrer Morei

Up the hill from the Museu de Mallorca, c/Portella leads into **Carrer Morei** where, at no. 9, you'll find **Can Oleza** (no public access), a sixteenth-century mansion with an elegant shaded courtyard embellished by a handsome balustrade and a set of Ionic columns. Nearby, in c/Almudaina, are the chunky remains of the old east gate, the **Arc de L'Almudaina**, a rare remnant of the Moorish fortifications topped with medieval barbicans. Beyond the old gate, at 9 c/Almudaina, is **Can Bordils**, one of the city's oldest mansions, now housing municipal offices with just two splendidly carved windows and a pair of thick stone doorway arches left to recall its better days.

Església de Santa Eulalia

Plaça Santa Eulalia • Mon–Fri 7am–12.30pm & 5.45–8.30pm, Sat 7am–1pm & 4.30–8.45pm, Sun 8am–1pm & 6.30–8.30pm • Free

Overshadowing the square at the top of c/Morei, the **Església de Santa Eulalia** was built on the site of a mosque in the mid-thirteenth century. It took just 25 years to complete and consequently possesses an architectural homogeneity that's unusual for ecclesiastical Palma, though there was some later medieval tinkering, and nineteenth-century renovators added the belfry and remodelled the main (south) facade. The church is typically Gothic in construction, with a yawning nave originally designed – as in the cathedral – to give the entire congregation a view of the high altar. The bricked-up windows of today – as well as the darkness of the stained glass – keep out much of the light and spoil the effect, but suggestions that they be cleared have always been ignored. Framing the nave, the aisles accommodate twelve shallow **chapels**, one of which (the first on the right) sports a delightful Gothic panel-painting in finely observed Flemish style. In kitsch contrast, the other chapels are standard-issue Baroque, though they pale into insignificance when compared with the hourglass-shaped **high altarpiece**, a flashy Baroque extravagance of colossal proportions. This holy ground witnessed one of the more disgraceful episodes of Mallorcan history. During Easter week, 1435, a rumour went round that **Jewish** townsfolk had enacted a blasphemous mock-up of the Crucifixion. There was no proof, but the Jews were promptly robbed of their possessions and condemned to be burnt at the stake unless they adopted Christianity. The ensuing mass baptism was held here at Santa Eulalia.

Can Vivot

C/Can Savella 4

Can Vivot, which lies behind the church of Santa Eulalia, is an especially opulent early eighteenth-century mansion, whose spacious main courtyard, with its handsome columns and arches, is distinguished by a lovely staircase. Built on top of a Moorish palace, the mansion has an interior decorated in fine Neoclassical style, especially the sumptuous library, though the house is rarely open to the public.

The Basílica de Sant Francesc

Plaça Sant Francesc • Daily 9.30am–12.30pm & 3.30–6pm; closed Sun afternoon • €1.50 • ☎ 971 71 12 12

A short walk east of Plaça Santa Eulalia, the **Basílica de Sant Francesc** is a domineering pile that occupies the site of the old Moorish soap factory. Built for the Franciscans towards the end of the thirteenth century, the original church was a vast Gothic edifice that benefited from royal patronage after King Jaume II's son, also named Jaume, became a member of the monkish order in 1300. Subsequent remodellings replaced the initial wooden ceiling with today's single-span, vaulted stone roof of imposing dimensions and added grandiloquent chapels to the nave and apse. The Basílica became the most fashionable church in medieval Palma and its friars received handsome kickbacks for entombing the local nobility within its precincts. Increasingly eager to enrich themselves, the priests came to compete for possession of the corpses, while the various aristocratic clans vied with each other in the magnificence of their sarcophagi. These tensions exploded when a certain Jaume Armadams had a jug of water emptied over his head inside the church on All Saints' Day, 1490. The congregation went berserk and more than three hundred noblemen fought it out in the nave before the priests finally restored order. The scandal caused the Basílica to be closed by decree for several decades. In the seventeenth century the church was badly damaged by lightning, prompting a thoroughgoing reconstruction, which accounts for most of its present-day appearance.

The main facade

Dating from the seventeenth century, the **main facade** displays a stunning severity of style, with its great rectangular sheet of dressed sandstone stretching up to an arcaded and balustraded balcony. It is pierced by a gigantic rose window of Plateresque intricacy and embellished by a **Baroque doorway**, the tympanum of which features a triumphant Virgin Mary engulfed by a wriggling mass of sculptured decoration. Above the Madonna is the figure of St George and to either side and below are assorted saints – look out for the scholar and missionary Ramon Llull (see p.62), shown reading a book. The strange statue in front of the doorway of a Franciscan monk and a young Native American celebrates the missionary work of **Junipero Serra** (see p.162), a Mallorcan priest despatched to California in 1768, who subsequently founded the cities of San Diego, Los Angeles and San Francisco.

The interior

Approached through a neat and trim Gothic cloister, the church's **interior** is distinguished by its monumental **high altar**, a gaudy Baroque affair featuring balustrades, lattice-work and clichéd figurines beneath a painted wooden statue of *St George and the Dragon*. It's heady stuff, as are the rolling scrollwork and trumpeter-angel of the **pulpit** on the wall of the nave, and the ornate Gothic-Baroque frontispiece of the **organ** just opposite. Beside the high altar, recessed chapels enclose the

1

A CATHOLIC HERO: THE LIFE AND TIMES OF RAMON LLULL

The life of **Ramon Llull** (1235–1315) – a figure much beloved of Catholic propagandists – was an exercise in redemption through carnal excess. As a young man, Llull was an ebullient rake in the retinue of the future Jaume II. His sexual adventures were not impeded in the least by his marriage, but they ground to a dramatic halt when a certain Ambrosia de Castillo, his latest amatory target, whom he had pursued into the church of Santa Eulalia on horseback, revealed to him her diseased breasts. A deeply shocked Llull devoted the rest of his life to the Catholic faith, becoming a fearless missionary and dedicated scholar of theology, philosophy and alchemy. Exemplifying the cosmopolitan outlook of thirteenth-century Mallorca, Llull learnt to read, write and speak several languages, including Arabic, and travelled to France, much of Spain and North Africa. He also founded a monastery and missionary school on **Puig Randa** (see p.164), east of Palma, where he spent ten years in seclusion, writing no fewer than 250 books and treatises. It was Llull's scholarship that attracted the attention of his old friend Jaume II, who summoned him to court in 1282. With royal patronage, Llull then established a monastic school of Oriental languages in the mountains near Valldemossa, and it was here he trained his future missionary companions. Llull was **killed** on his third evangelical excursion to Algeria in 1315, his martyrdom ensuring his subsequent beatification.

ambulatory with the first chapel on the left holding the **tomb of Ramon Llull**, whose bones were brought back to Palma after his martyrdom in Algeria in 1315. Considering the sanctity of the man's remains, it's an odd and insignificant-looking memorial, with Llull's alabaster effigy set high up on the wall to the right of the chapel altarpiece at a disconcertingly precarious angle.

The Templar chapel
C/Temple • In theory, Mon–Fri 9.30am–1pm & 3.30–7pm, Sat 9.30am–1pm • Free

At the end of c/Ramon Llull, a large and distinctive thirteenth-century fortified **gateway** marks what was once the entrance to the castle-like compound of the **Knights Templar**, a military order founded to support the Crusades. The knights established bases right across the Mediterranean and this was one of the more important – though they were soon to be dispossessed. The order was rich and secretive, its independence resented by the papacy and just about every secular ruler in Europe. In 1312, following trumped-up charges of heresy, sorcery and bestiality, the pope disbanded the order and their Palma compound passed into the hands of the Hospitallers of St John, a rival knightly order. The Knights Hospitallers survived until 1802, when the Spanish king disbanded them and confiscated their property.

An alley leads through the gateway to the only other surviving part of the military compound, the **Templar chapel**, whose gloomy, rib-vaulted, Gothic-Romanesque nave is supported by a set of narrow columns and flanked by arcaded galleries.

Plaça Sant Jeroni
South of the Templar gateway, along c/Temple, **Plaça Sant Jeroni** is a pretty little piazza set around a dinky water fountain. The severe stone walls of a former convent, now a college, dominate one side of the square, while the **Església de St Jeroni** fills out another. The church facade is mostly a plain stone wall, but it is broken up by two doorways, the one on the left displaying a swirl of carved foliage and garlands of fruit. The door's tympanum portrays the well-known story of Saint Jerome in the desert, during which the saint endures all sorts of tribulations and temptations, but still sticks true to the faith; above, two heraldic lions stand rampant. The **interior**, with its heavy stone vaulting is mostly seventeenth-century, but it's rarely open to the public – a shame given that the church holds several good paintings by the Mallorcan Primitives. From the square, it's a five-minute walk to Plaça Cort (see p.64).

CLOCKWISE FROM TOP LEFT OLD TOWN DOOR KNOCKER; COLL, SA GERRERIA (P.75); FUNDACIÓ MIRÓ (P.80); CATHEDRAL (P.47) >

1

Plaça Cort

Bustling **Plaça Cort**, with its elegant nineteenth-century facades and grizzled olive tree, was named after the various legal bodies – both secular and religious – which were once concentrated here. Along with the rest of Spain, Mallorca possessed a truly Byzantine legal system until the whole caboodle was swept away and rationalized during the Napoleonic occupation. Today, one side of the square is dominated by the **Ajuntament** (Town Hall), a debonair example of the late Renaissance style: pop in for a look at the grand and self-assured foyer, which mostly dates from the nineteenth century, and the six folkloric *gigantones* (giant carnival figures) stored here – four in a corner, the other two tucked against the staircase.

From Plaça Cort, it's a pleasant five-minute stroll to Plaça de la Reina via **c/Sant Domingo**, which weaves down a hill lined by attractive nineteenth-century townhouses with wrought-iron grilles and stone balconies. Alternatively, it's a short walk from Plaça Cort along c/Palau Reial to the Palau March (see p.56) and the cathedral (see pp.47–54).

Plaça de la Reina

Tiny, leafy **Plaça de la Reina** is at the very heart of Palma with one of the city's most sociable avenues – the Passeig d'es Born – extending north, and Avinguda d'Antoni Maura running south. Also, a wide and good-looking flight of steps, the **Costa de la Seu**, leads up from the square beneath the spiky walls of the Palau de l'Almudaina to the cathedral (see pp.47–54) and the Palau March (see p.56). The *palau* originally extended right down to the Plaça de la Reina, incorporating what is now the *Cappuccino* café as well as the tiny Biblioteca March Servera (library), but these parts were hived off years ago.

Avinguda d'Antoni Maura

South of Plaça de la Reina, **Avinguda d'Antoni Maura** slices down to the wide breakwater that marks the start of Palma harbour. Until recently, the avenue was a traffic-clogged mess, but it's been prettied up with a long line of cafés on one side and tiered gardens that stretch up towards the cathedral on the other. It takes its name from **Antoni Maura** (1853–1925), a Mallorcan who served as prime minister of Spain four times between 1903 and 1921. An outstanding orator and extraordinarily forceful personality, Maura was a conservative who saw universal suffrage – which was in place from 1887 – as "the politics of the mob", preferring a limited franchise and a constitution that gave power to the middle classes, as long as they marched to the tune of Church and Crown. In a backward, largely agrarian society, most Spaniards were largely indifferent to national issues and power was concentrated in the hands of district bosses, or *caciques*, who would bring out the vote for any candidate provided they were guaranteed control of political patronage. Some bosses ruled by intimidation, others by bribery, but the end result was a dense mixture of charity and jobbery, dubbed *caciquismo*, which made national government well-nigh impossible. Maura struggled against this chicanery, and his assertive nationalism was quite enough for Franco to have this avenue named after him; no one has bothered to change it since.

The Passeig d'es Born

North of Plaça de la Reina, the **Passeig d'es Born** is distinguished by its long line of plane trees and by the stone sphinxes at its top and bottom. The avenue has been the city's principal promenade since the early fifteenth century, when the stream that ran here was diverted following a disastrous flash flood. In recent years, it has suffered badly from traffic congestion, but newly imposed restrictions have restored some of its more pleasing features and a concerted effort has also been made to clean up its decaying mansions, large and decorous affairs that once housed the island's most powerful families. One of the last to receive the treatment was **Can Alomar**, an imposing stone extravagance at the corner of c/Sant Feliu that now accommodates luxury shops.

Can Solleric

Passeig d'es Born 27 • Tues–Sat 10am–2pm & 5–9pm, Sun 10am–1.30pm • Free • ☏ 971 72 20 92

Built for a family of cattle-and olive oil-merchants in 1763, **Can Solleric** is perhaps the grandest mansion on the Passeig d'es Born. It's a lavish affair of heavy wooden doors, marble columns and vaulted ceilings as well as a fine Italianate loggia and an elegant double stone stairway leading up from an internal courtyard. The house now displays temporary exhibitions of modern art and has a small tourist information desk.

El Puig de Sant Pere

The ancient neighbourhood of **El Puig de Sant Pere** (St Peter's Mount) covers the area west of the Passeig d'es Born and north to Avinguda Jaume III. The district comprises a cobweb of narrow lanes and alleys that shelter a sprinkling of old stone mansions, though most were divided up years ago to cater for the district's sailors, dockers and fishermen. It's the general flavour of Sant Pere that appeals rather than specific sights, but it's still worth seeking out two late Renaissance facades on c/Sant Feliu, which runs off Passeig d'es Born. At no. 8 is **Can Moner**, whose ornate doorway sports telamons, cherubs and cornucopia, whilst no. 10, **Can Pavesi**, offers a mythical beast with its tongue stuck right out.

There's a gruesome story behind the name of a lane off nearby c/Estanc. **Mà del Moro**, "The Hand of the Moor", harks back to Ahmed, an eighteenth-century slave who murdered his master in a house on this alley. Ahmed was executed for the crime, and his hand was chopped off and stuck above the doorway of the house where the murder was committed – "pour encourager les autres" as Voltaire would have it.

Avinguda Jaume III

Avinguda Jaume III marches west from the top of Passeig d'es Born flanked by a matching set of long and sturdy stone arcades, which encase some of the island's chicest clothes shops and downtown's biggest department store, **El Corte Inglés** (see p.77). Dating from the 1940s, this is Francoista architecture at its most appealing – very symmetrical and self-consciously Spanish – and there's something very engaging about the airs and graces of the avenue, with its jostle of be-shorted tourists and be-suited Spaniards. Furthermore, the web of ancient alleys immediately to the north of the avenue, focused on **c/Concepció**, is another attractive corner of the city, all high stone walls and dignified old mansions.

Passeig Mallorca and La Feixina

At the top of Avinguda Jaume III, the **Passeig Mallorca** is a busy boulevard bisected by the deep, walled watercourse that once served as the city moat – and is now an especially handsome feature of the city. On the other side of the footbridge spanning the Passeig Mallorca is **La Feixina**, a pleasant terraced **park**, whose trees, lawns, flower beds and fountains step south to the foot of **Avinguda Argentina**, just east of the fenced-off jetties where the fishing boats come in. The park's only scenic blot is the whopping **column** erected by Franco to honour those Balearic sailors who were loyal to the Fascist cause.

1

Es Baluard museu d'art modern i contemporani

Plaça Porta Santa Catalina • Tues–Sat 10am–8pm, Sun 10am–3pm • €6 • ☎ 971 90 82 00, ⊛ esbaluard.org

Es Baluard museu d'art modern i contemporani (Es Baluard Modern and Contemporary Art Museum) has a spectacularly handsome setting, nestled within the stern lines of a mighty stone bastion that looks out over the harbour. Outside, the museum begins with a series of large, geometric **sculptures** carefully positioned across the top of the fortification in a perfect match of style and setting. Inside, the museum, which spreads over three floors, does not quite live up to its setting, but it does host a lively programme of temporary exhibitions, which affect exactly what parts of the permanent collection are on display – and where. That said, the ground floor usually has one room devoted to **Joan Miró**, with examples of his early landscape paintings through to his more characteristic cartoon-like squiggles, and a section dedicated to the Mallorcan landscapes of **Hermen Anglada Camarasa** (1871–1959). On the first floor, you can expect to see the museum's pride and joy, a rare and unusual sample of **Picasso** ceramics, most memorably a striking white, ochre and black vase-like piece entitled *Big Bird Corrida*. There are more sculptures on the museum's rooftop walkway, complemented by panoramic views over the harbour and the city.

Around Carrer Unió

Running east from Plaça Rei Joan Carles I, **Carrer Unió** is a new if rather unimaginative appellation – it means "unity" – for a street Franco had previously named after **General Mola**, one of the prime movers of the Nationalist rebellion of 1936. Mola was killed in a plane accident during the Civil War, possibly to Franco's relief. Hitler, for one, thought that Mola was the more competent, remarking that his death meant that "Franco came to the top like Pontius Pilate in the Creed". Near the start of c/Unio, at no. 3, **Can Balaguer** is a sprawling Renaissance mansion with imposing doors and a grand cobbled courtyard. A mouldy sort of place, it has long been in need of a major refurbishment – and one has at last just started; the plan is to turn the place into an art gallery. Flanking c/Unió, **Plaça Mercat** is a crowded little square that is overseen by two identical *Modernista* buildings commissioned by a wealthy baker, Josep Casasayas, in 1908. Each is a masterpiece of flowing, organic lines tempered by graceful balconies and decorated with fern-leaf and butterfly motifs.

Plaça Weyler

Plaça Weyler is home to a number of *Modernista* extravagances, with the **Forn des Teatre** (theatre bakery), at no.9, boasting floral motifs and a gaily painted wooden doorway. The bakery is downright playful, but across the street is a much more imposing *Modernista* edifice, the **Gran Hotel** of 1903. Recently cleaned and buffed, the hotel's facade boasts a dinky turret-tower, balconies, columns and bay windows enlivened with intricate floral trimmings and brilliant polychrome ceramics inspired by Hispano-Arabic designs. The *Gran Hotel* now houses a café on the ground floor (see p.74) and the Caixa Forum art gallery up above (see below).

Caixa Forum art gallery

Plaça Weyler 3 • Tues–Sat 10am–9pm, Sun 10am–2pm • Free • ☎ 971 17 85 00

Inside the *Gran Hotel* (see above), the spacious **Caixa Forum art gallery** organizes an excellent and wide-ranging programme of temporary exhibitions. Its permanent collection is essentially confined to a large sample of work by the Catalan Impressionist-Expressionist **Hermen Anglada Camarasa** (1871–1959). Camarasa is best known for the evocative Mallorcan land- and seascapes he produced during his sojourn on the island from 1914 to 1936. However, the gallery only possesses one or two of these scenes and instead Camarasa is poorly represented here by two huge and drearily folkloric canvases entitled *Valencia* and *El Tango de la Corona*, though a couple of sombre women's portraits are rather more inspiring.

Plaça Major and Plaça Marquès del Palmer

On either side of the Neoclassical Teatre Principal on c/Riera (see p.76), a steep flight of steps leads up to **Plaça Major**, a large pedestrianized square built on the site of the former headquarters of the **Inquisition**. The square, a rather plain affair with a symmetrical portico running around its perimeter, once housed the fish and vegetable market, but nowadays it's mainly popular for its pavement cafés.

On the south side of Plaça Major lies the much smaller **Plaça Marquès del Palmer**, a cramped setting for two fascinating *Modernista* edifices. The more dramatic is **Can Rei**, a six-storey apartment building splattered with polychrome ceramics and floral decoration, its centrepiece a gargoyle-like face set between a pair of winged dragons. The facade of the adjacent **L'Àguila** building is of similar ilk, though there's greater emphasis on window space, reflecting its original function as a department store. Close by, the shopping area stretching south from Plaça Marquès del Palmer to Plaça Cort retains an agreeably old-fashioned air, with the three- and four-storey buildings that frame its main streets – principally pedestrianized **c/Jaume II** – embellished with an abundance of fancy iron-grilled balconies.

Carrer Sant Miquel

Cutting north from Plaça Major, **Carrer Sant Miquel** is a popular and pleasant shopping street that runs past the main city market, on Plaça Olivar (see p.78), before pressing on towards Plaça Espanya. Near the start of the street, at no. 11, a branch of the **Banca March** occupies a fine Renaissance mansion whose *Modernista* flourishes date from a tasteful refurbishment in 1917. The building has two entrances, one to the bank, the other leading upstairs to the Museu Fundación Juan March.

Museu Fundación Juan March

C/Sant Miquel 11 • Mon–Fri 10am–6.30pm, Sat 10.30am–2pm • Free • ☎ 971 71 35 15, ⓦ march.es/arte

The **Museu Fundación Juan March** showcases a prime sample of contemporary art drawn from the collection of the March family (see p.57). The collection features seventy works by 52 twentieth-century Spanish artists, the intention being to survey the Spanish contribution to modern art – a theme which is further developed by temporary exhibitions. The earliest piece, Picasso's *Tête de femme* (1907), is of particular interest, being one of the first of the artist's works to be influenced by the primitive forms that were to propel him, over the following decade, from the re-creation of natural appearances into abstract art. Miró and Dalí are also represented, and there's one still life by the Spanish Cubist Juan Gris, as well as a number of harsh abstractions by the leading contemporary Catalan artist Antoni Tàpies (1923–2012). Rather harder to negotiate are the allegedly "vigorous" abstractions of both the El Paso (Millares, Feito, Canogar) and the Parpalló (Sempere, Alfaro) groupings of the late 1950s.

Església Sant Miquel

C/Sant Miquel 67 • Mon–Sat 8am–1.30pm & 4.30–7.30pm • Free • ☎ 971 71 54 55

From the Museu Fundación Juan March, it's a brief stroll north along c/Sant Miquel to the **Església Sant Miquel**, whose sturdy exterior is the result of all sorts of architectural meddlings. Inside, the barrel-vaulted nave is almost entirely windowless, a dark and gloomy space where the one highlight is the high altarpiece, a Baroque classic with a central image celebrating St Michael in smiting mode. The altarpiece is a good example

1

of the intricate work of **Francesc Herrara** (1590–1656), a much-travelled Spanish painter of religious and genre subjects known for his purposeful compositions and tangy realism.

Along the harbourfront

The various marinas, shipyards, fish docks and ferry and cargo terminals that make up Palma's **harbourfront** extend west for several kilometres from the bottom of Avinguda d'Antoni Maura to the edge of Cala Major (see p.80). The harbour is at its prettiest along its eastern, city-centre-skirting stretch, where a cycling and walking path hugs the seashore, with boats to one side and bars, restaurants, apartment blocks and the smart hotels of the **Avinguda Gabriel Roca** – often dubbed the Passeig Marítim – across the main road on the other.

Sa Llotja

Plaça Llotja s/n · Tues–Sun 11m–1pm, but exhibition hours vary · ☎ 971 71 17 05

A harbourfront landmark, the fifteenth-century **Sa Llotja** once housed the city's stock exchange, but now hosts regular art exhibitions. Designed by Mallorca's own **Guillermo Sagrera**, one of the most original European architects of his day, this carefully composed, late-Gothic structure is distinguished by its four octagonal turrets, slender, spiralling columns and tall windows. It also boasts a series of fierce-looking gargoyles and a muscular angel – appropriately the Guardian Angel of Commerce – above the front door.

Consolat de Mar

The dignified **Consolat de Mar**, next door to Sa Llotja on Passeig de Sagrera, was built in the 1660s to accommodate the Habsburg officials who supervised maritime affairs in this part of the empire. Today, as the home of the president of the Balearic islands, it's closed to the public, but the outside is worth a second look for its pair of crusty old cannons and elegant Renaissance gallery. The forlorn-looking gate between the Consolat and Sa Llotja – the **Porta Vella del Moll** – originally stood at the end of Avgda d'Antoni Maura, where it was the main entrance into the city from the sea; it was moved here when portions of the town wall were demolished in the 1870s.

Parc Quarentena

A 20min walk west of Avgda Argentina along the harbourfront

With its cool and shaded terraces that clamber up the hillside from the harbourfront, the delightful **Parc Quarentena** is one of the city's best-kept parks, a verdant tangle of flowering shrubs and plants spreading beneath a canopy of palm trees. You can exit at the top on c/Patrimoni, metres from Plaça Gomila and Avgda Joan Miró.

The Poble Espanyol

C/Son Dureta 39 · Daily 9am–7.30pm · €8 · ☎ 971 73 70 70 · The Poble Espanyol is about 2.5km northwest of the city centre and served by Citysightseeing double-decker buses (see p.71)

The ever-so kitsch **Poble Espanyol** (Spanish Village) was constructed between 1965 and 1967, its Francoist intentions apparent in its celebration of everything Spanish. Walled like a medieval city, the "village" contains accurate, scaled-down reproductions of a number of old and important buildings, such as Barcelona's Palau de la Generalitat, Seville's Torre del Oro, a segment of Granada's Alhambra, El Greco's house in Toledo, and the Ermita de San Antonio in Madrid. These are dotted round the village's streets and squares, where you'll also find souvenir shops, restaurants and bars. It's all a bit daft – and school parties swamp the place during the day – but it is, perhaps, one way of introducing yourself to Spanish architecture.

The Castell de Bellver

C/Camilo José Cela s/n • May–Aug Tues–Sun 10am–7pm; Sept & Oct Tues–Sun 10am–6pm; Nov–Feb Tues–Sun 10am–5pm • €4 • ☎ 971 73 50 65, ⊛ cultura.palma.es • Served by Citysightseeing double-decker buses (see p.71), or take EMT bus #3 to Plaça Gomila, then it's a stiff, 30min walk uphill

Boasting superb views of Palma and its harbour from a wooded hilltop some 3km west of the city centre, the **Castell de Bellver** is a handsome, strikingly well-preserved fortress built for Jaume II at the beginning of the fourteenth century. Of canny circular design, the castle's immensely thick walls and steep ditches encircle a central **keep** that incorporates three imposing towers. In addition, an overhead, single-span **stone arch** connects the keep to a massive, freestanding **tower**, built as a final refuge. To enhance defence, the walls curve and bend and the interconnecting footbridges are set at oblique angles to each other. It's all very impressive – and looks well-nigh impregnable – but the castle was also intended to serve as a royal retreat from the summer heat, and so the austere outside walls hide a genteel-looking **circular courtyard**, surrounded by two tiers of inward-facing arcades that once belonged to the residential suites. The whole construction is ingenious, incorporating many skilful touches: the flat roof, for example, was designed to channel every drop of rainwater into a huge underground cistern. Soon after its construction, however, improvements in artillery rendered the original fortress obsolete and although modifications were made, they were never very convincing. Neither did it last long as a royal residence. As early as the 1350s the keep was in use as a prison, a function it performed until 1915, before finally becoming a **museum**.

The museum

Inside the castle, the ground floor houses a plodding exhibition on the history of the city, along with a small display on the castle's most distinguished prisoner, the eighteenth-century reformer Gaspar Jovellanos. Much better, however, is the delightful collection of **Roman statuary** on the floor above. A local antiquarian and ecclesiastical bigwig by the name of **Cardinal Antonio Despuig** (1745–1817) gathered together these classical pieces and bequeathed the whole lot to the city on his death. The only problem is that there's no labelling, so unless you're a classical expert it's impossible to know quite what you're looking at. Nevertheless, amongst the miscellany of busts and effigies, there's no mistaking a rare and perfectly preserved column of strikingly patterned *cippolino* marble and, most extraordinary of all, a small and exquisite alabaster of a sleeping **hermaphrodite**, apparently troubled by a confusing dream, half-in but mainly out of her toga. Other exhibits include carved seals, marble inscriptions, first-century medallions, a funeral stele, and a fearsome bust of **Medusa**, her head crawling with snakes.

ARRIVAL AND DEPARTURE
PALMA

BY PLANE

Mallorca international airport Mallorca's airport (☎ 971 78 90 00, ⊛ mallorcaairport.co.uk) is 11km east of the city centre, immediately behind the resort of Ca'n Pastilla. It has one enormous terminal, which handles both scheduled and charter flights, with Arrivals downstairs and Departures upstairs. On the Arrivals floor, a flotilla of car rental outlets jostles for position by the luggage carousels. Beyond, through the glass doors, is the main Arrivals Hall, with 24hr ATMs and currency exchange facilities, dozens of package-tour agents plus a provincial tourist office.

AIRPORT INFORMATION

Both Arrivals and Departures floors have information desks. In the Arrivals Hall, the provincial tourist office (Mon–Sat 8.30am–8pm, Sun 9am–1.30pm; ☎ 971 78 95 56) is currently beside Exit 3, though there are plans to move it elsewhere within the Arrivals Hall. It has a wide range of brochures, public transport timetables, maps and lists of hotels and *hostales*, but can't arrange accommodation.

TRANSPORT FROM THE AIRPORT

By car The airport is linked to the city and the Bay of Palma resorts by a busy highway, which shadows the shoreline from S'Arenal in the east to Palma Nova and Magaluf in the west.

By bus The least expensive way to reach downtown Palma from the airport is by EMT bus #1 (daily every 15min

1

6am–1am; €2.50), which leaves from outside the main entrance of the terminal building, just behind the taxi rank. They reach the city's inner ring road near the foot of Avgda Gabriel Alomar i Villalonga, at the c/Joan Maragall junction, then head on to Plaça Espanya, on the north side of the centre, before continuing west to the Passeig Mallorca and then south to the top of Avgda Jaume III, stopping frequently en route.

By taxi A taxi from the airport to the city centre costs about €20; taxi rates are controlled and a list of island-wide fares is available from the provincial tourist office in the Arrivals Hall.

BY FERRY

Palma car ferry and catamaran terminal is about 4km west of the city centre: Acciona Trasmediterranea (☎ 902 45 46 45, ☜ trasmediterranea.es) and Iscomar (☎ 902 11 91 28, ☜ www.iscomar.com) boats arrive at Terminal 2; Balearia boats (☎ 902 16 01 80, ☜ balearia.com) at Terminal 3, about 150m away. Ferry and high-speed catamaran tickets can be bought online, by phone, and at the ferry port, though the ticket offices at the port are only open before and just after sailings (see p.22). EMT bus #1 (daily every 15min 6am–1am; €1.50) runs from outside Terminal 2 to the Plaça Espanya. There are also taxi ranks outside both terminal buildings; the fare to the city centre is about €10.

BY BUS

Almost all long-distance buses arrive and depart from Palma's combined bus and train station, the Estació Intermodal, adjoining Plaça Espanya. There's an information desk at the Estació – and the city's two main tourist offices (see opposite) supply public transport timetables too. There's also an all-embracing website, covering both train and bus services, on ☜ tib.org, or call ☎ 971 17 77 77 (though you'll probably need to speak Spanish or Catalan). Long-distance buses are operated by a variety of companies, but EMT has a monopoly on Palma buses (see opposite).

Destinations Alcúdia (every 1–2hr; 1hr); Andratx (1–2 hourly; 1hr); Artà (2–5 daily; 1hr 20min); Banyalbufar (4–7 daily; 1hr); Binissalem (3–6 daily; 30min); Cala d'Or (Mon–Sat 6 daily, 3 on Sun; 1hr 15min); Cala Figuera (May–Oct Mon–Sat 2 daily; 1hr 45min); Cala Major (every 30min–1hr; 20min); Cala Millor (Mon–Sat every 1–2hr, 3 on Sun; 2hr); Cala Rajada (2–5 daily; 2hr); Colònia de Sant Jordi (3–5 daily; 1hr 20min); Coves del Drac (May–Oct Mon–Sat 4 daily, 1 on Sun; 1hr 15min); Deià (5–7 daily; 45min); Esporles (Mon–Fri hourly, 4 on Sat & Sun; 40min); Estellencs (4–7 daily; 1hr 15min); Lluc (Mon–Sat 2 daily, Sun 1 daily; 1hr 10min); Magaluf (1–2 hourly; 1hr); Peguera (1–2 hourly; 1hr); Pollença (Mon–Fri hourly, 7 on Sat & Sun; 45min); Port d'Alcúdia (every 1–2hr; 1hr); Port d'Andratx (1–2 hourly; 1hr 20min); Port de Pollença (every 1hr–2hr; 1hr 15min); Port de Sóller, via the tunnel (Mon–Fri hourly, Sat 8 daily, Sun 5 daily; 35min); Port de Sóller, via Valldemossa (5–7 daily; 1hr 30min); Porto Cristo (May–Oct Mon–Sat 8 daily, 3 on Sun; Sept–April 2–3 daily; 1hr 15min); Sóller, via the tunnel (Mon–Fri hourly, Sat 8 daily, Sun 5 daily; 30min); Sóller, via Valldemossa (5–7 daily; 1hr 15min); Valldemossa (Mon–Fri every 1–2hr, Sat 8 daily, Sun 5 daily; 30min).

BY TRAIN

Trains on Mallorca's principal train line arrive and depart from the Estació Intermodal, adjoining Plaça Espanya. This line travels east–west across the island linking Palma with the likes of Binissalem, Inca, Manacor and Muro. Both main tourist offices (see opposite) as well as the information desk at the Estació Intermodal issue train timetables. Alternatively, check out ☜ tib.org, or phone ☎ 971 17 77 77 (if you speak Spanish or Catalan). Mallorca's second train line, aimed principally at tourists, links Palma with Sóller (see box, p.91), from a separate station a few metres from the Estació Intermodal.

Destinations Binissalem (every 20min; 30min); Inca (every 20min; 40min); Lloseta (every 20min; 35min); Manacor (hourly; 1hr); Muro (hourly; 50min); Petra (hourly; 55min); Sineu (hourly; 50min).

BY CAR

Driving into Palma is straightforward enough, though you would do well to avoid the narrow lanes and complicated one-way system of the old town, sticking instead to the zigzag of boulevards that encircle the centre from Avgda Gabriel Alomar i Villalonga in the east to the Passeig Mallorca in the west.

PARKING

Trying to find an on-street parking space in downtown Palma can be a nightmare, and you're well advised to either leave your vehicle on the city's outskirts, or head for one of several car parks – the Parc de la Mar near the cathedral often has spaces when others do not. Car parks charge around €1.70/hr). If you're staying downtown, choose a hotel which either has its own car park or has an arrangement with a local one (some hotels offer parking discounts).

Tickets On-street parking in the city centre requires an ORA ticket during busy periods (Mon–Fri 9am–2pm & 4.30–8pm, Sat 9am–2.30pm); outside these hours parking is free. Tickets are available from ORA meters but parking is limited to just 2hr: although the cost is reasonable (around €2.50 for 2hr), the fines for over-staying your time are immediate and steep. Note that if the time allowed overlaps into a free period, your ORA ticket is still valid when restricted time begins again.

INFORMATION

Tourist offices There's a provincial tourist office in the centre of Palma just off Passeig d'es Born at Plaça de la Reina 2 (Mon–Fri 9am–8pm, Sat 9am–2pm; ☎ 971 71 22 16), while the main municipal tourist office is on the north side of Plaça Espanya (daily 9am–8pm; ☎ 902 10 23 65). These both provide city- and island-wide information, free maps, accommodation lists, bus schedules, ferry timetables, lists of car rental firms and leaflets, including the useful *Shopping Mallorca* brochure, which details many of the island's most distinctive shops. Another, smaller municipal office inside Can Solleric, at Passeig d'es Born 27 (daily 10am–8pm; ☎ 902 10 23 65), provides a limited range of city information, and there's a provincial tourist office at the airport (see p.69).

Website Palma's official website, ⊚ palmademallorca.es, is multilingual and has a battery of information.

CITY TOURS

By bus Palma Citysightseeing (☎ 902 10 10 81, ⊚ city -sightseeing.com) operates double-decker, hop-off, hop-on bus trips around the major sights (daily: May–Sept 10am–8pm; Oct–April 10am–6pm; every 20–30min), heading round the city centre's enclosing boulevards and west as far as the ferry terminal. Tickets (€15) are available on board all their buses, and are valid for 24hr. The most popular departure point is at the top of Avgda d'Antoni

Maura, near the cathedral. Citysightseeing buses are useful for visiting Poble Espanyol (see p.68) and the Castell de Bellver (see p.69), which are not served by EMT buses, otherwise frankly EMT buses (see opposite) are a better bet.

By horse and carriage One very popular way to see central Palma is by horse and carriage, which line up next to the cathedral; tours cost around €30 per carriage for 30min, €50/hour.

GETTING AROUND

BY BUS

City buses are operated by EMT (Empresa Municipal de Transports; ☎ 971 21 44 44 in Spanish or Catalan, ⊚ emtpalma.es) and almost all their services, which combine to link the centre with the suburbs and the nearer tourist resorts, pass through Plaça Espanya; several of the more useful services also pass through Plaça de la Reina. In the city centre, each EMT bus stop displays a schematic route map and timetable for the buses that stop there, as well as an electronic display showing when the next bus will arrive. Tickets are available from the driver and cost €1.50 per journey within the city limits.

Destinations Airport (#1: daily every 15min; 25–45min); Cala Major (#3: every 10–20min; 15min); Illetes (#3; every 10–20min; 20min); S'Arenal (#15; every 10–20min; 45min).

BY BIKE

Bike rental Palma on Bike rents out city and mountain bikes from €14/day from its central outlet at Avgda

d'Antoni Maura 10 (☎ 971 71 80 62, ⊚ palmaonbike.com). Reservations, at least 24hr in advance, are advised. It also rents out kayaks and roller-blades.

BY CAR

Car rental Mallorca's airport heaves with car rental companies, and there's a concentration of both large and small companies west of Palma's centre along the harbourfront on Avgda Gabriel Roca. The city's two main tourist offices (see above) can supply a complete list, or try Europcar, at Avgda Gabriel Roca 19 (☎ 971 73 75 89; airport ☎ 971 78 91 36; ⊚ europcar.com) or Hertz, at Avgda Gabriel Roca 13 (☎ 971 73 47 37; airport ☎ 971 78 96 70; ⊚ hertz.com).

BY TAXI

Taxi fares are reasonable. There are several city-centre ranks, with one on Plaça Espanya, another on Avgda Jaume III and a third on Avgda d'Antoni Maura; alternatively, phone Taxis Palma (☎ 971 40 14 14).

ACCOMMODATION

Many of Palma's more enticing hotels and *hostales* are in the centre, by far the most engaging part of the city. There's a cluster of **budget** places along the narrow, cobbled side streets off the Passeig d'es Born and a number of more modern **mid-range hotels** on the Passeig Mallorca, where two sections of old city wall run down the middle of the boulevard on either side of a deep watercourse-cum-moat. Modern high-rises, including some quite plush places, cluster to the west of the centre, overlooking the waterfront along Avgda Gabriel Roca (also known as the Passeig Marítim), but the city's most **distinctive hotels** are concentrated in the old town, in a string of beautifully converted old mansions.

Booking a room Despite the substantial number of hotels and *hostales*, you still need to book ahead in peak periods, most notably June, early July and September. Surprisingly, things are not usually as busy from the middle of July to late August, when many Spaniards avoid the searing heat of the city, but even so vacant rooms can still be sparse. The city's tourist offices (see above) can provide a full list of hotels and *hostales*. Note that many of the

1

budget hotels and *hostales* may have some ropey rooms as well as good ones – if you are not satisfied, insist on a transfer.

CENTRAL PALMA

Hotel Almudaina Avgda Jaume III, 9 ☎971 72 73 40, ⓦ hotelalmudaina.com; map pp.52–53. Dapper modern rooms in one of the attractive 1940s blocks overlooking the city's premier shopping street. It's popular with Spanish business folk, and has great rooftop views from the uppermost floors. €130

Hostal Apuntadores c/Apuntadors 8 ☎971 71 34 91, ⓦ hostalapuntadores.com; map pp.52–53. A long-established *hostal* with simple, straightforward rooms in a centrally located old house just off Passeig d'es Born. Some rooms are en suite (€15 extra), others have shared facilities, but light sleepers should bag a room at the back as c/Apuntadors can get very noisy at night. €70

★ **Hotel Born** c/Sant Jaume 3 ☎971 71 29 42, ⓦ hotelborn.com; map pp.52–53. Delightful hotel in an excellent downtown location, set in a refurbished mansion with big wooden doors and a lovely courtyard, where you can have breakfast under the palm trees. The rooms, most of which face onto the courtyard, are comfortable and decorated in a traditional style. It's a popular spot, so book early in high season. €110

Hotel Casa Padrina c/Tereses 2 ☎971 42 53 00, ⓦ casapadrina.com; map pp.52–53. Run by the owners of the *Hotel Dalt Murada* (see below), this six-room hotel occupies a late nineteenth-century townhouse complete with beamed ceilings and antique Spanish furniture. It's all very pleasant and competitively priced – the location is good too, right in the centre of town, albeit in the side streets off the Passeig de la Rambla. €90

Hotel Convent de la Missió c/de la Missió 7A ☎971 22 73 47, ⓦ conventdelamissio.com; map pp.52–53. Über-cool, fourteen-room hotel, whose slick minimalism has been intelligently shoehorned into the wide spaces of a former convent. The location, however, is really rather drab – on a dull side street off c/Sant Miquel. Also home of the headline-hitting *Simply Fosh* restaurant (see p.75). €225

★ **Hotel Dalt Murada** c/Almudaina 6 ☎971 42 53 00, ⓦ daltmurada.com; map pp.52–53. Arguably the most delightful hotel in the city, this family-run place occupies a splendid old mansion down a cobbled alley metres from Plaça Cort. The house retains many of its original eighteenth-century – and even earlier – features, and there is a lovely roof-terrace with views of the cathedral. The 23 guest rooms are all characterful, large and well appointed, and most hold antique furnishings, such as age-old chandeliers and paintings. The pick have balconies overlooking the courtyard, where breakfast is served. €120

Hotel H M Jaime III Passeig Mallorca 14 ☎971 72 59 43, ⓦ hmjameiii.com; map pp.52–53. Four-star hotel with smart modern rooms kitted out in crisp, minimalist style. The public areas are a little over-done – what on earth is a canoe sculpture doing in the foyer? – but that's hardly a major drawback. The front guest rooms, overlooking the Passeig Mallorca, have the advantage of a balcony, but try to keep to the upper floors away from the noise of the traffic. €140

Hotel Palacio Ca Sa Galesa c/Miramar 8 ☎971 71 54 00, ⓦ palaciocasagalesa.com; map pp.52–53. Charmingly renovated seventeenth-century mansion set amongst the narrow alleys of the oldest part of town, with just twelve luxurious and tastefully furnished rooms and suites. There's an indoor heated swimming pool (set in a renovated ancient Roman bath) and fine views of the city from the rooftop terrace. Opened in the early 1990s, this was one of the first deluxe hotels to occupy an old island mansion and its success has set something of a trend. €290

Hotel Palau Sa Font c/Apuntadors 38 ☎971 71 22 77, ⓦ palausafont.com; map pp.52–53. This smooth and polished four-star hotel, decorated in earthy Italian colours and graced by modern works of art, manages to be both stylish and welcoming. There's a small pool on the roof terrace, and some rooms enjoy inspiring views of the cathedral. €160

Hotel Puro Oasis Montenegro 12 ☎971 42 54 50, ⓦ purohotel.com; map pp.52–53. Self-conscious designer hotel in an old house amongst the narrow side streets west of the Passeig d'es Born. Aimed at the "hip" city dweller, it has details such as rugs on the ceiling, cushions on the floor, and ambient music in the public areas. As you might expect, the guest rooms are similarly slick and modish. €200

Hostal Ritzi c/Apuntadors 6 ☎971 71 46 10, ⓦ hostalritzi.com; map pp.52–53. Long-established one-star *hostal* that is generally well regarded and occupies an ancient but well-kept five-storey house in the centre of the city, just off Passeig d'es Born. Although the rooms, both with shared facilities and en suite (€10 extra), could hardly be described as super-comfortable, they are perfectly adequate. €55

Hotel San Lorenzo c/Sant Llorenç 14 ☎971 72 82 00, ⓦ hotelsanlorenzo.com; map pp.52–53. Amongst the narrow lanes of what was once the fishermen's quarter of Sant Pere, this chi-chi four-star hotel has been cleverly squeezed into an old seventeenth-century mansion. The antique details have been lovingly preserved, while all mod cons, including a swimming pool in the garden, have been tastefully added. €170

★ **Hotel Santa Clara** c/Sant Alonso 16 ☎971 72 92 31, ⓦ santaclarahotel.es; map 52–53. In an intriguing corner of the Old Town, this four-star hotel occupies an old stone mansion, but the interior has been entirely

PALMA'S TOP 5 HOTELS
Hotel **Araxa** See below
Hotel **Born** See p.72
Hotel **Dalt Murada** See p.72
Hotel **Santa Clara** See p.72
Hotel **Saratoga** See below

remodelled to accommodate ultra-modern rooms of sharp and crisp design. €160

★ **Hotel Saratoga** Passeig Mallorca 6 ☎ 971 72 72 40, ⍟ hotelsaratoga.es; map pp.52–53. Bright, modern, centrally located hotel in a tidy seven-storey block complete with a garden swimming pool. The rooms are neat and trim, with marble floors and balconies either overlooking the boulevard (which can be noisy) or an interior courtyard (much quieter). Substantial banquet-breakfasts too. €160

Hostal Terminus Plaça Espanya 5 ☎ 971 75 00 14, ⍟ terminushostal.com; map pp.52–53. Two-star establishment with a quirkily old-fashioned foyer and reasonably large but distinctly frugal rooms beyond: en-suite rooms cost an extra €10. Very handy for the Palma–Sóller train station, but also within earshot of the traffic-clogged inner ring road. €60

OUTSIDE THE CENTRE

AC Ciutat de Palma Plaça Pont 3 ☎ 971 22 23 00, ⍟ marriott.com; map pp.48–49. Gleaming chain hotel in a stylishly revamped, six-storey high-rise on the edge of the groovy Santa Catalina quarter. The interior is resolutely modern, all angular lines and big vases, while the 85 bedrooms are very comfortable with all mod cons. On EMT bus route #3, which serves the city centre, including Plaça

Rei Joan Carles I. Rates can soar in peak periods, but it's normally reasonably priced. €140

★ **Hotel Araxa** c/Pilar Juncosa 22 ☎ 971 73 16 40, ⍟ hotelaraxa.com; map pp.48–49. Attractive four-storey modern hotel with pleasant gardens and an outdoor swimming pool, located in a quiet residential area about 2km west of the centre, not far from the Castell de Bellver. Most of the rooms, which are decorated in comfortable modern style, have balconies. To get there by public transport, take EMT bus #3 from Plaça Rei Joan Carles I and get off at c/Marquès de la Sènia, just before the start of Avgda Joan Miró; it's a 10min walk from the bus stop. €120

Hotel Catalonia Majórica c/Garita 3 ☎ 971 40 02 61, ⍟ hoteles-catalonia.com; map pp.48–49. Big, modern four-star hotel overlooking the coast, with some 170 rooms kitted out in brisk and efficient chain-hotel style – ask for a room with a sea view. About 4km west of the centre, it's handy for the ferry port and reasonably priced. €100

Hotel Feliz Avgda Joan Miró 74 ☎ 971 28 88 47, ⍟ hotelfeliz.com; map pp.48–49. The *Feliz* occupies a well-kept, tastefully kitted out modern block 3km west of the centre, at the junction of Avgda Joan Miró and c/Patrimoni. There are forty-odd guest rooms, some with sea-facing balconies, and each room is decorated in shades of white and cream interspersed with bold splashes of colour. The hotel also has a cool lounge-bar, an outside pool, a rooftop sun terrace and a mini-library. On EMT bus route #3, giving access to several points in the city, including Plaça Joan Carles I. €100

Hotel Melià Palas Atenea Avgda Gabriel Roca 29 ☎ 971 28 14 00, ⍟ melia.com; map pp.48–49. A vast, really rather classy 1960s-style foyer, which looks like it has been imported from Las Vegas, leads to attractively furnished, comfortable rooms with balconies overlooking the bay. €180

EATING AND DRINKING

There's more gastronomic variety in Palma than anywhere else in Mallorca, with most of the city's cafés, restaurants and tapas bars geared up for the tourist trade to some extent at least. **Multilingual menus** (in English, German, Catalan and Castilian) are commonplace, though we have also provided a useful Menu Reader at the back of the guide to help you identify some of the dishes you may come across (see pp.275–279).

CAFÉS AND TAPAS BARS

Cafés and tapas bars are liberally distributed around the city centre, with a particular concentration in the main tourist zone, amongst the side streets off the Passeig d'es Born and Avgda d'Antoni Maura, though those on and around c/Apuntadors, at the heart of the city's nightlife, tend to charge over the odds. Some downtown cafés are up and running by 9am, but – with most visitors taking breakfast at their hotel – there's not much demand for early-morning cafés and things only get going around 11am. Tapas can cost as little as €5 per dish and should never cost more than €14.

Bar Bosch Plaça Rei Joan Carles I ☎ 971 72 11 31; map

pp.52–53. One of the most popular and inexpensive tapas bars in town, the traditional haunt of the city's intellectuals and usually humming with conversation. At peak times you'll need to be assertive to get served. Daily 8am–1am.

Bon Lloc c/Sant Feliu 7 ☎ 971 71 86 17; map pp.52–53. One of the few vegetarian café-restaurants on the island, with good food at low prices – and an informal, homely atmosphere in old and pleasant wood-beamed premises; mains at around €10. Mon–Sat 1–4pm.

Café Lirico Avgda d'Antoni Maura 6 ☎ 971 72 11 25; map pp.52–53. Unlike most of Palma's downtown cafés that have been modernized to better or worse effect, this

1

old stalwart has kept undue progress pretty much at bay, its large mirrors, imitation marble and weather-beaten clientele reminiscent of Spanish cafés of yesteryear. There's a pleasant shaded terrace too. Good place for coffee and a Spanish brandy. Daily 8am till late.

Café Roma c/Baró de Pinopar ☎971 72 03 21; map pp.52–53. Well beyond the tourist scrum, this straightforward modern café does a good line in bocadillos and tapas – the meat balls are especially tasty – from as little as €4. Mon–Fri 7.30am–8.30pm, Sat 9am–7pm.

Ca La Seu c/Corderia 17 ☎871 57 21 57; map pp.52–53. One of the grooviest spots in the Sa Gerrería neighbourhood (see box, p.75), this café-cum-bar occupies high-ceilinged premises that were formerly an ever-so-traditional rope and twine shop. The tapas are cheap and filling – at just €2–3 each. Tues–Fri 7pm–2am.

★ **Ca'n Joan de S'Aigo** c/Can Sanç 10 ☎971 71 07 59, ⓦ canjoandesaigo.webs-sites.com; map pp.52–53. Long-established coffee house offering wonderful, freshly baked *ensaimadas* (spiral pastry buns), the thickest, richest hot chocolate imaginable, and fruit-flavoured mousses to die for. Charming decor too, from the kitschy water fountain to the traditional Mallorcan green-tinted chandeliers. On a narrow alley near Plaça Santa Eulalia. Daily except Tues 8am–9pm.

Cappuccino Palau March c/Conquistador 13 ☎971 71 72 72, ⓦ grupocappuccino.com; map pp.52–53. Occupying the lower part of the Palau March (see p.56), this attractive terrace café (one of a small island chain) offers nicely presented sandwiches (€5–10) and salads. Service is attentive, the furnishings and fittings slick and the soundtrack jazzy, all of which contribute to making this a very popular spot. Daily 8.30am–midnight.

Es Rebost Café Avgda Jaume III, 20 ☎971 71 00 00; map pp.52–53. This new self-service café serves authentic Balearic cuisine made from local ingredients, wherever possible – try the *Panzanella Mallorquina* of tomatoes, roasted red peppers, olives and cheese. Mon–Fri 8.30am–8.30pm, Sat 9am–9pm.

Gran Hotel Café Plaça Weyler 3 ☎971 17 85 00; map pp.52–53. Smart, modern café on the ground floor of the eponymous hotel, a handsome *Modernista* building of 1903. The café makes a good spot for coffee and a snack with tables inside or out on a pleasant little square. Daily 11am–11pm.

La Bodeguilla c/Sant Jaume 1–3 ☎971 71 82 74, ⓦ la -bodeguilla.com; map pp.52–53. Located in a glossily refurbished old townhouse just off Avgda Jaume III, this establishment is half restaurant, and half wine-cum-tapas bar. It's the tapas bar you want, offering a tasty range of tapas from €10: try, for example, the oxtail cannelloni in a red wine sauce. Daily 1–11pm.

La Taberna del Caracol c/Sant Alonso 2 ☎971 71 49 08, ⓦ taberna.name; map pp.52–53. Deep in the old town, this pint-sized tapas bar-cum-restaurant occupies charming old premises, all wooden beams and ancient arches. Choose from thirty different sorts of tapas ranging from €5–20 – and look out for the daily market specials. The meat balls are especially tasty and cost just €6.50. Reservations recommended. Mon 7.30–11pm, Tues–Sun 1–3.30pm & 7.30–11pm.

Orient Express c/Llotja de Mar 6 ☎971 71 11 83; map pp.52–53. Beside Sa Llotja, this idiosyncratic, split-level café-restaurant justifies its name by having an interior like a railway carriage, festooned with a platoon of vintage French advertising posters. Crêpes are the speciality – served every which way and costing €4–8. Mon–Sat 1.30–4pm & 8.30pm–midnight.

RESTAURANTS

There's often little distinction between tapas bars and restaurants, as many of the former serve full meals as well as snacks – and, of course, put a couple of tapas together and you've got a full meal anyway. In fact, the differences often have more to do with appearance than food: if you've got a tablecloth, for instance, you're almost certainly in a restaurant. Many Palma restaurants concentrate on Catalan and Mallorcan dishes, but there are lots of Spanish places too as well as a couple of vegetarian café-restaurants. At all but the most expensive of places, €20/€25 should cover the price of a main course in the evening, and you can usually cut costs by opting for a lunchtime *menú del día*.

Caballito del Mar Passeig de Sagrera 5 ☎971 72 10 74, ⓦ caballitodemar.info; map pp.52–53. Harbourside restaurant metres from Sa Llotja, which has long been a favourite with well-heeled British holidaymakers. There was a time when this was undoubtedly the best seafood restaurant in town and although this isn't the case today, it does excel with its house speciality – the *daurada amb sal al forn* (sea bream baked in salt). The terrace is the place to eat here, since the interior is really rather glum. Main courses average €25, but the extras soon mount up. Reservations well-nigh essential. Daily 1–11.30pm.

★ **Celler Pagès** c/Felip Bauza 2, off c/Apuntadors at ☎971 72 60 36; map pp.52–53. Small, intimate restaurant with an easy-going family atmosphere that occupies a pleasantly decorated two-room basement. It serves traditional Mallorcan food – try the stuffed marrows with home-made mayonnaise on the side, the delicious roast leg of duck with dried plums and grilled vegetables or the tongue with capers. Mains are a real bargain here – from just €12. Reservations pretty much essential. Mon–Sat 1–3.30pm & 8–11pm.

Forn de Sant Joan c/Sant Joan 4 ☎971 72 84 22, ⓦ forndesantjoan.com; map pp.52–53. Set in an old bakery, this extremely popular restaurant may be something of a tourist trap, but it does offer a wide-ranging menu that specializes in Mallorcan dishes. The regular main courses average about €25, the tapas €10 – try the red peppers stuffed with shellfish, followed by a lemon and cinnamon mousse. It's bang in the centre of the city's nightlife area, so get ready for the crowds. Daily 1–4pm & 7–11.30pm.

La Cuchara Passeig Mallorca 18 ☎971 72 22 23, ⓦlacucharapalma.com; map pp.52–53. With its neat and trim modern decor, this appealing restaurant offers a well-balanced menu featuring both Mallorcan and Spanish dishes – including a tasty range of paellas. You can eat outside on the terrace or inside – and there's a great wine cellar too. Mains €14–18. Daily 1–3pm & 8–11pm.

Las Olas Bistro c/Can Fortuny 5 ☎971 21 49 05, ⓦlasolasbistro.com; map pp.52–53. Cosy, very informal, family-run restaurant that serves an inventive mix of Vietnamese/Cambodian and French/Mediterranean dishes: try, for example, the wonton soup followed by bream in a rich sauce with beans and rice. Main courses cost as little as €10. Mon & Tues 12.30–4pm, Wed–Sat 12.30–4pm & 8.30–11.30pm.

Misa Braseria Can Maçanet 1 ☎971 59 53 01, ⓦmisabraseria.com; map pp.52–53. In the deluxe *San Miquel Hotel*, this smart, brasserie-style restaurant – part of the Marc Fosh group – offers a shortish but creative

menu with a Spanish twist. Try the hake with saffron parmentier and tomato compote. It's all first rate – but the portions are a bit stingy. Mains range from €18–28. Mon–Sat 1–3.30pm & 7.30–10.30pm.

★ **Simply Fosh** Hotel Convent de la Missió, c/de la Missió 7A ☎971 72 01 14, ⓦsimplyfosh.com; map pp.52–53. Taking its name from Mallorca's leading chef, Marc Fosh, this top-notch restaurant has garnered lavish praise from all and sundry. The premises are super-cool/very minimalist and you can eat either inside or on the shaded terrace. The food is light, well balanced and finely flavoured with local, seasonal ingredients to the fore. Try such delights as smoked ham in a pea and truffle broth or pork belly with orange and rosemary. A two-course meal with a glass of wine costs an affordable €40–50 and there's a *menú del día* for around €20. Great service too. Reservations essential. Mon–Sat 1–3.30pm & 7.30–10.30pm.

Trattoria Sant Ambros Plaça Coll 11 ☎971 72 52 26; map pp.52–53. There's a *Sant Ambros* café on one side of this little square, the trattoria on the other. The trattoria menu covers all the Italian classics and although the food isn't great, it is inexpensive (pizzas from €9) and Plaça Coll, on the edge of the Sa Gerrería neighbourhood, is a delightful spot to while away a couple of hours. Mon–Sat 1–3.30pm & 6–11pm.

NIGHTLIFE AND ENTERTAINMENT

LATE-NIGHT BARS

Most of the cafés and tapas bars that we've reviewed are happy to ply you with drink until midnight or beyond, but there is also a cluster of lively late-night bars – mostly with music as the backdrop rather than the main event – amongst the narrow and ancient side streets backing onto Plaça Llotja. This is, however, the main tourist zone and if you're after close encounters with the Catalans, then the best bet is the huddle of bars in the Sa Gerrería neighbourhood, just southeast of Plaça Major. Sa Gerrería has a relaxed, informal vibe – the area is popular with students. If it's high heels and flexed muscles you want, there are a number of modish bars west of the centre, dotted along Avgda Gabriel Roca in the vicinity of the Jardins La Quarentena.

Abaco c/Sant Joan 1 ☎971 71 49 39, ⓦbar-abaco.com; map pp.52–53. Set in a charming old mansion in the city

centre, just off c/Apuntadors, this is Palma's most unusual bar, with an interior straight out of a Busby Berkeley musical: fruits cascading down its stairway, caged birds hidden amid patio foliage, elegant music and a daily flower bill you could live on for a month. Drinks, as you might imagine, are extremely expensive (cocktails cost as much as €20) but you're never hurried into buying one. It is, however, rather too sedate to be much fun if you're up for a big night out. Sun–Thurs 8pm–1am, Fri & Sat 8pm–3am.

Bar Flexas c/Llotgeta 12 ☎971 42 59 38, ⓦbarflexas .com; map pp.52–53. Enough to make Franco turn in his grave, this might well be the most idiosyncratic – even weird – bar in the Sa Gerrería neighbourhood. The tiled bar is a vintage relic; the furniture ricketty-racketty; the modern paintings on the wall are eye-catching – but the phallic toys are perhaps a step too far. Snacks and light

---

LA RUTA MARTIANA – THE ROUTE OF THE MARTIANS

The **Sa Gerrería neighbourhood** was once one of Palma's tattiest, but it's been reinvented with more than twenty boho bars and cafés clustered amongst its narrow lanes and alleys. At least part of the revamp has been down to the creation of the so-called **La Ruta Martiana**, a distinctly odd name – with odd little street signs to match – that takes you from one bar to the next. Tuesday night is the most popular night as it's the time when most of the bars and cafés offer mini tapas for €1 each.

1

meals, but this is really a place to drink. Mon–Sat 1–5pm & 8pm–12.30am.

Escape Bar Plaça Draçana 13 ☎971 72 49 68; map pp.52–53. Friendly little café-bar, and always lively, located just off a square that gets busier if not exactly prettier every year. Has a boho, international feel from breakfast time through to the wee hours. Mon 5pm–1am, Tues–Thurs 10am–1am, Fri & Sat 10am–3am, Sun 10am–1am.

Gaudí Café Plaça de la Quartera 5; map pp.52–53. Plain and straightforward Sa Gerreria haunt with a graffiti wall and an über-casual-meets-careworn look. Also serves tapas (from €3.75), which you can devour either inside or outside on the pavement terrace. Daily 5pm–1am.

Jazz Voyeur Club c/Apuntadors 5 ☎971 72 07 80, ⓦjazzvoyeur.com; map pp.52–53. Pocket-sized jazz club in the heart of the city, metres from Sa Llotja. Live sounds most nights – check the website for who's coming when. Daily 8.30pm–1am.

La Lonja c/Llotja de Mar 2 ☎971 72 27 99; map pp.52–53. A popular, well-established haunt, with revolving doors and pleasantly old-fashioned decor; the background music caters for (almost) all tastes and you can sit outside in the square – right in front of Sa Llotja. Mon–Sat 10am–1am, Sun 11am–1am.

CLUBS

The area around Avgda Gabriel Roca and the Jardins La Quarentena hums at night with fashionable locals dressed to the nines, the main pull being its several nightclubs (*discotecas*). Clubs are not perhaps Palma's forte, but there are certainly enough to be going on with, though they are rarely worth investigating until around 1am. Entry charges cost anything up to €20, depending on the night and what's happening, although admission is sometimes free. The door staff mostly operate an informal dress code of one sort or another – if you want to get in, avoid beach gear and (heaven forbid) white trainers. There is a modest range of gay clubs and bars in the somewhat careworn suburb of El Terreno, about 3km west of the centre below the Castell de Bellver, but the scene is something of a moveable feast, so check out ⓦmallorcagaymap.com for the latest news.

Abraxas Avgda Gabriel Roca 42 ☎971 45 59 08, ⓦabraxasmallorca.com; map pp.48–49. This loud, popular and raucous superclub has a gyrating dance floor and a couple of bars inside, as well as a bar outside in the garden. A 10min walk west of the Jardins La Quarentena - and 800m east of the ferry terminal. Dress up to get in – no

dullards. July & Aug daily 11pm–6am; Sept–June Thurs–Sat 11pm–6am.

El Garito Dàrsena de Can Barbarà s/n ☎971 73 69 12, ⓦgaritocafe.com; map pp.48–49. Cool club that caters for all musical tastes, from house to disco classics, with regular live bands too. West of the centre, just off Avgda Joan Miró. Wed–Sat 8pm–4am.

Tito's Plaça Gomila 3 ☎971 73 00 17, ⓦtitosmallorca .com; map pp.48–49. With its stainless steel and glass exterior, this long-established nightspot looks a bit like something from a sci-fi film. Outdoor lifts carry you up from Avgda Gabriel Roca (the back entrance) to the dance floor, which pulls in huge crowds from many countries – or you can go in through the front entrance on Plaça Gomila. The music (anything from house to mainstream pop) lacks conviction, but it's certainly loud. The Avgda Gabriel Roca entrance is just on the city-centre side of the Jardins La Quarentena. June to early Sept daily 11.30pm–5am; Oct–May Fri–Sun 11.30pm–5am.

PERFORMING ARTS

Palma has a couple of major performing arts venues and puts on a busy cultural programme in the open-air during the summer. There's almost always something going on at the Parc de la Mar, just below the cathedral, and other summer venues for music and dance include the Castell de Bellver (see p.69). Ask at the tourist office (see p.71) for a complete listing of upcoming events.

Auditorium de Palma Avgda Gabriel Roça 18 ☎971 73 47 35, ⓦauditoriumpalma.com; map pp.48–49. Large, modern harbourfront auditorium used for both conferences and a range of performing arts – opera, ballet, theatre etc – often by visiting troupes from far and wide.

Teatre Principal c/Riera 2A ☎971 21 97 00, ⓦteatreprincipal.com; map pp.52–53. Housed in a nineteenth-century building, whose tympanum sports a relief dedicated to the nine Muses of Greek mythology, Palma's main performing arts venue offers a mixed bag of classical concerts, opera, theatre, dance and cabaret. Gala nights here are some of the biggest social events on the island.

SPECTATOR SPORTS: FOOTBALL

Mallorca's premier football team is Real Club Deportivo Mallorca (ⓦrcdmallorca.es) – and very good they are too. They play at the Iberostar Estadi on the north side of town. Check the website for fixture details or contact the tourist office.

SHOPPING

Like every other big city in Spain, Palma has its share of multinational stores and most of them have extended opening hours, whereas the smaller, more local companies tend to stick to the traditional norm – Monday to Friday 9/10am to 1.30/2pm and 5/6pm to 8.30/9pm and Saturday 9/10am to 1/2pm. Two of the city's perennial favourite purchases are

Mallorcan wine, which is sold at most large supermarkets and at a number of specialist stores, and artificial pearls, which are also made on the island. The largest manufacturer of these pearls is Majorica (www.majorica.com), whose products are on sale at scores of Palma's shops and stores, but the main outlet is El Corte Inglés (see below).

ARTS AND CRAFTS

Fet a Mà c/Sant Miquel 52 ☎ 971 71 10 95; map pp.52–53. For pottery and other handmade wares, including flowers in bottles, try this cosy and old-fashioned little shop. Also sells *siurells*, white clay whistles flecked with red and green paint and shaped to depict a figure, an animal or a scene (a man sitting on a donkey, for instance); *siurells* have been given as tokens of friendship in Mallorca for hundreds of years. Mon–Fri 9.30am–1.30pm & 4.30–8pm, Sat 9.30am–1.30pm.

Gordiola c/Victoria 2 ☎ 971 71 15 41; map pp.52–53. Glass-making is a traditional island craft and *Vidrios Gordiola*, near the Ajuntament, has a fine range of clear and tinted glassware, from bowls, vases and lanterns through to some wonderfully intricate chandeliers. Mon–Fri 10.15am–2pm & 4.30–8pm, Sat 10.15am–2pm.

BOOKS AND MAPS

Fine Books c/Morei 7 ☎ 971 72 37 97; map pp.52–53. There's nothing quite like this English-owned and -run bookshop in the rest of Palma, indeed the whole of the Balearics – a secondhand bookshop whose interior heaves with dishevelled tomes on every subject under the sun. Great for browsing. Mon–Fri 9am–7pm, Sat 9am–4pm, Sun 9am–1pm.

La Casa del Mapa c/Sant Domingo 11 ☎ 971 22 59 45; map pp.52–53. In the mini-arcade below c/Conquistador, this is easily the best map shop in town, funded by the city council and with a wide selection of town, cycling and hiking maps (see p.34) for every part of Mallorca. Mon 9.30am–2pm, Tues–Fri 9.30am–7pm.

CLOTHES AND SHOES

There's a cluster of international-brand and designer clothes shops on and around Avgda Jaume III - Plaça Rei Joan Carles I, for example, has two Zaras, an H&M, and a Loewe – while the streets around Plaça Cort tend to have more local companies.

Camper Avgda Jaume III, 16 ☎ 971 71 46 35, camper.com; map pp.52–53. Fashionable and extremely popular, Camper shoes are made in Mallorca, but the company now has an international reach with outlets all over the world. They have several stores in Palma, but this is the most central and it carries a wide range of their footwear. Mon–Sat 10am–6.30pm.

Carmina c/Unio 4 ☎ 971 22 90 47, carminashoemaker.com; map pp.52–53. Mallorca has a long tradition of shoe-making. The Carmina company is at the top end of the men's market with shops in several European capitals and one here, right in the city centre. The

shoes begin at €190, so may not be for everyone, but there is no disputing the quality. Mon–Sat 10am–6pm.

S'Avarca Sant Domingo 14 ☎ 971 712 058; map pp.52–53. Neat and trim little shop located in the mini-arcade below c/Conquistador and offering a wide selection of S'avarca, the simple but stylish leather sandals made in Menorca. Mon–Sat 10am–2pm & 5–8.15pm.

DEPARTMENT STORE

El Corte Inglés Avgda Jaume III, 15 ☎ 971 77 01 77, elcorteingles.es; map pp.52–53. The biggest and best department store in the city centre, selling just about everything you can think of, including all the familiar fashion and electronic brands. In the basement, there is a first-rate food and drinks section with an especially wide range of both Spanish and Mallorcan wine, all at competitive prices – a top-notch Binissalem red only costs about €8. The book section sells a small and rather eccentric assortment of English-language novels from Ken Follett to Anne Frank alongside a modest selection of Mallorca guidebooks and maps. Mon–Sat 9.30am–9.30pm, Sun 11am–8pm.

FOOD AND DRINK

Colmado Santo Domingo c/Sant Domingo ☎ 971 71 48 87, colmadosantodomingo.com; map pp.52–53. This tiny, cave-like, old-fashioned store is packed with hanging sausages and local fruit and veg; it's right in the city centre, metres from Plaça Cort. The sausages to try carry the "Sobrasada de Mallorca de Cerdo Negro" label, which guarantees they are made from the island's own indigenous black pig. Mon–Sat 10.30am–8pm.

Forn Fondo c/Unió 15 ☎ 971 71 16 34; map pp.52–53. Palma has a platoon of good cake and pastry shops (*pastelerías*) and this is certainly one of the best – the fig cake (*higos* in Castilian) is especially delicious for starters. They also sell the freshly baked *ensaimadas* (spiral pastry buns) that are so much a feature of island life. Mon–Sat 8am–8.30pm, Sun 8am–2pm.

Frasquet c/Orfila 4 ☎ 971 72 13 54, confiteriafrasquet.com; map pp.52–53. Just off Plaça Mercat, beside the church, this traditional confectioners and chocolatier occupies fine old premises whose fancy, Art Nouveau frontage dates back to the 1890s. The window displays are bound to make your mouth water – and that's before you actually go in: try the *torrons*, almond-paste balls doused in roasted pine nuts. Mon–Fri 9.30am–2pm & 5–8pm, Sat 9.30am–2pm.

★ **Son Vivot** Plaça Porta Pintada 1 ☎ 971 72 07 48, sonvivotpalma.com; map pp.52–53. Exemplary shop specializing in Balearic produce and products; more than

1

300 items from honeys and jams to olives, cheeses, pork Sobrasada black sausages and liqueurs. Also has an especially fine selection of Mallorcan wines. Mon–Sat 10am–6.30pm.

MARKETS

Flower market Passeig de la Rambla; map pp.52–53. Shaded by plane trees, this open-air flower market stretches out along the *passeig*, its long line of flower stalls popular with locals and expats alike. Mon–Fri 8am–2pm & 5–8pm, Sat 8am–2pm.

★ **Mercat de l'Olivar** Plaça de l'Olivar ☎ 971 72 03 14, ⓦ mercatolivar.com; map pp.52–53. The city's main covered market is a flourishing affair, jam-packed with stalls selling all the island's varied produce, from sausages to cheese, olives to tomatoes. The separate fish section is simply superb. Mon–Thurs & Sat 7am–2pm, Fri 7am–2pm & 2.30–8pm.

Rastrillo Avgda Gabriel Alomar i Villalonga, between Plaça Porta d'es Camp and c/Manacor; map pp.48–49. Palma's biggest and best open-air flea market takes place weekly and sells everything from old and battered statues of saints to flared trousers, handbags by the truck load and piles of vinyl records. Sat 8am–2pm.

DIRECTORY

Banks and exchange There are plenty of banks on and around the Passeig d'es Born and Avgda Jaume III. ATMs are commonplace across the city centre – there are two on Plaça Cort.

Consulates Ireland, c/Sant Miquel 68A ☎ 971 71 92 44; UK, c/Convent dels Caputxins 4 ☎ 971 71 24 45; USA c/ Porto Pi 8 ☎ 971 40 37 07.

Doctors and dentists Most hotel receptions will be able to find an English-speaking doctor or dentist. For complete lists look under *metges* (Castilian, *médicos*) or *clíniques dentals* (*clínicas dentales*) in the Yellow Pages (ⓦ paginasamarillas.es).

Emergencies ☎ 112.

Internet Most hotels and *hostales* provide internet access for their guests either free or at minimum cost. Otherwise, head for the library (see below).

Library There's a quaint old municipal library offering free internet access inside the Ajuntament (Town Hall) on Plaça Cort (Mon–Fri 8.30am–8.30pm, Sat 9am–1pm).

Pharmacies Farmacia Buades, Plaça Rei Joan Carles I, 3 (daily 9am–midnight; ☎ 971 71 15 34) is centrally located. For a full list of pharmacies, see Yellow Pages (ⓦ paginasamarillas.es) under *farmàcies* (Castilian *farmacias*).

Post office The central *correos/correu* is at c/Constitució 5 (Mon–Fri 8.30am–8.30pm, Sat 9.30am–2pm).

Around Palma

Spread around the sheltered waters of the **Badía de Palma** are the package tourist resorts that have made Mallorca synonymous with the cheap and tacky. In recent years the Balearic government has done its best to improve matters – greening resorts, restricting high-rise construction and redirecting traffic away from the coast – but their inherited problems remain. In the 1960s and 1970s, the bay experienced a **building boom** of almost unimaginable proportions as miles of pristine shoreline sprouted concrete-and-glass hotel towers, overwhelming the area's farms and fishing villages. There were few planning controls, if any, and the legacy is the mammoth sprawl of development that now extends, almost without interruption, for 30km along the coast from **S'Arenal** in the east to **Magaluf** in the west – with Palma roughly in the middle. To make matters worse, it is also debatable as to whether the recent move away from high-rise construction is well conceived. The villa complexes that are now the fashion gobble up the land at an alarming rate and multiply traffic. Furthermore, although the new villas are rarely more than three storeys high and built in a sort of pan-Mediterranean style they end up looking remorselessly suburban. As a consequence, although this stretch of

TOP 5 SANDY BEACHES AROUND PALMA

Camp de Mar See p.83
Magaluf See p.82
Palma Nova See p.82

Peguera See p.82
Platja de Palma See p.84

1

coast is divided into a score or more resorts, it's often impossible to pick out where one ends and the next begins. That said, most of the resorts have evolved their own identities, in terms of the nationalities they attract, the income group they appeal to, or the age range they cater for. Despite the aesthetic gloom there are a couple of noteworthy attractions – primarily the one-time home and studio of **Joan Miró** – as well as a clutch of appealing hotels and a string of excellent **beaches**.

West of Palma

West of Palma, the coast bubbles up into the low, rocky hills and sharp coves that prefigure the mountains further west. The sandy **beaches** here are very small – and some are actually artificial – but the terrain makes the tourist development seem less oppressive. **Cala Major**, the first stop, was once the playground of the jetset. It's grittier today, but some of the grand old buildings have survived and the **Fundació Pilar i Joan Miró**, which exhibits a fine selection of Miró's work, makes an enjoyable detour. The neighbouring resort of **Illetes** is more polished, boasting comfortable hotels and attractive cove beaches, and is the best place to stay in the area, especially when compared with its westerly neighbours: **Portals Nous**, known hereabouts for its swanky marina; **Palma Nova**, a major package holiday destination popular with Brits; and **Magaluf**, where the modern high-rise hotels, thumping nightlife and substantial sandy beach cater to a youthful and very British crowd. West of Magaluf, the coastal highway leaves the Badia de Palma for large and sprawling **Santa Ponça** before pushing on to **Peguera**, a rambling resort with attractive sandy beaches and a relaxed family atmosphere. Next door – and much more endearing – is tiny **Cala Fornells**, where pretty villas thread along the coastal hills and a brace of first-rate hotels overlook a wooded cove – and concrete-slab beaches, which are not as bad as they sound. The development is fairly restrained here and, if you're after a straightforward resort holiday on this part of the coast, this is as good as it gets. From Cala Fornells, it's another short hop to the good-looking bay that encloses the burgeoning resort of **Camp de Mar**.

Cala Major

Beginning just a couple of kilometres to the west of Palma's ferry port, cramped and crowded **CALA MAJOR** snakes its way along a hilly stretch of coastline bisected by its main street (the Ma-1C). This modest, modern pile-up is brightened by the occasional *Modernista* building, reminders of halcyon days when Cala Major was a byword for elegance – hence the ritzy, coast-hugging *Hotel Nixe Palace* (see p.83), restored after years of neglect and now the finest hotel hereabouts by a long chalk. There's also a royal palace, the **Palacio de Marivent**, and although it's not open to the public, you can glimpse it from the main street – it's beside the Ma-1C at the east end of the resort.

Fundació Pilar i Joan Miró

C/Joan de Saridakis 29, Cala Major · Mid-May to mid-Sept Tues–Sat 10am–7pm, Sun 10am–3pm; mid-Sept to mid-May Tues–Sat 10am–6pm, Sun 10am–3pm · €6 · ☏ 971 70 14 20, ⊛ miro.palmademallorca.es · The Fundació is signed off the main Ma-1C road through Cala Major; EMT bus #46 (every 20–30min) from central Palma stops 100m below the entrance

One of Mallorca's most enjoyable attractions, the **Fundació Pilar i Joan Miró** was where the painter **Joan Miró** (1893–1983) lived and worked for much of the 1950s, 1960s and 1970s. Initially – from 1920 – the young Miró was involved with the **Surrealists** in Paris and contributed to all their major exhibitions: his wild squiggles, supercharged with bright colours, prompted André Breton, the leading theorist of the movement, to describe Miró as "the most Surrealist of us all". In the 1930s he adopted a simpler style, abandoning the decorative complexity of his earlier work for a more minimalist use of symbols, though the highly coloured forms remained. Miró returned to Barcelona, the city of his birth, in 1940, where he continued to work in the Surrealist tradition, though as an avowed opponent of Franco his position was uneasy. In 1957 he moved to Mallorca, its relative isolation offering a degree of safety. His wife and mother were both Mallorcan, which must have influenced his decision, as did the chance to work in his own purpose-built studio with its view of the coast. Even from the relative isolation of Franco's Spain he remained an influential figure, prepared to experiment with all kinds of media, right up until his death here in Cala Major in 1983.

The Edifici Moneo

The expansive hillside premises of the Fundació fan out from the **Edifici Moneo**, an angular modern gallery which displays a rotating and representative sample of the artist's work. Miró was nothing if not prolific, and the Fundació owns 134 paintings, 300 engravings and 105 drawings, as well as sculptures, gouaches and preliminary sketches – more than six thousand works in all. There are no guarantees as to what will be on display, but you're likely to see a decent selection of his paintings, most notably the familiar dream-like squiggles and half-recognizable shapes that are intended to conjure up the unconscious, with free play often given to erotic associations. The gallery also hosts temporary exhibitions of modern and contemporary art, which are often well reviewed.

The Taller Sert

From the Edifici Moneo, it's a brief stroll up to the **Taller Sert** (Sert Workshop), a striking Modernist structure with a roof partly shaped like seagull wings. The workshop takes its name from the architect who designed it, Josep Sert, but this was very much Miró's studio and where he spent a large slice of his life. The interior has been left pretty much as it was at the time of the artist's death and it certainly gives the flavour of how the man worked – tackling a dozen or so canvases at the same time.

Son Boter

Just beyond the Taller Sert, **Son Boter** is a traditional Mallorcan farmhouse dating from the seventeenth century. Miró bought the place in 1959 and used it as a reserve studio for some of his larger compositions. He also doodled on the walls and his graffiti has survived intact – and a delightful sample of his work it is too.

Illetes

Busy **ILLETES**, just off the Ma-1C immediately to the west of Cala Major, spreads along the coast, its ribbon of restaurants, hotels and apartment buildings bestriding the steep hills that rise high above a rocky shoreline. A string of tiny cove beaches punctuates the coast here, the most attractive being the pine-shaded **Platja Cala Comtesa**, right at the southern end of the resort.

Portals Nous

Nudging tight against the coast to the west of Illetes, **PORTALS NOUS** is a ritzy settlement where polished mansions fill out the green and hilly terrain between the coast and the dull and drab main street (Ma-1C). There's a tiny **beach**, set beneath the cliffs and reached via a flight of steps at the foot of c/Passatge del Mar, but the main draw is the **marina**, one of Mallorca's most exclusive, where the boats look more like ocean liners than pleasure yachts. What you make of all this glitz and the flock of celebrities that it attracts is very much a matter of taste (and politics), but the marina is certainly a lively spot.

Marineland

C/Garcilaso de la Vega 9, Costa d'en Blanes • Early March to Oct daily 9.30am–6pm • €23, children €17 • ☎ 971 67 51 25, Ⓦ marineland .es/marineland/mallorca

All the fun of the fair – or to be more accurate a nautical theme park – is here at **Marineland**, from performing dolphins and seals to a shark aquarium, penguins,

1

stingrays and pelicans. Young children love the place; adults mostly suffer in silence. Marineland is in Costa d'en Blanes, the westerly extension of Portals Nous.

Palma Nova

Old Mallorca hands claim that **PALMA NOVA**, 4km west of Portals Nous, was once a beauty spot, and certainly its wide and shallow bay, with its excellent beaches and pine-clad headlands, still has its moments. But for the most part, the bay has been engulfed by a broad, congested sweep of tourist facilities. With the development comes a vigorous (mainly British) nightlife and a platoon of hotels on or near the seashore – though, as elsewhere, most are block-booked by tour operators throughout the season.

Calvià

Tucked away in the hills behind the coast, about 7km north of Palma Nova, is the tiny town of **CALVIÀ**, the region's administrative centre – hence the oversized town hall, paid for by the profits of the tourist industry. The parish church of **Sant Joan Baptista** is the town's key building, a large and much modified thirteenth-century structure whose Gothic subtleties mostly disappeared during a nineteenth-century refurbishment – hence the crude bas-relief carving of the Garden of Gethsemane above the main door. There are pleasant views across the surrounding countryside from outside the church, and the adjacent square is home to a modern mural showing a neat depiction of the island's history.

Magaluf

Torre Nova, on the chunky headland at the far end of Palma Nova, is a cramped and untidy development that slides into **MAGALUF**, whose high-rise towers march across the next bay down the coast. For years a cheap-as-chips package holiday destination, Magaluf finally lost patience with its youthful British visitors in 1996. The local authorities won a court order allowing them to demolish twenty downmarket hotels in an attempt to end the annual binge of "violence, drunkenness and open-air sex" that, they argued, characterized the resort. The high-rise hotels were duly dynamited and an extensive clean-up programme freshened up the resort's appearance. These draconian measures have brought some improvement, but the resort's British visitors remain steadfastly determined to create, or at least patronize, a bizarre caricature of their homeland: it's all here, from beans-on-toast with Marmite to endless supplies of lager.

Western Water Park

Ma-1, Exit 13 • May–Sept daily 10am–5/6pm • €26, children 2–12 years €18 • ☎ 971 13 12 03, ⓦ westernpark.com

Stuck on the western edge of Magaluf, **Western Water Park** contrives to weld together a replica Wild West town – one of the most incongruous sights in Spain – with a platoon of water rides and water chutes. It's all very odd, but very popular.

Santa Ponça

West of Magaluf, the Ma-1 trims the outskirts of **SANTA PONÇA**, one of the less endearing of the resorts that punctuate this stretch of coast. Mostly a product of the 1980s, this sprawling conurbation has abandoned the concrete high-rises of yesteryear for a pseudo-vernacular architecture that has littered the hills with suburban-looking villas. More positively, the setting is attractive, with rolling hills flanking a broad bay, and the resort's white sandy beaches offer safe bathing.

Peguera

PEGUERA, about 6km northwest of Santa Ponça, strings out along a lengthy, partly pedestrianized main street – the Avinguda Peguera – immediately behind several generous sandy beaches. There's nothing remarkable about the place, but it does have an easy-going air and is a favourite with families and older visitors. The Ma-1 loops right round Peguera and the easiest approach, if you're just after the **beach**, is from the south. Head into the resort along the main street and park anywhere you can before you reach the pedestrianized zone, where the town's baffling one-way system sends you weaving through the resort's side streets – best avoided, if possible.

Cala Fornells

Next door to Peguera, the much prettier – and much smaller – resort of **CALA FORNELLS** is reached via either of two signed turnings on the Avinguda Peguera just to the west of the pedestrianized centre. Take the more easterly turning and the road climbs up to a string of chic, *pueblo*-style houses that perch on the sea cliffs and trail round to the tiny centre of the resort, where a wooded cove is set around a minuscule beach and concreted sunbathing slabs. Although Cala Fornells tends to be overcrowded during the daytime, at night the tranquillity returns, and it makes a good base for a holiday, especially as it has a particularly appealing hotel (see below).

Camp de Mar

Burgeoning **CAMP DE MAR**, flanking a hilly cove just 3km west of Peguera, has an expansive beach and fine bathing, though the scene is marred by the presence of two thumping great **hotels** dropped right on the seashore. Camp de Mar and its surroundings are also in the middle of a massive expansion, with brand-new villa complexes trailing back from the beach in an all-too-familiar semi-suburban sprawl. All the same, the **beach** is an amiable spot to soak up the sun, and it's hard to resist the eccentric café stuck out in the bay and approached via a rickety walkway on stilts. A minor road twists west from Camp de Mar over wooded hills to **Port d'Andratx** (see p.120).

ARRIVAL AND DEPARTURE   WEST OF PALMA

By bus Bus services along the coast west from Palma are fast and frequent. The nearer resorts (Cala Major and Illetes) are served by EMT (see p.71) with buses departing from several points in central Palma. The resorts to the west of Illetes are served by a number of other bus companies, but almost all buses start and terminate at Palma's main bus station, the Estació Intermodal, off Plaça Espanya. There's a transport information desk at the Estació, and the city's two main tourist offices (see p.71) supply bus timetables too, or check ⊛ tib.org, or call ☎ 971 17 77 77 (Spanish or Catalan only).

Destinations Palma to: Cala Major (EMT #3: every 10–20min; 15min); Calvià (every 2hr; 40min); Camp de Mar (1–2 hourly; 1hr); Illetes (EMT #3; every 10–20min; 20min); Magaluf (1–2 hourly; 1hr); Palma Nova (1–2 hourly; 55min); Peguera (1–2 hourly; 1hr 30min); Portals Nous (1–2 hourly; 45min); Santa Ponça (1–2 hourly; 1hr 15min).

ACCOMMODATION

Although the Badía de Palma resorts boast hundreds of **hotels**, *hostales* and apartment buildings, the bulk are block-booked by the package tourist industry from May or June through to September or October, with frugal pickings for the independent traveller; out of season, many places simply close down. We've selected some of the more interesting and enjoyable package hotels where there's a reasonable chance of finding a vacancy independently in high season; it's also worth checking out their full- and half-board deals.

CALA FORNELLS

Cala Fornells c/Cala Fornells s/n ☎ 971 68 69 50, ⊛ calafornells.com. In a handsome location on a hill looking straight out to sea, this charming hotel has 94 well-appointed guest rooms as well as indoor and outdoor pools, fitness facilities and a sauna. **€140**

CALA MAJOR

Hotel Nixe Palace Avgda Joan Miró 269 ☎ 971 70 08 88, ⊛ hotelmallorcanixepalace.com. There was a time when this grand hotel was the chi-chi haunt of socialites and although those days are long gone – and the furnishings and fittings now lack a little élan – it's still a handsome building with Art Nouveau flourishes, wide sun terraces and its very own sandy cove beach. **€180**

ILLETES

Hotel Bon Sol Passeig de Illetes 30 ☎ 971 40 21 11,

1

ⓦhotelbonsol.es. This popular, long-established hotel spreads down the hillside in the heart of Illetes in a sort of pan-Andalucian style that is really rather appealing. The interior has a stately, country-house feel, the gardens are lush and the hotel's assorted terraces tumble down the cliffs to the seashore – and its own little cove beach. €125

PORTALS NOUS

H10 Punta Negra c/Punta Negra s/n ☎ 971 68 07 62, ⓦh10hotels.com. Spread over two rugged coves beside crystal clear waters, this deluxe, four-star, 135-room modern resort boasts a fine location and every modern facility. Lies just south of the old coastal road, the Ma-1C, 3km west of Portals Nous. €180

East of Palma

The **coastal motorway** zips **east** out of Palma with tourist resorts on one side and the airport on the other. The flatlands backing onto the coast were once prime agricultural land, hence the multitude of ruined **windmills**, built to pump water out of the marshy topsoil and now gaunt reminders of earlier, more pastoral times. The alternative route, along the **old coastal road**, is a bit more interesting and a lot slower: take the turning off the motorway just beyond the city walls (signposted to Ca'n Pastilla) and follow the road as it tracks through a series of resorts, beginning with **Es Portixol**, once down-at-heel but now really rather pleasant. Thereafter, things get distinctly dull – and the route east is easy to lose – but ultimately you reach **Ca'n Pastilla**, the first substantial tourist resort on this part of the coast, its fifty-odd hotels and apartment buildings set in a rough rectangle of land pushed tight against the seashore. The place is short on charm and certainly too close to the airport for sonic comfort, but it does herald the start of the fine **Platja de Palma beach**, which stretches round to **S'Arenal** in a great sandy arc. Make no mistake, the **beach** is superb, but the flat shoreline behind it accommodates an unprepossessing, seemingly interminable strip of cheap restaurants and souvenir shops with dozens of pounding bars and all-night clubs mainly geared up for young German tourists.

Es Portixol

ES PORTIXOL, just a couple of kilometres east of Palma Cathedral, was once the preserve of local fishermen, who docked their boats at either of its sheltered coves. The district hit the skids in the 1960s, but it's now championed as an exemplar of urban renewal, its terrace houses all cleaned and dusted, one cove turned into a marina, the other into a tiny beach resort.

Sometimes, Ses Maravelles and S'Arenal

The **Platja de Palma**, the 4km stretch of sandy beach that defines the three coterminous (and indistinguishable) resorts of **SOMETIMES**, **SES MARAVELLES** and **S'ARENAL**, is crowded with serious sun-seekers, a sweating throng of bronzed and oiled bodies slowly roasting in the heat. The beach is also a busy pick-up place, the spot for a touch of verbal foreplay before the night-time bingeing begins. It is, as they say, fine if you like that sort of thing – though older visitors can't but help look marooned. A wide and pleasant walkway lined with palm trees runs behind the beach and this, in turn, is edged by a long sequence of bars, restaurants and souvenir shops. A toy-town tourist "train" shuttles up and down the walkway, but there's so little to distinguish one part of the beach from another that it's easy to become disoriented. To maintain your bearings, keep an eye out for the series of smart, stainless-steel beach bars, each numbered and labelled, in Castilian, "*balneario*", dotted along the shore.

Palma Aquarium

C/Manuela de los Herreros i Sorà s/n, Ca'n Pastilla (Ma–19, Exit 10) • Daily 10am–6pm • €22, children €18 • ☎ 902 70 29 02, ⓦpalmaaquarium.com

A watery world with bells and whistles, **Palma Aquarium**, at the western end of the Platja de Palma, has around fifty different tanks displaying sea creatures in various marine habitats, including a Tropical Sea, a Mediterranean Sea, a tank full of jellyfish and the "Big Blue", the deepest shark tank in Europe. In addition, there's a jungle area, a mock-up of an old sailing ship, and a play area that will appeal to most young children.

Aqualand

Ma–19, Exit 13 • Mid-May to late Sept daily 10am–5/6pm • €26, children (over 2 years) €18 • ☎ 971 44 00 00, ⓦ aqualand.es

On its eastern edge, about 15km east of Palma, S'Arenal boasts Mallorca's largest waterpark, **Aqualand**, a huge leisure complex of swimming pools, water flumes and children's playgrounds. One of the chutes resembles a wriggling snake, another features a giant dragon – and it's all great fun for the kids.

ARRIVAL AND DEPARTURE
EAST OF PALMA

By bus The excellent EMT (see p.71) bus #15 runs every 10–20min from Palma to Es Portixol (25min) and S'Arenal (45min).

ACCOMMODATION

ES PORTIXOL

Hotel Portixol c/Sirena 27 ☎ 971 27 18 00, ⓦ portixol .com. This high-rise, seafront hotel in the recently revamped former fishing village of Es Portixol is a very urban and urbane spot, with all sorts of finessed details, from creative backlighting through to guest room TV cabinets that look like mini beach huts. It's all good fun, but if you're paying this much, it's worth splashing out the extra €75 for a room with a sea view. There's an outside swimming pool and a restaurant, where you can dine either inside or outside looking out over the ocean. **€225**

Western Mallorca

91 Sóller

95 Port de Sóller

98 Biniaraix

98 Fornalutx

99 Jardins d'Alfàbia

100 Raixa

100 Orient

102 Castell d'Alaró

102 Alaró

103 Deià

107 Son Marroig

108 Miramar

108 Valldemossa

112 Port de Valldemossa

112 La Granja

116 Esporles

116 Banyalbufar

117 Estellencs

118 Andratx

119 Sant Elm

120 Port d'Andratx

DEIÀ

Western Mallorca

As he approached the northwest coast of Mallorca in 1888, the British traveller Charles Wood was moved to write "Nothing could be more beautiful than the views of sea and land. The island rounded in a succession of curves and bays. One headland after another opened out magnificently". And no wonder: few would argue that Mallorca is at its scenic best in the gnarled ridge of the Serra de Tramuntana, the imposing mountain range that stretches the length of the island's northwestern shore, its rearing peaks and plunging sea cliffs intermittently punctuated by valleys of olive and citrus groves.

Midway along and cramped by the mountains is **Sóller**, an antiquated merchants' town that serves as a charming introduction to the region, especially when reached on the vintage narrow-gauge **train line** from Palma. From Sóller, it's a short hop down to the coast to **Port de Sóller**, a one-time port and fishing village that has become a popular resort set around a deep and handsome bay: this geographical arrangement – the town located a few kilometres inland from its port – is repeated across Mallorca, a reminder of more troubled days when marauding corsairs forced the islanders to live away from the coast. The mountain valleys in the vicinity of Sóller were once remote and isolated, but today they shelter three bucolic stone-built villages – **Biniaraix**, **Fornalutx** and **Orient** – and two of the island's finest gardens, the oasis-like **Jardins d'Alfàbia** and the Italianate terraces of **Raixa**.

Southwest of Sóller, the principal coastal road, the **Ma-10**, threads up through the mountains to the beguiling village of **Deià**, tucked at the base of formidable cliffs and famous as the former home of Robert Graves. Beyond lies the magnificent Carthusian monastery of **Valldemossa**, whose shadowy cloisters briefly accommodated George Sand and Frédéric Chopin in the 1830s, and the *hacienda* of **La Granja**, another compelling stop. Continuing southwest, the Ma-10 wriggles high above the shoreline, slipping through a sequence of mountain hamlets, of which **Banyalbufar** and **Estellencs** are the most picturesque, their tightly terraced fields tumbling down the coastal cliffs. A few kilometres further on you leave the coast behind, drifting inland out of the mountains and into the foothills that precede the market town of **Andratx**. Beyond, on Mallorca's western tip, lies the underrated resort of **Sant Elm**, where you can hike out into the mountains or catch the boat to **Sa Dragonera**, a humpy island nature reserve with both hiking trails and an abundant bird population. Nearby are the safe waters of **Port d'Andratx**, a medium-sized resort and sailing centre draped around a handsome inlet.

GETTING AROUND   WESTERN MALLORCA

By car Several fast roads link Palma with the northwest coast – the prettiest runs to Valldemossa – and a delightful network of country roads pattern the foothills, but the key sights and the best scenery are most readily reached along

Western Mallorca's Top 5 beaches p.91
Vintage trains and trams: Palma to Sóller and Port de Sóller p.91
Sa Fira i Es Firó p.95
Walks around Biniaraix p.98
The Ma-2100 – a scenic drive through forested foothills p.100

Robert Graves in Deià p.104
The ups and downs of the Archduke Ludwig Salvator p.107
George Sand at Valldemossa p.110
A circular hike from Valldemossa to Puig d'es Teix by the Archduke's path p.114
The hike to La Trapa p.119

JARDINS D'ALFÀBIA

Highlights

❶ Palma-Sóller train Ride the antique train over the mountains from Palma to Sóller for a wonderful introduction to the island's jagged, rearing mountains. **See p.91**

❷ Sóller This delightful town boasts handsome stone mansions, a dinky main square and an exquisite setting amidst craggy mountains – and it's still within easy striking distance of the beach. **See pp.91–95**

❸ Jardins d'Alfàbia First established by the Moors, these are the finest gardens in Mallorca, with lush trellises and terraces leading to the sweetest of lily-choked pools. **See p.99**

❹ Deià One of Mallorca's most beguiling villages, where a huddle of ancient stone houses are set against a spectacular mountain backdrop. **See p.103**

❺ Hiking in the Serra de Tramuntana Crisscrossed by scores of exhilarating trails, the rugged mountains that range along the length of the island's northwest shore offer the finest hiking in the Balearics. **See p.98, p.114 & p.119**

❻ Valldemossa Monastery The old stone town of Valldemossa zeroes in on its splendid medieval monastery, whose echoing cloisters once sheltered George Sand and Frédéric Chopin. **See p.108**

HIGHLIGHTS ARE MARKED ON THE MAP ON P.90

2

the main coastal road, the Ma-10. Distances are small – from Andratx to Sóller via the Ma-10 is only about 70km – and the roads are good, but parking can be a real pain: all the villages hereabouts have small car parks, but in summer finding a space between about 10am or 11am and 5pm can be problematic. Parking is easier in Sóller, the largest town on this stretch of the coast, though its one-way system is tricky to negotiate.

By train Vintage trains run along the line from Palma to Sóller (see box opposite).

By bus There is a regular bus service from Palma to Sóller and Port de Sóller via either the tunnel or

Valldemossa and Deià. Another bus runs from Palma to Esporles, La Granja, Banyalbufar and Estellencs. There are also fast and frequent buses from Palma to Andratx and Port d'Andratx. The only major gaps are along the Ma-10 coast road between Estellencs and Andratx and between Banyalbufar and Valldemossa – for timetable details, check ⓦ tib.org.

By taxi Distances between destinations are short, so taxis can be a reasonable proposition, especially if you're in a group: the fare for the 70km trip from Sóller to Andratx, for instance, is about €70; Sóller to Valldemossa costs €35; and the 13km trip from Sóller to Deià is just €21.

INFORMATION AND ACCOMMODATION

Information There are tourist offices in Sant Elm, Sóller and Port de Sóller, and almost all the region's hotels and *hostales* carry information, from bus and boat timetables to details of local restaurants.

Accommodation Port d'Andratx, Deià, Sóller and Port de

Sóller have the widest range of accommodation, but all the villages in the region have at least a couple of places to stay. Nevertheless, from June to early September (and sometimes beyond), vacancies can be thin on the ground and advance reservations are advised.

ACTIVITIES

HIKING

The Serra de Tramuntana provides the best hiking on Mallorca, with scores of hiking trails latticing the mountains. There are trails to suit all aptitudes and levels of enthusiasm, and generally speaking paths are well marked, though apt to be clogged with thorn bushes.

Trails The region is crossed by Mallorca's main long-distance hiking trail, the Ruta de Pedra en Sec (Dry-stone Route, the GR221), which begins in Sant Elm and threads its way through the mountains to Sóller before proceeding

onto Pollença (see p.132).

Hostels There are two hikers' hostels (*refugis*; ⓦ conselldemallorca.net) on the Sant Elm–Sóller section of the GR221 – one each at Deià (see p.106) and Port de Sóller (see p.97) – and one more is under construction at Sant Elm.

Guides & Maps Hiking guides and maps are best purchased before you arrive (see p.34), though you can buy the *Editorial Alpina* and *Triangle Postals* maps and guides in Sóller (see p.94).

WESTERN MALLORCA'S TOP 5 BEACHES

Port de Sóller Thin, artificial sandy beach at its best at the back of the port's horse-shoe shaped bay. See p.98

Cala Deià A shingle strip, great for swimming. See p.105

Port de Valldemossa A handsome shingle strip of beach. See p.112

Cala Estellencs Wild, windswept shingle beach. See p.118

Sant Elm A pleasant, if rather short, sandy strip – the best beach on this part of the island. See p.119

2

Sóller

One of the most laidback and enjoyable towns on Mallorca, **SÓLLER** lies at the end of the train line from Palma, and makes an ideal and inexpensive base for exploring the Serra de Tramuntana. Rather than any specific sight, it's the general flavour of the town that appeals, with its narrow, sloping lanes cramped by eighteenth- and nineteenth-century **stone houses** adorned with fancy grilles and big wooden doors – the former dwellings of the area's wealthy fruit merchants. A scattering of low-key attractions fills out a stroll around the town, though hikers will soon want to head off into the surrounding mountains.

Sóller train station

Plaça Espayna • **Exhibition rooms** Daily 10.30am–6.30pm • Free

Sóller **train station** is a handsome building, its imposing, *hacienda*-like facade and wide stone staircases witnessing the days when it was crucial to the town's merchants. Five of the station's rooms have been turned into **exhibition** areas – two displaying a selection of cheery, sometimes tongue-in-cheek ceramics by **Picasso** and three for the flamboyant squiggles of his friend **Miró**, whose maternal grandfather came from Sóller. In the main station hall, there are also a couple of **photos** showing Miró and Picasso together – the former looking rather crumpled when compared with his handsome friend.

Although the railway was welcomed in Sóller by the town's merchants, the country folk hereabouts were less convinced. They had already proved themselves reluctant to accept technological change in the 1860s, when **telegraph poles** were erected between Sóller and Palma. At first, groups of farm labourers had snipped the wires and chopped the poles down, but when they heard that messages could be sent down the wires, they

VINTAGE TRAINS AND TRAMS: PALMA TO SÓLLER AND PORT DE SÓLLER

The 28km **train journey** from Palma to Sóller is a delight, dipping and cutting through the mountains and fertile valleys of the **Serra de Tramuntana**. The line was completed in 1911 on the profits of the orange and lemon trade: the railway was built to transport the fruit to Palma, at a time when it took a full day to make the trip by road. The rolling stock is tremendously atmospheric too, with narrow carriages – the gauge is only 914mm – that look like something from an Agatha Christie novel, though frankly it is rather a clanky, bumpy ride. Once past the scratchy suburbs of Palma, the train runs across pancake-flat farmland with the impenetrable-looking peaks of the Serra de Tramuntana dead ahead. After a short stop at **Bunyola**, it threads upwards to spend five minutes tunnelling through the mountains, where the noisy engine and dimly-lit carriages give the feel of a rollercoaster ride. Beyond, out in the bright mountain air, are the steep valleys and craggy thousand-metre peaks at the heart of the Serra de Tramuntana, and everywhere there are almond groves, vivid with blossom in January and February. From its terminus at Sóller train station, **vintage trams**, some of which date from 1912, clank their way down to the coast at Port de Sóller, 5km away. For schedule and prices, see p.93.

2

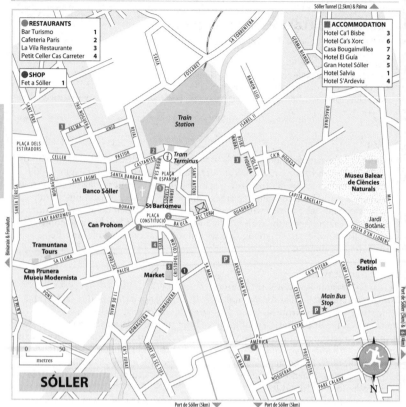

concluded that the same applied to goods. As a result, according to a visiting British captain, J. W. Clayton, "bundles of clothes, pairs of knickerbockers, petticoats, baskets of edibles, and even wigs…[were] neatly ticketed and addressed" and hung on the wires for onward transmission.

Plaça Constitució

In Sóller, all streets lead to the main square, **Plaça Constitució**, an informal, pint-sized affair of big old plane trees, crowded cafés and mopeds just down the hill from the train station. The square is dominated by the hulking mass of the church of **St Bartomeu** (Mon–Thurs 11am–1pm & 3–5pm, Fri & Sat 11am–1pm, Sun noon–1pm; free), a crude but somehow rather fetching neo-Gothic remodelling of a medieval original with a couple of Art Nouveau flourishes thrown in. Its most appealing features are the enormous and precisely carved rose window stuck high in the main facade and the heavy-duty but apparently pointless balustrade above it. Inside, the cavernous, barrel-vaulted nave is suitably dark and gloomy, the penitential home of a string of gaudy Baroque altarpieces. Next door, the **Banco de Sóller**, now Banco Santander, is a *Modernista* extravagance, sheathed in a coat of roughly dressed stone and adorned by miniature balconies and wrought-iron grilles, all the work of **Joan Rubiò** (1870–1952), a Gaudí acolyte. Just off the square at c/Sa Lluna 16, the grand eighteenth-century mansion of **Can Prohom** is more traditional, with massive wooden doors and overhanging eaves; it was here that the district's landed gentry used to stay when they came to town.

Can Prunera Museu Modernista

c/Sa Lluna 86 • March–Oct daily 10.30am–6.30pm; Nov–Feb Tues–Sun 10.30am–6.30pm • €5 • ☎ 971 63 89 73, ⦿ canprunera.com

The elaborate stone facade of **Can Prunera**, designed by Joan Rubiò, has recently been converted into the **Museu Modernista**. The museum's two lower floors are distinguished by their graceful *Modernista* furnishings and fittings, while the top floor is given over to sketches by a wide range of artists, both foreign and Spanish – though for the most part they are lesser pieces.

Museu Balear de Ciències Naturals

2

Carretera Palma–Port de Sóller s/n • Mon–Sat: March–Oct 10am–6pm; Nov–Feb 10am–2pm • €5 • ☎ 971 63 40 14, ⦿ jardibotanicdesoller.org

In an old merchant's villa, the mildly diverting **Museu Balear de Ciències Naturals** (Balearic Museum of Natural Sciences) houses a series of modest displays, with temporary exhibitions on the top floor and the **permanent collection** on the two floors below. The latter begins with a fairly good section on the leading botanists of yesteryear, including Archduke Ludwig Salvator (see p.107), and continues with an assortment of island fossils and rocks. The labelling is in Catalan, but English leaflets are available in each room. Outside, the neat and trim **Jardí Botànic** rolls down the hillside divided into thirteen small areas, half of which (M1–M6) are dedicated to Balearic species, including dune and sea cliff species in M2, shade-loving plants in M4, and mountain plants in M5. A free English-language brochure identifying and illustrating many of the plants is issued at the main gate (for both the house and the gardens).

ARRIVAL AND DEPARTURE

SÓLLER

BY TRAIN

Sóller train station is in the centre of town on Plaçe Espanya. From March to October, there are 7 trains daily from Palma station and 5 from Sóller; from November to February, there are 5 from Palma and 4 from Sóller. The journey takes just under 1hr and a one-way ticket costs €12.50, a return €19.50. For further information, call ☎ 902 36 47 11, or check ⦿ trendesoller.com.

BY TRAM

Sóller tram terminus is outside the train station, on Plaça Espanya. The trams (daily 7am–7pm) depart for Port de Sóller every hour on the hour, returning on the half hour. The 15min journey costs €5 each way – pay the conductor.

BY BUS

Main bus stop The bus stop is on the west side of the centre, just off the Ma-11 on c/Cetre; from here, it's a 5- to 10min walk to Plaça Constitució. If you are heading east along the coast to Lluc or Pollença, the bus is often full; to be sure of a seat, it's best to catch it down in Port de Sóller, where the service originates. Note that the fastest Palma–Sóller buses use the Ma-11 – and its tunnel – while the slower, more scenic service runs via Deià and Valldemossa. And finally note that there are no buses from Sóller to points west along the coast beyond Valldemossa.

Destinations Biniaraix (Mon–Fri 4 daily, Sat 2 daily; 10min); Deià (5–7 daily; 25min); Fornalutx (Mon–Fri 4 daily, Sat 2 daily; 15min); Lluc (May–Oct Mon–Sat 2 daily;

1hr); Palma (via the tunnel: Mon–Fri hourly, Sat 8 daily, Sun 5 daily; 30min); Palma via Valldemossa (5–7 daily; 1hr 30min); Pollença (May–Oct Mon–Sat 2 daily; 1hr 35min); Port de Pollença (May–Oct Mon–Sat 2 daily; 1hr 50min); Port de Sóller (Mon–Fri hourly, Sat & Sun every 1–2hr; 10min); Valldemossa (5–7 daily; 55min).

BY CAR

The Ma-11 Fast and straight, the Ma-11 cuts across the island from Palma to Sóller, tunnelling straight through the mountains as it approaches its destination. The 27km journey takes about 30min, and the tunnel, which is 3023m long and ends 2.5km from the centre of Sóller, costs €4.90 per car. Note that cyclists are not allowed to use the Ma-11 tunnel because of vehicle fumes.

The Ma-11A You can avoid the tunnel – and the toll – by taking the scenic route over the mountains: as you approach the tunnel, follow the signs for the Ma-11A, a minor road that hairpins its way up and over the mountains in fine style. En route, there are splendid views out along the coast at the Coll de Sóller, a rocky pass with a lookout point – and the whole detour only adds 7km to the journey.

Parking On-street parking in Sóller is almost impossible – especially as the town's streets are very narrow and the one-way system byzantine. There's a car park behind the main bus stop on c/Cetre and a more central (unpaved) car park off Avgda Gran Via. There's rarely a problem finding a vacant slot at either.

2

GETTING AROUND

By taxi There's a taxi rank beside the tourist office, or call ☎971 63 84 84. Tariffs are fixed – and reasonable: the taxi ride to Deià costs €21; Lluc €50; Pollença €80; Valldemossa €33.

By bike Bike rental is available from Tramuntana Tours, c/

Sa Lluna 72 (☎971 63 24 23, ⊕tramuntanatours.com). They have several different types of bike with the least expensive costing €12 per day. They also have an outlet in Port de Sóller (see p.96).

INFORMATION

Tourist office Sóller tourist office occupies an old train carriage just outside the train station in the middle of Plaça d'Espanya (Mon–Fri 9.30am–2pm & 3–5pm, Sat & Sun 10am–1pm; ☎971 63 80 08, ⊕sollernet.com). They have a

wide range of local information, including bus timetables, and sell *Editorial Alpina* and *Triangle Postals* hiking guides (see p.34), which can also be bought at the Libreria Papereria, on Plaça Constitució, and the Libreria Calabruix, at c/Sa Lluna 7.

ACTIVITIES

Tours Tramuntana Tours, at c/Sa Lluna 72 (March–Sept Mon–Fri 9am–1.30pm & 3–7.30pm; Oct–Jan Tues & Thurs 10am–1.30pm & 5–8pm, Sat 10am–1.30pm; ☎971 63 24 23, ⊕tramuntanatours.com), runs mountain-bike tours, canyoning, fishing trips, sea-kayaking and a range of guided day walks to suit most aptitudes. There are, for example, medium-to-difficult guided walks to the Puig

d'es Teix (16km) and up the Barranc de Biniaraix (17km); a difficult clamber down the Torrent de Pareis gorge (8km); and an easy jaunt round the Sóller valley (7km). Costs vary, but reckon on a minimum of €30 per trip per person. Transport is provided to and from the trailhead as required and the operators will, within reason, collect hikers from where they are staying.

ACCOMMODATION

⭐ **Hotel Ca'l Bisbe** Bisbe Nadal 10 ☎971 63 12 28, ⊕hotelcalbisbe.com. This appealing four-star hotel occupies a creatively refurbished former bishop's palace, complete with beamed ceilings, pool and garden. Each of the 25 guest rooms is generously appointed, unfussily decorated with cream colour to the fore and comes with every mod con. The best rooms also have smashing views out towards the mountains. **€110**

Casa Bougainvillea c/Sa Mar 81 ☎971 63 31 04, ⊕casa-bougainvillea.com. An enjoyable B&B that occupies an old, sympathetically modernized three-storey terrace house on a busy side street a short walk from Plaça Constitució. There are eight guest rooms here, all en suite, and each is decorated in a pleasingly unfussy style. Weather permitting, breakfast is served in the garden, where guests can idle away their time reading and relaxing. **€100**

⭐ **Hotel Ca's Xorc** Carretera Sóller–Deià (Ma-10: Km 56.1) ☎971 63 82 80, ⊕casxorc.com. Located high in the hills, about 4km west of Sóller, this superb hotel occupies a renovated old olive mill in which each of the twelve guest rooms has been decorated in sleek modern style. There's an outside pool and handsome terraced gardens, and the food is fabulous, featuring local ingredients and variations on traditional Mallorcan dishes. Reservations well-nigh essential. **€200**

Hotel El Guía c/Castanyer 2 ☎971 63 02 27, ⊕sollernet.com/elguia. This long-established, family-run place is rather engaging. Set behind a pretty little

courtyard, the hotel's layout and decor are very traditional and although the guest rooms are a tad spartan, they are perfectly adequate and spotlessly clean. Great location, too – just 2min from the train station: turn right at the station entrance. Closed late Nov to mid-March. **€90**

Gran Hotel Sóller c/Romaguera 18 ☎971 63 86 86, ⊕granhotelsoller.com. There are four good things about this five-star hotel: the central location, the rooftop pool and breakfast bar, the garden, and the building, a grand structure whose *Modernista* flourishes date back to the 1880s – amazingly enough, considering its size, the building started out as a private house. Less positively, the interior has been kitted out in a plush but pedestrian modern style and although the guest rooms have every convenience, they hardly stir the imagination. **€300**

Hotel Salvia c/Palma 18 ☎971 63 49 36, ⊕hotelsalvia .com. The *Salvia* is one of Sóller's smartest small hotels, its six guest rooms cleverly inserted into a fine old stone mansion complete with period furnishings and fittings. There's an outside pool, gardens, a shaded terrace and long views of the surrounding mountains. It's a luxurious spot – and you pay for it. **€210**

Hotel S'Ardeviu c/Vives 14 ☎971 63 83 26, ⊕sollernet .com/sardeviu. Down an unbecoming alley a stone's throw from the main square, the *S'Ardeviu* is a small, family-run hotel in an intelligently revamped old mansion. Many of the house's original features have been maintained and the bedrooms are smart and well appointed. **€100**

EATING AND DRINKING

Sóller's main square and its immediate surroundings heave with **cafés** and **café-bars**, and although prices are reasonable, the quality of the food on offer is often disappointing. The **restaurant** scene is similarly constrained and although there are one or two good spots, you're much better popping down to Port de Sóller (see below), where there is a whole gaggle of excellent restaurants (see p.97).

Bar Turismo Avgda d'es Born 8 ☎971 63 00 92. By the tram lines just up from Plaça Constitució, this convivial and rather old-fashioned little bar is a pleasant spot to nurse a drink. Daily 9am–10pm.

Cafeteria Paris Plaça Constitució 4 ☎971 63 00 03. This family-run café may be in standard-issue modern premises, but it serves up the best coffee in town – and filling snacks, too. Daily 9am–10pm.

La Vila Restaurante Plaça Constitució 14 ☎971 63 46 41, ⓦlavilahotel.com. On the ground floor of a handsome *Modernista* building on the main square, the inside dining area of this restaurant may be gloomy, but the outside area is more agreeable. The menu is short, but well chosen, the

Spanish dishes given an international twist, and there is a good-value fish of the day too. Patchy service – take something to read, just in case. Mains average €20. Daily noon–3.30pm & 7.30–10.30pm.

Petit Celler Cas Carreter c/Cetre 4 ☎971 63 51 33, ⓦcascarreter.net. Long-established, family-run restaurant in a cleverly recycled old wheelwright's workshop – the large and conspicuous wine barrel bottoms were added later. Offers a mixture of well-presented Spanish and Mallorcan dishes – try the snails – with mains averaging €14. Tues–Sat noon–4pm & 7.30–11pm, Sun noon–4pm.

SHOPPING

Fet a Sóller c/Romaguera 12 ☎971 63 88 39, ⓦfetasoller.com. Sweet little shop, part of a community initiative, selling all things local, including nuts, olives,

wine, fruit juices and jam. Attached to an ice-cream parlour, where they sell locally made ice cream in a variety of alarming colours. Daily 10am–9pm.

Port de Sóller

One of the most photographed places on the island, **PORT DE SÓLLER** has a lovely setting, its wide, horseshoe-shaped bay, ringed by forested hills. One of the west coast's most enjoyable resorts, it's a low-key, family-oriented place with a string of classy hotels and restaurants grafted onto an old fishing port and naval base. A decade ago, the resort looked tired and sad, but now – with traffic directed away from the waterfront by means of a tunnel (1290m) – Port de Sóller is on the up, with private investment following in the slipstream of government subsidy. The only fly in the ointment is the **beach**: a narrow strip of imported sand encircling the east side of the bay, it's a scrawny affair except at the back of the bay, where the **Platja d'en Repic** just about passes muster.

The town makes for a pleasant wander and the **vintage tram**, which gambols round the east side of the bay, provides an appealing backcloth. It's also worth making the enjoyable hour-long hike – or brief drive – west to the **lighthouse** (*far*) guarding the cliffs of Cap Gros above the western entrance to the bay. From here, the views out over the wild and rocky coast and back across the harbour are truly magnificent, especially at sunset. There's a narrow surfaced road all the way: from the tram terminus, walk round the southern side of the bay past Platja d'en Repic and keep going, following the signs.

SA FIRA I ES FIRÓ

If you're around Sóller and Port de Sóller in the second week of May, don't miss the **Sa Fira i Es Firó**, which commemorates the events of May 1561 when a large force of Arab pirates came to a sticky end after sacking Sóller. The Mallorcans had been taken by surprise, but they ambushed and massacred the Arabs as they returned to their ships and took grisly revenge by planting the raiders' heads on stakes. The story – bar decapitations – is played out in chaotic, alcoholic fashion every year at the festival. The re-enactment begins with the arrival of the pirates by boat, and continues with fancy-dress Christians and Arabs battling it out through the streets of the port, to the sound of blanks being fired in the air from antique rifles. On the days preceding this knees-up, there are also sporting and cultural events as well as a large, open-air market. The tourist office (see opposite) can give you a rough idea of the schedule of events, plus details of the dances and parties that follow.

2

ACCOMMODATION

Hotel Aimia	3
Hotel Espléndido	5
Hotel Es Port	2
Jumeirah Port Sóller Hotel	1
Hotel Los Geranios	7
Hotel Marina	6
Refugi Muleta	4

RESTAURANTS

Restaurant-bar Agapanto	5
Restaurant El Pirata	1
Restaurant Es Canyís	6
Restaurant Es Faro	3
Restaurant Espléndido	4
Restaurant Randemar	2

PORT DE SÓLLER

ARRIVAL AND INFORMATION

By bus Buses stop at the roundabout on Avgda 11 de Maig, from where it's a 5min walk to the waterfront.

Destinations Biniaraix (Mon–Fri 4 daily, Sat 2 daily; 15min); Deià (5–7 daily; 30min); Fornalutx (Mon–Fri 4 daily, Sat 2 daily; 120min); Lluc (May–Oct Mon–Sat 2 daily; 1hr 10min); Palma (via the tunnel: Mon–Fri hourly, Sat 8 daily, Sun 5 daily; 35min; via Valldemossa: 5–7 daily; 1hr 35min); Pollença (May–Oct Mon–Sat 2 daily; 1hr 40min); Port de Pollença (May–Oct Mon–Sat 2 daily; 1hr 50min); Sóller (Mon–Fri hourly, Sat & Sun every 1–2hr; 10min); Valldemossa (5–7 daily; 1hr).

By tram The vintage tram from Sóller (see box, p.91) travels along the east side of the bay; the tram terminus is right in the centre of town beside the jetties.

Tourist information Port de Sóller tourist office is located about 3min walk from the tram terminus, beside the church at c/Canonge Oliver 10 (Mon–Fri 9.30am–1pm & 3–6pm, Sat 10am–1pm; ☎ 971 63 30 42, ⓦ sollernet.com).

TOURS AND ACTIVITIES

Boat trips The main boat company is Barcos Azules (☎ 971 63 01 70, ⓦ barcosazules.com) and their most popular excursion is to Sa Calobra (May–Oct Mon–Sat 2–3 daily in each direction; €25 return). Boats leave from the dock beside the tram terminus.

Tours Tramuntana Tours, Passeig Es Través 12 (March–Oct daily 9am–7.30pm; ☎ 971 63 27 99, ⓦ tramuntanatours .com). This well-regarded company has a seasonal outlet here in the port and a larger outlet in Sóller (see p.94).

ACCOMMODATION

Most of the port's hotels and *hostales* overlook the bay and although **rooms** are hard to find in high season thanks to the tour operators, there are usually lots of vacancies the rest of the year. Pleasingly, there are no massive hotel tower blocks here, but rather a ring of 1960s three- to four-storey blocks, several of which have benefited from the resort's recent upgrading.

Hotel Aimia c/Santa Maria del Camí 1 ☎ 971 63 12 00, ⓦ aimiahotel.com. In this slick, medium-sized four-star hotel the guest rooms have the unmistakeable signs of a designer's touch with flush ceiling lights and several shades of brown. Naturally, there's a spa, a gym and a pool – and it's all reassuringly smart, comfortable and expensive. **€185**

Hotel Espléndido Passeig des Través 5 ☎ 971 63 18 50, ⓦ esplendidohotel.com. The stylish remodelling of a 1950s, five-storey hotel block has created this ultra-chic establishment, where the guest rooms have been equipped in Modernist style with lots of greys and whites plus crafty overhead lighting. The better guest rooms have a sea-facing balcony and there's a large outside pool, spa and garden. **€200**

Hotel Es Port c/Antoni Montis s/n ☎ 971 63 16 50, ⓦ hotelesport.com. In its own lush gardens at the back of the port, a few minutes' walk from the waterfront, this is one of the resort's more distinctive hotels. Most of the public areas are in a seventeenth-century country house, whose interior displays many charming original features – including a Baroque family chapel. The guest rooms in the old section are commodious and have an antique feel, with wood-beamed ceilings, but most of the rooms are housed in a modern annexe at the back. There are also indoor and outdoor pools. **€150**

Jumeirah Port Sóller Hotel c/Bélgica s/n ☎ 971 63 78 88, ⓦ jumeirah.com. The latest thing to hit Port de Sóller is this super-duper deluxe hotel, a massive affair that perches high above the resort with exquisite views over the bay and coast. No expense has been spared in its construction, from the neo-baronial stone staircase to the wonderfully positioned outside pool. There are panoramic vistas from many of the guest rooms, which are large and über-modern with every facility. And, of course, there's a spa too, plus bars and a restaurant. **€300**

Hotel Los Geranios Passeig de Sa Platja 15 ☎ 971 63 14 40, ⓦ www.hotel-losgeranios.com. Straightforward seafront hotel with four stars that overlooks the Platja d'en Repic. Has twenty-odd rooms on four floors, mostly with sea views. The place is independently managed, but the rooms are equipped in standard chain style. **€130**

Hotel Marina Passeig de Sa Platja 3 ☎ 971 63 14 61, ⓦ hotelmarinasoller.com. Large, long-established and competitively priced hotel overlooking the Platja d'en Repic. The rooms are decorated in standard-issue modern style, but most of them are spacious with balconies, and many have cooking facilities. Recently upgraded with a new spa. Closed Dec. **€80**

Refugi Muleta Cap Gros s/n ☎ 971 63 42 71, ⓦ www .conselldemallorca.net. Government-run hikers' hostel in an old stone building beside the lighthouse up on the headland immediately to the west of Platja d'en Repic. The hostel is also within easy walking distance of the GR221 long-distance hiking trail (see p.90). Offers dormitory accommodation in bunk beds; breakfast is €4.50 extra. Open all year; advance reservations required. Dorms **€11**

EATING AND DRINKING

Port de Sóller is awash with **restaurants** and standards are generally very high – indeed the port has some of the finest restaurants in Mallorca. Most of the prime places have bayside locations and the majority mix Mallorcan and Spanish dishes, though in many the big deal is the seafood, some of it caught by local fishermen.

★ **Restaurant-Bar Agapanto** Camí del Far 2 ☎ 971 63 38 60, ⓦ agapanto.com. At the west end of Platja d'en Repic, right beside the seashore, the *Agapanto* is a modish restaurant with a stylish, inventive menu featuring subtle sauces and imaginatively prepared vegetables. Try, for example, the scallops and pea purée (€11) followed by the fish of the day (€26). Outstanding service too, plus an "ambient" soundtrack. Daily noon–4pm & 7–11pm; bar till 1am.

Restaurant El Pirata Santa Catalina d'Alexandria 8 ☎ 971 63 14 97, ⓦ chilimontes.com. The decor of this busy café-restaurant is a little off-putting – it's much too garish for most tastes – but they do serve a good line in grilled seafood as well as home-made pastas and salads both inside and outside on their bayfront terrace. Mains average €17. Daily 11am–11pm.

★ **Restaurant Es Canyís** Passeig de Sa Platja 21 ☎ 971 63 14 06, ⓦ escanyis.es. Bright and cheerful bistro-style restaurant offering an excellent and extensive range of Spanish dishes from its bayside premises behind the Platja d'en Repic. The snails are a house speciality, but the paella is also tempting, as is the chicken breast in almond sauce. Main courses begin at €15. Tues–Sat 1–4pm & 8–11pm, Sun 1–4pm.

Restaurant Es Faro Cap Gros s/n ☎ 971 63 37 52. This well-known restaurant has a wonderful location, high up on the cliffs at the entrance to the harbour (and a 1.6km drive – or stiff walk – up from Platja d'en Repic). However, the spectacular views often exceed the quality of the evening meal, so it's perhaps a better bet for lunch when the *menú del día* is really very good – and a lot cheaper. Reservations essential in the evening. March–Oct daily noon–4pm & 6.30–9.30pm; Nov–Feb daily noon–4pm.

Restaurant Espléndido Passeig des Través 5 ☎ 971 63 18 50, ⓦ esplendidohotel.com. In the hotel of the same name, this fast-moving bistro has smashing bay views and an all-purpose menu featuring everything from fish and chips to classic Spanish dishes. Mains average €15–20. Daily noon–midnight.

★ **Restaurant Randemar** Passeig des Través 16 ☎ 971 63 45 78, ⓦ randemar.com. Much-praised

restaurant occupying a good-looking 1920s villa and its spacious, leafy terrace down by the bay. Covers many of the Spanish classics, but it's the Italian dishes that steal the limelight – lip-smacking pasta dishes and pizzas from €16 for a main course. Loungey/jazzy music is the background track. March–Nov daily 12.30–11.30pm.

2 Biniaraix

Nestled in the foothills of the Serra de Tramuntana, the tiny hamlet of **BINIARAIX** is extraordinarily pretty, its cluster of old stone houses cuddling up to a dilapidated church and the smallest of central squares. It's around an hour's walk east of Sóller along **c/Sa Lluna** (and its several continuations), a little longer and much quieter via the GR221 which loops round the northern edge of town past orchards and farmland. Biniaraix also makes a useful starting point for **hikes** into the surrounding mountains.

ARRIVAL AND DEPARTURE   BINIARAIX

By bus The bus to Biniaraix stops near the main square. Destinations Fornalutx (Mon–Fri 4 daily, Sat 2 daily; 5min); Port de Sóller (Mon–Fri 4 daily, Sat 2 daily; 15min);

Sóller (Mon–Fri 4 daily, Sat 2 daily; 10min).
By car Try not to drive into Biniaraix: the streets are incredibly narrow and there is hardly anywhere to park.

Fornalutx

Good-looking **FORNALUTX**, about 4km northeast of Sóller, is often touted as the most attractive village on Mallorca, and it certainly has a superb location, its honey-coloured stone houses huddling against a mountainous backdrop with the surrounding valley perfumed by orange and lemon groves. Matching its setting, the quaint centre of Fornalutx fans out from the minuscule main square, its narrow cobbled streets stepped to facilitate mule traffic, though nowadays you're more likely to be hit by a hikers' rucksack than obstructed by a mule: tourists, and ex-pats, love the place and flock here in their hundreds.

ARRIVAL AND DEPARTURE   FORNALUTX

By bus Buses to Fornalutx stop at the foot of c/Sol, on the southwest edge of the village, a 3min walk from the main square, Plaça d'Espanya.

Destinations Biniaraix (Mon–Fri 4 daily, Sat 2 daily; 5min); Port de Sóller (Mon–Fri 4 daily, Sat 2 daily; 20min); Sóller (Mon–Fri 4 daily, Sat 2 daily; 15min).

WALKS AROUND BINIARAIX

From Biniaraix, the most popular hiking route is the stiff, but particularly scenic, 2hr haul up to the L'Ofre farmhouse at the top of the **Barranc de Biniaraix**, a beautiful ravine of terraced citrus groves set in the shadow of the mountains. To get to the Biniaraix **trailhead**, walk uphill from the main square along c/Sant Josep. After about 200m you'll reach a spring and cattle trough, where a sign offers a choice of hiking trails, including the one east up the *barranc*, on (one small part of) the **GR221** long-distance footpath (see p.90). Sections of the trail up the *barranc* use the old **cobbled roadway** that was once part of the pilgrims' route between Sóller and the monastery at Lluc (see p.129). Built in the fifteenth century, the roadway proved a real headache to maintain for a long line of bishops: sometimes they had to threaten the peasantry with fines to keep the road in good order, sometimes they offered indulgences, but the snail hunters who regularly broke down the retaining walls to collect these tasty creatures proved indifferent to both. At the top of the ravine, you can extend your walk by clambering west up to the **Es Cornadors** viewpoint – allow 45 minutes each way – or by heading northeast to the Cúber reservoir (see p.128), a comparatively easy walk across even ground on the GR221 – allow about 2hr. Otherwise, the quickest way to get back to Sóller is by returning the way you came.

By car If you're driving from Sóller, the easiest way to get to Fornalutx is to take the Ma-10 east and watch for the turn; this will bring you straight to the car parks at the north end of the village.

ACCOMMODATION

★ **Fornalutx Petit Hotel** c/Alba 22 ☎971 63 19 97, ⓦfornalutxpetithotel.com. Charming hotel in an immaculately furnished and spotlessly clean old stone house with a terraced garden and pool. Smart and appealing, it offers splendid views down the valley below. Reservations are essential. **€170**

EATING

★ **Ca N'Antuna** c/Arbona Colom 14 ☎971 63 30 68. Well-regarded restaurant where the emphasis is on island dishes. Baked lamb is the house speciality, though the lemon tart is a close rival and famous from one end of Mallorca to the other. Has a lovely shaded terrace with views down the valley. Mains average €15. Tues–Sat 12.30–4pm & 7.30–11pm, Sun 12.30–4pm.

Es Turó c/Arbona Colom 4 ☎971 63 08 08. The homely *Es Turó* offers good-quality Mallorcan cuisine at very reasonable prices – mains begin at about €15. The restaurant has a pleasant outside terrace with valley views and is located just a couple of minutes' walk uphill from the main square near the car park. Daily except Thurs 8am–11pm; closed Dec & Jan.

2

Jardins d'Alfàbia

Carretera Palma–Sóller Km17 • April–Oct Mon–Sat 9.30am–6.30pm; Nov & Jan–March Mon–Fri 9.30am–5.30pm, Sat 9.30am–1pm • €6.50 • ☎971 61 31 23, ⓦjardinesdealfabia.com • The Palma–Sóller bus stops right outside the gardens (every 1–2hr)

The lush terraced gardens of the **Jardins d'Alfàbia**, a few metres from the south end of the Palma–Sóller tunnel (see p.93), are one of Mallorca's most enjoyable attractions. Shortly after the Reconquista, Jaume I granted the estate of Alfàbia to a prominent Moor by the name of **Benhabet**. Seeing which way the historical wind was blowing, Benhabet, as governor of Pollença, had given his support to Jaume, provisioning the Catalan army during the invasion. There was no way Jaume I could leave his Moorish ally in charge of Pollença (and anyway it was already pledged to a Catalan noble), but he was able to reward him with this generous portion of land. Benhabet planned his new estate in the Moorish style, channelling water from the surrounding mountains to irrigate the fields and fashion oasis-like gardens. Generations of island gentry added to the estate without marring the integrity of Benhabet's original design, thus creating the lovely gardens of today.

The gardens

From the roadside entrance, you follow a stately avenue of plane trees towards the gatehouse. In front of the gatehouse is the **ticket office**; a sign here directs visitors up a wide flight of stone steps and into the **gardens**, where the footpath leads through trellises of jasmine and wisteria, creating patterns of light and shade. Near the start there's even a visitor-operated water feature – press the button and retire. Thereafter, brightly coloured flowers cascade over narrow terraces to the sound of gurgling watercourses and, at the end of the path, lies a verdant jungle of palm trees where bullrushes tangle a tiny pool choked with water lilies. It's an enchanting spot, especially on a hot summer's day, with an outdoor **bar** (usually) selling glasses of freshly squeezed orange juice – a snip at just €2.

The house and gatehouse

The estate **house** is a rather routine *hacienda* with a wide veranda and a handful of high-ceilinged rooms that hold an eccentric mix of antiques and curios, including paintings of local bigwigs and exotic animals, most memorably a particularly odd-looking elephant. Pride of place, however, goes to a superb **oak chair**, made in the fifteenth century in Flanders and adorned with delightful bas-relief scenes depicting the legend of **Tristan and Isolde**. On the front of the chair the two protagonists are shown playing chess, an innocent enough pastime, but one that stirs the jealousy of Isolde's husband the king. On the back of the chair, the king's head appears in the tree peering down at the two of them as they walk in the garden – and you know it will all end in tears.

At the front of the house, the cobbled **courtyard** is shaded by a giant plane tree and surrounded by good-looking, rustic outbuildings. Beyond lies the **gatehouse**, an imposing structure sheltering a fine coffered ceiling of Mudéjar design, with an inscription praising Allah.

2 Raixa

Carretera Palma–Sóller (Ma-11) Km12 · Closed for refurbishment till late 2013 · ☎ 971 21 97 41, ⊛ raixa.cat

At the end of a short (1km) unpaved lane, **Raixa** was once the country estate of the eighteenth-century antiquarian Cardinal Antonio Despuig, whose collection of classical sculpture can be seen in Palma (see p.69). The cardinal carved a sequence of terraced **gardens** out of the hill beside his elegant country home and then proceeded to decorate them with Neoclassical statues, water fountains and bits of old masonry recovered from medieval buildings in Palma – all in the fashionable Italian style of his day. Despuig saw himself as a leading light of the Enlightenment, but beneath his cultured cassock lurked medieval piety: he died in Italy and on his deathbed he left instructions for his heart to be cut out and buried close to the body of Mallorca's favourite saint, Catalina Thomàs (see p.111). At the time of writing, the gardens are being restored and the house is being turned into a museum devoted to the Serra de Tramuntana mountains.

Orient

With a resident population of around thirty, **ORIENT** is the tiniest of hamlets, its scattering of old houses straddling a wooded gulch on the edge of the Vall d'Orient, a slender valley where steep hills crimp and crowd olive and almond groves. The main part of the village slopes up the hill from the road and at the top is a sturdy little parish **church** named in honour of Sant Jordi (St George), whose effigy cuts a striking pose on the high altar. For most of its long history, Orient's isolation made life hard hereabouts, but tourism has transformed the place and now the locals share their bucolic retreat with second-home owners and several smart, rural-chic hotels.

ARRIVAL AND DEPARTURE ORIENT

By bus The only bus to Orient is from Bunyola (2 daily; 20min), on the Palma–Sóller train line. Seats on the bus need to be reserved at least a day beforehand on ☎ 617 36 53 65.

ACCOMMODATION AND EATING

★ **Hotel Rural Son Palou** Plaça de l'Església s/n ☎ 971 14 82 82, ⊛ sonpalou.com. First impressions of this lovely hotel are misleading: the entrance is narrow, almost cramped, squeezed into the square at the top of the village beside the

---

THE MA-2100 – A SCENIC DRIVE THROUGH FORESTED FOOTHILLS

On the landward side of the Serra de Tramuntana, a few kilometres south of Sóller, a country road – the **Ma-2100** – forks east off the Ma-11 to loop past the sun-bleached walls of **Bunyola** before negotiating the range's forested foothills. It's a beautiful drive, with mountains to either side – though some of the bends are nerve-jangling – and after about 12km you reach the extraordinary pretty hamlet of **Orient** (see above). Thereafter, there's more fine scenery as the Ma-2100 zigzags up to slip along the narrow valley of the Torrent d'en Paragon for around 3km before veering south to pass between a pair of molar-like hills whose bare rocky flanks tower above the surrounding forest and scrub. The more westerly of the two sports the sparse ruins of the **Castell d'Alaró** (see p.102), with the attractive little towns of **Alaró** (see p.102) and Binissalem (see p.189), the centre of Mallorca's wine industry, just beyond.

church. In fact, the hotel comprises a series of immaculately restored old farm buildings and the surrounding estate, with lovely gardens. The twelve guest rooms are comfortable and well appointed, and the outside pool is delightful – as are the views. It's a popular spot – so book early. **€160**

Hotel L'Hermitage Carretera Alaró-Bunyola ☎ 971 18 03 03, ⓦ hermitage-hotel.com. About 1km east of Orient on the Ma-2100, the smooth and polished *L'Hermitage* is a combined hotel and spa whose lush gardens surround a complex of old stone buildings: some of these date from its earliest incarnation as a monastery, others from its days as a manor house – including an attractively modernized old

olive mill. It has twenty rooms with a handful in the old buildings and the rest in the surrounding chalets. Full- and half-board available. **€200**

★ **Restaurante Orient** c/Orient s/n ☎ 971 61 51 53. At the west end of the village, beside the Ma-2100, this delightful restaurant is a low-key, informal affair with a relaxing outside terrace. Few would praise the decor, but who cares when the food is this good, featuring a range of Mallorcan favourites, including snails, suckling pig partridge with mushrooms and rabbit with prawns; mains average €17. Mon–Sat 10am–10pm, Sun 10am–7pm; closed in July.

Castell d'Alaró

Originally a Moorish stronghold but rebuilt by Jaume I, **Castell d'Alaró** is visible for miles around on its lofty perch. It looks impregnable and certainly impeded the Aragonese during their invasion of 1285. When an Aragonese messenger was despatched to suggest terms for surrender, the garrison's two commanders responded by calling the Aragonese King Alfonso III "fish-face", punning on his name in Catalan (*anfos* means "perch"). After the castle finally fell, Alfonso got his revenge by having the two roasted alive.

The **side road** that leads up towards the castle branches off the Ma-210 just to the north of Alaró – watch for the signposted right turn near the Km-18 stone marker. The first 3km of this side road are bumpy and narrow but reasonably easy, whereas the last 1.3km is gravel and dirt with a perilously tight series of hairpins negotiating a very steep hillside – especially hazardous after rain. The road ends at a car park and an old **farmstead**, now the *Es Verger* restaurant (see below), from where the views down over the plain are sumptuous. From here, the ruins of the **castle** are clearly visible above, about an hour and a half's walk away along a clearly marked track. The trail leads to the castle's stone gateway, beyond which lies an expansive wooded plateau accommodating the fragmentary ruins of the fortress, a hikers' hostel (see below) and the tiny **pilgrims' church** of Mare de Déu del Refugi.

ACCOMMODATION AND EATING

Hostatgeria Castell d'Alaró ☎ 971 18 21 12, ⓦ castellalaro.cat. Recently opened, this straightforward hikers' hostel occupies a sympathetically modernized old building in the precincts of the castle. It says much for the determination of the local council that it ever got finished at all – much of the heavier tackle had to be lifted in by helicopter. The hostel has sixteen bunk beds in four dormitories, though more are planned, and there is a café too. Reservations are not required, but you'd be pretty crazy

to climb up here without booking first – or checking when they serve food. Half-board costs €24 per person per day. Dorm **€12**

Restaurante Es Verger Castell d'Alaró ☎ 971 18 21 26. High up on the mountain, on the way to the castle, this rustic restaurant, with its wooden benches and long tables, is famous for its lamb (*cordero*), slow-cooked in beer in a wood-fired oven and served with *patatas bravas* (Spanish-style potatoes). Daily 10am–8pm.

Alaró

Just south of the Castell d'Alaró turn-off, the town of **ALARÓ** is a sleepy little place of old stone houses blossoming out from an attractive main square, **Plaça Vila**. An elegant arcaded gallery flanks one side of the square, and a second is shadowed by the **church**, a fortress-like, medieval affair of honey-coloured sandstone embellished by a fancy Baroque doorway. The town was once at the centre of the trade between the mountains and the plain, with farm produce going one way, animal skins and charcoal the other, but it hit the headlines in 1901 when it became the first place on the island to install electric street lighting – even before Palma, much to the chagrin of that city's ruling council. Just south of Alaró, you leave the foothills of the Serra de Tramuntana and slip down onto the central plain, Es Pla, near **Binissalem** (see p.159).

ARRIVAL AND DEPARTURE ALARÓ

By bus Alaró's main bus stop is on Avgda de la Constitució (Ma-2022), about 350m southeast of the main square, Plaça Vila. There are no buses from Alaró to Orient or Bunyola, but Alaró can be easily reached by bus from Consell train station, on the Palma–Inca line (1–2 hourly; 15min).

ACCOMMODATION AND EATING

Can Xim Hotel Plaça Vila 7 ☎ 971 87 91 17, ⓦcanxim .com. On Alaró's main square, this small, family-owned hotel with eight guest rooms occupies an attractive old stone building. It's a pleasant place to stay, although the rooms are a tad frugal. **€160**

Traffic Restaurant Plaça Vila 7 ☎971 87 91 17, ⓦcanxim.com. Alaró's main square holds several cafés and restaurants where local families gather at the weekend, and the pick of the bunch is *Traffic*, part of the *Can Xim Hotel*. Here, Mallorcan specialities – notably casseroles – are served either inside or in the spacious garden at the back. Mains average €15. Daily except Tues noon–4pm & 8–11.30pm.

Deià

Ten kilometres west of Sóller, **DEIÀ** is beautiful. An ancient mountain village glued to the steep terraced slopes that rise high above the seashore, this is where the mighty Puig d'es Teix (1064m) meets the coast, retaining a formidable, almost mysterious presence, especially in the shadows of a moonlit night. Deià's long main street, Arxiduc Lluis Salvador, doubles as the coastal highway (Ma-10), skirting the base of the Teix to show off the bulk of the village's hotels and restaurants to fine advantage. It was Robert Graves (see box, p.104) who made Deià famous, holed up in his den, **Ca N'Alluny**, and at its peak, in the 1960s and 1970s, the village heaved with writers and poets, painters and musicians. Today, the literati have moved on and the affluent have moved in, but although Deià's main drag can be too congested to be much fun, the tiny heart of the village, tumbling over a high and narrow ridge on the seaward side of the road, still retains a surprising tranquillity.

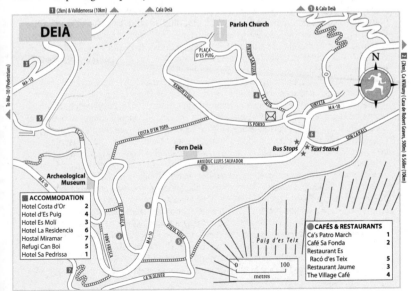

Deià church

On Deià's seaward side, labyrinthine alleys of old peasant houses curl up to a pretty **parish church**, in the precincts of which lies **Robert Graves**, his headstone marked simply "Robert Graves: Poeta, E.P.D." (*En Paz Descanse*, "Rest In Peace"). From the graveyard, there are memorable views out over the coast and of the Teix, with banks of tightly terraced fields tumbling down from the mountain towards the sea. The gloomy, barrel-vaulted church is itself unremarkable, but one of its outbuildings does hold a modest **Museu Parroquial** (no fixed opening hours; €2), which possesses a folksy assortment of religious bric-a-brac.

Ca N'Alluny: La Casa de Robert Graves

Carretera Deià–Sóller • Mon–Fri 10am–5pm, Sat 10am–3pm • €7 • ☎ 971 63 61 85, ⓦ lacasaderobertgraves.com

Graves put Deià on the international map and his old home, **Ca N'Alluny** (the "Far House" in Catalan), is a substantial stone building overlooking the coast about

ROBERT GRAVES IN DEIÀ

The English poet, novelist and classical scholar **Robert Graves** (1895–1985) spent two periods living in Deià, the first in the 1930s, and the second from the end of World War II until his death. During his first stay he shared a house at the edge of the village with **Laura Riding**, an American poet and dabbler in the mystical. Riding had arrived in England in 1926 and, after she became Graves's secretary and collaborator, the two of them began an affair that was to break up both their marriages. Their relationship created such a furore that they decided to leave England, settling in Mallorca on the advice of Gertrude Stein in 1930. The fuss was not simply a matter of morality – many of their friends were indifferent to adultery – but more to do with the self-styled "**Holy Circle**" they had founded, a cabalistic and intensely self-preoccupied literary-mystic group. The last straw came when Riding, in her attempt to control the group, jumped out of a window, saying "Goodbye, chaps", and the besotted Graves leapt after her. No wonder his mate T.E. Lawrence (of Arabia) wrote of "madhouse minds" and of Graves "drowning in a quagmire".

Both recovered, but the dottiness continued once they'd moved to Deià, with Graves acting as doting servant to Riding, whom he reinvented as a sort of all-knowing matriarch and muse. Simultaneously, Graves thumped away at his prose: he had already produced *Goodbye to All That* (1929), his bleak and painful memoirs of army service in the World War I trenches, but now came his other best-remembered books, **I, Claudius** (1934) and its sequel **Claudius the God** (1935), historical novels detailing the life and times of the Roman emperor. Nonetheless, to Graves these "potboilers", as he styled them, were secondary to his poetry – usually carefully crafted love poems of melancholic tenderness in praise of Riding – which were well received by the critics of the time.

At the onset of the Spanish Civil War, Graves and Riding left Mallorca, not out of sympathy for the Republicans but to keep contact with friends and family. During their exile Graves was ditched by Riding, and he subsequently took up with a mutual friend, **Beryl Pritchard**. After Graves had returned to Deià in 1946, he worked on *The White Goddess*, a controversial study of prehistoric and classical myth that argued the existence of an all-pervasive, primordial religion based on the worship of a poet-goddess. Pritchard joined him in the midst of his labours (the book was published in 1948), and in 1950 they were married in Palma. Graves, however, had a predilection for young women, claiming he needed female muses for poetic inspiration, and whilst his wife outwardly accepted this, she did so without much enthusiasm.

Meanwhile, although Graves's novels became increasingly well known and profitable, his poetry, with its preoccupation with romantic love, fell out of fashion, and his last anthology, *Poems 1965–1968*, was widely criticized by the literary establishment. Nevertheless, Graves's international reputation as a writer attracted a steady stream of visitors to Deià from the ranks of the literati, as well as the occasional film star. By the middle of the 1970s, however, just as an acclaimed BBC TV production of *I, Claudius* was bringing his books to a wider public in his native country, Graves had begun to lose his mind and he ended his days in sad senility. The house where Graves lived in Deià from 1946 onwards is now open to the public (see above).

500m east of the village. Opened to the public in 2006, **La Casa de Robert Graves** has been returned to something like its 1940s appearance and comes complete with the family's own furnishings and fittings. A visit begins with a short and well-made film introducing the author's life and times and then it's onto the house, where the living rooms seem surprisingly modest and very homely. The study, where Graves produced much of his finest work, is of modest proportions too, and beyond is an exhibition area with yet more biographical information, old photographs, letters and manuscripts, plus a recording of Graves reading a poem – *The Face in the Mirror*. There are photos, too, of Graves here in Deià with a bevy of famous friends, from Kingsley Amis to Alec Guinness and Ava Gardner. Finally, you emerge into the small but well-kept garden, where there are olive, carob, fruit and almond trees.

2

Deià Archeological Museum
Es Clot s/n • Tues, Thurs & Sun 5–7pm • Free • ☎ 971 63 90 01

Deià's **Archeological Museum** is hidden away in a leafy ravine below the main road. The archeologists William and Jacqueline Waldren founded the museum in 1962 to display the items they had retrieved from a number of local prehistoric sites. In particular, during their investigations into a prehistoric cave dwelling near Deià the couple found a great hoard of bones, the remains of a veritable herd of *Myotragus balearicus*, a small species of goat unique to the Balearics, whose precise prehistoric importance has sparked much debate. The Waldrens asserted that the animal was a dietary mainstay and that attempts had been made to domesticate it. What's more, they claimed that the goat bones were found at a level in the subsoil that pushed back the date at which the earliest islanders settled here by several hundred years – to 4000 or even 5000 BC. Few experts now agree and many believe that the goat was actually extinct before humans arrived. The Waldrens carried on with their archeological explorations after their important discovery, and the museum displays many of the key finds they retrieved in forty years of work.

Cala Deià
Much loved by Graves, **Cala Deià** is the nearest thing the village has to a beach, comprising some 200m of seaweed and shingle at the back of a handsome, hoop-shaped cove of jagged cliffs, boulders and white-crested surf. It's a great place for a swim – the water is clean and cool, and there are two summer-only beach bar-restaurants (see p.106). It's a popular spot, especially at weekends, when parking can be a nightmare – so get there early (by 11am). To drive, head northeast along the main road out of Deià and watch for the (easy-to-miss) sign about 700m beyond the *Hotel La Residencia*. To walk, the most obvious route is signed from the bend in the road 80m or so northeast of the bus stop; this leads down a wooded ravine and takes about thirty minutes. Even more bucolic, however, is the path that threads through the wooded and terraced gulch between the old centre of the village and the *Hotel Es Molí*; this takes about forty minutes.

ARRIVAL AND INFORMATION DEIÀ

Deià's main street is a 10min walk from end to end, but it takes much longer to explore the village's nooks and crannies, from the old church above the road to the ravine below.

By bus Buses from points east and west along the coast scoot through Deià along the Ma-10, stopping towards the east end of the village.
Destinations Palma (3–6 daily; 1hr); Port de Sóller (3–6 daily; 30min); Sóller (3–6 daily; 25min); Valldemossa (3–6 daily; 30min).

By taxi There's a one-berth taxi stand on the south side of the main road, 10m from the bus stop. To call a cab, ring ☎ 609 38 61 68.

Tourist information There's no tourist information office as such, but most of the hotels and *hostales* can provide advice on local walks and have bus timetables.

2

ACCOMMODATION

IN THE VILLAGE

★ **Hotel d'Es Puig** c/Es Puig 4 ☎971 63 94 09, ⓦhoteldespuig.com. A smart and tastefully furnished hotel with eight bedrooms in an elegantly converted, four-storey old stone house located in the centre of the village – between the Ma-10 and the church. It's worth paying a few euros more for a room with a balcony. Closed Jan. **€155**

Hotel Es Molí Carretera Deià-Valldemossa s/n ☎971 63 90 00, ⓦesmoli.com. Overlooking the main road from wooded slopes, this long-established, four-star hotel has an excellent reputation. Inside, the public areas are smart and spacious, with around ninety well-appointed, a/c bedrooms and suites divided between the main building, some of which dates from the seventeenth century, and an annexe at the back. The rooms are decorated in a comfortable, reassuring style and most have a balcony with wide coastal views. The lovely terraced gardens provide a lush setting for the pool, and the breakfast terrace is charming. The hotel minibus takes guests – the majority of whom are British – to a private (rocky) beach, a 20min drive to the east. Closed Nov to March. The hotel prefers longer bookings (at least seven nights) to short stays. **€200**

Hotel La Residencia c/Son Canals s/n ☎971 63 90 11, ⓦhotel-laresidencia.com. Models with nannies, big cars and flash clothes are the order of the day here in one of Mallorca's ritziest hotels. The decor is minimalist-meets-rustic and the hotel itself is an extended extrapolation of two old stone manor houses overlooking the main village drag. Currently owned by Orient-Express, it has facilities aplenty – pools, bars, restaurants, tennis court, a spa and so on. **€700**

★ **Hostal Miramar** c/Ca'n Oliver s/n ☎971 63 90 84, ⓦpensionmiramar.com. You don't get many good deals in Deià, but this is one of them – a family-run *hostal* in a traditional stone *finca* perched high above the main road about halfway through the village. There are nine pleasant rooms here – some en suite, some with shared facilities – and the views over the village from the courtyard in front of the house are stunning. On foot, it's a stiff 10min walk up from the main road. **€90**

Refugi Can Boi c/Es Clot 5 ☎971 63 61 86, ⓦwww.conselldemallorca.net. Government-run hikers' hostel in a neat and trim old stone building with 32 bunk beds in dorms. It's handily located in the valley below the church and is on the GR221 long-distance footpath. Advance reservations required. Dorm **€11**

OUTSIDE THE VILLAGE

Hotel Costa d'Or Llucalcari ☎971 63 90 25, ⓦhoposa.es. This four-star hotel enjoys a wonderful setting, overlooking an undeveloped slice of coast and surrounded by pine trees and olive groves. There's a shaded terrace bar and an outdoor swimming pool. The rooms are kitted out in slick, modern style, with the best looking over the ocean. The hotel – and the hamlet of Llucalcari – are located 2km east of Deià along the Ma-10 coast road. Closed Nov–March. **€190**

Hotel Sa Pedrissa Carretera Deià–Valldemossa s/n ☎971 63 91 11, ⓦsapedrissa.com. This hotel, set on its own about 2km west of Deià on the Ma-10, occupies an immaculately revamped old stone farmhouse, perched high above – and with wide views over – the coast. Stone-and-marble floors, exposed wooden beams and oodles of white paint set the tone, and each of the nine bedrooms is impeccably turned out. There's also a terrace pool. **€160**

EATING AND DRINKING

You're spoiled for choice when it comes to eating out in Deià. Dotted along the main street are several smart and polished **restaurants** plus a number of more modest **café-bars**, ideal for nursing a drink and people-watching. The village also has a good **grocery-store-cum-bakery**, Forn Deià, about 200m west of the main bus stop.

Café Sa Fonda c/Arxiduc Lluís Salvador 5 ☎971 63 93 06. If you're looking for island simplicities, Deià is the wrong place, but this busy café-bar, up a flight of steps off the main drag, is the nearest thing you'll get to a locals' favourite. There's a large shaded terrace and although drinks are the main event, they serve snacks and light meals too. Daily Tues–Sun noon–midnight.

★ **Ca's Patro March** Cala Deià ☎971 63 91 37. The better of the two café-bars down in Cala Deià, this lovely place occupies a rustic-looking tumble of old stone buildings that culminate in a shaded terrace looking straight out to sea. The speciality is seafood caught and brought here by the owner's son. Easter to late Oct daily 12.30–6pm.

Restaurant Es Racó d'es Teix c/Vinya Vella 6 ☎971 63 95 01, ⓦesracodesteix.es. Delightful restaurant in an old stone house with an attractive shaded terrace; it's a steep 30m or so above the main road, about halfway into the village – watch for the sign. The Mediterranean cuisine features local ingredients and is strong on island dishes, but it doesn't come cheap, with main courses from €30. Reservations well-nigh essential. Wed–Sun 1–3pm & 7.30–10.30pm; closed late Nov to Jan.

Restaurant Jaume c/Arxiduc Lluís Salvador 22 ☎971 63 90 29, ⓦrestaurantejaume-deia.com. First-rate, family-owned terraced restaurant specializing in traditional Mallorcan cuisine – try, for instance, the pork in cabbage leaves. Every dish is carefully prepared and the service is attentive; main courses average around €25. Reservations advised. Daily except Thurs 1–3.30pm & 7.30–10.30pm, but restricted opening hours for much of the winter.

★ **The Village Café** c/Felip Bauça 1 ☎ 971 63 91 99, ⓦ villagecafedeia.com. Lively place with an inventive menu and an appealing shaded terrace overlooking the coast. The menu is fairly short, but manages to cover lots of cuisines – from Spanish to Italian and Greek – with one of the highlights being its burgers. Mains are competitively priced at around €13. Mid-Feb to Oct Thurs–Mon noon–11pm, Wed 5–11pm.

FESTIVALS

Deià International Music Festival ☎ 678 98 95 36, ⓦ dimf.com. Deià is the haunt of long-term ex-pats, who club together to sustain several cultural festivals, most notably this one, whose assorted classical concerts begin in April and end in September.

2

Son Marroig

Carretera de Valldemossa–Deià (Ma-10) • April–Sept Mon–Sat 9.30am–6pm; Oct–March Mon–Sat 9.30am–1pm & 3.30–5.30pm • €4 • ⓦ sonmarroig.com

Three kilometres beyond Deià, **Son Marroig** is an imposing L-shaped mansion perched high above the seashore – and just below the Ma-10. The house dates from late medieval times, but was refashioned in the nineteenth century to become the favourite residence of the Habsburg archduke **Ludwig Salvator** (see box below). Dynastically insignificant but extremely rich, the Austrian aristocrat first visited Mallorca aged 19, fell head-over-heels in love with the place, and returned to buy Son Marroig along with a sizeable slice of the west coast between Deià and Port de Valldemossa.

The house and garden

The Son Marroig estate comprises the house, its gardens and the headland below. Despite its setting and long history, the **house** is actually rather dull, with all its key

---

THE UPS AND DOWNS OF THE ARCHDUKE LUDWIG SALVATOR

Cousin to the Habsburg Emperor Franz Josef of Austria, the young **Ludwig Salvator** (1847–1915) was supposed to join the imperial army, but he cleared off and took his sea captain's certificate instead. Annoyed at this insubordination, the emperor appointed him the Governor of Bohemia hoping it would settle him down. It might have worked, too, but for a freak accident: Salvator's young wife, **Mathilde**, was watching the archduke inspect his soldiers from a balcony, when the cigarette that she was smoking set her dress on fire and she burnt to death. Out of sympathy, his family indulged Salvator's wanderlust and the archduke headed south to the Mediterranean in 1866. It was on his travels that the archduke first visited Mallorca, which it made such an impression on him that he returned to live here, buying a chunk of the west coast and building (or at least adopting) no fewer than **three homes** – Son Marroig (see above), Miramar (see p.108) and S'Estaca, now owned by Michael Douglas.

Once in residence, Ludwig immersed himself in all things *Mallorquín*, learning the dialect and chronicling the island's topography, archeology, history and folklore in astounding detail. He churned out no fewer than **seven volumes** on the Balearics and, perhaps more importantly, played a leading role as a proto-environmentalist, conserving the coastline of his estates and paying for a team of geologists to chart the Coves del Drac (see p.178). Salvator may have been hard working, but he also squeezed in a lot of R&R, allegedly sleeping with a platoon of local women and fathering a merry band of children. Back at Habsburg HQ, rumours of Salvator's antics went down badly: it was not so much that "Don Balearo", as he was nicknamed, slept with peasant girls, but more that he recognized them and their (his) children, giving them money and land. He even brought one of his women – **Catalina Homar** – back to the Habsburg court in Vienna and, after her untimely death, publicly dedicated one of his books to her. It was, however, World War I rather than Vienna's disapproval that brought a sudden end to the archduke's stint in Mallorca. In 1914, at the outbreak of war, Salvator was summoned back to the Austro-Hungarian Empire to do his royal duty; he died within a year.

exhibits piled into one, sometimes two, large and gloomy first-floor rooms. Here you'll find a small sample of Hispano-Arabic pottery; a handful of classical Greek figurines; a beautifully carved, medieval bas-relief diptych; and a display featuring some of the archduke's manuscripts and pamphlets alongside several ducal photographs – which show the duke ballooning up from a regular-sized young man to a real heavyweight. More appealing, however, is the **garden**, whose terraces are graced by a Neoclassical belvedere of Tuscan Carrara marble that provides gorgeous views along the jagged, forested coast.

Sa Foradada

Below the house is a slender shank of a promontory known as **Sa Foradada**, "the rock pierced by a hole", where the archduke used to park his yacht. The hole in question is a strange circular affair sited high up in the rock face at the end of the promontory. It takes about forty minutes to **walk** the 3km down to this rock, a straightforward excursion to a delightfully scenic spot, though the estate itself is a little scruffy and ill-kempt. The walk begins at the gate just up the slope and to the left of the house, where a sign insists you need to get permission at Son Marroig before setting out, but this is just to make sure you pay the admission fee. Walkers usually have to clamber over the gate's stile – though sometimes the gate is left open – and then, about 100m further on, need to keep right at the fork in the track; as you approach the tip of the promontory, think carefully before deciding to attempt the precarious climb beyond the old jetties. On your return, you can slake your thirst at one of the two **café-bars** overlooking the coast from beside the car park near the house.

Miramar

Carretera de Valldemossa–Deià (Ma-10) · Mon–Sat 10am–5.30pm · €4

Just 2km southwest of Son Marroig, **Miramar** was once the site of a medieval monastery – hence the signs for the "**Monestir de Miramar**" – and the last of the three houses bought by the Archduke Salvator. The house and its grounds hold an improbable assortment of remains and memorials, beginning with a line of thirteenth-century **stone pillars**, which, marooned in the garden, are all that is left of the original monastery built for the scholar-missionaries of Ramon Llull (see p.62). Beyond the pillars is the **house**, whose handful of rooms holds a mock-up of part of the archduke's yacht, the *Nixe II*, two rooms devoted to the life of Ramon Llull, a recreation of a monk's cell, and a ridiculously romantic stone memorial to the archduke's first secretary, Vratislav Vyborny, who died in Palma when he was in his twenties. Outside, in the **grounds** are some strange geometric shapes allegedly laid out by Llull, as well as a fancy stone shrine built by the archduke in Llull's honour, though the high point is the short **path** that meanders down through the olive groves to a fine vantage point offering tremendous views along the coast.

Valldemossa

Beyond Miramar, the Ma-10 stays high above the coast, twisting through what was once the archducal estate en route to the inordinately pretty hill-town of **VALLDEMOSSA**, whose ancient **monastery** has made it one of the most visited places on Mallorca. The origins of Valldemossa date from the early fourteenth century, when the asthmatic **King Sancho** built a royal palace here in the hills where the air was easier to breathe. Later, in 1399, the palace was gifted to Carthusian monks from Tarragona, who converted and extended the original complex into a monastery, which has survived in prime condition. An enjoyable place to spend the night, especially as the tourist hordes leave the town by early evening, Valldemossa has two appealing hotels as well as a couple of good restaurants and it's also within easy striking distance of its old seaport,

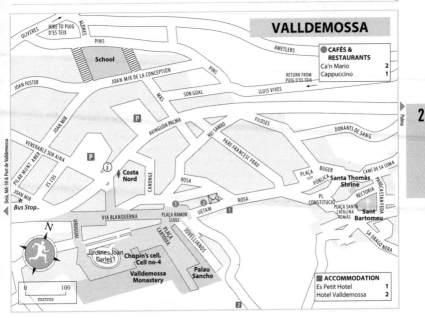

2

Port de Valldemossa, whose gaggle of modern villas and tiny beach are reached along the dramatic hairpins of a narrow country road.

Valldemossa Monastery

Plaça de la Cartoixa • April–Sept Mon–Sat 9.30am–7pm, Sun 10am–1pm; Oct, Nov, Feb & March Mon–Sat 9.30am–5.30pm, Sun 10am–1pm; Dec & Jan Mon–Sat 9.30am–3.30pm, Sun 10am–1pm • €8, which includes the Palau Sancho and the Chopin concerts; Cell No.4 costs €3 extra • ☎ 971 61 29 86, ⓦ cartujadevalldemossa.com

Remodelled and restructured on several occasions, most of Valldemossa's **Real Cartuja de Jesús de Nazaret** (Royal Carthusian Monastery of Jesus of Nazareth) is of seventeenth- and eighteenth-century construction. It owes its present notoriety almost entirely to the novelist and republican polemicist **George Sand** (1804–76), who, with her companion, the composer **Frédéric Chopin** (1810–49), lived here for four months in 1838–39. They arrived just three years after the last monks had been evicted during the suppression of the monasteries, and so were able to rent a comfortable set of vacant cells. Their stay is commemorated in Sand's *A Winter in Majorca*, a sharp-tongued and sharp-eyed epistle (see p.110), that expresses Sand's frustration with the ossified social structures on the island, though her diatribes against reaction sometimes merge into a mean-spirited contempt for her Spanish neighbours. Ungraciously, Sand explains that her nickname for Mallorca, "Monkey Island", was coined for its "crafty, thieving and yet innocent" inhabitants, who, she asserts, are "heartless, selfish and impertinent". Quite what the islanders made of Sand is unknown, but her trouser-wearing, cigar-smoking image – along with her "living in sin" – could hardly have made her popular in the rural Mallorca of that period.

The monastery church and pharmacy

A visit begins in the gloomy **church**, a square and heavy construction, which is distinguished by its late Baroque ceiling paintings and barrel vaulting. It also possesses a kitsch high altar and a fanciful bishop's throne, which somehow manages to look a little self-conscious. Beyond the church lie the shadowy **cloisters**, where the first port of call is the **pharmacy**, which survived the expulsion of the monks to serve the town's medicinal needs well into the twentieth century. Its shelves are crammed with a host of beautifully decorated majolica jars, antique glass receptacles and painted wooden boxes, each carefully inscribed with the name of a potion or drug.

The prior's cell

Despite its name, the **prior's cell** is a comfortable suite of bright, sizeable rooms, enhanced by access to a private garden with splendid views down the valley. The cell incorporates a chapel, a library, an audience chamber, a dining room and a bedroom – all graced by a potpourri of religious objets d'art. These include a number of handsome majolica pieces and two unattributed medieval triptychs displayed in the library. The triptychs are the *Adoration of the Magi*, a charmingly naive painting in the Flemish style, and an intricate marble sculpture celebrating the marriage of Pedro II of Aragón (1174–1213), who died in battle against the army of Simon de Montfort outside Toulouse. This degree of luxury was clearly not what the ascetic **St Bruno** had in mind when he founded the **Carthusian order** in the eleventh century. Nevertheless, it's hard to blame the monks at Valldemossa for lightening what must have been a very heavy burden. Bruno's rigorous regime, inspired by his years as a hermit, had his monks in almost continuous isolation, gathering together only for certain church services and to eat in the refectory on Sundays. At other times, lay brothers fed the monks through hatches along the cloister corridors: three days a week the monks had only bread and water, and they never ate meat. The diet and the mountain air, never mind the celibacy, seem to have suited them: the longevity of the Valldemossa monks was proverbial.

GEORGE SAND AT VALLDEMOSSA

Of the many foreigners writing about Mallorca in the nineteenth century, the most celebrated was **George Sand** (1804–76), the pen name of the French aristocrat Armandine Lucile Aurore Dupin, the Baroness Dudevant. Sand married the eponymous baron in 1822, then left him nine years later for the literary life of Paris, where she embraced the Republican cause. A prolific author, dramatist and journalist, Sand became a well-known figure in French political circles and her occasional travels included an extended stay in Valldemossa (1838–39) with her partner, the pianist and composer **Frédéric Chopin**. Sand was not overly impressed with the islanders, but she did take a liking to Valldemossa, as she recorded in her **memoir** of the time, *A Winter in Majorca*:

"To reach the Cartuja [Valldemossa monastery] you have to leave the coach, for it is impossible for any vehicle to clamber up the stony track that leads to it. It is a fascinating approach with its sudden twists and bends among magnificent trees, and with wonderful views that are unfolded at every step, and increase in beauty the higher one rises. ... At the head of the valley ...[the Carthusian monks]... have made a vast garden ... [which occupies]... the whole inclined background of the valley, and rises in a succession of wide terraces on the lower slopes of the mountain. By moonlight, when its irregularity is masked by the darkness, it could be taken for an amphitheatre carved out for the battles of giants....

The Cartuja, situated at the highest point of this gorge, looks on the north side over an extensive valley, which widens out and rises in a gentle slope to the coastal cliffs, whose base is battered and eroded by the sea. One arm of the cordillera points towards Spain, and the others towards the Orient. From this picturesque Carthusian monastery therefore, the sea can be glimpsed or sensed on two sides. Whilst its roar is audible to the north, it can be descried to the south like a fine, brilliant line beyond the descending mountain slopes and the immense plain which is revealed to the eye. It is a surpassing picture, framed in the foreground by dark, pine-covered crags; beyond that by the sharply outlined profiles of mountains set off by superb trees; and in the background by the rounded humps of hills, which the setting sun gilds with the warmest shades, and on whose crests one can still distinguish, from a distance of a league, the microscopic outlines of the trees, as fine as the antennae of butterflies, as black and distinct as a trace of Chinese ink on a backdrop of sparkling gold."

Cells no. 2 and 4

Along the cloister corridor, **Cell no. 2** exhibits miscellaneous curios relating to **Chopin and Sand**, from portraits and photos to musical scores and letters; it was in this cell that the composer wrote his *Raindrop* Prelude. Next door is **Cell no. 4**, which now charges €3 to enter either from the cloisters or from a separate entrance outside the monastery. Pride of place here goes to Chopin's piano, which was finally installed just three weeks before the couple left for Paris. Considering the hype, these incidental Chopin mementos are something of an anticlimax and you'll soon be moving onto the ground-floor galleries of the adjacent Museu Municipal.

Museu Municipal

Just along the cloister corridor from Cell no. 4 is the **Museu Municipal**, whose first room traces the endeavours of Archduke Ludwig Salvator (see box, p.107). On display is a photograph of his favourite mistress, Catalina Homar, and a copy of the booklet the archduke dedicated to her, as well as several photos of the island's hermit-monks. The museum's second room is devoted to a modest collection of local landscape paintings, amongst which the bright, cheerful and very folksy canvases of **Joan Fuster** (1870–1943) are the pick.

Museu Municipal Art Contemporani

Upstairs, the **Museu Municipal Art Contemporani** has a small but surprisingly good collection of modern art. There's a platoon of characteristic squiggles by Joan Miró, works by international artists such as Max Ernst and Francis Bacon, and a substantial collection of paintings by the Spanish modernist **Juli Ramís** (1909–90), from geometric abstractions through to forceful, expressionistic paintings like *The Blue Lady* (*Dama Blava*).

Palau Sancho

From the prior's cell a doorway leads outside the cloisters and across the courtyard to the **Palau Sancho** (Palace of King Sancho). It's not the original medieval palace – that disappeared long ago – but this fortified mansion is the oldest part of the monastery complex and within its imposing walls, which mostly date from the sixteenth century, lie a string of appealing period rooms cluttered with faded paintings and other curios, from fans, vintage engravings and a head of a suffering Christ to old halberds and muskets. The palace was the first home of the monks, but it has also seen service as the residence of local bigwigs and as a political prison, its most celebrated internee being the liberal reformer **Gaspar de Jovellanos**, a victim of the royal favourite Manuel de Godoy, who had him locked up here from 1801 to 1802.

Valldemossa town

The monastery is very much the main event in Valldemossa, though there are a couple of minor attractions amongst the cobbled lanes and old stone houses of the **town centre**, which tumbles prettily down the hillside beneath it. First is the church of **Sant Bartomeu**, an imposing Gothic edifice with a handsome Baroque bell tower that lords it over a tiny piazza. Nearby, round the back along a narrow alley at c/Rectoria 5, is the humble birthplace of **Santa Catalina Thomàs**, a sixteenth-century nun revered for her piety. The interior of the house has been turned into a simple little shrine, with a statue of the saint holding a small bird.

ARRIVAL AND INFORMATION **VALLDEMOSSA**

By car The prettiest approach to Valldemossa is from the south, along the Ma-1110, which squeezes through a narrow defile, passing high above terraced orchards and olive groves as it clambers towards the town's sloping jumble of houses and monastic buildings. The Ma-10, meanwhile, approaches via the town's workaday western outskirts.

Parking There are several car parks beside the ring road – Avgda Palma – but spaces can get thin on the ground between about 10am and 4pm.

2

By bus The main bus stop is beside the most westerly of the car parks flanking the ring road.

Destinations Deià (3–6 daily; 30min); Palma (3–6 daily; 30min); Port de Sóller (3–6 daily; 1hr); Sóller (3–6 daily; 55min).

Tourist information The town tourist office is beside the ring road (Mon–Fri 9am–1.30pm & 3–5pm, Sat 10am–1pm; ☎ 971 61 21 06, ⓦ valldemossa.com).

ACCOMMODATION

Es Petit Hotel c/Uetam 1 ☎ 971 61 24 79, ⓦ espetithotel -valldemossa.com. This lovely hotel occupies a tastefully renovated old stone house metres from the monastery. There are eight en-suite guest rooms here, each decorated in a pleasant, unfussy style with creams and browns to the fore; several also have smashing views down the valley. **€130**

Hotel Valldemossa Carretera Vieja de Valldemossa s/n ☎ 971 61 26 26, ⓦ valldemossahotel.com. A grand Italianate stairway climbs up to what was originally a pair of nineteenth-century hilltop farmhouses, but is now the sleek, rural-chic *Valldemossa* hotel with a heated indoor pool, a restaurant and an expansive terrace. Verdant gardens tumble down the hillside and the twelve rooms – three doubles and nine suites – come with every mod con. All very chi-chi. **€340**

EATING AND DRINKING

The centre of Valldemossa is packed with cafés and restaurants, but many are geared up for the day-trippers and offer pretty dire food at inflated prices. That said, there are one or two exceptions, as detailed below, and/or you can enjoy locally made ice cream from the kiosk opposite the monastery entrance.

Ca'n Mario c/Uetam 8 ☎ 971 61 21 22. In an old and handsome terraced house, the first-floor *Ca'n Mario* is a family-run place with engagingly old-fashioned decor. They serve traditional Mallorcan food here with main courses averaging around €15. Mon–Wed 1.30–3.30pm, Thurs–Sun 1.30–3.30pm & 8–10pm.

Cappuccino Plaça Ramon Llull 5 ☎ 971 61 60 59, ⓦ grupocappuccino.com. Part of a small Mallorcan chain, this slick and modern café-restaurant has fast service, though the prices are a tad over the odds. The menu changes with the time of day, from breakfast in the morning to hot dishes – beef carpaccio, lasagne and so forth – from lunchtime onwards. Daily 9am–midnight.

Port de Valldemossa

Valldemossa may not have a beach, but you can go for a paddle or swim at **PORT DE VALLDEMOSSA**, where a handful of seaside villas huddle together in the shadow of the mountains at the mouth of a narrow, craggy cove. There's no public transport, but the drive down to the port, once Valldemossa's gateway to the outside world, is stimulating: head west out of Valldemossa to rejoin the Ma-10 and, after about 1.5km, turn right at the sign and follow the twisty side road for 6km down through the mountains. Port de Valldemossa's **beach** is small and shingly, and tends to get battered by the surf, but the scenery is stunning.

EATING AND DRINKING

PORT DE VALLDEMOSSA

Es Port c/Ponent s/n ☎ 971 61 61 94, ⓦ restaurantesport.es. With a terrace overlooking the ocean, the only restaurant in Port de Valldemossa has a justifiably good reputation for seafood – try the shellfish and lobster paella at just €24 per head; times may vary, so ring ahead to confirm. Daily: Feb–June & Sept–Nov 10am–6pm; July & Aug 10am–10pm.

La Granja

Carretera Banyalbufar s/n · Daily May–Sept 10am–7pm; Oct–April 10am–6pm · €14 · ☎ 971 61 00 32, ⓦ lagranja.net · The Palma/ Estellencs bus stops by the entrance to La Granja (4–8 daily)

Southwest of Valldemossa, the Ma-10 threads a scenic route along the coastal mountains for 8km until it reaches the turning for **La Granja**, a grand *hacienda* nestling in a tranquil wooded and terraced valley. The house and its grounds make for a popular package-tourist trip, but, despite the many visitors, the estate just about manages to maintain a languorous air of old patrician comfort. La Granja was occupied until fairly

VALDEMOSSA (P.108) >

2

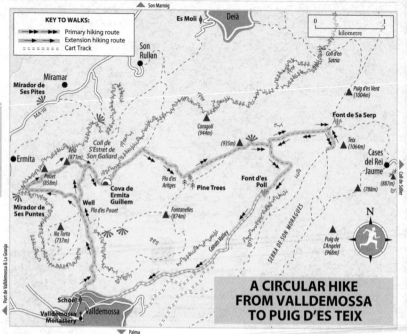

A CIRCULAR HIKE FROM VALLDEMOSSA TO PUIG D'ES TEIX

A CIRCULAR HIKE FROM VALLDEMOSSA TO PUIG D'ES TEIX BY THE ARCHDUKE'S PATH

12.5km • 674m of ascent • 4hr 30min–5hr • Medium difficulty • Trailhead: N39.71089°, E002.62091° • Optional extensions: the Mirador de Ses Puntes & Veià (an additional 1.5km; 116m of ascent; 45min); and Puig d'es Teix (2.5km; 186m of ascent; 60min)

The terrain between **Valldemossa and Deià** is mountainous and wild, abounding in steep cliffs and rocky summits; the lower slopes are wooded but the tops are almost devoid of vegetation, with numerous dramatic viewpoints, many of them overlooking the ocean. The land is rough but the mountains are crisscrossed by footpaths first made by charcoal burners, olive growers and hunters. Although these tracks can be stony, the archduke **Ludwig Salvator** (see box, p.107) had some wonderful paths constructed so that he could ride around on horseback admiring the scenery. This **circular walk** – which can be lengthened or shortened to suit – is a classic, showing the area to its best advantage.

THE ROUTE

From near the monastery on Valldemossa's bypass (Avgda Palma), proceed along **c/Venerable Sor Aina** past the **car park** and take the first right up to the school. Climb the **steps** at the left-hand side of the school, then turn right and almost immediately left onto c/Alzines. Follow this road round, turn right onto c/Oliveres and then continue through a chained entry next to **Son Gual Petit** (house), down a stony path that leads into the woods, entered by a ladder over a locked gate. The path winds uphill steeply through the woods to reach an opening in the wall at the edge of a wooded plain, the **Pla d'es Pouet**, where there is a crossroads. Continue straight ahead here until you reach an old **well** (now polluted) in a large clearing. This well is a vital reference point in a confusing area and it is essential that you take your bearings carefully here.

At this point you can extend the walk to take in the Mirador de Ses Puntes (see below), or take the path from the well that bears slightly right and leads easily up to the **Coll de Son Gallard**. At a T-junction, turn right past some V-shaped stone seats. The main path continues uphill. South of this path lies the **Cova de Ermita Guillem**, a hermit's cave with a shrine and assorted icons – look for a branch path on the right, which leads to the enclosure in front of the cave. From the cave, retrace your steps back to the main path and continue. A short stiff climb takes you to the stone **Archduke's path**. Here, turn left uphill, winding up to the edge of the cliffs for breathtaking views across the island and of the coastline below; this is a great place for a picnic.

Continue along the path and as you skirt the summit of **Puig de Caragolí** (944m), you can spy Port de Sóller down on the coast and the mountains Major, Teix and Galatzó rising high above the seashore. The descent is gentle, over the sloping, arid plain of **Pla d'es Aritges**. A clearly signposted junction at an isolated group of pine trees offers a shortcut, heading right, back to Valldemossa via Fontanelles. To stay on the main route, continue straight on, heading northeast, which brings you over a 935m top and, shortly after, to a viewpoint overlooking Deià. After this the path swings southeast and begins to descend to the Teix path junction.

A 1m-high **cairn** and waymark clearly identifies the **Teix path junction**, where those heading for the Teix summit (see below) steer left. Otherwise, continue straight ahead to follow the interminable cement track's descent into the **Cairats valley**. First you'll come to an old "snowhouse" (a deep hole used for storing ice in winter), then a stone mountain refuge, the *Refugi de Son Moragues*, and below that a spring and picnic site, the **Font d'es Poll** (Well of the Poplar). The wide track beyond is stony but you'll have no trouble finding the route. On the way down the valley you'll see the remains of a *sitja*, a charcoal-worker's shelter, and a lime kiln. Keep on the main track down the Cairats valley, going over a wall via stone steps. The main path bends round to the left to lead down to the main road to the east of Valldemossa.

The **more direct route** back to town is to head down a path to your right, before vineyards, where the dirt track eventually leads down to join c/Xesc Forteza. From here, bear left into c/Lluis Vives at the end of which is a large old house with a square tower. Take a moment to stop here and admire the splendid views over the old part of Valldemossa. Then, continue on down c/San Gual, turn left into c/Mas and right onto Avgda Palma, which will bring you directly into the town centre.

MIRADOR DE SES PUNTES EXTENSION

From the well (see above), take the path to your left, which leads northwest before zigzagging uphill and swinging west. Fork left shortly after passing an old and long-defunct bread oven to reach the **Mirador de Ses Puntes**. From this superb viewpoint, return to the fork and take the left branch, which rises through the trees to the top of **Pouet** (858m) and, after a little dip, **Veià** (871m). For much of the way, the path is the wide bridleway built by the archduke and from it you can look down on Sa Foradada, a rocky headland near his old house, Son Marroig (see p.107). From the ruined shelter on Veià the path descends to the **Coll de Son Gallard**, where you rejoin the main path a little up from the well. You'll need to re-orientate yourself at the well.

PUIG D'ES TEIX SUMMIT EXTENSION

For the hour-long detour to the **Puig d'es Teix summit**, turn left at the waymarked Teix path junction, taking a path that scrambles up a little gully and then continues over a sandy plateau towards a high stone wall. Cross this using the ladders provided and walk on to the **Pla de Sa Serp**, a plain where there is a spring – the **Font de Sa Serp**. A well-used path then leads up to the col between the two summits and on to the main west summit of **Puig d'es Teix** (1064m). From here the views over the Sóller valley and the western summit of Puig Major are especially fine, while the tops of Cornadors, L'Ofre and the Alfàbia ridge form a stunning skyline. Return to the Teix path junction by the same route (avoid the difficult-to-follow route southwest from Teix towards Sa Bussa) and turn left to continue the walk.

2

recently by the Fortuny family, who took possession in the mid-fifteenth century; after about the 1920s it seems that modernization never crossed their minds. Pick up the leaflet outlining the numbered **self-guided tour** just before you reach the ticket office.

The house

From the ticket office, which is immediately in front of the main forecourt, signs direct you up round the back of the house, past a collection of well-weathered agricultural tackle and farmyard animals. At the back of the house, you proceed up to the old bath house, which offers a wide view over the estate, then onto the **house** itself, where a sequence of rooms is strewn with domestic clutter. A highlight is the delightful little theatre, where plays were once performed for the household in a manner common among Europe's nineteenth-century rural landowners. Amongst much else, there's a children's games room, an ironing room, a graceful first-floor loggia and a dining room, which, with its faded paintings and tapestries, has a real touch of country elegance.

The workshops

Tagged onto the house, a series of **workshops** recall the days when La Granja was a profitable and almost entirely self-sufficient concern. A wine press as well as almond and olive-oil mills prepared the estate's produce for export, whilst plumbers, carpenters, cobblers, weavers and rope makers all kept pace with domestic requirements. After the workshops, you can either go for a twenty minute **walk** through the surrounding woods, or head directly to the **cellars**, the site of the farm kitchen. The Fortunys were one of Mallorca's more enlightened landowning families, and employees were well fed by the kitchen staff, who made cheeses, bread and preserves. Also in the cellars are two entirely unauthentic additions – a display of torture instruments and a torture chamber.

The chapel and forecourt

After the cellars, you soon reach the family **chapel**, a diminutive affair with battered religious paintings and sculptures, and then the expansive **forecourt**, shaded by plane trees and surrounded by antiquated workshops where costumed artisans "practise" traditional crafts such as wood-turning and candle-making. This part of the visit is more than a little bogus, but fun all the same – and the home-made pastries and doughnuts (*bunyols*) are lip-smacking. Your visit may coincide with a mildly diverting display of Mallorcan **folk dancing**, usually held in the forecourt.

Esporles

A couple of kilometres south of La Granja, **ESPORLES** is an amiable, leafy little town whose elongated main street runs parallel to the line of an ancient stone watercourse. This is Mallorca away from the tourist throng, with the town's finest building being a massive, heavily buttressed thirteenth-century **church** overlooking **Plaça Espanya** – though the *plaça* here is not a square but a street. In 1452, Miquel Forns, the leader of a local peasants' revolt that had spread across the whole of Mallorca from the Esporles district, was tortured to death on Plaça Espanya and his body left swinging on a gibbet as a warning.

ARRIVAL AND DEPARTURE ESPORLES

By bus Buses to and from Esporles pull in on c/Jaume I, just west of the main street (the Ma-1100), towards the north end of town, and a couple of blocks south of Plaça Espanya.

Destinations Banyalbufar (4–8 daily; 20min); Estellencs (4–8 daily; 35min); Palma (every 1–2hr; 35min).

Banyalbufar

Approaching from the east, the Ma-10 offers spectacular views as it nears **BANYALBUFAR**, a drowsy little village whose terraced fields cling gingerly to the coastal cliffs. The land here has been cultivated since Moorish times, with a spring above the village providing water that's still channelled down the hillside along slender watercourses into open storage cisterns, the unlikely looking home for a few carp. The village is bisected by the Ma-10, also its main street, with ancient houses and steep cobbled lanes to either side. The cute main square, **Plaça de la Vila**, perches above the Ma-10, overlooked by a chunky, barrel-vaulted parish **church** dating from the fifteenth century. Banyalbufar is a fine place to unwind and there's a rough and rocky **beach** a steep fifteen-minute walk down the hill – just follow the signs to the *Hotel Sa Coma* and keep going. About 1.5km west of Banyalbufar on the Ma-10, the **Torre del Verger**, a sixteenth-century watchtower built as a sentinel against pirate attack, provides stunning views along the coast. There's no tourist office in the village, but a good range of accommodation and a busy café and restaurant scene.

ARRIVAL AND DEPARTURE
BANYALBUFAR

By bus Buses to and from Banyalbufar travel the length of the main street, with services to Estellencs stopping west of the main square: those heading east stop across from the square.

Destinations Esporles (4–8 daily; 20min); Estellencs (4–8 daily; 15min); Palma (4–8 daily; 1hr 10min).

ACCOMMODATION

Hotel Mar i Vent c/Major 49 ☎971 61 80 00, ⓦ hotelmarivent.com. In a conspicuous 1940s building on the main street towards the east end of the village, this traditional hotel has thirty rooms, the best of which are reasonably large and have sea-facing balconies with fantastic views along the coast. There's also an outside pool and staff will park your car for you – a blessing given the village's steep and narrow lanes. **€100**

Hotel Sa Baronia c/Baronia 16 ☎971 61 81 46, ⓦ hbaronia.com. Traditional – some would say old-fashioned – hotel, parts of which inhabit an ancient fortified house. The forty-odd guest rooms are simple and straightforward, all white walls and varnished furniture, and all have sea-facing balconies. It has a large outside pool and is handily located at the west end of the village, beside the main street. Closed Nov–March. **€80**

★ **Hotel Sa Coma** Camí des Molí 3 ☎971 61 80 34, ⓦ hotelsacoma.com. Banyalbufar has a clutch of traditional, family-run hotels and this is one of them. In a straightforward, three-storey modern block, it has fittings and furnishings reminiscent of the 1970s, but the whole ensemble is engaging and most of the rooms have mini-balconies with sea views. There's an outdoor pool too. The hotel is located down below the main drag on the way to the beach. Closed Nov–April. **€125**

Hotel Son Borguny c/Borguny 1 ☎971 14 87 06, ⓦ sonborguny.com. A short walk up from the main street, this hotel occupies a sympathetically modernized three-storey stone house that dates from the fifteenth century. The seven guest rooms are kitted out in a cheerful version of modern-meets-traditional style, though few have sea views. **€95**

EATING AND DRINKING

Pegasón y el Pajarito Enmascarado c/Pont 2 ☎971 14 87 13, ⓦ pegasonyelpajaritoenmascarado.com. The liveliest place in town, this bar and restaurant is in cellar-like premises almost underneath the main street across from the main square. With twin rooms adorned with bizarre-cum-Baroque furnishings and fittings, it has a short but well-chosen menu that includes traditional Mallorcan dishes as well as pizzas and the like. Check out, too, the fish of the day (€20). Mon–Wed, Sat & Sun 12.30–4pm & 7.30–10.30pm, Fri 7.30–10.30pm.

Restaurante 1661 Cuina de Banyalbufar c/Baronia 1 ☎971 61 82 45. Bang on the high street, this smart new restaurant offers a temptingly varied menu with Spanish/Catalan dishes at its core: main courses average €20. Daily 12.30–4pm & 7.30–10.30pm.

★ **Restaurante Son Tomas** c/Baronia 17 ☎971 61 81 49. At the west end of the village, this agreeable restaurant occupies modern premises with a large, sea-facing terrace. Service is punctilious and the steaks are good, but the seafood is even better – look out for the fish of the day. Main courses average €15. April to late Oct Mon 12.30–4pm, Wed–Sun 12.30–4pm & 7.30–10.30pm; late Oct to March daily except Tues 12.30–4pm.

Estellencs

Eight kilometres west of Banyalbufar, **ESTELLENCS** is similar to its neighbour, with steep coastal cliffs and tight terraced fields – if anything it's even prettier, its narrow, winding alleys crimped by old stone houses and one-time agricultural buildings. The village has one notable structure, a fortress-like **church**, dating from the fifteenth century when pirate attack was likely. From the west side of the village, a steep and very narrow 2km lane leads down past olive and orange orchards to **Cala Estellencs**, a rocky, surf-buffeted cove that shelters a rough shingly beach, a fishing jetty and a summertime bar. There's a superb vantage point over the coast 3.5km southwest of Estellencs on the Ma-10 at the **Mirador Es Grau**, where a flight of stone steps climbs up to an ancient tower.

ARRIVAL AND DEPARTURE ESTELLENCS

By bus Buses stop in the centre on the main street. Destinations Esporles (4–8 daily; 35min); Banyalbufar (4–8 daily; 15min); Palma (4–8 daily; 1hr 15min).

ACCOMMODATION

Hotel Maristel c/Eusebi Pacscual s/n ☎ 971 61 85 50, ⓦ hotelmaristel.com. One of the best things about this large four-star hotel is the expansive sea views. Straddling the main road at the west end of the village, its two substantial modern blocks house fifty or so large and well-appointed rooms, many of which have sea-facing balconies. There's also an attractive pool. **€80**

★ **Hotel Nord** Plaça d'es Triquet 4 ☎ 971 14 90 06, ⓦ hotelruralnord.com. The charming *Hotel Nord*, below the main street in the middle of Estellencs, is a family-run place, in a cleverly reworked and modernized old stone house and olive press. There are eight guest rooms, two with

a private terrace and one with a balcony, each decorated in ochres and whites but featuring the original architecture – especially the wooden beamed ceilings. They serve evening meals here too and there's a lovely, courtyard patio for drinks. It's hard to find, though: keep your eyes peeled for the sign on the west side of the village (it's approached via the road to the beach). Closed Nov–Jan. **€100**

Sa Plana Hotel c/Eusebi Pascual s/n ☎ 971 61 86 66, ⓦ sa plana.com. The delightful *Sa Plana Hotel* is a rustic, family-run *finca* just above the main road at the west end of the village. It comprises five guest rooms, each with a distinctly period appearance, and there's an outside pool. **€100**

EATING AND DRINKING

★ **Montimar** Plaça Constitució 7 ☎ 971 61 85 76. The pick of the village's several restaurants, up a flight of steps from the main street near the church. The menu here bristles with Mallorcan favourites like suckling pig, snails

and rabbit and every effort is made to source things locally. The building is attractively ancient, too, and there's a pleasant outside terrace; mains average €15. Tues–Sun noon–3.30pm & 7–10pm.

SHOPPING

Vall–Hermós c/Eusebi Pascual s/n ☎ 971 61 86 10, ⓦ vallhermos.com. Attached to a café that bears the same name, this tiny little shop offers a good range of Mallorcan

wines and other assorted products. Daily except Wed 10am–11pm.

Andratx

Just 23km from Palma and 24km southwest of Estellencs, **ANDRATX** is a busy if rather modest little place with a popular **Wednesday morning market**. The old houses and narrow streets of the upper town form a harmonious ensemble that culminates in the fortress-like walls of the thirteenth-century church of **Santa Maria**, built high and strong to deter raiding pirates: its balustraded precincts offer panoramic views down to the coast.

CCA Andratx Art Centre

c/Estanyera, 1km east of Andratx on the Ma-1031 to Capdellà • Tues–Fri 10.30am–7pm, Sat & Sun 10.30am–4pm • €6 • ☎ 971 13 77 70, ⓦ ccandratx.com

Mallorca's largest centre of contemporary art, the **CCA Andratx** occupies a whopping modern structure built in the style of a *hacienda* complete with an expansive, internal courtyard. The gallery runs an enterprising artists-in-residence programme – the complex incorporates a set of apartments – but the key note is its temporary exhibitions of contemporary art (three or four a year), featuring an international crew of artists. The gallery's literature claims that the exhibitions are "challenging" – and indeed they are.

ARRIVAL AND DEPARTURE	ANDRATX

By bus Buses loop through Andratx with one of the more central stops being roughly halfway along Avgda Joan Carles I (the Ma-10).

Destinations Palma (1–2 hourly; 1hr); Peguera (1–2 hourly; 15min); Port d'Andratx (1–2 hourly; 10min); Sant Elm (7 daily; 40min).

Sant Elm

Three kilometres west of Andratx, the hillside hamlet of **S'Arracó** is the prelude to a pretty, orchard-covered landscape that buckles up into wooded hills and dipping valleys as it approaches the seashore, another 5km or so away. At the end of the road is the low-key resort of **SANT ELM**, whose main street strings along the shoreline with a pretty, sandy cove **beach** at one end and a **harbour** at the other – and, mercifully, no tower blocks in between.

2

Parc Natural de Sa Dragonera

April–Sept daily 10am–5pm; Oct–March daily 10am–3pm • Free • Cmcenos Margarita boats from Sant Elm (Feb & March Mon–Sat 7 daily to the island, 4 daily return) cost €11 return and take 15min (☎ 639 61 75 45, ⓦ crucerosmargarita.com)

From Sant Elm's tiny harbour, boats shuttle across to the austere offshore islet that comprises the **Parc Natural de Sa Dragonera**. This uninhabited hunk of rock, some 4km long and 700m wide, lies at an oblique angle to the coast, with an imposing ridge of sea cliffs dominating its northwestern shore. Behind the ridge, a rough road/path runs the length of the island, linking a pair of craggy capes and their lighthouses. The boat docks at a tiny cove-harbour – **Cala Lladó** – about halfway up the east shore, which puts both ends of the island within comfortable walking distance, though the excursion north to **Cap de Tramuntana** is both shorter and prettier – allow about an hour each way. There's also a much more challenging, three- to four-hour trail that clambers up to the **Puig de na Pòpia** (352m) lighthouse on the northwest coast. Most people visit Sa Dragonera for the scenic solitude, but the island is also good for **birdlife** – ospreys, shags, gulls and other seabirds are plentiful, and you may also see several species of raptor. To confirm **sailing times**, call ahead or ask at the tourist office (see below), and be sure to check the times of your return boat on the outward journey.

ARRIVAL AND INFORMATION	SANT ELM

By bus Buses thread their way through the resort, but the main bus stop is at the south end of the main street, metres from the beach.

Destinations Andratx (7 daily; 40min); Port d'Andratx (7 daily; 30min).

By car The large, partly shaded dirt car park at the south end of the main street – and across from the beach – usually has spaces, but things can get tight after 10am on summer weekends; a flat-rate ticket costs €3.50.

By ferry Cruceros Margarita (☎639 61 75 45, ⓦ crucerosmargarita.com) runs a ferry service between Sant Elm and Port d'Andratx (Feb & March Mon–Sat 1 daily; April–Oct 1 daily; 30min; €8 each way).

Tourist information Sant Elm tourist office, Avgda Jaume I, 28 (May–Sept Mon–Thurs 9am–4pm, Fri 9am–3pm, Sat 9am–2pm, Sun 9am–4pm; ☎ 971 23 92 05), is on the main street, roughly halfway between the beach and the harbour. They have information on local hikes and rudimentary hiking maps, issue bus timetables, and have the sailing times of the boat to Sa Dragonera (see above).

THE HIKE TO LA TRAPA

The rugged coastal district just to the north of Sant Elm is devoid of development and boasts several enjoyable **hikes**. The most popular is the hour-long (5km) hike along the GR221 (see p.90) to **La Trapa**, a small monastery built by Trappist monks, who arrived here in 1810 having escaped from Revolutionary France. Part of the hiking route from Sant Elm is along a steep and narrow path that offers superlative views over the coast, though the final ascent involves some rock scrambling. The hike begins from the north side of Sant Elm: follow the shoreline until you reach Plaça Mossen Sebastia Grau (where buses terminate). From this square, take Avgda La Trapa and keep going.

2

ACCOMMODATION

One of the pleasures of Sant Elm is its relative lack of development: there are, it's true, a fair number of second homes and holiday apartments, but it is all pretty inconspicuous and there are only two hotels. One of them is package-tour territory, the other – a *hostal* – is your best bet for an on-spec room. A hikers' hostel is also planned for La Trapa (see p.27).

Hotel Aquamarín c/Cala Es Conills s/n ☎ 971 23 91 05, ⓦ universaltravel.ch. Overlooking the beach at the south end of the resort, this package-tour favourite occupies a distinctive concrete structure built in the style of an old watchtower. Rooms tend to be block-booked, but it's worth a try. Closed Nov–April. **€110**

Hostal Dragonera c/Jaume I, 5 ☎ 971 23 90 86, ⓦ hostaldragonera.net. A well-kept, modern *hostal* in a prime location halfway along the main drag and with views over the sea. The rooms are clean and neat with the pick having sea-facing balconies. Top-notch breakfasts too. At peak times, the minimum stay is one week. Excellent value. Closed Nov–Feb. **€80**

EATING

Sant Elm's main street is awash with cafés and restaurants, but the best two places are right by the harbour. Both specialize in seafood, some of which is caught locally. For a snack, *Gelati Telmo*, also on the main street, sells tasty, locally made ice cream.

Restaurante de Na Caragola c/Jaume I, 23 ☎ 971 23 90 06, ⓦ restaurantenacaragola.com. Right by the harbour, this long-established restaurant is also the resort's prettiest, its long, sea-facing terrace festooned with greenery. Seafood is its forte, simply served with a minimum of fuss. Mains cost around €17. Daily except Wed 1–4pm & 7–11pm.

Restaurante Vista Mar c/Jaume I, 46 ☎ 971 23 75 47. Straightforward, modern restaurant right by the harbour and with a pleasant sea-view terrace. Offers a wide range of fresh fish – the sardines and the fish soup are especially tasty. Main courses from around €17. Daily except Tues 1–4pm & 7–11pm.

Port d'Andratx

In recent years, a splash of low-rise shopping complexes and Spanish-style villas has sprung up in the picturesque port and fishing harbour of **PORT D'ANDRATX**, 6km southwest of Andratx. Nevertheless, the heart of the **old town**, which slopes up from the south side of the bay, preserves a cramped network of ancient lanes, and there's no denying the prettiness of the setting, with the port standing at the head of a long and slender inlet flanked by wooded hills. Sunsets show the place to best advantage, casting long shadows up the bay, and it's then that the old town's gaggle of restaurants crowd with well-heeled, nautical holidaymakers and ex-pats. Port d'Andratx lacks a sandy **beach**, however – the nearest is east over the hills at Camp de Mar (see p.83).

ARRIVAL AND DEPARTURE   PORT D'ANDRATX

By bus Port d'Andratx is easy to reach by bus, with the main bus stop at the back of the bay at the northerly end of the old town, a brief stroll from the marina.
Destinations Andratx (every 30min to hourly; 10min); Camp de Mar (every 30min to hourly; 20min); Palma (every 30min to hourly; 1hr 10min); Sant Elm (7 daily; 30min).
By ferry Cruceros Margarita (☎ 639 61 75 45,

ⓦ crucerosmargarita.com) runs a ferry between Port d'Andratx and Sant Elm (Feb & March Mon–Sat 1 daily; April–Oct 1 daily; 30min; €8 each way).
By taxi There's a taxi rank at the back of the bay at the northerly end of the old town. Alternatively, call Radio Taxi Andratx (☎ 971 13 63 98); the fare to Camp de Mar is about €6, €10 to Sant Elm.

ACCOMMODATION

Hotel Brismar Avgda Almirante Riera Alemany 6 ☎ 971 67 16 00, ⓦ hotelbrismar.com. A modern block of modest proportions in a prime harbourside location, this long-established three-star hotel has recently been upgraded. It has 48 spotless if somewhat frugal en-suite rooms, the pick of which have port-facing balconies

(though avoid these if you're a light sleeper – there are a couple of bars nearby). Closed Dec–Feb. **€95**
★ **Hostal Catalina Vera** c/Isaac Peral 63 ☎ 971 67 19 18, ⓦ hostalcatalinavera.es. This delightful *hostal* is the best place to stay in Port d'Andratx. There are 15 guest rooms here, a couple in a building at the back, but the

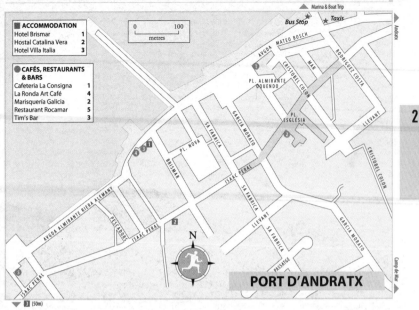

PORT D'ANDRATX

majority in a neatly shuttered and whitewashed, 1950s two-storey house in a quiet but central location. Each room is smartly turned out in traditional Spanish style with its own balcony: those at the front have a sea view. A small orchard and a lovely garden surround the *hostal* – there is even a selection of cactuses on the rear stairway – and the foyer is packed with house plants. **€75**

Hotel Villa Italia Cami Sant Carles 13 ☎ 971 67 40 11, ⓦ hotelvillaitalia.com. Set behind a steeply terraced garden just beyond the west end of the old town, this opulent hotel occupies a handsome – and immaculately modernized – 1950s twin-towered Italianate mansion. Features include an outdoor pool, a spa and gorgeous views over the bay. There are rooms and suites both in the old villa and in the more modern annexe. Substantial off-season discounts. **€280**

EATING AND DRINKING

The old town is packed with cafés and restaurants, most of which are along the harbourfront and the more central portions of c/Isaac Peral. Standards are generally high with seafood a local feature – it's good almost everywhere and occasionally superb. There are several bars too, lively little spots that hum till the early hours throughout the summer.

Cafeteria La Consigna Avgda Mateo Bosch 19 ☎ 971 67 16 04. Down by the harbourside, this popular coffee house-cum-patisserie is a straightforward modern affair whose cakes and breads are made nearby at Andratx. Daily 9am–9pm.

La Ronda Art Café c/Almirante Riera Alemany 8 ☎ 971 69 87 19, ⓦ laronda-artcafe.com. The flashiest bar in town, with a wide range of sounds – from house through to jazz – and imaginative decor, including bizarre-baroque art installations in the courtyard. Daily noon–1am.

Marisquería Galicia c/Isaac Peral 37 ☎ 971 67 27 05, ⓦ marisqueriagalicia.es. Bistro-style Galician place, where the seafood is the main event – vegetables are second-class citizens. Here you can sample everything from

hake to octopus, barnacles to monkfish at prices that are significantly less than those down on the harbour. Mains average €22. Daily noon–11pm.

Restaurant Rocamar c/Almirante Riera Alemany 27 ☎ 971 67 12 61, ⓦ restaurant-rocamar.com. Well-established restaurant at the west end of the harbourfront, away from the crowds. The interior is nothing special, but the ocean-facing terrace is a lovely spot and they serve a good range of seafood. Main courses around €20. Closed mid-Nov to early March. Daily noon–11pm.

Tim's Bar c/Almirante Riera Alemany 7 ☎ 971 67 18 92. Cosy, even intimate, little bar down on the harbourfront that attracts a well-heeled, nautical crew. The cocktails go down a storm and there are occasional DJ nights too. Daily noon–11pm.

Northern Mallorca

127 The northern coast

127 Gorg Blau

128 Cala Tuent

128 Sa Calobra

129 Escorca and the Torrent de Pareis

129 Monestir de Nostra Senyora de Lluc

132 Selva and around

132 Pollença

137 Cala Sant Vicenç

138 Port de Pollença

142 Península de Formentor

144 Badía d'Alcúdia

144 Alcúdia

147 The Alcúdia peninsula

149 Port d'Alcúdia

152 Parc Natural de S'Albufera

152 Muro

CAP DE FORMENTOR FROM POLLENÇA

Northern Mallorca

The magnificent Serra de Tramuntana mountains reach a precipitous climax in the rearing peaks of northern Mallorca. This is the wildest part of the island, long the haunt of brigands and monks – the monastery at Lluc is one of the island's undoubted highlights – and even today the ruggedness of the terrain forces the main coastal road, the Ma-10, to duck and weave inland, offering only the occasional glimpse of the sea. The mountains fade away as they near Pollença, one of Mallorca's prettiest towns and within easy striking distance of the region's two prime resorts, Port de Pollença and Port d'Alcúdia, as well as the island's top-ranking birdwatching site, the Parc Natural de S'Albufera.

3

Heading northeast from Sóller, the **Ma-10** soon snakes its way up into the mountains, threading round the stern flanks of Puig Major before passing the extraordinary side road that wiggles and wriggles down to both overcrowded **Sa Calobra** and the attractive beach at **Cala Tuent**. Nonetheless, it's the lovely monastery of **Lluc** that remains the big draw hereabouts, for religious islanders – who venerate an effigy of the Virgin known as La Moreneta – and tourists alike. Pushing on along the coast, the Ma-10 emerges from the mountains to reach **Pollença**, a tangle of stone houses clustered around a fine, cypress-lined Way of the Cross. Pollença is one of Mallorca's most appealing towns and it's also within easy reach of both the solitary coastal resort of **Cala Sant Vicenç** and the wild and rocky **Península de Formentor**, the bony, northernmost spur of the Serra de Tramuntana. This peninsula shelters the northern shore of the **Badía de Pollença**, which is home to the laid-back and low-key resort of **Port de Pollença**, whilst the next bay down holds the more upbeat **Port d'Alcúdia**. Here also the old walled town of **Alcúdia** has a clutch of modest historical sights, but the star turn is the **Parc Natural de S'Albufera**, which takes the prize as the best birdwatching wetland in the Balearics. The long, golden strands that stretch round the bays of Pollença and Alcúdia are Northern Mallorca's finest **beaches**: elsewhere – for example at Cala Tuent – the beaches are rougher and stonier, but you do escape the crowds.

GETTING AROUND

By bus and taxi Bus services around northern Mallorca are generally excellent, though one of the most popular tourist routes – along the north coast from Port de Sóller and Sóller to Pollença and Port de Pollença via Lluc – is seasonal and fairly infrequent (May–Oct Mon–Sat 2 daily), so some advance planning is necessary. All the area's tourist offices carry bus timetables; you could also check the island's official public transport website, ⓦ tib .org. Where the bus won't take you, a taxi will, and rates, especially if you're travelling in a group, are very reasonable.

By car If you have your own vehicle, be aware that parking in all the populous towns can be a pain in summer between 10 or 11am and 5pm.

ACCOMMODATION

The resorts of northern Mallorca are predominantly package territory, and from June to early September, independent travellers are advised to make **advance reservations**. In the shoulder season and in winter things are easier and

Top 5 places to stay p.1247
Majolica p.130
Mallorcan walking tours p.138
A valley hike from Port de Pollença to Cala Bóquer p.141

A circular hike on the Alcúdia peninsula p.148
Northern Mallorca's Top 5 beaches p.150

BEACH, PORT DE POLLENÇA

Highlights

❶ **Monestir de Nostra Senyora de Lluc**
Home to the Balearics' most venerated icon, La Moreneta, this intriguing monastery also makes a smashing base for mountain hikes. **See p.129**

❷ **Ermita de Nostra Senyora del Puig** A rambling assortment of old stone buildings, this is one of the most appealing of Mallorca's several hilltop monasteries. **See p.135**

❸ **The Davallament** Held in the beguiling little town of Pollença, the torchlit Lowering of the Cross – the Davallament – is the most evocative

of the many events celebrating Easter Holy Week. **See p.135**

❹ **Port de Pollença beach** A long arc of sand and safe shallows make this one of Mallorca's best beaches. **See p.138**

❺ **Península de Formentor** This tapered promontory of bleak sea cliffs and pine-clad hills offers gorgeous views and is a fruitful area for birdwatching. **See p.142**

❻ **Parc Natural de S'Albufera** A pocket of wetland offering the best birdwatching on the island, especially in spring. **See p.152**

HIGHLIGHTS ARE MARKED ON THE MAP ON P.126

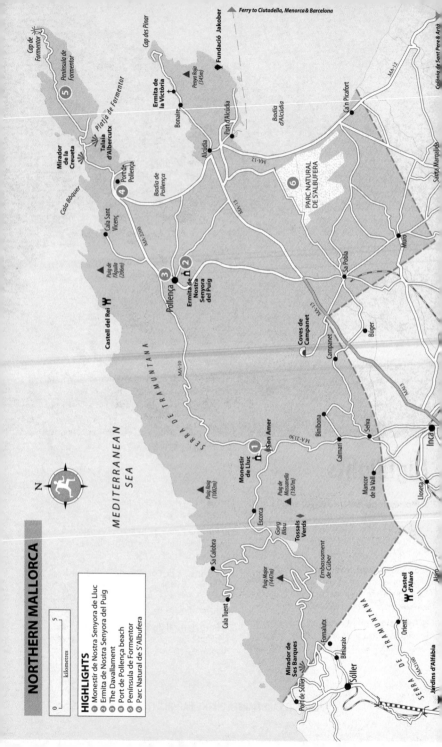

NORTHERN MALLORCA

HIGHLIGHTS

1. Monestir de Nostra Senyora de Lluc
2. Ermita de Nostra Senyora del Puig
3. The Davallament
4. Port de Pollença beach
5. Península de Formentor
6. Parc Natural de S'Albufera

0   5
kilometres

N

MEDITERRANEAN
SEA

Ferry to Ciutadella, Menorca & Barcelona

Cap de Formentor
Península de Formentor
5
Platja de Formentor
Mirador de la Creueta
Talaia d'Albercutx
Cap des Pinar
Fundació Jakober
Ermita de la Victòria
Penya Roja (345m)
Bonaire
Port d'Alcúdia
Can Picafort
Cala Bóquer
Port de Pollença
4
Badia de Pollença
Alcúdia
Badia d'Alcúdia
MA-12
Colònia de Sant Pere & Artà
Cala Sant Vicenç
Puig de l'Àguila (206m)
MA-2200
3
2
Pollença
Ermita de Nostra Senyora del Puig
Castell del Rei
Coves de Campanet
PARC NATURAL DE S'ALBUFERA
6
Muro
Sa Pobla
Santa Margalida
Búger
Campanet
MA-13
S E R R A   D E   T R A M U N T A N A
MA-10
Binibona
Selva
Sa Calobra
Puig Roig (1002m)
Escorca
Gorg Blau
Puig de Massanella (1367m)
Tossals Verds
San Amer
1
Monestir de Lluc
MA-2130
Caimari
Mancor de la Vall
Inca
Lloseta
Embassament de Cúber
Cala Tuent
Puig Major (1447m)
Embassament de Cúber
MA-13
MA-11
Mirador de Ses Barques
Fornalutx
Biniaraix
Castell d'Alaró
Orient
Alaró
Port de Sóller
Sóller
S E R R A   D E   T R A M U N T A N A
MA-2100
Jardins d'Alfàbia

cheaper, though many places do close down. More promisingly, the number of **inland hostales and hotels** is increasing – Pollença and Alcúdia both have places to stay – and there's not the seasonal crush here that there is on the coast. Alternatively, you could stay at one of the region's two **monasteries** – at Lluc (see p.131) and just outside Pollença (see p.136): the rooms are frugal but inexpensive, and there's usually space at any time of year. In addition, the region boasts three **hikers' hostels** (*refugi*; ⓦ www.conselldemallorca.net), all on the long-distance hiking route, the GR221 (see p.90): *Tossals Verds* (see p.128) in the mountains east of the Embassament de Cúber; *Son Amer*, near Lluc (see p.131); and *Pont Romà* in Pollença, though this is currently closed and it is not certain if it will open again.

HIKING

This part of the Serra de Tramuntana offers superb hiking. Suggestions for several comparatively easy and/or short walks are given in the text, and we have also described in detail a half-day hike beginning in Port de Pollença (see p.141) and a longer, tougher hike near Alcúdia (see p.148). The region is also traversed by Mallorca's main **long-distance hiking trail**, the **Ruta de Pedra en Sec** (Dry-stone route; officially known as the **GR221**), which runs in from Sóller and worms its way through the mountains bound for Pollença (see p.90).

The northern coast

3

Beyond Sóller, the **Ma-10** forges through the highest and harshest section of the Serra de Tramuntana. For the most part, the mountains drop straight into the sea – precipitous and largely unapproachable cliffs with barely a cove in sight. The accessible exceptions are the comely beach at **Cala Tuent** and the overly commercialized hamlet of **Sa Calobra** next door. The best place to break your journey, however, is inland at the monastery and pilgrimage centre of **Lluc**, which offers a diverting museum, excellent mountain hiking trails and a reliable supply of inexpensive rooms.

There's more low-priced monastery accommodation at the hilltop **Monestir de Nostra Senyora del Puig**, just outside **Pollença**, a beguiling old town of honey-coloured stone mansions sitting at the foot of a beautiful "calvary" walkway. Nearby, just down at the coast, is **Port de Pollença**, a medium-sized, agreeable resort with a long sandy beach draped around the Badía de Pollença. The port is a popular summertime retreat for the inhabitants of Palma and abounds in places to stay; it's also within easy striking distance of the dramatic sea cliffs of the **Formentor Peninsula** at the northernmost tip of the island.

GETTING AROUND   THE NORTHERN COAST

By bus There are excellent bus services to and between the towns and resorts stretching along the coast between Port de Pollença/Pollença and Ca'n Picafort. There are also daily buses from Palma to Lluc. However, the coastal bus linking Port de Sóller and Sóller with Lluc, Pollença and Port de Pollença only operates twice daily (May–Oct Mon–Sat). What's more, the buses get busy, and you will have a better chance of a seat if you get on at Port de Sóller rather than the second stop, Sóller.

Gorg Blau

Northeast of Sóller, the Ma-10 zigzags up into the mountains. After about 5km, the road passes the steep turning down to Fornalutx (see p.98) before offering a last lingering look over the coast from the **Mirador de Ses Barques** vantage point. Thereafter, the road snakes inland and tunnels through the western flanks of **Puig Major** (1447m), the island's highest mountain. Beyond the tunnel is the **Gorg Blau** (Blue Gorge), a bare and bleak ravine that was a well-known beauty spot until a hydroelectric scheme scarred the gorge and its immediate surroundings with a trio of puddle-like reservoirs. The second of the

> **TOP 5 PLACES TO STAY**
> **Monestir de Lluc** See p.131
> **Es Castell** See p.132
> **Posada de Lluc** See p.136
> **Hotel Llenaire** See p.140
> **Petit Hotel Hostatgeria la Victòria**
> See p.147

three – 3km beyond the tunnel – is the **Embassament de Cúber** (Cúber reservoir), an unappetizing expanse of water redeemed by its abundant birdlife, notably several different types of raptor. For a better look, stop at the lay-by to follow the easy footpath that circumnavigates the reservoir – it only takes a couple of hours to complete. The reservoir is also an obvious starting point for the four-hour hike west to the Barranc de Biniaraix along (part of) the **GR221** long-distance footpath; alternatively, it's a two-hour hike southeast to the *Refugi Tossals Verds* **hikers' hostel** (see below) in a remote spot high in the mountains. The *refugi* is also on the GR221, but getting there involves a detour from the main route between Biniaraix and Lluc.

To the immediate north of the reservoir rear the bare and craggy flanks of **Puig Major**, but the dramatic trail that twists up to the summit from the military base beside the main road remains off limits on account of its radar station. This makes **Puig de Massanella** (1367m), which looms over the Gorg Blau to the east, the highest mountain that can be climbed on Mallorca.

3

ACCOMMODATION	GORG BLAU

Refugi Tossals Verds ☎971 18 20 27, reservations ☎971 17 37 00, ⓦconselldemallorca.net. Up in the mountains, a 2hr hike southeast of the Embassament de Cúber reservoir, this hikers' hostel is one of several owned and operated by the state. There are thirty bunk beds here at €11 per person per night, with breakfast costing a further €4.50, and one double room; reservations must be made at least five days beforehand. **Dorm €11, double €22**

Cala Tuent

At the far end of the Gorg Blau, the Ma-10 bores into the mountains to emerge just short of a left turn leading down to Sa Calobra (see below) and Cala Tuent (unsigned). This turn-off – the **Ma-2141** – makes for an exhilarating, ear-popping detour to the seashore, the well-surfaced road hairpinning its way down the mountain slopes so severely that at one point it actually turns 270 degrees to run under itself.

About 10km down this road, there's a fork: head left over the hills for the 5km journey to **CALA TUENT**, where a smattering of villas cling to the northern slopes of Puig Major as it tumbles down towards the seashore. Ancient orchards temper the harshness of the mountain, and the gravel-and-sand beach is one of the quietest on the north coast. It's a lovely spot and – provided you stay close to the shore – the swimming is safe, though there's no public transport here, nor is there anywhere to stay. Parking is tricky too, especially at weekends.

EATING AND DRINKING	CALA TUENT

★ **Es Vergeret** Cala Tuent ☎971 51 71 05, ⓦesvergeret.com. On the far side of the cove, this excellent restaurant has a gorgeous location, its long, shaded terrace nudging out into the sea. It serves up a tasty range of fish and meat dishes from €14 – all accompanied by the sound of the roll of the ocean. Mid-Feb to Oct daily 12.30–4.30pm, plus July & Aug Sat 8.30–10.30pm.

Sa Calobra

The Ma-2141 continues beyond the Cala Tuent turning, wriggling its way down to the seashore at **SA CALOBRA**, where a scattering of houses occupy a pint-sized cove in the shadow of the mountains. The setting is gorgeous, but tour operators deposit busloads of tourists here every day in summer and the crush can be unbearable. The reason so many people come is to visit the impressive box canyon at the mouth of the **Torrent de Pareis** (River of the Twins). It takes about ten minutes to follow the partly tunnelled walkway round the coast from the village to the mouth of the canyon. Here, with sheer cliffs rising on every side, the milky-green river trickles down to the thick bank of sandy shingle that bars its final approach to the sea – though the scene is transformed after heavy rainfall, when the river crashes down into the canyon and out into the ocean.

ARRIVAL AND DEPARTURE

SA CALOBRA

By bus Buses stop in the large car park just up the road from the village.

Destinations Alcúdia (May–Oct Mon–Sat 1 daily; 3hr); Cala Sant Vicenç (May–Oct Mon–Sat 1 daily; 2hr 40min);

Lluc (May–Oct Mon–Sat 1 daily; 1hr); Pollença (May–Oct Mon–Sat 1 daily; 2hr 30min); Port d'Alcúdia (May–Oct Mon–Sat 1 daily; 3hr 20min); Port de Pollença (May–Oct Mon–Sat 1 daily; 2hr 50min).

Escorca and the Torrent de Pareis

About 4km northeast of the Cala Tuent/Sa Calobra turning, the Ma-10 passes through **ESCORCA**, a poorly defined scattering of houses that marks the starting point for the descent of the **Torrent de Pareis**, a formidable, 7km-long limestone gorge and river which drops from here to Sa Calobra (see opposite). It's a well-known, very testing and potentially dangerous hike-cum-climb which requires some basic rock-climbing skills, and takes about five hours to negotiate. The descent is not practicable in winter, spring, or after rainfall, when the river may be waist-high and the rocks dangerously slippery. The descent starts at the **sign** on the main road opposite the conspicuous *Restaurant Escorca*. The gorge is almost always hotter than its surroundings, so take lots of water.

Monestir de Nostra Senyora de Lluc

Just off the Ma-10, about 10km east of Escorca • Daily: April–Sept 10am–11pm; Oct–March 10am–8pm • Free

Tucked away in a remote valley, the austere, high-sided dormitories and orange-flecked roof tiles of the **Monestir de Nostra Senyora de Lluc** (Monastery of Our Lady of Lluc) stand out against the greens and greys of the surrounding mountains. It's a magnificent setting for what has been Mallorca's most important place of pilgrimage since the middle of the thirteenth century, though its religious significance goes back much further: the valley's prehistoric animistic inhabitants deified the local holm-oak woods, and the **Romans** picked up on the theme, naming the place from *lucus*, the Latin for "sacred forest". Thereafter, the **monks** who settled here after the Reconquista invented the story of a shepherd boy named Lluc (Luke) stumbling across a tiny, brightly painted **statue** of the Virgin in the woods. Frightened by his discovery, the lad collared the nearest monk and when the pair returned, heavenly music filled played, bright lights dazzled them, and celestial voices declared the statue to be an authentic heaven-sent image.

The monastery church

The **monastic complex** is an imposing and formal-looking affair mostly dating from the eighteenth and early nineteenth centuries. At its centre is the main shrine and architectural highlight, the **Basílica de la Mare de Déu de Lluc**, which is graced by an elegant Baroque facade. To reach it, pass through the monastery's stately double-doored entrance and keep straight on till you reach the second – and final – courtyard, where there's a dreary statue of Bishop Campins, who overhauled Lluc in the early part of the last century and is shown kneeling and facing the entrance to the church. Dark and gaudily decorated, the interior of the church is dominated by heavy jasper columns, the stolidness of which is partly relieved by a dome over the crossing. On either side of the nave, stone steps extend the aisles round the back of the Baroque high altar to a small chapel. This is the holy of holies, built to display the statue of the Virgin, which has been commonly known as **La Moreneta** ("the Little Dark-Skinned One") ever since the original paintwork peeled off in the fifteenth century to reveal brown stone underneath. Just 61cm high, the Virgin looks innocuous, her face tweaked by a hint of a smile and haloed by a much more modern jewel-encrusted gold crown. In her left arm she cradles a baby Jesus, who holds the "Book of Life" open to reveal the letters alpha and omega.

The **Escolania de Lluc choir** performs in the basilica during the daily 11am Mass and again at evensong (Mon–Fri at 4.30pm). Founded in the early sixteenth century with the stipulation that it must be "composed of natives of Mallorca, of pure blood, sound in grammar and song", the choir is nicknamed *Els Blauets*, "The Blues", for the colour of their cassocks. At the start of proceedings, a sliding door whizzes opens to reveal La Moreneta to the assembled congregation in the main body of the church.

The monastery museum

Daily 10am–1.30pm & 2.30–5pm • €4

Just inside and to the right of the basilica's main entrance a small door leads through to a corridor that runs past the stairway up to the enjoyable **Museu de Lluc**. Immediately beyond the museum ticket desk, the exhibits begin with a section devoted to archeological finds from the Talayotic and Roman periods and then it's on into the **Sala del Tresor** (Treasure Room), packed with all manner of folkloric items brought here to honour La Moreneta, from painted fans, medallions, rosaries and crosses through to walking sticks discarded when the supplicants found they were no longer lame. A further room displays examples of traditional island costume and then there's a section devoted to religious carvings, followed by a substantial collection of **majolica** (see box below), glazed earthenware mostly shaped into two-handled drug jars and show dishes or plates. Some two or three hundred majolica pieces are on display, the pick coming from the eighteenth century, when the designs varied from broad and bold dashes of colour to carefully painted naturalistic designs. The colours, however, remained fairly constant, restricted by the available technology to iron red, copper green, cobalt blue, manganese purple and antimony yellow. There is also a good sample of Catalan and Valencian **lustreware**, brown earthenware with a sheen – or lustre – and manufactured between the sixteenth and the eighteenth centuries. The final rooms on this floor are, by comparison, rather tame, devoted to the uninspiring island land- and village-scapes of **José Coll Bardolet** (1912–92).

A flight of stairs beside the ticket office leads up to an excellent cross section of **Mallorcan art**, either by native artists or artists once resident here. Among them are the Goya-esque works of Salvador Mayol (1775–1834); the romantic landscapes of Bartomeu Sureda (1769–1851); the finely observed mountain landscapes of Antoni Ribas Oliver (1845–1911); and the Neo-Impressionist canvases of Llorenç Cerdà Bisbal (1862–1955). Oliver is arguably the most talented artist on display here. In particular, look out for his *Gorg Blau*, painted long before the gorge's rugged beauty disappeared under the waters of a reservoir (see p.128).

Camí dels Misteris del Rosari

A few metres to the west of the monastery's double-doored entrance • Open access • Free

A large and conspicuous rough-hewn column marks the start of the **Camí dels Misteris del Rosari** (Way of the Mysteries of the Rosary), a broad pilgrims' footpath

---

MAJOLICA

The fifteenth century witnessed a vigorous trade in decorative pottery sent from Spain to Italy via Mallorca. The Italians coined the term **"majolica"** to describe this imported Spanish pottery after the medieval name for the island through which it was traded, but thereafter the name came to be applied to all tin-glazed pottery. The process of making majolica began with the mixing and cleaning of clay, after which it was fired and retrieved at the "biscuit" (earthenware) stage. The biscuit was then cooled and dipped in a liquid glaze containing tin and water. The water in the glaze was absorbed, leaving a dry surface ready for decoration. After painting, the pottery was returned to the kiln for a final firing, which fused the glaze and fixed the painting. Additional glazings and firings added extra lustre. Initially, majolica was dominated by greens and purples, but technological advances in the fifteenth century added blue, yellow and ochre. Majolica of one sort or another was produced in bulk in Mallorca up until the early twentieth century.

that winds its way up the rocky hillside directly behind the monastery. Dating from 1913, the solemn granite stations marking the way are of two types: simple stone pediments and, more intriguingly, rough trilobate columns of Gaudí-like design, each surmounted by a chunky crown and cross. The prettiest part of the walk is round the back of the hill, where the path slips through cool, green woods with rock overhangs on one side and views out over the bowl-shaped **Albarca valley** on the other, with **Puig Roig** (1003m) rearing up beyond. It takes about ten minutes to reach the top of the hill, where a wrought-iron *Modernista* cross stands protected by ugly barbed wire. It's possible to stroll down into the Albarca valley on the country lane that begins to the left (west) of the monastery's main entrance, though the road fizzles out at a remote farmhouse long before you reach the coast, and the landowner only allows access on Sundays.

Jardí Botanic

Mon–Sat 10am–5pm • Free

On the east side of the monastery are the **Jardí Botanic** (Botanical Gardens) – they're signed through the conspicuous arches on the right as you face the main entrance. The gardens are laid out with local plants as well as exotics, plus small ponds and waterfalls, little footbridges and even a windmill. It takes about fifteen minutes to walk through the gardens on a well-defined path.

3

ARRIVAL   MONESTIR DE NOSTRA SENYORA DE LLUC

By bus Buses stop in the large car park right outside the monastery.

Destinations Alcúdia (May–Oct Mon–Sat 2 daily; 1hr 10min); Cala Sant Vicenç (May–Oct Mon–Sat 2 daily; 35min); Palma (2 daily; 1hr 10min); Pollença (May–Oct Mon–Sat 2 daily; 40min); Port d'Alcúdia (May–Oct

Mon–Sat 2 daily; 1hr 15min); Port de Pollença (May–Oct Mon–Sat 2 daily; 50min); Port de Sóller (May–Oct Mon–Sat 2 daily; 1hr 20min); Sa Calobra (May–Oct Mon–Sat 1 daily; 1hr); Sóller (May–Oct Mon–Sat 2 daily; 50min).
By car Parking costs €4.

INFORMATION

There's an information desk inside the monastery (daily 10am–8pm; ☎ 971 87 15 25) and a small Serra de Tramuntana information office, Ca L'Amitger, beside the main car park (daily 9am–4pm). The latter sells hiking leaflets and mini-guides.

ACCOMMODATION AND EATING

The obvious place to stay in Lluc is at the monastery, which also has the best restaurant. If you don't fancy a sit-down meal, however, you could try any of several cafés between the monastery and the car park: the nearest to the monastery serves fresh and tasty meat and pea pies – *empanadas* – to eat in or take out.

★ **Monestir de Lluc** ☎ 971 87 15 25, ⊕ lluc.net. Accommodation here is highly organized, with simple, self-contained, en-suite cells and slightly more comfortable apartments (for up to six people) which offer self-catering but do not provide any utensils. Book ahead in summer; at other times simply ask at the monastery's information office on arrival. There's usually an 11pm curfew, except for the apartments, which have their own separate entrance. Singles €34, doubles €48, six-person apartment €162

Refugi Son Amer Escorca ☎ 971 51 71 09, reservations ☎ 971 173 700, ⊕ www.conselldemallorca.net. The main alternative to the monastery is this *Refugi*, an all-year hikers' hostel in an attractively restored old farmhouse on a

hillside close to the Ma-10. It's a 10min walk from Lluc monastery on the GR221 long-distance hiking route (see p.90). The hostel has a dining room and several bunk-bed dormitories with shared facilities. Breakfast is available for €4.50, dinner for €8. There are no double rooms. Flat-rate per person €11

Sa Fonda Lluc ☎ 971 51 70 22. Lluc's gastronomic star turn is the monks' former refectory, *Sa Fonda*, a beautifully restored old hall complete with wooden beams, wide stone arches and marble pillars. The food is traditional Spanish, with main courses from around €14; the meat dishes are much better than the fish. March–Oct daily 1–4pm & 7–9pm; Nov–Feb Mon 1–4pm, Wed–Sun 1–4pm & 7–9pm.

Selva and around

South of Lluc, the **Ma-2130** drifts its way up and over the mountains in what is one of the island's most beautiful journeys. After about 12km, the road slips through **SELVA**, an amiable country town set amongst the foothills of the Serra de Tramuntana. The town's main square – Plaça Major – is especially pleasant and overlooked by a fortress-like church, whose frontispiece appears to have been glued to the Gothic nave as an afterthought. The oldest part of town nudges up to the church, its narrow lanes crowded by the old stone buildings where the local peasantry once rested after their long days in the surrounding olive groves.

From Selva, the Ma-2130 continues onto Inca (see p.160), but it's more enjoyable to head east along the narrow country lanes that traverse the foothills in one of the quietest parts of the island. The obvious target is the handful of remote chi-chi houses that make up **BINIBONA**.

ARRIVAL AND DEPARTURE   SELVA AND AROUND

By bus Buses travel through Selva sticking to – and stopping on – the Ma-2130.

Destinations Inca (2 daily; 10min); Lluc (2 daily; 25min); Palma (2 daily; 1hr).

ACCCOMMODATION AND EATING

★ **Es Castell** c/Binibona s/n ☎971 87 51 54, ⓦfincaescastell.com. Deep in the countryside, 1.2km from Binibona, this is one of Mallorca's finest *finca*-hotels comprising a tastefully restored stone *finca*, parts of which date from the fourteenth century. Entered via a delightful antique courtyard, it occupies a superb location with the mountains behind and the plains stretching out below, flanked by olive groves, carob, almond, orange and lemon trees. There's an outside pool and twelve smart and unfussy guest rooms, each featuring rustic stonework. The excellent restaurant uses homegrown ingredients – oranges, lemons, honey, figs and a superb olive oil. €160

Pollença

Founded in the thirteenth century, the pretty little town of **POLLENÇA** nestles among a trio of bulging hillocks where the Serra de Tramuntana mountains fade into coastal flatland. Following standard Mallorcan practice, the town was established a few kilometres from the seashore to militate against sudden pirate attack, with its harbour, Port de Pollença (see p.138), left as an unprotected outpost. For once the stratagem worked. Unlike most of Mallorca's old towns, Pollença successfully repelled a string of piratical onslaughts, the last and most threatening of which was in 1550, when the notorious Turkish corsair Dragut came within a hair's breadth of victory. In the festival of **Mare de Déu dels Àngels** on August 2, the townspeople celebrate their escape with enthusiastic street battles, the day's events named after the warning shouted by the hero of the resistance, a certain Joan Más: "Mare de Déu dels Àngels, assistiu-mos!" ("Our Lady of Angels, help us!").

Lined by lovely old houses, Pollença's maze of streets attract a well-heeled, mainly British crew in sufficient numbers to support several first-rate **restaurants** and **hotels**. The town is also within easy striking distance of both **Cala Sant Vicenç**, a brisk, modern resort on the island's northern shore, and, of course, **Port de Pollença**.

Plaça Major

Little of Pollença's medieval town has survived and the handsome stone houses that now cramp the twisting lanes of the centre mostly date from the seventeenth and eighteenth centuries. The heart of the town is **Plaça Major**, an especially amiable main square, which accommodates a cluster of laidback cafés and restaurants and is also the site of a lively fruit and veg market on most Sunday mornings. Overlooking the square is the severe facade of the church of **Nostra Senyora dels Àngels**, a sheer cliff-face of sun-bleached stone pierced by a rose window. Dating from the thirteenth century, but extensively remodelled in the Baroque style five centuries later, the church's gloomy

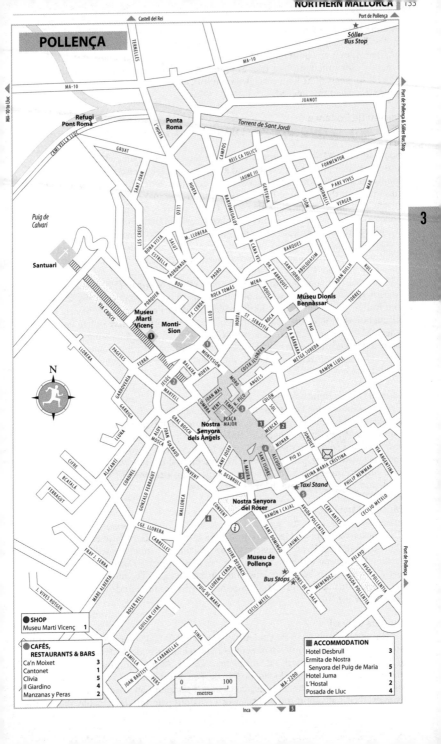

3

POLLENÇA

Castell del Rei

Port de Pollença

Sóller
Bus Stop

MA-10

MA-10 to Lluc

Port de Pollença & Sóller Bus Stop

MA-10

JUANOT

Refugi
Pont Romà

Ponta
Roma

Torrent de Sant Jordi

CAMI VELLA LLUC

GRUAT

TERNELLES

L'HORTA

CAMPOS

REIS CA TOLICS

FORMENTOR

SANT JOAN

JAUME III

GERTERIA

PARE VIVES

HORTA

BARTOMEU LLOY

BINIMELIS

VERGER

MAR

Puig de
Calvari

LES CREUS

BONA VISTA

D311

M. LLOBERA

B. CAMP VES

BARQUES

SLOM

SIOM

Santuari

ESTRELLA

SALJUT

PADRONADA

PADRO

MENA

DE I. ABREQUES

SANT JORDI

ABDULQASIM

ADAN DIELM

RULL

BOU

ROCA TOMAS

Museu Martí
Vicenç

VIA CRUCIS

PORQUER

P.S. CERDA

LLEO

HORTA

AGUILA

ROCA

ST. SEBASTIÀ

Museu Dionís
Bennàssar

TORRES

PAU

Monti-
Sion

PAGESES

FERRA

MONTESION

COSTA LLOBERA

ST A BARBARA

METGE SOREDA

RAMON LLULL

LLOBERA

GAMBOVERIA

JESUS

BALAIXA

HORTA

MORO

ANGELS

GARRIGA

MARTELL

JOAN MAS

OMBRA

VENT

TEMPLE

R. PICO

COLOM

SOL

N

LLUNA

ALACANTI

GRAL BOSCH

JOAN GUARAUD

ALOY

MOSCA

Nostra
Senyora
dels Àngels

PLAÇA
MAJOR

MERCAT

MUNAR

JUNQUET

VIA ARGENTINA

CIFRE

B.CATALA

CORONEL

GONZALO TERRAGUT

CONVENT

SANT JOSEP

M. DESBRULL

A. MAURA

SANT ISIDRE

ALCUDIA

PIO XI

REINA MARIA CRISTINA

PHILIP NEWMAN

CECILIO METELO

TERRAGUT

MALLORCA

Nostra Senyora
del Roser

RAMON I CAJAL

AVGDA POLLENTIA

CERVANTES

FRAY J. SERRA

CGE. LLOBERA

CABRELLES

CONVENT

i

SANT DOMINGO

JAUME I

PELAYO

J. VIVES ROYGER

MARE ALBERTA

ROSER VELL

GUILLEM CIFRE

BISBE DESBACH

Museu de
Pollença

Bus Stops

LLOREN CERDA

PUIG DE MARIA

DONES DE C. CALA

MENENDEZ

AVGDA POLLENTIA

AVGDA POLLENTIA

SINIA

A. CABANELLAS

JOAN BAUTIST

PERS

CAMILIA

CECILI METEL

MA-2200

Inca

5

Taxi Stand

Port de Pollença

SHOP
Museu Martí Vicenç   1

**CAFÉS,
RESTAURANTS & BARS**
Ca'n Moixet   3
Cantonet   1
Clivia   5
Il Giardino   4
Manzanas y Peras   2

ACCOMMODATION
Hotel Desbrull   3
Ermita de Nostra
   Senyora del Puig de Maria   5
Hotel Juma   1
L'Hostal   2
Posada de Lluc   4

0   100
metres

interior, with its mighty single-vaulted nave, has a mildly diverting sequence of ceiling and wall paintings, as well as a whopping, tiered and towered high altarpiece. The original church was built for the Knights Templar (see p.62) and passed to another knightly order, the Hospitallers of St John, after the pope suppressed them in 1312. The Hospitallers of St John struggled on until 1802, when the Spanish king appropriated all they owned.

Museu de Pollença

c/Guillem Cifre s/n • July–Sept Tues–Sat 10am–1pm & 5.30–8.30pm, Sun 10am–1pm; Oct–June Tues–Fri 10.30am–1pm • €2 • ☎ 971 53 11 66

South of Plaça Major, c/Antoni Maura leads into a leafy square, whose greenery surrounds an antique water wheel and a stumpy, much battered watchtower. Behind looms the austere facade of Nostra Senyora del Roser, a deconsecrated church which, together with the adjoining monastery complex, now makes up the **Museu de Pollença**. Inside, the former **monks' quarters** hold a surprisingly good and regularly rotated collection of contemporary paintings, photography and video art, including pieces by winners of the town's annual art competition. There's also a modest assortment of local archeological finds, though these are poorly labelled, and a room of **Mallorcan primitive paintings**, most memorably a warm, tender and exquisitely detailed *Virgin and Musical Angels* by Francesc Comes (1379–1415).

In the **cloisters**, look out for the memorial to **Philip Newman** (1904–66), the Manchester-born violinist who took a real shine to Pollença in the 1950s, founding and fostering its main musical festival, the **Festival de Pollença**, still held here every year throughout July and August (ⓦ festivalpollenca.org), with the likes of flamenco star Diego El Cigala and Catalan folk legend Joan Manuel Serrat appearing in recent years. Next to the cloisters is the **church**, whose truncated, barrel-vaulted nave is a gloomy affair with an enormous gilded altar; the church is sometimes used for temporary exhibitions.

Museu Dionís Bennàssar

c/Roça 14 • Tues–Sun 10.30am–1.30pm • €2 • ☎ 971 53 09 97, ⓦ museudionisbennassar.com

A short stroll northeast of Plaça Major, the **Museu Dionís Bennàssar** occupies the former home of Dionís Bennàssar (1904–67), who recovered from a wound he sustained as a soldier in the Spanish army in Morocco to become one of the island's most talented and respected artists. The museum holds a tidy collection of his Neo-impressionist paintings, brightly coloured canvases amongst which the Mallorcan land- and village-scapes are the most interesting.

Museu Marti Vicenç

c/Calvari 10 • Tues–Sat 10.30am–5.30pm, Sun 10.30am–2pm • Free • ☎ 971 532 867, ⓦ martivicens.org

The pocket-sized **Museu Marti Vicenç**, lodged inside an ancient beamed house near the foot of the Via Crucis, is given over to the striking textiles created by Marti Vicenç (1926–95). Vicenç was born into a family of local weavers, whose traditional patterns and motifs he extrapolated into abstract designs. The museum shares its premises with a fabric and textile **shop** that sells its products under the label Teixits Vicens (see p.136).

Puig de Calvari

Pollença's pride and joy is its **Via Crucis** (Way of the Cross), a long, steep and beautiful stone stairway, graced by ancient cypress trees, which ascends the **Puig de Calvari** (Calvary Hill) on the north side of the town centre. At the top, a much-revered thirteenth-century statue of **Mare de Déu del Peu de la Creu** (Mother of God at the Foot of the Cross) is lodged in a simple, courtyarded **santuari** (sanctuary), whose whitewashed walls sport some of the worst religious paintings imaginable, though the views out over coast and town are sumptuous. On Good Friday, a figure of Jesus is slowly carried by torchlight down from the *santuari* to the church of Nostra Senyora dels Àngels, a procession known as the **Davallament** (Lowering), one of the most moving religious celebrations on the island.

Pont Roma

Although it doesn't merit a huge detour, the **Pont Roma**, on the northern edge of town, is worth a peep. The old Roman bridge spans the Torrent de Sant Jordí, though in summer you'll be lucky to spot a stream, never mind a river. The finely worked stone bridge consists of two slightly different arches and although in itself it's not a remarkable structure, it has at least survived intact despite all the historical odds.

Ermita de Nostra Senyora del Puig

There are magnificent views over the Pollença area from the **Ermita de Nostra Senyora del Puig**, a rambling, mostly eighteenth-century monastery perched on top of the Puig de Maria, a 330m high hump facing the south end of town. The monastic complex, with its fortified walls, courtyard, chapel, refectory and cells, has had a chequered history, alternately abandoned and restored by both monks and nuns. The Benedictines now own the place, but the monks are gone and today a custodian supplements the order's income by renting out cells to tourists (see p.136). There's nothing specific to see, but the setting is extraordinarily serene and beautiful, with the mellow honey-coloured walls of the monastery surrounded by ancient carob and olive trees.

It takes around an hour to **walk** to the monastery from the centre of town: head for the main Pollença–Inca road (Ma-2200), where a signed turning leads up a steep lane that fizzles out after 1.5km to be replaced by a cobbled footpath winding up to the monastery's entrance. It's possible to drive to the top of the lane, but unless you've got nerves of steel, you're better off parking elsewhere. Note that there have been reports of cars left at the foot of the lane overnight being vandalized; although this is unusual, you might prefer to park in town instead.

ARRIVAL AND DEPARTURE
POLLENÇA

By car To avoid the baffling one-way streets of Pollença, enter the town from the south, turning off the main Palma road – the Ma-2200 - onto Avgda Pollentia (where there is almost always parking).

By bus Buses to Pollença from Palma, Inca, Port de Pollença and Cala Sant Vicenç pull in on the south side of the centre on c/Cecili Metel, a 5min walk from the main square, Plaça Major. Less conveniently, buses from Port de Sóller, Sóller and Lluc currently drop passengers on the north side of town, beside the Ma-10, a good 1km from Plaça Major.

Destinations Alcúdia (May–Oct 1–4 hourly; Nov–April hourly; 15min); Cala Sant Vicenç (5 daily; 25min); Lluc (May–Oct Mon–Sat 2 daily; 30min); Palma (Mon–Fri hourly, 7 on Sat & Sun; 45min); Port d'Alcúdia (May–Oct 1–4 hourly; Nov–April hourly; 20min); Port de Pollença (May–Oct 1–4 hourly; Nov–April hourly; 15min); Port de Sóller (May–Oct Mon–Sat 2 daily; 1hr 45min); Sóller (May–Oct Mon–Sat 2 daily; 1hr 35min).

By taxi Although the centre of Pollença is best explored on foot, its outlying attractions, such as the resort of Cala Sant Vicenç (see p.137), can be reached either by bus (see above) or taxi. There's a taxi rank in the centre at the corner of Avgda Pollentia and c/Reina Maria Cristina, or call ☎ 971 86 62 13.

INFORMATION

Information The town's tourist office is a 3min walk from Plaça Major, in the walls of the old convent on c/Guillem Cifre (Nov–April Mon–Fri 8am–3pm; May–Oct Mon–Fri 9am–1.30pm & 2–4pm, Sat & Sun 10am–1pm; ☎ 971 53 50 77, ⓦpollensa.com).

ACCOMMODATION

Pollença has a string of quality hotels right in the centre and several of them occupy creatively modernized old stone townhouses. There's also bargain accommodation at a hilltop **monastery** on the outskirts of town. The state-run *Refugi Pont Romà*, a hikers' **hostel** on the northern edge of Pollença on Camí Vell a Lluc, is currently closed but will probably re-open in 2013: check the website for the latest news (ⓦwww.conselldemallorca.net).

3

Hotel Desbrull c/Marquès Desbrull 7 ☎971 53 50 55, ⓦdesbrull.com. Small and smart, this family-owned hotel occupies an old stone villa in the centre of town. It has six double rooms, each kitted out in an attractive modern style but with the house's older features – like beamed ceilings – still on show. **€100**

Ermita de Nostra Senyora del Puig de Maria 2km south of town (see p.135) ☎971 18 41 32. At this hilltop monastery, the original monks' quarters have been renovated to provide simple rooms with shared facilities, sleeping between two and six guests. A single room costs €14, triples €29, quads €36 and five-bedded rooms €43. To be sure of a room, book ahead, but be warned that it can get cold and windy at night, even in the summer. There's a refectory on site, but the food is only average. **€22**

Hotel Juma Plaça Major 9 ☎971 53 50 02, ⓦpollensahotels.com. Right in the middle of town, overlooking the main square, this enjoyable small hotel occupies an old stone merchant's house that functions rather like a traditional *pension* with reception on the first floor, a café down below and the a/c rooms up above. The rooms are bright and cheerful and the best have balconies with views over the centre. **€120**

L'Hostal c/Mercat 18 ☎971 53 52 81, ⓦpollensahotels .com. In a lavishly updated old stone house, this appealing hotel has six en-suite rooms decorated in a bright and breezy modern style with flashes of the old – beamed ceilings and bare stone walls. The central courtyard is a good place to unwind, and you are just metres from the main square. **€130**

★ **Posada de Lluc** c/Roser Vell 11 ☎971 53 52 20, ⓦposadalluc.com. This small and very comfortable hotel occupies an attractively restored old stone house in the centre of town. The monks from Lluc monastery (see p.129) used to lodge here when they popped into Pollença to pick up supplies – hence the statue of the Madonna over the front door – and many of the original features have been kept, notably the deep stone arches and masonry walls. There's a small outside pool and each of the a/c guest rooms has been equipped in a traditional style but with modern comforts. **€130**

EATING AND DRINKING

Pollença does very well for restaurants, which are popular with the villa owners who congregate here each evening, strolling in from the surrounding countryside. The café and bar scene is less convincing, but there are several reasonably lively spots on and around Plaça Major. Almost all the town's cafés and bars serve food of some description, mostly tapas.

Ca'n Moixet Plaça Major 2 ☎971 53 42 14. Every other place on the main square may heave with the well-heeled and the well-tanned, but the renegades – or at least the semi-renegades – gather here at this old-fashioned, locals' favourite under the sign "Bar Espanyol". Drinks are the big deal, but they also serve filling and inexpensive snacks. Daily 10am–midnight.

Cantonet c/Monti-Sion 20 ☎971 53 04 29. This amenable restaurant just north of Plaça Major offers first-rate international/Italian cuisine from a short but well-chosen menu with main courses starting from as little as €14. The home-made pastas are particularly delicious – try the ravioli. In the summer, you can eat out on the terrace of the large church just up the street. Daily except Mon 1–3pm & 7–11pm.

★ **Clivia** Avgda Pollentia 5 ☎971 53 36 35. Very hospitable restaurant, and long-time ex-pat favourite, offering an excellent range of Spanish dishes – try the squid in ink. If you choose fish, the waiter brings the uncooked version to the table so you can inspect it before buying. The decor is traditional Spanish and attracts an older clientele. Mains average €25. Reservations advised. Daily except Wed 1–3pm & 7–10.30pm.

Il Giardino Plaça Major 11 ☎971 53 43 02, ⓦgiardinopollensa.com. One of the best restaurants in town, this smart bistro-style place offers a superb range of Italian dishes from about €14, and pastas from €10, all prepared with vim and gusto and featuring the best of local ingredients; the ravioli stuffed with wild mushrooms is particularly good. To be sure of a seat on the terrace – where you will probably want to eat – either come early or book ahead. Great house wines too. Mid-March to mid-Nov daily 12.30–3pm & 7–11pm.

★ **Manzanas y Peras** c/Martell 6, Plaça Seglars ☎971 53 22 92, ⓦmanzanasyperas.es. In an attractive location, on a little square beside the Via Crucis, this excellent and mildly boho café-restaurant has every reason to be proud of its fresh and tasty menu, featuring everything from salads (€8) and home-made burgers (€9) through to pork *filet* with prunes, mushrooms and a mustard sauce (€14). Sun 10am–4pm, Mon 11am–4pm, Tues–Fri 11am–4pm & 7–11pm.

SHOPPING

Museu Marti Vicenç c/Calvari 10 ☎971 532 867, ⓦteixitsvicens.com. Sharing its premises with the Museu Marti Vicenç (see p.134), this small textile shop features the island-made fabrics and textiles of Teixits Vicens. Their most distinctive offerings are in the traditional, striped fabric known as *robes de llengues*. Tues–Sat 10.30am–5.30pm, Sun 10.30am–2pm.

Cala Sant Vicenç

There's no denying that **CALA SANT VICENÇ**, a burgeoning, modern resort just 6km northeast of Pollença, boasts an attractive, solitary setting amongst a set of bare rocky outcrops that nudge gingerly out into the ocean. The only problem – if indeed there is one – is the resort itself: some visitors like the modern villas that spill over and around the wooded ravine at its heart, others think they are dreary, but most are agreed that the *Hotel Don Pedro*, plonked on the minuscule headland separating two of the resort's beaches, is crass in the extreme. If you are staying in Cala Sant Vicenç, it may be comforting to know that it's easy enough to escape all the development by **hiking north** out onto the wild and wind-licked seashore. The obvious targets are the remote *calas* that punctuate the coastline, but you could also undertake the moderately strenuous hoof up to the top of **Puig de l'Àguila** (206m), from where there are grand views. This 6km-long hike takes around three hours; the first part uses a rough dirt-and-gravel road, the second follows a well-defined path that leads to the base of Puig de l'Àguila – but you'll still need a proper hiking map to find your way. If that sounds too much like hard work, you could simply enjoy the resort's four sandy **beaches**: two on either side of the *Hotel Don Pedro* and two more on the east side of Cala Sant Vicenç on the far side of a dividing headland.

ARRIVAL AND DEPARTURE

CALA SANT VICENÇ

By bus Buses to Cala Sant Vicenç stop in the centre of the resort on both Avgda Cavall Bernat and on c/Temporal. Destinations Alcúdia (May–Oct Mon–Sat 2 daily; 20min); Lluc (May–Oct Mon–Sat 2 daily; 40min); Pollença (4–5 daily; 25min); Port de Pollença (4–5 daily; 15min); Port de Sóller (May–Oct Mon–Sat 2 daily; 1hr 50min).

INFORMATION

Tourist information The tourist office is in a little wooded dell just back from the beach on Plaça Sant Vicenç (June–Sept Mon–Fri 9am–1.30pm & 2–4pm, Sat 10am–1pm; ☎ 971 53 32 64, ⊛ pollensa.com).

ACCOMMODATION AND EATING

Ca'l Patró c/Cala Clara s/n ☎ 971 53 38 99. Amongst the resort's several cafés and restaurants, this is the pick – just down the steps to the left of the *Hotel Don Pedro*. The focus is firmly on seafood: the catch of the day is usually first-rate and costs in the region of €25. Daily except Tues noon–3pm & 6–10pm.

Hostal Los Pinos c/Can Botana s/n ☎ 971 53 12 10, ⊛ hostal-lospinos.com. Cala Sant Vicenç is package territory,

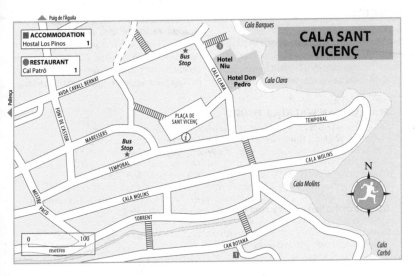

so on-spec, vacant rooms are extremely thin on the ground, but you might try this two-star *hostal*, which occupies an attractive modern villa with Art Deco flourishes on a wooded hillside on the south side of the resort. The rooms here are furnished in a spick-and-span version of traditional Spanish style, and there's an outside pool. Closed mid-Oct to April. **€75**

Port de Pollença

With the mountains as a shimmering backcloth, **PORT DE POLLENÇA** is a pleasantly low-key, family-orientated resort that arches through the flatlands behind the Badía de Pollença. The **beach** is the focus of attention here, a narrow, elongated sliver of sand, which is easily long enough to accommodate the crowds, with sheltered waters that are ideal for swimming. A rash of apartment buildings and hotels blights the edge of town, but there are no high-rises to speak of and the resort is dotted with attractive whitewashed and stone-trimmed villas. Altogether it's quite delightful, especially to the north of the marina, where a portion of the old beachside road – along **Passeig Anglada Camarasa** and **Passeig Voramar** – has been pedestrianized. When – or if – you get bored by the beach, you can also hire a bike and **cycle** out into the surrounding countryside, make the enjoyable hike across to Cala Bóquer (see p.141), or head off to the wondrous mountain scenery of the neighbouring Península de Formentor (see p.142).

ARRIVAL AND DEPARTURE

PORT DE POLLENÇA

By bus Buses to Port de Pollença stop right in the centre of the resort at the foot of the main drag, c/Joan XXIII, and a few metres from the marina.
Destinations Alcúdia (May–Oct every 15min; Nov–April hourly; 15min); Cala Sant Vicenç (4–5 daily; 15min); Ca'n Picafort (May–Oct every 15min; Nov–April hourly; 1hr 15min); Lluc (May–Oct Mon–Sat 2 daily; 50min); Palma (hourly to 2 hourly; 1hr 15min); Platja de Formentor (May–Oct Mon–Sat 3 daily; 20min); Pollença (May–Oct 1–4 hourly; Nov–April hourly; 15min) Port d'Alcúdia (May–Oct every 15min; Nov–April hourly; 30min); Port de Sóller (May–Oct Mon–Sat 2 daily; 2hr); Sóller (May–Oct Mon–Sat 2 daily; 1hr 50min).

INFORMATION

Information The tourist office is bang in the centre of the resort at Passeig Saralegui s/n (May–Sept Mon–Fri 9am–8pm, Sat 9am–4pm; Oct–April Mon–Fri 9am–3pm, Sat 9am–1pm; ☎ 971 86 54 67, ✇pollensa.com), with lots of local information, including accommodation lists, bus- and boat-trip timetables and details of car rental companies.

ACTIVITIES

BOAT TRIPS

Boat trips of various descriptions are extremely popular in Port de Pollença and they all leave from the west side of the marina. The main company is Lanchas La Gaviota (☎ 971 86 40 14, ✇lanchaslagaviota.com), which runs regular excursions out into the Badía de Pollença (June–Sept Mon–Thurs 1 daily; 2hr; €22) and to Cap de Formentor (June–Sept 3 weekly; 2hr 30min; €22). The most popular trip, however, is the 20min hop over to the golden sands of the Platja de Formentor (May–Oct 2–5 daily; €11 return).

MALLORCAN WALKING TOURS

Port de Pollença is home to the island's best hiking company, the small, independent **Mallorcan Walking Tours** (MWT; ☎ 609 70 08 26, ✇mallorcanwalkingtours.puertopollensa .com), which runs an outstanding range of **day-long guided hikes** from September to June. There is something to suit most levels of fitness and they cover the whole of the Serra de Tramuntana as well as the hilly uplands north of Artà (see p.167) and Sant Elm (see p.119). Costs vary depending on the hike but begin at €28 per person including transport to the trailhead, though walkers need to take their own food and water. MWT also lead a **week-long traverse of the Serra de Tramuntana** from Valldemossa to Pollença for around €540 per person. You need to book (by phone or online) a minimum of 24 hours beforehand, much more for the longer hikes. MWT also provides route advice and moves luggage between destinations for **self-guided treks**.

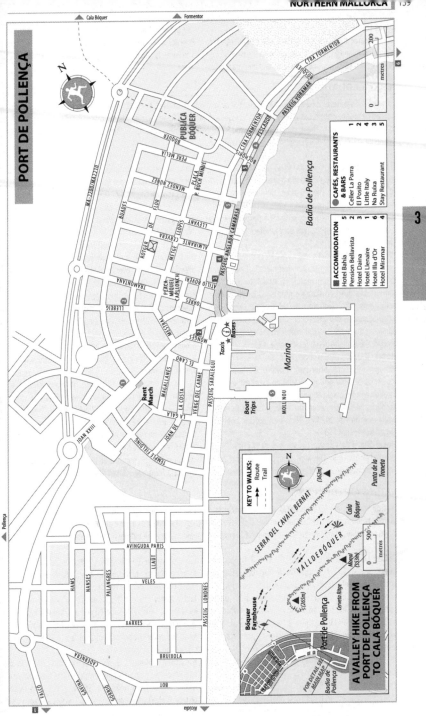

PORT DE POLLENÇA

N

Cala Bóquer

Formentor

PUBLICA BOQUER

MA-2200/PM-2210

MESTRAL

JOAN XXIII

Pollença

HAMS

NANSES

PALANGRES

AVINGUDA PARIS

LLAUT

VELES

PASSEIG LONDRES

XARXES

BRUIXOLA

CADERNERA

GAVINA

GORRIÓ

FALCO

BOT

Alcúdia

Badia de Pollença

CTRA FORMENTOR

BOSCH OS

PASSEIG VORAMAR

PESCADOR

BOQUER

PERE MELIA

MENDEZ NUÑEZ

PLAÇA P. ROCH MIQUEL

FLOR

BUADES

ROGER DE LLÉVANT

SIDOTI CRAVERA

MEGE

ALMIRANTE

PASSEIG ANGLADA CAMARASA

TRAMONTANA

PLAÇA MIGUEL CAPLLONCH

TORRES

ATILIO BOVERI

LLEBEIG

MONGES

EL CANO

MAGALLANES

LA COSTA

VERGE DEL CARME

PASSEIG SARALEGUI

LA GALA

JOAN DE

TEMPLE FIELDING

Rent March

Taxis
Buses

Marina

Boat Trips

MOLL NOU

KEY TO WALKS:

→ Route
---- Trail

N

SERRA DEL CAVALL BERNAT

(342m)

Punta de la Troneta

Cala Bóquer

VALLDEBÓQUER

Moixol (353m)

(260m)

Cererola Ridge

(353m)

Bóquer Farmhouse

FOR DETAIL SEE MAIN MAP

Port de Pollença

Badia de Pollença

Pollença

A VALLEY HIKE FROM PORT DE POLLENÇA TO CALA BÓQUER

0   500   metres

0   200   metres

● **CAFÉS, RESTAURANTS & BARS**

Celler La Parra	1
El Posito	2
Little Italy	4
Na Ruixa	3
Stay Restaurant	5

■ **ACCOMMODATION**

Hotel Bahia	5
Pension Bellavista	2
Hotel Daina	3
Hotel Llenaire	1
Hotel Illa d'Or	6
Hotel Miramar	4

3

CYCLING

The rusticated flatlands edging the Badía de Pollença and stretching inland as far as Pollença make for easy, scenic cycling. Bikes (€20/day or €110/week) and mountain bikes can be rented from Rent March, in the centre of Port de Pollença at c/Joan XXIII, 89 (Mon–Sat 9am–1pm & 4–8pm, Sun 9am–12.30pm; ☎ 971 86 47 84, ⓦ rentmarch.com).

ACCOMMODATION

Port de Pollença has around a dozen hotels and not quite as many *hostales*. Needless to say, most of the rooms are block-booked by tour operators, but there's a reasonably good chance of finding a vacancy in the places listed below, especially in the shoulder season. The part of town you want is the pedestrianized Passeig Anglada Camarasa; try to avoid Passeig Saralegui unless you're indifferent to the hum of traffic.

Hotel Bahía Passeig Voramar 31 ☎ 971 86 65 62, ⓦ hoposa.es. In a great location a few minutes' walk north of the marina along the seashore, this three-star hotel occupies one of the town's older villas with many period details surviving in the public areas. The thirty rooms are bright and breezy and the pick have sea-facing balconies. Closed Nov–March. **€150**

★ **Pension Bellavista** c/Monges 14 ☎ 971 86 46 00, ⓦ pensionbellavista.com. Funkiest place in town with a laidback vibe and a handful of straightforward, but comfortable, clean, en-suite rooms in a 1930s house a brief walk from the seafront. Breakfasts are vegetarian extravaganzas – and are taken in the shaded café/bar area adjoining the hotel. Very different from the chain hotels all around – and all the better for it. A snip. **€60**

Hotel Daina c/Atilio Boveri 2 ☎ 971 86 62 50, ⓦ hoposa.es. Straightforward, tower-block hotel with four stars, seventy-odd rooms and an excellent seashore location beside Passeig Anglada Camarasa. The public areas are slick and modern, as are the bedrooms with shades of white and grey to the fore. There's an outside pool too. Closed Nov–Feb. **€170**

Hotel Illa d'Or Passeig Colom 265 ☎ 971 86 51 00, ⓦ hotelillador.com. This well-equipped, four-star hotel sits by the waterfront on the northern edge of the resort. Set in its own grounds with a private jetty and beach, the hotel is built in traditional Spanish style and dates from the 1920s though the interior is ultramodern and the decor a tad pedestrian. Good facilities include saunas, pools and a gym. Closed Nov–March. **€200**

★ **Hotel Llenaire** Camí de Llenaire s/n ☎ 971 53 52 51, ⓦ hotelllenaire.com. Just 5km from the town centre, this handsome Mallorcan manor house sits on the brow of a hill with wide views over the Badía de Pollença. The owner still runs a farm here, with sheep munching away and groves of almond and olive trees, but the house is now a charming country hotel with most of its eighteenth-century features sympathetically revamped. There are eleven guest rooms, each decked out in lavish period style, an outside infinity pool and a sauna. The hotel is signposted from the inner ring road running just inland from the seashore. **€275**

Hotel Miramar Passeig Anglada Camarasa 39 ☎ 971 86 64 00, ⓦ hotel-miramar.net. Pleasant, three-star hotel in an elegant building – all iron grilles and stone lintels – that dates back to 1912, when it must have been pretty much the only building on the beach. The rooms are standard-issue modern affairs, but it's worth paying the extra €30 or so for a room with a sea view and a balcony – or you might be plonked at the back looking out over Carretera Formentor. Closed Nov–March. **€140**

EATING AND DRINKING

Port de Pollença heaves with **cafés and restaurants**. Most of them offer run-of-the-mill tourist fodder, but others skilfully blend Catalan and Castilian cuisines and serve the freshest of seafood. As a general rule, competition keeps prices down to readily affordable levels, with around €15 covering a main course at all but the ritziest establishments.

Celler La Parra c/Juan XXIII 84 ☎ 971 86 50 41, ⓦ cellerlaparra.com. Distinctive, family-run restaurant with a rustic feel – it's in an old *celler* (warehouse) where wine was once bought and sold. The menu pretty much sticks to all things Mallorcan (which is no bad thing) and everything is freshly prepared. They have wood-burning ovens and main courses start at around €12. Daily 8am–11.30pm; kitchen 1–3pm & 7.15–11pm (10.30pm in winter). Nov–March closed Mon.

El Posito c/Llebeig 8 ☎ 971 86 54 13. Unassuming modern restaurant with old sepia photos on the wall. Its (Spanish) menu is a mixed bag; featuring such delights as suckling pig and rabbit with lobster. Mains around €20. Daily 12.30–4pm & 7–10.30pm.

Little Italy Passeig Voramar 57 ☎ 971 86 67 49, ⓦ litaly.es. Nothing too special perhaps, but this low-key, very informal Italian restaurant right by the beach offers large and authentic pizzas from as little as €9. Electric-fast service too. Daily noon–10pm.

Na Ruíxa c/Mendez Nunez 3 ☎ 971 86 66 55. On a pedestrianized side street just off the beach, this pleasant restaurant, with its traditional Spanish decor and large terrace, is especially strong on seafood. Mains average €18.

A VALLEY HIKE FROM PORT DE POLLENÇA TO CALA BÓQUER

6km • 107m of ascent • 45min to 1hr each way • Easy • Trailhead: N39°54.602, E03°05.201

The walk through the sheltered **Vall de Bóquer** is an attractive, easy stroll over the gently undulating, verdant ground that lies between the Serra del Cavall Bernat and the Cerveta Ridge, across the neck of the **Península de Formentor**. The headland at the end of the walk offers splendid views of the severe sea cliffs that characterize the northern coast, with the cove and beach below. The walk is suitable for most ages and abilities – though the last leg down to the beach is uneven and can be difficult for young children. The hike is especially popular with birdwatchers, who favour early morning or evening visits, but at any time this is a popular route with the antics of frolicking, feral goats to keep you entertained.

THE ROUTE

Start by heading north along the seafront from Port de Pollença's marina and then turn left up **Avinguda Bocchoris** until you reach the triple-carriageway ring road. Cross this main road at the roundabout (which has a small car park on its right and provides a good alternative start to the walk) and continue up the dirt track with the ridge of the Serra del Cavall Bernat straight ahead. Approximately 300m further on, the path passes through an **iron gate**, passing the **Bóquer farmhouse** on the right. There's a splendid view of the Badía de Pollença from here and some fine examples of the *Agave americana*, a succulent whose flower spikes reach heights of 3m.

Beyond the farmhouse, the path turns round to the right, heading north through a small **iron gate**, then ascends steadily for about 500m, passing between large rocks. Niches in the rocks are occupied by clumps of dwarf fan palms, and you'll probably see the blue rock thrushes that inhabit the area. Here and further along the walk, you may also spot wheatears, black-eared wheatears, black redstarts, rock sparrows and wrynecks, as well as buzzards, peregrines, kestrels, booted eagles, the occasional osprey, Eleonora's falcons in spring and in summer, stonechats and goldfinches. Various warblers pass through this area during migration too, but the big ornithological thrill is the **black vulture**, with a wingspan of around 2m, which glides the air currents of the north coast. There's a fairly good chance of spotting one from the Vall de Bóquer and if you're really lucky you'll get a close view, its large, black body contrasting with a brownish head, beak and ruff.

Beyond the boulders the path descends, becoming less rocky, then passes through a gap in a dry-stone wall before ascending gently for about 150m – a scattering of pine trees 50m to the left offers a shady spot for a picnic. The valley's semi-wild goats have heavily grazed the area, leaving the vegetation sparse and scrubby. The most noticeable plant is *Asphodelus microcarpus*, which grows up to 2m high, bearing tall spikes of white flowers with a reddish brown vein on each petal. Not even the goats like it. Other common shrubs are the *Hypericum balearicum*, a St John's Wort whose yellow flowers are at their best in spring and early summer, and the narrow-leaved cistus and spurges, whose hemispherical bushes bear bright yellow glands. At the top of the next incline the path passes through another wall. About 50m off to the right of the junction of wall and path, more or less due south, is a 1.5m-high **tunnel**, inside which is a spring. Be careful, however, if you venture in, as it's popular with goats, who like the water and shade.

Further on, at some carved stone seating, the **path forks**, with the route to the **beach** to the left, whilst the right path, to the **headland**, splits into as many paths as there are goats. The beach route runs alongside a dried-up watercourse amidst the cries of sea birds and the whispering of the tall carritx grass. Patches of aromatic blue-flowered rosemary line the path. The beach at **Cala Bóquer** is disappointing, being predominantly shingle, but the water is clean and it's a good place for a swim. To return to Port de Pollença, simply retrace your steps.

Mid-March to mid-Oct daily except Tues 1.30–3.30pm & 7–10.30pm.

Stay Restaurant Moll Nou jetty ☎971 86 40 13, ⓦstayrestaurant.com. This long-established restaurant is renowned for its wide-ranging menu and the quality of its seafood – though the main courses tend towards the small size. The decor is crisp and modern, and prices a bit above average, though well worth it for the setting out on the pier; there's a top-notch wine list too. It's a popular spot, so reservations are advised in the evening when mains are anywhere between €16 and €50. Prices are much lower in the daytime. Daily noon–11pm.

Península de Formentor

Port de Pollença has been popular with middle-class Brits for decades – witness Agatha Christie's story *Problem at Pollensa Bay* – but the hoi polloi were kept away from the adjoining **Península de Formentor** by an Argentine swank called Adan Diehl. In 1928, Diehl bought the whole peninsula, a wild and stunningly beautiful 20km spur of the Serra de Tramuntana, and then built the *Hotel Formentor* (see p.144) for his friends and contacts. Since then, the Diehl family and then the government have permitted almost no development and you can now drive along the narrow, twisting road to the rugged cape at the end without a villa in view. In summer, however, the road can heave with cars and buses and you're best travelling before 10am or after 6pm.

Mirador de la Creueta

Heading northeast out of Port de Pollença, the ring road clears the far end of the resort before weaving up into the hills at the start of the peninsula. At first, the road travels inland, offering grand views back over the port, but then, after about 3.5km, it reaches a wonderful viewpoint, the **Mirador de la Creueta**, where a string of lookout points perch on the edge of plunging, north-facing sea cliffs. There are further stunning views over the southern shore from the **Talaia d'Albercuix** watchtower, though you'll have to brave the wiggly side road that climbs the ridge opposite the Mirador.

Platja de Formentor

Beyond the Mirador, the road cuts a handsome route as it threads its way along the peninsula, somehow negotiating the sheerest of cliffs before slipping down to a fork in the road, where it's straight on for the cape (see below) and right for the 900m detour to the *Hotel Formentor* (see p.144). The fork is a couple of hundred metres from the start of the **Platja de Formentor**, a narrow strip of golden sand that stretches east for about 1km beneath a low, pine-clad ridge. It's a beautiful spot, with views over to the mountains on the far side of the bay, though it can get crowded in peak season.

Cap de Formentor

Beyond the turn-off for the Hotel Formentor, the main peninsula road runs along a wooded valley before climbing up to tunnel through Mont Fumat. Afterwards, it emerges on the rocky mass of **Cap de Formentor**, a tapering promontory of bleak sea cliffs, which offers magnificent views and top-notch **birdwatching**. The silver-domed lighthouse stuck on the cape's windswept tip is out of bounds, but you can explore the rocky environs, where the sparse vegetation offers a perfect habitat for lizards and small birds, especially the deep-blue feathered rock thrush and the white-rumped rock dove. You can also see the steep, eastward-facing sea cliffs that shelter colonies of nesting Eleonora's falcons from April to October, whilst ravens, martins and swifts circle overhead. During the spring and summer migrations, thousands of sea birds fly over the cape, Manx and Cory's shearwaters in particular. For a closer look at the cape, take the steep but clearly marked **footpath** leading along the east coast from the lighthouse to the **Moll des Patronet viewpoint**; allow fifteen minutes each way.

ARRIVAL AND DEPARTURE   PENÍNSULA DE FORMENTOR

By car Most visitors drive to the peninsula, where there is a small car park on the cape at the end and a much larger one (€7) at the start of the Platja de Formentor.

By bus There's no public transport to the far end of the peninsula, but buses do run as far as the car park at the start of the Platja de Formentor.

Destinations Alcúdia (May–Oct Mon–Sat 3 daily; 35min); Port d'Alcúdia (May–Oct Mon–Sat 3 daily; 50min); Port de Pollença (May–Oct Mon–Sat 3 daily; 20min).

By boat In summer, Lanchas La Gaviota (☎971 86 40 14, ⓦ lanchaslagaviota.com) runs a regular passenger ferry service from Port de Pollença to the Platja de Formentor (May–Oct 2–5 daily; €11 return).

VIA CRUCIS, POLLENÇA TOWN (P.132) >

ACCOMMODATION AND EATING

Hotel Formentor ☎ 971 89 91 00 or ☎ 902 10 10 01, ⊚ barcelo.com. Opened in 1930, the *Formentor* was once the haunt of the rich and fashionable – Charlie Chaplin and F. Scott Fitzgerald both stayed here – and although its socialite days are long gone, the hotel preserves an air of understated elegance befitting its hacienda-meets-Art-Deco architecture. Breakfast is taken on the splendid upper-floor loggia with spectacular views over the bay, and you can stroll around the hotel's wonderful terraced gardens and up the hillside behind. Now owned by the Barceló chain, the hotel has every facility, and while the rooms are not quite as grand as you might expect, they are still charming – it's well worth staying here if you have the cash. €300

Restaurant Platja Mar ☎ 971 89 91 00. As you might expect, there is a standard-issue café-bar down on the Platja de Formentor beach, but it's well worth stumping up the extra to eat here at its more upmarket neighbour, an outpost of the *Hotel Formentor*; the restaurant occupies a brisk, modern, two-storey building and serves up delicious grilled fish and tasty paella, with main courses around €25. April–Oct daily noon–8pm.

Badía d'Alcúdia

Moving south from Port de Pollença, it's just 10km round the bay to the pretty little town of **Alcúdia**, whose main claims to fame are its imitation medieval walls and the rubbly remains of the old Roman settlement of Pollentia. The place floods with tourists on market days – Tuesdays and Sundays – but otherwise is rather restrained and, with its brace of smart hotels, can make a useful base for exploring this part of the island. The obvious draw is the rugged **Alcúdia peninsula** that juts east from the town, its further recesses holding a fine old chapel, the **Ermita de la Victòria**, and some handsome mountain scenery readily explored on a four-hour **hike** (see p.148), though you will need a car to get to the trailhead. Just south down the road from Alcúdia lies the mega-resort of **Port d'Alcúdia**, where glistening sky-rises sweep around the glorious sandy beach of the **Badía d'Alcúdia**. In summer the resort is packed, but shoulder seasons are more relaxing and the beach comparatively uncrowded. In winter you'll barely see a soul, but then most of the hotels and many of the restaurants are closed.

Port d'Alcúdia's assorted hotels, villas and apartment blocks stretch around the bay to the resort of **Ca'n Picafort**, 10km to the south, almost without interruption. The developers drained the swampland that once extended behind this coastal strip years ago, but one small area of wetland has been protected as the **Parc Natural de S'Albufera**, a real birdwatchers' delight. Further behind the coast lies a tract of fertile farmland dotted with country towns, amongst which **Muro**, with its imposing church and old stone mansions, is the most diverting.

GETTING AROUND

BADÍA D'ALCÚDIA

By bus Transport connections, particularly from May to October, are very good. Frequent buses run along the coast linking Pollença, Port de Pollença, Alcúdia, Port d'Alcúdia and Ca'n Picafort, and there are regular buses to all of them from Palma. There is also a useful seasonal bus service from Port de Sóller and Sóller to Lluc, Pollença, Port de Pollença, Alcúdia and Port d'Alcúdia (May–Oct Mon–Sat 2 daily).

There is, however, no bus service east from Alcúdia to the Ermita de la Victòria.

By train Regular trains connect Palma and Inca with Muro – though Muro train station is a few kilometres out of town (with no bus connection) – and the rail line will eventually be pushed through to Alcúdia.

Alcúdia

To pull in the day-trippers, **ALCÚDIA** holds one of the largest open-air markets on the island, a sprawling, bustling affair held on Tuesdays and Sundays, its assorted tourist trinkets taking over the whole east end of the old centre. Otherwise, the town's salient feature is the **crenellated wall** that encircles its centre and although this is, in fact, a modern restoration of the original medieval defences, the sixteenth- to eighteenth-century stone houses within are the genuine article. It only takes an hour or so to

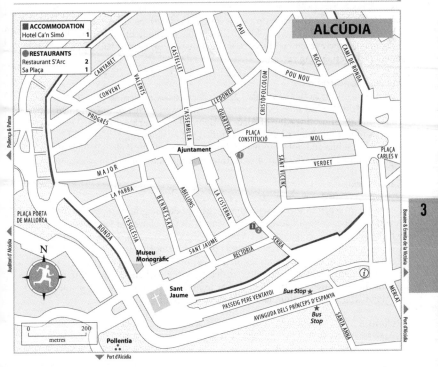

explore the ancient lanes of Alcúdia's compact **centre** and to check out the town wall and its fortified gates. This pleasant stroll can be extended by a visit to a series of minor sights, which combine to make an enjoyable whole, although none of them are especially compelling in themselves.

A brief history

Situated on a neck of land separating two large and sheltered bays, **Alcúdia** had a strategic value that was first recognized by the **Phoenicians**, who settled here in around 700 BC and used it as a staging-post for the sea trade between northwest Africa and Spain. A few Phoenician baubles have been unearthed here – including several fine examples of delicate, coloured-glass jewellery – but their town disappeared when the Romans razed the place and built their island capital, **Pollentia**, on top of the earlier settlement. In 426 AD, Roman Pollentia was, in its turn, destroyed by the Vandals and lay neglected until the **Moors** built a fortress in about 800 AD, naming it Al Kudia (On the Hill). After the Reconquista, the Christians began again, demolishing much of the Moorish town and establishing Alcúdia as a major trading centre for the western Mediterranean, a role it performed well into the nineteenth century, when the town slipped into a long and impoverished decline. And what a decline it was: "There is no difficulty in finding a place for shelter in Alcúdia both for man and beast", wrote E.G. Bartholomew in the 1860s, "for by far the greater number of houses are tenantless and doorless." This sorry state of affairs persisted until tourism eventually revived the town's economy.

Plaça Constitució and around

Beginning at the old town's eastern entrance, on **Plaça Carles V**, walk through the ancient stone gateway and keep to the main drag – here c/Moll – and you'll soon reach the slender **Plaça Constitució**, a pleasant square lined with pavement cafés. Just beyond, on c/Major, is Alcúdia's best-looking building, the **Ajuntament** (Town Hall), a handsome, largely seventeenth-century structure with an elegant balcony, a fancy bell tower and overhanging eaves.

Museu Monogràfic

c/Sant Jaume 30 • Tues–Fri 10am–4pm, Sat & Sun 10am–2pm • €3, including admission to Pollentia (see below) • ☎ 971 54 70 04

From c/Major, several side streets lead to the southwest corner of the old town, where you'll find the most diverting of Alcúdia's sights, the **Museu Monogràfic**. The museum consists of just one large room, but it's stuffed with a satisfying collection of archeological bits and bobs, primarily Roman artefacts from Pollentia, including amulets, miniature devotional objects, tiny oil lamps and some elegant statuettes.

Sant Jaume

c/Sant Jaume s/n • March–Oct daily except Wed 8am–5.30pm • €1 • ☎ 971 54 86 65

Across the street from the Museu Monogràfic and dominating this portion of the old town, is the heavyweight and heavily reworked Gothic church of **Sant Jaume**, part of which holds a modest religious museum. Amongst the museum's assorted vestments, chalices and crucifixes are a few medieval **panel-paintings** illustrative of the Mallorcan Primitives (see p.50). The paintings on display are of unknown provenance, but two sixteenth-century panels stand out: one depicting the Archangel Michael standing on a devil, who is painted red; the second of St John the Baptist, shown – as painterly fashion dictated – with almond-shaped eyes and full lips.

Pollentia

Avgda dels Prínceps d'Espanya s/n • Tues–Fri 10am–4pm, Sat & Sun 10am–2pm • €3, including admission to the Museu Monogràfic (see above) • ☎ 971 89 71 02

Beside the ring road lie the broken pillars and mashed-up walls of Roman **Pollentia**, the disappointingly meagre remains of what was once the island capital. Nearly all the stone was looted by the locals years ago, so you'll need lots of imagination to picture the Roman town, though at least the ruins are clearly labelled and the site is partly redeemed by the substantial, open-air remains of the **Teatre Romà** (Roman Theatre). Dating from the first century BC, this is the smallest of the twenty Roman theatres to have survived in Spain. Nonetheless, despite its modest proportions, the builders were able to stick to the standard type of layout with eight tiers of seats carved out of the rocky hillside and divided by two gangways, though the stage area, which was constructed of earth and timber, has of course disappeared. It's a pleasant spot, set amidst fruit and olive trees, though you do have to put up with the rumble of the traffic from the main road nearby.

ARRIVAL AND DEPARTURE
ALCÚDIA

By bus Buses to Alcúdia stop on the south side of the centre beside the ring road, Avgda del Prínceps d'Espanya.

Destinations Ca'n Picafort (May–Oct every 15min; Nov–April hourly; 1hr 15min); Palma (every 1–2hr; 1hr); Platja de Formentor (May–Oct Mon–Sat 3 daily; 35min); Pollença (April–Oct 3 daily; 30min); Port d'Alcúdia (May–Oct every 15min; Nov–April hourly; 10min); Port de Pollença (May–Oct every 15min; Nov–April hourly;15min); Port de Sóller (May–Oct Mon–Sat 2 daily; 2hr 15min); Sóller (May–Oct Mon–Sat 2 daily; 2hr).

INFORMATION

Information Alcúdia tourist office is in a flashy new building on the north side of the ring road, on Passeig Pere Ventayol s/n (May–Sept Mon–Fri 9.30am–8.30pm, Sat & Sun 9.30am–3pm; Oct–April Mon–Fri 9.30am–3pm; ☎ 971 54 90 22, ⊛ alcudia.net).

Cultural centre Alcúdia's ultra-modern cultural centre, the Auditori d'Alcúdia, Plaça de la Porta de Mallorca (☎ 971 89 71 85, ⊛ www.auditorialcudia.net), includes a library, theatre and arts centre; it's just outside – and to the west of – the city wall.

ACCOMMODATION AND EATING

★ **Restaurant S'Arc** c/Serra 22 ☎ 971 54 87 18, ⓦ restaurantsarc.com. An ambitious menu featuring local, seasonal ingredients is the hallmark of this attractive restaurant, which occupies part of a cleverly modernized old stone house and its lovely shaded terrace; the rest of the house holds the *Hotel Ca'n Simó* (see below). The *menú del día* is a snip at €10, otherwise mains average €17. April–Sept daily 12.30–3.30pm & 6–11pm; Oct–March restricted opening hours.

Hotel Ca'n Simó c/Sant Jaume 1 ☎ 971 54 92 60, ⓦ cansimo.com. Smashing hotel occupying a substantial, creatively refurbished, nineteenth-century stone townhouse. It has seven double bedrooms, each with deluxe furnishings and fittings that complement the building's original features. €110

Sa Plaça Plaça Constitució 1 ☎ 971 54 62 78. There are mixed reviews for this smart restaurant at the heart of the old town, but at its best the traditional Mallorcan/Catalan cuisine can be very good indeed – try the house speciality, salted fish (*bacalao*). Main courses average €15. Daily 11am–11pm.

The Alcúdia peninsula

The **Alcúdia peninsula**, a steep and rocky promontory to the east of Alcúdia town, pokes a wild finger out into the ocean, its **northern shore** traversed by a country road that begins at the easternmost intersection of Alcúdia's ring road. After about 2km, this promontory road runs past the turning for both the Fundació Yannick i Ben Jakober and the day-hike trailhead (see p.148) before threading its way through the suburban villas of **Bonaire**. Thereafter, the road emerges into more scenic terrain, offering fine views of the Badía de Pollença as it rolls over the steep, pine-clad ridges that fringe the coast.

Ermita de la Victòria

About 5km from Alcúdia town, a signed turning on the right climbs 700m up the wooded hillside to the **Ermita de la Victòria**, a fortress-like church built in the seventeenth century to hold and protect a crude but much-venerated statue of the Virgin. It was a necessary precaution: this part of the coast was especially prone to attack and, even with these defences, pirates still stole the statue twice, though on both occasions the islanders managed to ransom it back. The Virgin is displayed in the simple, single-vaulted chapel on the ground floor of the Ermita, but this plays second fiddle to the panoramic views out across the bay.

The Ermita is also a popular starting point for **hikes** along the promontory, whose severe peaks are dotted with ruined defensive installations, including a watchtower and an old gun emplacement. An obvious target is the **Talaia d'Alcúdia watchtower** (446m), from the top of which there are great panoramic views: it's a fifty-minute walk each way.

ACCOMMODATION AND EATING   ERMITA DE LA VICTÒRIA

Mirador de la Victòria Camí de la Victòria ☎ 971 54 71 73, ⓦ miradordelavictoria.com. This first-rate restaurant, which offers sweeping sea views from its expansive, shaded terrace, specializes in traditional Mallorcan dishes – try the snails, the suckling pig or the guinea fowl. Main courses cost €15. Feb to mid-April Tues–Sun 12.30–4pm; mid-April to Oct Tues–Sun 1–3.30pm & 7–11pm.

★ **Petit Hotel Hostatgeria la Victòria** ☎ 971 54 99 12, ⓦ lavictoriahotel.com. The old monastic quarters in the Ermita, directly above the chapel, have been turned into a delightful hotel, whose beamed ceilings, ancient stone arches and exposed masonry walls hold twelve en-suite guest rooms decorated in a suitably frugal, but highly buffed and polished style. Singles €51, doubles €74

Fundació Yannick i Ben Jakober

Es Mal Pas, Alcúdia 07400 • Tues 9.30am–12.30pm & 2.30–5.30pm, plus Wed–Sat pre-booked guided tours only at 11am & 3pm • €9 • ☎ 971 54 98 80, ⓦ fundacionjakober.org • From Alcúdia, take the Ermita de la Victòria road and turn sharp right at the *Bodega del Sol* bar onto Camí de la Muntanya; after 2km or so, you'll reach the Alcúdia Peninsula trailhead (p.148), from where it's a further 2km along a very bumpy dirt road to the Fundació

The **Fundació Yannick i Ben Jakober** is a bespoke art gallery housed in the subterranean water cistern of a sprawling mansion. Dating from the 1970s, the **house**, Finca Sa Bassa Blanca, has wide views over the ocean and was built in the manner of a

3

A CIRCULAR HIKE ON THE ALCÚDIA PENINSULA

10km • 450m of ascent • 5hr round trip, plus 1hr for diversion to Platja des Coll Baix • Moderately difficult • Trailhead N39.85133°, E003.15736°

This trek through the heart of the **Alcúdia peninsula** offers stunning sea views, including a 360° panoramic vista from the **Talaia d'Alcúdia**, at 445m the peninsula's highest point. The first part of the walk has moderate ascents on tracks, changing to a more strenuous ascent over exposed ground and a rock scramble to reach the Talaia peak. The second half of the walk steadily descends to the Coll Baix and returns through pine woods to the starting point. If time permits, a diversion can be made from the Coll Baix to the **Platja des Coll Baix**, a small, secluded and unspoilt beach, returning by the same route. There is **parking** at the trailhead.

THE ROUTE

Leave Alcúdia on the road to El Mal Pas and Bonaire. After about 2km, turn sharp right at the *Bodega del Sol* bar onto **Camí de la Muntanya** and continue straight on until you reach, after another 2km or so, Parque Victoria, a nature reserve administered by ICONA (National Institute for Nature Conservation). Leave your car just inside the park near the **iron gates**. The walk starts at this point: take the path on the uphill side of the gates, ignoring any signposts leading off right. Look and listen out for hoopoes in this area: these striking birds will appear as flashes of salmon-pink with black-and-white striped wings and crest in woodland glades, making a distinctive hoop-hoop-hoop call. The path climbs gently upwards and then drops into a shallow valley dotted with pine trees. Passing a row of newly built villas, head towards the large white **columned house** on the skyline. Pass this house on your left and descend for about 400m, ignoring the ladder stile on your left which heads into the housing estate, and instead following the path until you reach a T-junction with an information board. Turn right at this point to begin your **ascent to Coll de ses Fontanelles**. After 2–3 minutes you will arrive at a stream, partly dammed with a concrete wall. Ignore the uphill path straight ahead and take the path to the right signposted **Coll de na Benet**. Continue along this and wind your way up the stone path to the valley head (Coll de ses Fontanelles).

The **Coll de ses Fontanelles** is populated by a stand of trees including a large olive tree. These offer valuable shade on a hot day and make this a good spot to stop, rest, take a drink and get your bearings. At the signpost, take the unsigned path to the left. At this point you start the, at first, gradual climb to the **Teleia summit**. The ground here is exposed and rocky on what is the most arduous part of the walk. From here to the summit there's no clear path, and the best way up is to follow dabs of red paint marked on the rocks. Aim for the left-hand side of the stone building at the Teleia summit as the ridge on which it stands is too steep to tackle. At this stage, the scrambling and clambering may seem daunting but reaching the summit is easier than it seems. Nevertheless, you do need to negotiate a steep and short, if relatively easy, rock face. Once on the top don't be disconcerted by the patrolled military hut but head for the **Trig Point** (stone column) and be rewarded with superb panoramic views of the peninsula with the sea in every direction.

To descend, take the path at the other side of the Trig Point, which drops down to a path signposted "**Collet des Coll Baix**". The well-defined path provides a gentle descent, zigzagging past views of valleys to the left and right and eventually reaching the headland with views of the secluded beach of **Platja des Coll Baix** on the left. Continue your descent until, at the bottom, you reach a wooded area scattered with picnic tables, a water fountain (not drinking water) and much-needed shade. This is a popular spot for the only indigenous goats on the island (the Mallorcan goat) to gather in their search for picnic leftovers. The beach is also signposted here and worth the visit, although **swimming is not encouraged** due to strong undertows.

From the picnic area, it's a fairly long haul on the easily graded **dirt road** to the walk's starting point by the gates. En route you will pass through pine woods, which have an undergrowth of lentiscs, narrow-leaved cistus, carritx, dwarf fan palms, euphorbias, asphodels and the occasional giant orchid; there are also almond and carob groves.

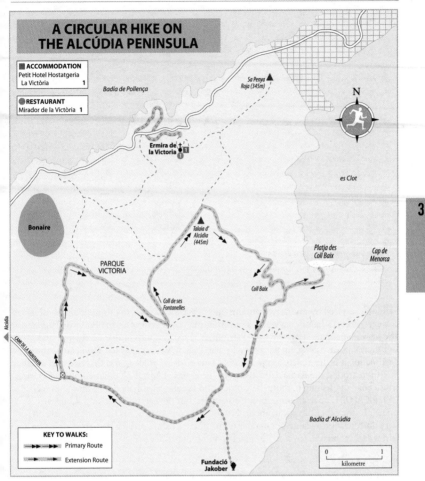

A CIRCULAR HIKE ON THE ALCÚDIA PENINSULA

■ ACCOMMODATION
Petit Hotel Hostatgeria
La Victòria   **1**

● RESTAURANT
Mirador de la Victòria **1**

Badia de Pollença

Sa Penya
Roja (345m)

N

Ermira de
la Victoria

es Clot

3

Bonaire

Talaia d'
Alcúdia
(445m)

PARQUE
VICTORIA

Platja des
Coll Baix

Cap de
Menorca

Coll Baix

Coll de ses
Fontanelles

Alcúdia

CAMI DE LA MUNTAYA

Badia d' Alcúdia

KEY TO WALKS:
▸▸▸ Primary Route
▸ ▸ ▸ Extension Route

Fundació
Jakober

0   1
kilometre

Moroccan fortified palace to a design by the Egyptian architect Hassan Fathy. The owners, the eponymous Jakobers, are art-loving sculptors and the house's **gardens** are dotted with large, modern sculptures. The gallery itself is entirely devoted to **children's portraits** dating from the seventeenth to the nineteenth century. It was Yannick who began the collection in the 1970s, when she picked up a striking *Girl with Cherries* by the nineteenth-century Mallorcan artist Joan Mestre i Bosch. None of the artists represented is particularly well known – and neither are the children – but together they provide an intriguing insight into the way the aristocracy of early modern Spain saw their children as miniature adults. Indeed, many of the portraits were hawked around the courts of Europe in search of a suitable bride or groom. Only from the 1750s onwards do the children seem more childlike, innocent and relaxed.

Port d'Alcúdia

PORT D'ALCÚDIA, 2km south of Alcúdia, is easily the biggest and busiest of the resorts in the north of the island, a seemingly interminable string of high-rise hotels and apartment

3

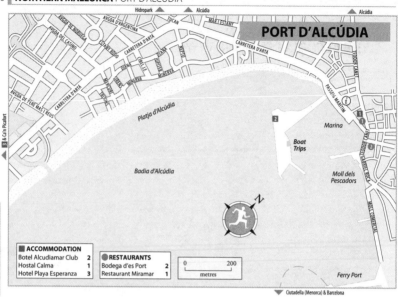

PORT D'ALCÚDIA

Hidropark Alcúdia Alcúdia

Platja d'Alcúdia

Badia d'Alcúdia

Marina

Boat Trips

Moll dels Pescadors

Ferry Port

Ciutadella (Menorca) & Barcelona

■ ACCOMMODATION	
Botel Alcudiamar Club	2
Hostal Calma	1
Hotel Playa Esperanza	3

● RESTAURANTS	
Bodega d'es Port	2
Restaurant Miramar	1

0 — 200 metres

buildings serviced by myriad restaurants and café-bars. Despite the superficial resemblance, however, Port d'Alcúdia is a world away from the seamy resorts on the Badía de Palma. The tower blocks are relatively well distributed, the streets are comparatively neat and tidy and there's an easygoing air, with families particularly well catered for. Predictably, the daytime focus is the **beach**, a superb arc of pine-studded golden sand that stretches south for 10km around the **Badía d'Alcúdia** from the jetties of Port d'Alcúdia's combined marina, cruise boat and fishing harbour. The beach and the sky-rises fizzle out as they approach **CA'N PICAFORT**, once an important fishing port, but now an uninteresting suburban sprawl. In the other direction, about 500m east of the marina, lies the **commercial and ferry port**, Mallorca's largest container terminal after Palma and the departure point for car ferries and catamarans over to Ciutadella, on Menorca (see p.228).

The beach

From June to September, a tourist **"train"** (on wheels, with clearly marked roadside stops) runs up and down Port d'Alcúdia every hour or so during the daytime, transporting sunbaked bodies from one part of the **beach** to another. Not that there's very much to distinguish anywhere from anywhere else – the palm-thatched **balnearios** (beach bars) are a great help in actually remembering where you are. There's also a **boardwalk** running along the back of much of the beach, which is usually less crowded the further south you venture.

ARRIVAL AND DEPARTURE   **PORT D'ALCÚDIA**

BY BUS

Port d'Alcúdia acts as northern Mallorca's summertime transport hub, with fast and frequent buses up and down the coast between Ca'n Picafort and Port de Pollença as well as regular buses to and from Palma. There's no bus station as such, but instead most local and long-distance buses travel the length of the Carretera d'Artà, the main drag, dropping off passengers at clearly signed stops along the way.

> **NORTHERN MALLORCA'S TOP 5 BEACHES**
> **Cala Tuent** See p.128
> **Cala Sant Vicenç** See p.137
> **Port de Pollença** See p.138
> **Platja de Formentor** See p.142
> **Port d'Alcúdia** See p.149

Destinations Alcúdia (May–Oct every 15min; Nov–April hourly; 10min); Ca'n Picafort (May–Oct every 15min; Nov–April hourly; 45min); Palma (every 1–2hr; 1hr); Platja de Formentor (May–Oct Mon–Sat 3 daily; 50min); Pollença (April–Oct 3 daily; 20min); Port de Pollença (May–Oct every 15min; Nov–April hourly; 30min); Port de Sóller (May–Oct Mon–Sat 2 daily; 2hr 30min); Sóller (May–Oct Mon–Sat 2 daily; 2hr 20min).

BY FERRY

Balearia (☎ 902 16 01 80, ⊛ balearia.com) operates a

fast-ferry catamaran service (1–2 daily) from Port d'Alcúdia to Ciutadella on Menorca (see p.228). The journey time is just over 1hr and one-way passenger fares start at about €60 (driver and car €150). In addition, Iscomar (☎ 902 11 91 28, ⊛ www.iscomar.com) operates car ferries from Port d'Alcúdia to Ciutadella once or twice daily except in the depths of winter; the journey time is 2hr 30min, the one-way passenger fare costs about €50, and vehicles up to 4.5m in length are charged around €72 more. Note that Balearic car rental firms do not allow their vehicles to leave the island they were rented on.

GETTING AROUND

Car, moped and bike rental There's a super-abundance of car, moped and bike rental companies strung out along the main drag, Carretera d'Artà. The best of the bike shops

is Bimont Bicicletes, Carretera d'Artà 38 (☎ 971 544 964, ⊛ bimont.com).

INFORMATION

Tourist office The main tourist office occupies a distinctive kiosk in what is the effective centre of the resort, just behind the marina on Passeig Marítim, (May–Oct Mon–Fri 10am–1.30pm & 3–5.30pm, Sat 9am–1pm;

☎ 971 54 72 57, ⊛ alcudiamallorca.com). They have all sorts of local information, including useful free maps marked with all the resort's hotels and apartments.

ACTIVITIES

Boat trips Several companies operate boat trips from the marina in Port d'Alcúdia, with the prime targets being the rocky, mountainous coastlines of the Alcúdia and Formentor peninsulas. The main company is Brisa (☎ 971 54 58 11, ⊛ www.tmbrisa.com), whose least expensive excursion is to the Cap des Pinar at the tip of the Alcúdia peninsula (May–Oct 2–3 daily; 2hr; €18). The longer cruises continue round the Cap des Pinar and cross the bay to the Platja de Formentor (May–Oct 1 daily; 4hr, including 1hr on Platja de Formentor; €23).

Water parks A kilometre or so inland, on Avinguda del

Tucán, Hidropark (May to early Oct daily 10.30am–6pm; ☎ 971 89 16 72, ⊛ hidropark.com; €20 for 12 and overs, €10 for 3–11-year-olds) is a major kids' attraction with its large and high undulating water slide and wiggly spiral water tube.

Watersports Watersports Mallorca (☎ 606 35 38 07, ⊛ watersportsmallorca.com), who operate from two beachside locations to the south of Port d'Alcúdia near the national park, offer a variety of sports, including windsurfing, kitesurfing and paddlesurfing.

ACCOMMODATION

In season, you'd be well advised to book ahead as vacant **rooms** are few and far between, though there's still a chance of finding something amongst the budget *hostales* clustered behind the marina in the oldest – and least appealing – part of the resort. In winter, most of the **hotels** and **hostales** close, but in the shoulder seasons it's often possible to get a good deal at one of the plusher hotels.

Botel Alcudiamar Club Passeig Maítim 1 ☎ 971 89 72 15, ⊛ botelalcudiamar.es. The prime selling point of this modern hotel is its location – right at the end of a jetty with water (almost) all around. There are sea-view terraces, an outdoor pool and a mini-spa. The rooms are decoratively uninspiring, but the best have sea-facing balconies. €190

Hostal Calma c/Teodor Canet 25 ☎ 971 54 84 85, ⊛ hostalcalma.de. The pick of the inexpensive *hostales* handily located close to the marina and a short hop from the beach, but on a busy street. This family-run place has

thirty a/c, en-suite rooms decorated in a straightforward, traditional style. The rooms are small, but the price is right. Good breakfasts and free wi-fi; bike rental is available too. €50

Hotel Playa Esperanza Avgda S'Albufera s/n ☎ 971 89 05 68, ⊛ esperanzahoteles.com. Whopping, four-star hotel in a grand location away from the crowds – and directly behind the beach about 5km south of the marina. Has a full range of facilities, splendid, well-tended gardens and a large self-service restaurant. €150

3

EATING AND DRINKING

Bodega d'es Port c/Teodor Canet 8 ☎971 54 96 33, ⓦbodegadesport.com. Set on the waterfront, between the marina and the commercial port, and decked out in an appealing version of traditional *bodega* style with wide windows, wooden chairs and a stone facade, this is one of the resort's better restaurants. The prime offering here is the first-rate selection of tapas from as little as €8. Daily 8am–11.30pm. Closed Nov & Dec.

Restaurant Miramar Passeig Marítim 2 ☎971 54 52 93, ⓦrestaurantmiramar.es. Well-established seafront restaurant with an expansive pavement terrace. It serves a top-notch range of seafood – try the hake with spinach – with dishes costing anywhere between €17 and €30. Daily 1–10.30pm, but restricted hours in winter.

Parc Natural de S'Albufera

The park entrance is clearly signposted on the Ma-12, about 6km round the bay from Port d'Alcúdia's marina; from the entrance, a country lane leads just over 1km inland to the Sa Roca reception centre (see below) • Daily: April–Sept 9am–6pm; Oct–March 9am–5pm • Free, but visitors need a permit, which is issued at the Sa Roca information centre • ☎971 89 22 50, ⓦmallorcaweb.net/salbufera

Given all the high-rise development strung along the Badía d'Alcúdia, the pristine wetland that makes up the 2000-acre **Parc Natural de S'Albufera**, between Port d'Alcúdia and Ca'n Picafort, is a welcome relief. Swampland once extended round most of the bay, but large-scale reclamation began in the nineteenth century, when a British company dug a network of channels and installed a steam engine to pump the water out. These endeavours were prompted by a desire to eradicate malaria – then the scourge of the local population – as much as by the need for more farmland. Further drainage schemes accompanied the frantic tourist boom of the 1960s, and only in the last decade or two has the Balearic government recognized the ecological importance of the wetland and organized a park to protect what little remains.

Footpaths and **cycle trails** fan out from Sa Roca into the reedy, watery tract beyond, where a dozen or so well-appointed **hides** and observation decks allow excellent **birdwatching** – the best on the island. More than two hundred different types of bird have been spotted here, including resident wetland-loving birds from the crake, warbler and tern families; autumn and/or springtime migrants such as grebes, herons, cranes, plovers and godwits; and wintering egrets and sandpipers. Such rich pickings attract birds of prey in their scores, especially kestrels and harriers. The open ground edging the reed beds supports many different wild flowers, the most striking of which are the orchids that bloom during April and May.

ARRIVAL AND DEPARTURE   PARC NATURAL DE S'ALBUFERA

By car Visitors are not allowed to drive down the lane to Sa Roca, but there is a small car park beside the Ma-12 just south of the park entrance.

By bus Buses running between Port d'Alcúdia and Ca'n Picafort stop close to the entrance.

Destinations Alcúdia (May–Oct every 15min; Nov–April hourly; 45min); Ca'n Picafort (May–Oct every 15min; Nov–April hourly; 15min); Port d'Alcúdia (May–Oct every 15min; Nov–April hourly; 30min); Port de Pollença (May–Oct every 15min; Nov–April hourly; 1hr).

By bike In summer, there's usually a bike rental kiosk at the start of the lane leading to Sa Roca (€12/day).

INFORMATION

Sa Roca information centre At this information centre (daily 9am–4pm), you can pick up a free map of the park and a list of birds that you might see. The map is marked with four colour-coded walking/cycling trails; the shortest is 725m, the longest 11km. Note, however, that the map is not especially accurate and, although it's perfectly adequate for these four routes, anything more ambitious – say, walking to Ca'n Picafort – is not advised as you would almost certainly get lost. Sa Roca also sells birdwatching guides and there is a small wildlife display in an adjacent building, Can Bateman.

Muro

Perched on a hill in the midst of a pancake-flat, windmill-studded landscape, **MURO** is a sleepy little place whose old stone townhouses date back to the early nineteenth century. The town is at its liveliest on January 16 during the **Revetlla de Sant Antoni**

Abat (Eve of St Antony's Day), when locals gather round bonfires to drink and dance, tucking into specialities like sausages and eel pies (*espinagades*), made with eels from the nearby marshes of S'Albufera. Quite what St Antony – an Egyptian hermit and ascetic who spent most of his long life in the desert – would have made of these high jinks it's hard to say, but there again he certainly wouldn't have been overwhelmed by temptation if he had stuck around Muro for the rest of the year.

Plaça Constitució

Muro's main square, **Plaça Constitució**, is an attractive, airy piazza overseen by the domineering church of **St Joan Baptista**, a real hotchpotch of architectural styles, its monumental Gothic lines uneasily modified by the sweeping sixteenth-century arcades above the aisles. A slender arch connects the church to the adjacent **belfry**, an imposing seven-storey construction partly designed as a watchtower; it's sometimes possible to go to the top, from where the views out over the coast are superb. The church's cavernous interior holds a mighty vaulted roof and an immense altarpiece, a flashy extravaganza of columns, parapets and tiers in a folksy rendition of the Baroque.

Museu Etnològic

c/Major 15 • Wed, Fri & Sat 10am–3pm, Thurs 5–8pm; Sun 10am–2pm; closed Aug • €3 • ☎ 971 86 06 47

A five-minute walk south of the main square is the **Museu Etnològic**, though it's is poorly signed and the town centre is labyrinthine – ask around to find your way. This is one of the least-visited museums on the island, and the custodians seem positively amazed when a visitor actually shows up. It occupies a rambling old mansion and showcases a motley assortment of local bygones, from old agricultural implements, pottery and apothecary jars through to Mallorcan bagpipes and traditional costumes. Amongst the agricultural equipment there's a broken-down example of a mule- or donkey-driven water wheel, a **noria**. Introduced by the Moors, these were common features of the Mallorcan landscape for hundreds of years, though there are few left today. Among the pottery, look out for the **siurells**, miniature white-, green- and red-painted figurines created in a naive style. Once given as presents, but now debased as a mass-produced tourist trinket, these are whistles – hence the spout with the hole – shaped in the form of animals, humans and mythological or imaginary figures.

ARRIVAL AND DEPARTURE

MURO

By train Muro's train station is 4km or so away to the west of the town centre, with regular services to Inca (every 15–30min; 15min) and Palma (every 15–30min; 50min).

By bus Buses from Ca'n Picafort (every 1–2hr; 20min) and Inca train station (every 1–2hr; 30min) pull in on the west side of the centre on c/Santa Anna.

EATING AND DRINKING

Sa Fonda c/Sant Jaume 1. On a hot summer's day you'll be glad of a drink at one of the cafés around the main square and this traditional little place, which also serves a range of inexpensive tapas, is as good as any. Located just off Plaça Constitució across from the church. Daily 9am–8pm.

Southern Mallorca

159 Binissalem
160 Inca
161 Sineu
162 Petra and around
163 Gordiola glassworks
164 Puig Randa and around
165 Els Calderers de Sant Joan
165 Manacor
167 Artà
170 Colònia de Sant Pere
172 Capdepera
173 Cala Rajada
176 Coves d'Artà
176 Platja de Canyamel
176 Porto Cristo and around
179 Porto Colom
179 Felanitx and around
180 Cala d'Or
181 Porto Petro
182 Mondragó Parc Natural
182 Cala Mondragó
182 Santanyí
183 Cala Figuera
184 Cap de Ses Salines
184 Colònia de Sant Jordi
188 Es Trenc
188 Cabrera National Park
189 Campos
189 Llucmajor

CALA RAJADA

Southern Mallorca

Most of southern Mallorca comprises the island's central plain, Es Pla, a fertile tract bounded to the west by the mountainous Serra de Tramuntana and to the east by the hilly range that shadows the coast, the Serres de Llevant. Although Es Pla may seem today like a sleepy backwater, it pretty much defined Mallorca until the twentieth century: the majority of the island's inhabitants lived here, it produced enough food to meet almost every domestic requirement, and Palma's gentry were reliant on Es Pla estates for their income. This persisted until the 1960s, when the tourist boom turned everything on its head and the developers bypassed Es Pla to focus on the picturesque coves of the east coast.

Largely ignored by the tourist industry, the **towns of Es Pla** provide the full flavour of an older, agricultural Mallorca, whose softly hued landscapes are patterned with olive orchards, chunky farmhouses and country towns of low, whitewashed houses huddled beneath outsized churches. Admittedly, there's precious little to distinguish one settlement from another, but there are exceptions, most notably wine-growing **Binissalem**, with its streets of handsome old houses; **Sineu**, once the site of a royal palace and now one of the plain's prettiest towns; and **Petra**, with its clutch of sights celebrating the life and times of the eighteenth-century Franciscan monk and explorer Junípero Serra. Other sights are the impressive monastery perched on the summit of **Puig Randa** and, in the Serres de Llevant, the hilltop shrine at **Artà** plus the delightful medieval castle at **Capdepera**. All these destinations are readily accessible from either the **Ma-13** motorway – the island's busiest and fastest road, which links Palma with Alcúdia and passes one of the region's largest towns, **Inca** – or the Ma-15, which runs the 70km from Palma to Artà, via **Manacor**, noted for its artificial pearl factories.

The ancient fishing villages of the **east coast** have mostly been swallowed up within mega-resorts, whose endless high-rises and villa complexes blemish the land for miles. A couple of enjoyable seaside towns, however, have avoided the worst excesses of concrete and glass: **Cala Rajada**, a lively spot bordered by fine beaches and a beautiful pine-shrouded coastline, and **Cala Figuera**, which surrounds a lovely, steep-sided cove. The former fishing village of **Porto Petro** has also managed to retain much of its original charm, as has the ramshackle old port of **Porto Cristo**. Different again is tiny **Cala Mondragó**, where a slice of coast has been protected by the creation of a park. The east coast also boasts the cave systems of **Coves del Drac**, justifiably famous for their extravagant stalactites and stalagmites. On the **south coast**, the scenery changes again, with hills and coves giving way to sparse flatlands, whose star turn is the port-cum-resort of **Colònia de Sant Jordi**, from where boat trips leave for the bleached remoteness of **Cabrera** island.

GETTING AROUND
SOUTHERN MALLORCA

Direct **buses** link Palma with almost every resort and town in the region, but services between the towns of Es Pla and along the east coast are patchy. Fast and frequent **trains** run north and east from Palma to Binissalem, Inca, Sineu, Petra

The festivals of Binissalem p.159
Gordiola glass p.163
A walk to Ermita de Betlem p.170

The route to Cala Gat p.173
Porto Cristo's Republican landing p.177
Birdlife of the saltpans p.188

COVES DEL DRAC

Highlights

❶ Sineu The most attractive of the ancient agricultural towns of central Mallorca, home to the island's finest parish church and a bustling Wednesday market. **See p.161**

❷ Cala Rajada Perched on the edge of a bumpy headland, this busy resort is within easy striking distance of several excellent, pine-clad sandy beaches. **See p.173**

❸ Coves del Drac Perhaps the finest of eastern Mallorca's numerous cave systems, with fantastically shaped stalactites and stalagmites, as well as one of the world's largest subterranean lakes. **See p.178**

❹ Cala Mondragó This beautiful, secluded pair of sandy beaches, nestled in a pine-clad natural reserve, is popular with locals and tourists alike, but still unspoiled by mass tourism. **See p.182**

❺ Colònia de Sant Jordi Charming, low-key resort with several sandy beaches, smashing seafood restaurants and easy-going hotels and *hostales*. **See p.184**

❻ Cabrera The fiercely hostile terrain of this offshore islet makes for an unusual day's excursion – and lots of rare Lilford's wall lizards will help you with your sandwiches. **See p.188**

HIGHLIGHTS ARE MARKED ON THE MAP ON P.158

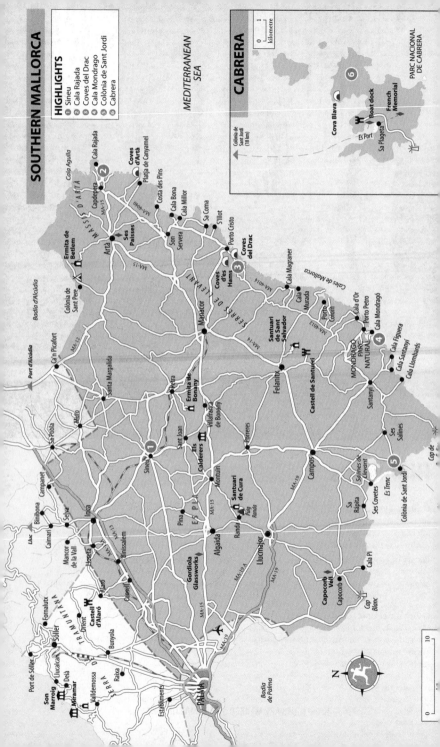

SOUTHERN MALLORCA

HIGHLIGHTS

1. Sineu
2. Cala Rajada
3. Coves del Drac
4. Cala Mondrago
5. Colònia de Sant Jordi
6. Cabrera

MEDITERRANEAN SEA

CABRERA

PARC NACIONAL DE CABRERA

Cova Blava
Boat dock
French Memorial
Es Port
Sa Plageta
Colònia de Sant Jordi (18 km)

and Manacor with **connecting bus services** leaving Inca and Manacor train stations for surrounding towns and villages. For further details on buses and trains in the region, call ☎ 971 17 77 77, or check out ⊕ tib.org.

ACCOMMODATION

Given the difficulty of finding a room in the coastal package resorts on spec and the general dearth of **accommodation** in the interior, **advance reservations** are a good idea – and pretty much essential in the height of the season. Towns with a healthy supply of non-package hotels and *hostales* include Artà, Cala Rajada, Porto Cristo and Colònia de Sant Jordi, though Binissalem and Sineu have some excellent hotels too. In addition, three of the region's former **monasteries** offer simple, inexpensive lodgings and usually have space at any time of year (see p.163, p.165 & p.180).

Binissalem

Long the centre of Mallorca's prime wine-growing area, **BINISSALEM** lies about 25km east of Palma. The tatty, semi-industrial sprawl that straddles the highway around the town camouflages an antique town centre of some architectural distinction, whose narrow streets hold a proud ensemble of old stone mansions dating from the seventeenth and eighteenth centuries. The Romans settled here, and so did the Moors – Binissalem could be derived from the Arabic "Bani Salaam", meaning Sons of Peace – but the town's commercial heyday began in the sixteenth century, boosted by its vineyards and stone quarries. These days the old town centre of Binissalem maintains a sleepy calm particularly attractive to those wanting to escape the tourist bustle of Palma.

Església Nostra Senyora de Robines

Binissalem's main square, the **Plaça Església**, is a pretty, stone-flagged piazza lined with benches where old-timers shoot the breeze in the shade of the plane trees. The northeast side of the square is dominated by the **Església Nostra Senyora de Robines**, whose clumpy, medieval nave is attached to a soaring neo-Gothic bell tower added in 1908. Inside, the single-vaulted nave is dark and gloomy, its most distinctive features being its glitzy Baroque altarpiece and the grooved stonework that appears above and beyond the high altar. This grooved stonework pops up all over town, representing the cockleshell emblem of **St James the Greater**, one of the apostles. Spanish legend insists that James preached in Spain and that his body was brought here from Jerusalem and buried at Santiago de Compostela in the far northwest of Spain. These tales have made St James one of Spain's most venerated saints.

Casa Museu Llorenç Villalonga

c/Bonaire 25 • Mon–Sat 10am–2pm; also Tues & Thurs 4–8pm • Free

A five-minute walk from Plaça Església via c/Concepció, **Can Sabater** is one of the town's most distinguished patrician mansions. This was once the home of the writer Llorenç Villalonga (1897–1980), whose most successful novel was *The Dolls' Room*, an ambiguous portrait of Mallorca's nineteenth-century landed gentry in moral decline. In his honour, the house has been turned into the **Casa Museu Llorenç Villalonga**, with detailed (Catalan) explanations of his life and times as well as his library and study. The house is typical of its type, with elegant stone arches and high-ceilinged rooms redolent of oligarchic comfort. It also has its own chapel: the island's richer families usually had their own live-in priests.

THE FESTIVALS OF BINISSALEM

An especially good time to visit Binissalem is in the third week of July, during the week-long **festivities** that precede St James' feast day on July 25. A second calendar highlight is the **Festa d'es Vermar** (Festival of the Grape Harvest) at the back end of September, when the town's cordoned-off streets are lined with trestle tables weighed down with all sorts of local wines and foods, proudly presented by their makers.

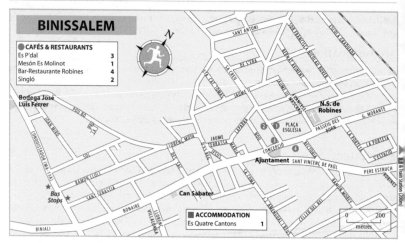

Bodega José Luis Ferrer

c/Conquistador 103 • **Winery** Mon–Fri 11am & 4.30pm • €6 • **Shop** Mon–Fri 9am–7pm, Sat 10am–2pm • ☎ 971 51 10 50, Ⓦ vinosferrer.com

From the Villalonga museum, it's a five-minute walk south along c/Bonaire to the Ma-13A, which doubles as c/Conquistador, and another five minutes or so west (towards Palma) for the **Bodega José Luis Ferrer**, which produces the best reds on the island. If you book ahead, you can tour parts of the winery during the working week, but most visitors are content to visit the **shop**, which stocks the full range of the company's wines.

ARRIVAL AND DEPARTURE   BINISSALEM

By bus Buses from Palma (6 daily, 4 on Sat, 3 on Sun; 30min) pull in beside the Ma-13A (c/Conquistador), a few metres to the west of c/Bonaire, which leads straight up towards Plaça Església.

By train Binissalem is on the train line from Palma to Manacor, and regular trains from both directions stop at the station on the northern edge of the town centre (every 20min; 30min from Palma; 40min from Manacor). From the train station, it's a 5- to 10- minute walk to Plaça Església: head straight down c/S'Estació, turn right at the end and then left at the end of this second street.

ACCOMMODATION AND EATING

Bar-Restaurante Robines Plaça Església 25 ☎ 971 51 11 36, Ⓦ barrestauranterobinesamericano.com. The town lacks a good restaurant and the best you'll do is the *Bar-Restaurante Robines*, an old-fashioned place serving all the Spanish classics with main courses averaging about €16. Daily except Tues 8am till late.

Es Quatre Cantons Carretera Biniali km 2.5 ☎ 971 87 01 62 Ⓦ esquatrecantons.com. Just outside town, the luxurious and picturesque *Es Quatre Cantons* is a lovingly restored *finca* hotel surrounded by terraces and gardens. Each of the twenty rooms has its own private patio and access. **€57**

Inca

Sprawling **INCA**, formerly a grimy town and Mallorca's third city, has long had a bad press as an industrial eyesore. In medieval times, one of the few ways to keep out of the clutches of the island's landowners was to practise a craft and then join the appropriate guild. As early as the fifteenth century, Inca had attracted enough **shoemakers** to become the centre of a flourishing shoemaking industry – and so it remains today with Camper's HQ and main factory-warehouse firmly ensconced here. This may not sound too enticing, but today it's a pleasant enough place with a re-energized and revamped old centre and the **walk** across its pedestrianized core, from the **train station** in the west to Plaça Orient in the east, is an agreeable way to spend an hour or so. Along the way, you'll spy a scattering of immaculate *Modernista* buildings and the town's main church, **Santa Maria la Major**, an imposing sandstone pile with all sorts of Baroque flourishes.

ARRIVAL AND DEPARTURE   INCA

By bus and train The bus and train stations are next to each other on Avgda del Tren. Inca is served by regular buses from Palma (Mon–Fri 10 daily, Sat & Sun 3–5 daily;

30min), and trains from both Palma (every 20min from Palma; 40min) and Manacor (every 20min; 30min).

EATING AND DRINKING

Ca'n Amer c/Pau 39 ☎971 50 12 61. As you might expect, Inca has oodles of cafés and restaurants, with one of the best being the long-established *Ca'n Amer*, a wonderfully old-fashioned cellar restaurant a short walk west of the main church. Main dishes cost approximately €10–17. May–Sept Mon–Fri 1–4pm & 7.30–11pm; Oct–April Mon–Sat same hours, but closed for hols most of Jan.

Joan Marc Plaça del Blanquer 10 ☎971 50 08 04, ⓦ joanmarcrestaurant.com. The local's choice for the best restaurant in town, the excellent, new *Joan Marc*, named after the restaurant's young owner, offers a chic but affordable take on classic Mallorquin dishes. Almost all ingredients and many of the wines are locally-sourced, and the à la carte menu of three to four courses, including a drink, comes in at around €30. Daily 1–4pm & 8–11.30pm.

Sineu

Without doubt, **SINEU**, 14km southeast of Inca, is one of the most interesting of the ancient agricultural towns of Es Pla. Glued to a hill at the geographical centre of the island, with winding, narrow streets cascading down into the valley, the town had obvious strategic advantages for the independent kings of fourteenth-century Mallorca. Jaume II built a royal palace here; his asthmatic successor, Sancho, liked the place for its upland air; and the last of the dynasty, Jaume III, slept in Sineu the night before he was defeated and killed at the battle of Llucmajor by Pedro of Aragón. The new Aragonese monarchs had no need of the Sineu palace, which disappeared long ago, but former pretensions survive in the form of Mallorca's grandest parish church, Nostra Senyora de los Angeles.

The best time to visit Sineu is on Wednesdays, when the cafés around the main square are packed and the town fizzes with one of Mallorca's liveliest fresh produce and clothes **markets** (the only one still licensed to sell large livestock). Replete with live gypsy jazz bands and bushels of garlic and chilli peppers hanging from hooks in the medieval town walls, the market sprawls up and down much of the old part of Seneu.

Nostra Senyora de los Angeles

Sa Plaça • Daily 9.30–4.30pm • €1

A charming medley of old stone buildings that slides into a string of narrow side streets, Sineu's main square, **Sa Plaça** is overlooked by the severe stone facade of **Nostra Senyora de los Angeles**. Built in the thirteenth century, the church was extensively remodelled three hundred years later, but the majestic simplicity of the original Gothic design is still plain to see. At the side, a single-span arch connects with the colossal freestanding **bell tower**, and close by, at the top of the steps, a big, modern and aggressive **statue** of a winged lion – the emblem of the town's patron, St Mark – stands guard, courtesy of Franco's cronies.

ARRIVAL AND INFORMATION   SINEU

By train Sineu is served by regular trains from Palma (hourly; 50min) and several other towns to the east and west. From Sineu train station, it's about 500m west up the

lightly sloping hill to Sa Plaça, the main square; there are no signs, you just follow your nose.

ACCOMMODATION AND EATING

Ca'n Font Sa Plaça 18 ☎ 971 52 02 95, ⓦ canfont.com. Located right on the main square, *Ca'n Font* has just seven fairly basic rooms, and an excellent restaurant in its cellar, with main courses costing around €10–15. Restaurant daily 9am–4pm & 7–11pm. **€52**

Celler Es Grop c/Major 18 ☎ 971 52 01 87. The best place to eat in Sineu is the *Celler Es Grop*, a few metres from Sa Plaça. This friendly place, whose cavernous interior doubles as a wine vault (hence the wooden barrels), serves first-rate Mallorcan meals, with main courses averaging around €12–17. Tues–Sun 9.30am–4pm & 7–11pm; also open Mon on festival days.

Sa Rota d'en Palerm Lloret de Vistalegre ☎ 971 52 11 00, ⓦ sa-rota.com. Around 6km southeast of Sineu, *Sa Rota d'en Palerm* is a charming rural retreat, set in a tastefully restored, eighteenth-century mansion with a large pool and period(ish) guest rooms. Breakfast features home-made products and you can reserve traditional Mallorquin food (much of it from the hotel's own orchards) for dinner beforehand, which will be delivered to your room. To reach the hotel from Sineu, take the road towards Lloret de Vistalegre. About 500m before you reach that village, take the left turn towards Montuïri and after about 800m there's a sign to the hotel on the left; continue for 2.5km to reach the hotel. **€156**

Hotel Son Cleda Plaça Es Fossar 7 ☎ 971 52 10 38, ⓦ hotelsoncleda.com. About 100m from Sa Plaça, in a handsome old mansion, the agreeable *Hotel Son Cleda* has friendly owners, views over the town, free wi-fi for guests, bikes for hire and a well-priced restaurant spilling out onto its front terrace. The hotel has just eight bedrooms, each kitted out in an attractive modern version of traditional Spanish style. **€70**

Petra and around

Nothing very exciting happens in **PETRA**, 11km southeast of Sineu and 10km northwest of Manacor (see p.165), but it was the birthplace of **Junipero Serra**, the eighteenth-century Franciscan friar who played an important role in the settlement of Spanish North America. Serra's missionary endeavours began in 1749 when he landed at Veracruz on the Gulf of Mexico. For eighteen years, Serra thrashed around the more remote parts of Mexico until political machinations back in Europe saved him from obscurity. In 1768, King Carlos III claimed the west coast of the North American continent for Spain and dispatched a small expeditionary force of soldiers and monks north from Mexico. Serra was made leader of the priests, and made the daunting walk from Mexico City to California: almost all of them survived to reach the Pacific Ocean somewhere near the present US–Mexico border in early 1769. Over the next decade, Serra and his small band of priests set about converting the Native Americans of coastal California to the Catholic faith, and established a string of nine missions along the Pacific coast, including San Diego, Los Angeles and San Francisco. Pope John Paul II beatified Serra in 1988.

Junipero Serra Museum

C/Barraca Alta 15 • Mon–Fri 9am–7pm • Donation requested

In the upper part of town, on c/Major, is the chunky church of **Sant Bernat**, behind which – down a narrow side street – lies a modest sequence of majolica panels honouring Junipero Serra's life and missionary work. At the end of the side street, further Serra tributes can be found at the self-effacing **Junipero Serra Museum**, in a pleasant old house where several rooms are devoted to the cult of Serra: the honours paid to him, books written about him, and paintings of him. Another room focuses on Serra's work in California, with photos and models of his foundations. A few doors up the street, at no. 6, is the humble stone **house** where he was born (same hours). The museum and house are sometimes locked, but there are instructions posted outside explaining how to collect the key from the custodian.

Ermita de Nostra Senyora de Bonany

Mon–Sat 10am–5pm • Free

The hilltop **Ermita de Nostra Senyora de Bonany**, about 5km southwest of Petra, offers extensive views over Es Pla. To get there, take the Felanitx road out of Petra and look out for the sign on the edge of the village. The monastery is at the end of a bumpy, 4km-long country lane, and takes its name from events in 1609 when desperate locals gathered here at the chapel to pray for rain. Shortly afterwards, the drought broke and the ensuing harvest was a good one – hence *bon any* ("good year"). The prettiest feature of the complex is the **chapel**, which is approached along an avenue of cypress and palm trees and comes complete with a rose window, twin towers and a little cupola. The monastery's conspicuous stone cross was erected in honour of Junipero Serra, who left here bound for the Americas in 1749.

ARRIVAL AND DEPARTURE

By train Served by 2 trains an hour from Palma (55min) and Manacor (9min), Petra's train station is on the northern edge of town, about 700m from Sant Pere, the large church

PETRA AND AROUND

at the north end of c/Major – and a further 500m or so from the church of Sant Bernat.

ACCOMMODATION AND EATING

Ermita de Nostra Senyora de Bonany, 5km southwest of Petra ☏ 971 82 65 68. The hilltop monastery (see opposite) rents out five simple double rooms: there's one shared bathroom with hot water, and cooking facilities, but you'll have to bring your own food and bedding. **€24**
Miratar Plaça des Caparrot 7 ☏ 971 56 19 20 ⓦ miratar .com. The (comparatively) funky, German-owned *Miratar* bar-cum-restaurant has sofas, a cellar bar and a huge garden next to Sant Pere. Expect a lively atmosphere, with live music, themed evenings and decent Mediterranean food. Mains come in at around €12–15. *Daily except Tues*

11am–4pm & 7pm–when the last drinker leaves.
Hotel Sa Plaça Plaça Ramon Llull 4 ☏ 971 56 16 46, ⓦ petithotelpetra.com. Central Petra's accommodation is limited to the *Hotel Sa Plaça* on the main square, which has just three double rooms with big, old furniture and a mix of whitewashed and rough-stone walls. It is also home to the town's best restaurant, an attractively old-fashioned place, where you can eat traditional Mallorcan cuisine either in the antique-filled interior or on the terrace outside; main courses are a little pricey at around €18. Restaurant 11am–2pm & 7–11pm. **€80**

Gordiola glassworks

Carretera Palma–Manacor Km19 • June–Sept Mon–Sat 9am–7pm, Sun 9am–1.30pm; Oct–May Mon–Sat 9am–6pm, Sun 9am–1.30pm • Free • ⓦ gordiola.com

Two kilometres west of Algaida on the Ma-15, **Gordiola glassworks** occupies a conspicuous castle-like building whose crenellated walls and loggias date from the 1960s. Don't be put off by the herd of tourist coaches outside, for here you can watch highly skilled **glassblowers** in action. Staff will explain the techniques involved – the fusion of silica, soda and lime at a temperature of 1100°C – before encouraging you towards the adjacent **gift shops**. These hold a massive assortment of glass and ceramic wares, from tourist tat to green-tinted **chandeliers** of traditional Mallorcan design costing from €2000 to €20,000 for a fanciful chandelier with coloured glass flowers; more affordably, a simple goblet will cost about €25.

> ### GORDIOLA GLASS
>
> The **Gordiola glassworks** were set up by the Gordiola family in the early eighteenth century, when Gordiola Rigal arrived in Mallorca from the Spanish mainland. The earliest Gordiola pieces were transparent jugs, whose frothy consistency was caused by trapped air bubbles: since the technology was so limited, it was impossible to maintain a consistently high temperature, so the glass could not be clarified or cleared of its imperfections. Aware of these deficiencies, **Bernardo Gordiola** (1720–91), went to Venice to learn from the leading glassmakers of the day, and greatly improved the quality of the glass. He also developed a style of Mallorcan-made jugs decorated with *laticinos*, glass strips wrapped round the object in the Venetian manner. Amongst later Gordiola work, kitchen- and tableware predominate – bottles, vases, jugs and glasses – in a variety of shades, of which green remains the most distinctive.

4

Museu del Vidre

Successive generations of the Gordiola family have accumulated an extraordinary collection of glassware, now exhibited in the **Museu del Vidre**, adjacent to the glassworks, whose thirty-odd cabinets are each devoted to a particular theme or country. Whilst the museum is dusty and neglected and the labelling is poor, there's no denying the quality of the items on display.

As well as a good collection of both early and later examples of Gordiola glassware (see box, p.163) the museum display pieces from all over the world, beginning with finds from **Classical Greece**, the Nile and the Euphrates. There's also an exquisite sample of **early Islamic glassware**, Spanish and Chinese opalescents, and superb **Venetian vases** dating from the seventeenth and eighteenth centuries. More modern items include goblets from Germany and Poland, traditional Caithness crystal from Scotland, and some striking **Swedish Art Nouveau glasswork**.

Puig Randa and around

At 540m, **Puig Randa** is the highest of a slim band of hills that lies between Algaida and Llucmajor. The road to the summit is a well-surfaced but serpentine affair, some 5km long, that starts by climbing through the village of **Randa**, a tiny little place of old stone houses.

Santuari de Nostra Senyora de Cura

Museum Daily 10.30am–1.30pm & 3–6pm • Donation requested • ⓦ www.santuariodecura.com

At the top, Puig Randa is flat enough to accommodate a substantial walled complex, the **Santuari de Nostra Senyora de Cura** (Hermitage of Our Lady of Cura), with Cura being the name of the upper part of the mountain. Entry is through a seventeenth-century portal, but most of the buildings beyond are plain and modern. These are the work of the last incumbents, Franciscan monks who arrived in 1913 after the site had lain abandoned for decades. The scholar and missionary **Ramon Llull** (see p.62) founded the original hermitage in the thirteenth century, and it was here that he prepared his acolytes for their missions to Asia and Africa. Succeeding generations of Franciscans turned the site into a centre of religious learning, and the scholastic tradition was maintained by a grammar school, which finally fizzled out in 1826. The Llull connection makes the monastery an important place of pilgrimage, especially for the **Benedicció del Fruita** (Blessing of the Crops), held on the fourth Sunday after Easter.

Nothing remains of Llull's foundation. The oldest surviving building is the quaintly gabled **chapel**, parts of which date from the 1660s. Situated to the right of the entrance, the chapel is homely and familiar, its narrow, truncated nave spanned by a barrel-vaulted roof. Next door, in the old school, there's a modest **museum** with a collection of ecclesiastical bric-a-brac and a few interesting old photos taken by the Franciscans before they rebuilt the place.

Santuari de Sant Honorat and Santuari de Gràcia

There are two other, less significant sanctuaries on the lower slopes of Puig Randa. Heading back down the hill, past the radio masts, it's a couple of kilometres to the easily missable sharp left turn for the **Santuari de Sant Honorat**, which comprises a tiny church and a few buildings of medieval provenance. Back on the main summit road, a further 1.2km down the hill, the more appealing third and final monastery, the **Santuari de Gràcia**, is approached through a signposted gateway on the left and along a short asphalt road. Founded in the fifteenth century, the whitewashed walls of this tiny sanctuary are tucked underneath a severe cliff face, which throngs with nesting birds. The simple barrel-vaulted church boasts some handsome majolica tiles, but it's the panoramic view of Es Pla's rolling farmland that holds the eye.

PUIG RANDA

Santuari De Cura 07629 Randa ☎971 12 02 60, ⓦ www.santuariodecura.com. The hotel at the Santuari De Cura has 31 sparse double rooms and four suites, all with basic facilities. Four of the rooms come with their own balcony (these cost an extra €20 per person per night). The sanctuary's terrace café offers average food and good coffee – but both are accompanied by superb views out across the island. **€62**

RANDA

★ **Es Reco de Randa** c/Font 21 ☎971 66 09 97, ⓦ esrecoderanda.com. This luxurious but affordable hotel has rooms decorated in traditional Spanish style, with an outdoor swimming pool on a balustraded terrace that offers panoramic views over the plain below. The place gets booked up months in advance in summer, but there are often vacancies out of season, and there's also a delightful restaurant, where the specialities include roast lamb and suckling pig. **€70**

Els Calderers de Sant Joan

Just outside the tiny village of Sant Joan, at the end of a lane 2km north of – and clearly signposted from – the Ma-15 between Montuïri and Vilafranca de Bonany • Daily: April–Oct 10am–6pm; Nov–March 10am–5pm • €8 • ⓦ www.elscalderers.com

Dating mostly from the eighteenth century, the charming country house of **Els Calderers de Sant Joan** bears witness to the wealth and influence once enjoyed by the island's landed gentry – in this case the **Veri family**. The house was the focus of a large estate that produced a mixed bag of agricultural produce. The main cash crop was originally grapes, but the phylloxera aphid destroyed the vineyards and the Veris switched to cereals, then a variety of other crops. At the beginning of the twentieth century the Veris were at the forefront of efforts to modernize Mallorcan agriculture, much to the consternation of some of their more traditional neighbours and workforce.

4

The house

Flanked by a pair of crumpled-looking lions, the entrance to the **house** leads to a sequence of handsome rooms surrounding a cool courtyard with a well. All are kitted out with antique furniture, *objets d'art* and family portraits, from the dainty music room to the hunting room, with assorted stuffed animal heads, and the **master's office**, with big armchairs and a polished desk. You can also see the family's tiny chapel (like every landowning family on the island, the Veris had a live-in priest), and there's more religious material upstairs in the assorted prints that line the walls. Attached to, but separate from, the family house are the living quarters of the *missatge* (farm manager), the barn and the farmworkers' kitchen and eating area. To complete your visit, take a stroll round the **animal pens**, though don't expect to see much farmyard activity in the heat of the day. The animals are breeds traditionally used on Mallorcan farms (notably black pigs, from which Mallorcan *sobrasada* spicy sausage is derived), though they're here to illustrate the past rather than to be of any practical use.

It takes an hour or so to wander round the house and the adjacent animal pens, more if you stop at the simple little **café**, where they serve traditional Mallorcan snacks: the *pa amb oli* (bread rubbed with olive oil) with ham and cheese is delicious.

Manacor

Hometown of the tennis star Rafael Nadal, industrial **MANACOR** declares its business long before you arrive, with vast roadside hoardings promoting its furniture, wrought-iron and artificial pearl factories. On the strength of these, Manacor has risen to become Mallorca's second city, much smaller than Palma, but large enough to have spawned unappetizing suburbs on all sides. Manacor locals, however, insist that Manacor is "un pueblo grande, no una ciudad" (a big town, not a city), and in keeping with this, its **old centre** has been attractively restored, with a string of bustling squares, pretty churches and an impressive convent.

Església Nostra Senyora Verge dels Dolors

Plaça Rector Rubí • Daily 8.30am–12.45pm & 5.30–8pm • Free, but donations requested

Abutting the busy Plaça Rector Rubí is Manacor's principal attraction, the **Església Nostra Senyora Verge dels Dolors**. This sprawling stone church was built on the site of the Moors' main mosque in the thirteenth century, though what you see today is mostly neo-Gothic. The imposing structure juts out from the surrounding architecture, with its thick stone walls and intricately carved bell tower.

Convent de Sant Vicenç Ferrer

Plaça Convent • Mon–Fri 8am–2pm & 5–8pm • Free

From Plaça Rector Rubí, it's a short walk northwest to Manacor's other main sight, the **Convent de Sant Vicenç Ferrer**, a good-looking Baroque complex dating from the late sixteenth century. The beautiful interior courtyard garden of the convent is surrounded on all sides by elegant pillared arches. Guests can scale the two storeys of the convent to look down into the centre quadrangle of the building. The convent is also home to a large library of theological texts.

Perlas Majorica artificial pearl factory

c/Pedro Riche • Oct–June Mon–Fri 9am–7pm, Sat & Sun 10am–1pm; July–Sept Mon–Sat 10am–8pm, Sun 10am–7pm • Free • Ⓦ www.majorica.com

Most visitors skip Manacor's centre and head to the north side of town, where the **Perlas Majorica artificial pearl factory**, signposted as the Pearl Centre, offers a somewhat perfunctory **factory tour** and a general insight into the manufacturing process. The core of the imitation pearl is a glass globule onto which are painted many layers of a glutinous liquid primarily composed of fish scales. Artificial pearls last longer than, and are virtually indistinguishable from, the real thing and are consequently expensive – as you will discover if you visit the showroom.

Museu d'Història de Manacor

Carretera Cales de Mallorca • Mid-June to mid-Sept Mon & Wed–Sat 9.30am–2.30pm & 6–8.30pm; mid-Sept to mid-June Mon & Wed–Sat 10am–2pm & 5–7.30pm, Sun 10.30am–1pm • Free • Ⓦ museu.manacor.org

Located just outside the city centre, in a medieval stone enclosure on the road to Cales de Mallorca, the **Museu d'Història de Manacor** holds a small but interesting collection of archeological finds, especially ceramics. In particular, look out for the well-preserved sixth-century mosaics.

ARRIVAL AND INFORMATION   MANACOR

By train Manacor train station is located on the northwest edge of the old centre, about 1km from Plaça Rector Rubí, and is served by hourly trains to Palma (1hr).

By bus As the terminus of the trainline, Manacor is a jumping-off point for buses to destinations up and down the coast, which leave from just outside the train station, about 1km from Plaça Rector Rubí.

Destinations Artà (6–8 daily; 30min); Cala Rajada (6–8 daily; 50min); Capdepera (6–8 daily; 45min); Colònia de Sant Jordi (2–4 daily; 1hr); Palma (Mon–Sat 10 daily, Sun 5 daily; 45min); Porto Cristo (6–8 daily; 30min); Santanyí (2–4 daily; 50min).

Tourist information The tourist office is about 300m south of Plaça Rector Rubí on Plaça Ramon Llull (Mon–Fri 9.30am–2pm; ☏ 971 84 72 41, Ⓦ manacor.org); they have a useful selection of local information, including a map marking the town's architectural high points.

ACCOMMODATION

Ca'n Guixa Hotel Gerrers 15 ☏ 971 55 36 97, Ⓦ canguixa.es. Centrally located, just metres from the Convent de Sant Vicenç Ferrer, this two-star hotel has just fifteen rooms and a reasonably priced restaurant: main courses cost around €12. **€50**

La Reserva Rotana Camí de Bendris Km3 ☏ 971 84 56 85, Ⓦ reservarotana.com. Four kilometres or so north of town, *La Reserva Rotana* is a luxury resort in a much extended and tastefully modernized old manor house. Facilities include a pool, spa and a nine-hole golf course. The fact that one of the owners is of royal stock is reflected in the opulence of the lodgings: suites are decorated with unusual antiques and there's a top-notch restaurant where the menu is firmly Mediterranean: count on around €60 a head for a full dinner. **€320**

Mayolet Agriturismo Camí de S´Avall Km3 ☎ 971 84 56 85, ⓦ mayolet.com. The secluded and affordable Mayolet Agriturismo has eight rooms (with all mod cons) kitted out in a modern rendition of traditional Spanish style. As well as its own golf course, there's also a large pool and a small terrace overlooking the vineyards. **€150**

EATING AND DRINKING

Bar Mingo Plaça Ramon Llull, next to the tourist information kiosk ☎ 971 55 26 62. For a taste of real Manacor, head to the locals' favourite: the down-to-earth Bar Mingo is well-known for its Bocadillo Mingo (Mingo Sandwich), a delicious but stomach-busting baguette stuffed with lamb, bacon, cheese and onions. Daily 7am–late.

Bor Cafeteria Plaça d'es Convent 7 ☎ 615 34 17 90.

Next to the Convent de Sant Vicenç Ferrer, Bor Cafeteria is a friendly café serving light bites and typical Spanish snacks, including bocadillos and tapas, as well as excellent coffee. Dishes cost around €5–8. Daily 7am–4pm.

Palau Café Plaça Rector Rubí 8 ☎ 971 84 44 92. This café on a busy square is a good place to sample the local speciality, sobrasada de cerdo negro, a spicy pork sausage made from black pig. Daily 7am–4pm.

Artà

The top end of the **Serres de Llevant** mountain range bunches to fill out Mallorca's eastern corner, providing a dramatic backdrop to **ARTÀ**, an ancient hill-town of sun-bleached roofs clustered beneath a castellated chapel-shrine. The town's historic beauty is complemented by a bohemian, artistic atmosphere – art and artists are everywhere – and there's a lively **market** on Plaça del Conqueridor every Tuesday and on Friday evenings. It's a delightful scene, even though at close quarters the town's cobweb of cramped and twisted alleys doesn't quite match the setting until you clamber up to the **Santuari de Sant Salvador**, long a place of pilgrimage and offering wonderous views back over the central plain, Es Pla.

Santuari de Sant Salvador

The ten-minute trek up to Artà's main attraction, the **Santuari de Sant Salvador**, is a must. It's almost impossible to get lost – just keep going upwards: from the foot of the town, follow the main street, c/Ciutat, as it slices across the edge of Plaça del Conqueridor, and then head straight on up to **Plaça de L'Ajuntament**, a leafy little piazza that is home to the town hall. Beyond, a short stroll through streets of gently decaying mansions brings you to the gargantuan parish church of **Sant Salvador**. From this unremarkable pile, steep stone steps and cypress trees lead up the **Via Crucis** (Way of the Cross) to the **santuari**, which, in its present form, dates from the early nineteenth century, though the hilltop has been a place of pilgrimage for much longer. During the Reconquista, Catalan soldiers demolished the Moorish fort that stood here and replaced it with a shrine accommodating an image of the Virgin Mary. This edifice was, in its turn, knocked down in 1820 in a superstitious – and ultimately fruitless – attempt to stop the spread of an epidemic that was decimating the local population. Built a few years later, the present chapel is hardly awe-inspiring inside – the paintings are mediocre and the curious statue of Jesus behind the altar has him smiling as if he has lost his mind – but the views are exquisite, with the picturesque town below and Es Pla stretching away to distant hills.

Ses Païsses

About 800m from the Artà ring road • April–Oct Mon–Sat 10am–12.30pm & 2.30–6pm; Nov–March Mon–Sat 9am–1pm & 2.30–5pm • €2 • ⓦ www.tourism-mallorca.com/sespaisses

On the southern peripheries of Artà lie the substantial and elegiacally rustic remains of the Talayotic village of **Ses Païsses**. To get there, walk east from c/Ciutat along the main through-road and watch for the signposted – and well-surfaced – country lane

4

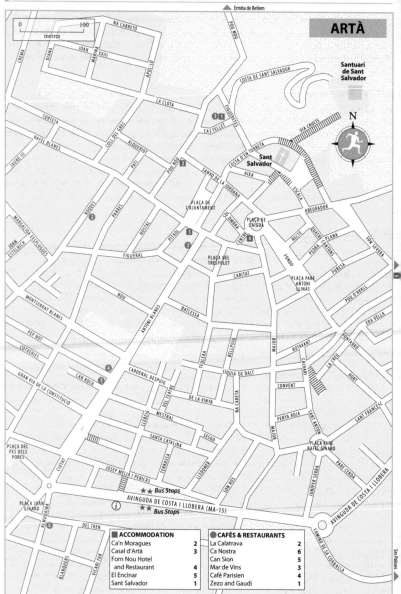

■ ACCOMMODATION		● CAFÉS & RESTAURANTS	
Ca'n Moragues	2	La Calatrava	2
Casal d'Artà	3	Ca Nostra	6
Forn Nou Hotel		Can Sion	5
and Restaurant	4	Mar de Vins	3
El Encinar	5	Café Parisien	4
Sant Salvador	1	Zezo and Gaudi	1

on the right. A clear footpath explores every nook and cranny of the site, and its numbered markers are thoroughly explained in the English-language **leaflet** available at the entrance.

Tucked away in a grove of olive, carob and holm-oak trees, the prehistoric village is entered through a **monolithic gateway**, whose heavyweight jambs and lintels interrupt the Cyclopean walls that still encircle the site. These outer remains date from the second phase of the Talayotic culture (c.1000–800 BC), when the emphasis was on consolidation and defence; in places, the walls still stand at their original size, around 3.5m high and 3m thick. Beside the gate, there's also a modern plinth erected in honour of Miquel Llobera, a local writer who penned romantic verses about the place. Beyond the gateway, the central **talayot** is from the first Talayotic phase (c.1300–1000 BC), its shattered ruins flanked by the foundations of several rooms of later date and uncertain purpose. Experts believe the horseshoe-shaped room was used, at least towards the end of the Talayotic period, for cremations, whilst the three rectangular rooms were probably living quarters. In the rooms, archeologists discovered iron objects and ceramics imported from elsewhere in the Mediterranean. Some of them were perhaps brought back from the Punic Wars (264–146 BC) by mercenaries – the skills of Balearic stone slingers were highly prized by the Carthaginians, and it's known that several hundred accompanied Hannibal and his elephants over the Alps in 218 BC.

ARRIVAL AND INFORMATION   ARTÀ

By bus Buses to Artà stop beside the Ma-15 on the southern edge of the town centre. From the bus stops, it's a couple of hundred metres west to the foot of the short main street, c/Ciutat.

Destinations Cala Rajada (Mon–Sat 8–18 daily, Sun 6–8 daily; 15min); Capdepera (Mon–Sat 8–17 daily, Sun 6–8 daily; 10min); Manacor train station (6–8 daily; 30min);

Palma (Mon–Sat 4–5 daily, Sun 2 daily; 1hr 20min); Platja de Canyamel (May–Oct Mon–Sat 1–3 daily; 20min).

Tourist information The town tourist office (Mon–Fri 10am–2pm; ☎ 971 83 69 81) is in the old train station on the western reaches of the Ma-15. They have a useful selection of local information, including a free town map and an illustrated heritage trail leaflet.

ACCOMMODATION

4

TOWN CENTRE
Ca'n Moragues Pou Nou 12 ☎ 971 82 95 09, ⓦ canmoragues.com. Decorated in calming shades of yellow and cream, some of this hotel's eight comfortable rooms overlook a courtyard garden with a small swimming pool and sauna – the two ground-floor rooms give directly onto the garden, the others are upstairs. Watch out for the two pet turtles, who are very willing to share your breakfast. **€90**

Casal d'Artà c/Rafael Blanes 19 ☎ 971 82 91 63, ⓦ casaldarta.de. Overlooking Plaça de L'Ajuntament, the *Casal d'Artà* occupies an immaculately restored, three-storey former grandee's mansion dating from the 1930s. It still has much of the original decor – stained glass, wooden ceilings, decorative ironwork, tiled walls and antique furniture, including several four-poster beds. There's a charming sun terrace on the roof too, and the hotel's owner, Karin, is a font of local knowledge. **€91**

Forn Nou Hotel and Restaurant C/Centre 7 ☎ 971 82 92 46, ⓦ fornou-arta.com. Newly opened in 2012 right in the centre of town, *Forn Nou* is petite, chic and stylish. The rooms are finished to a high standard, and the ground floor houses an excellent restaurant (main courses around €15).

Owner Toni is an attentive and friendly host and the hotel also boasts the best roof-terrace bar in town. **€100**

★ **Hotel Sant Salvador** c/Castellet 7 ☎ 971 82 95 55, ⓦ santsalvador.com. Once a grand *Modernista* mansion, the *Sant Salvador* is now a luxury hotel with an interior decorated in vibrant Almodóvar colours. Six of the eight rooms – each decorated in a different style and some with jacuzzis – have balconies overlooking the town. There are two top-notch restaurants (see p.170); live music is performed in the evenings from May–October, and the hotel organizes beach excursions, picnics and other events for guests. **€165**

OUT OF TOWN
El Encinar Carretera Artà-Son Servera (Ma-4041) ☎ 971 18 38 60 or ☎ 639 38 59 74, ⓦ elencinardearta .com. This handsomely restored and immaculately maintained country estate occupies an ideal spot 'twixt town and beach, about 5km from Artà on the Ma-4041 road to Son Servera. The eleven traditionally decorated rooms, sited in an airily modernized old manor house, ooze atmosphere, and the facilities include a pool, restaurant and lush garden. Closed Nov–Feb. **€105**

EATING AND DRINKING

Café Parisien c/Ciutat 18 ☎ 971 83 54 40, ⓦ cafeparisien .es. A bohemian little place with distressed sea-blue furniture and a shaded courtyard garden at the back. Their tasty and reasonably priced soups, salads and Italian-influenced dishes are based on what is fresh in the market. Daily 9am–late.

Ca Nostra c/Des Tren 1 ☎ 971 83 62 93, ⓦ ca-nostra.es. A down-to-earth restaurant close to the train station that is a local favourite for lunch. Main courses cost between €9 and €12, and the grilled fish is particularly good. Daily 9am–4pm & 6.30–11.30pm.

A WALK TO ERMITA DE BETLEM

Hidden away in the hills 10km northwest of Artà, the **Ermita de Betlem** is a remote and minuscule hermitage founded in 1805. In itself, the *ermita* is not a major pull, but the scenery hereabouts is lovely. The route begins on the north side of Artà, but the start is poorly signed and tricky to find: aim for c/Figueretes, go past the *Hotel Sant Salvador* and then follow the signs. The road's rough surface and snaking course make for a difficult drive, so an alternative is to **walk** – reckon on five or six hours for the return trip. The first portion is an easy stroll up along the wooded valley of the **Torrent des Cocons**, but then – after about 3km – the road squeezes through the narrowest of defiles, with the hills rising steeply on either side. Beyond, the road begins to climb into the hills of the Serres de Llevant – here the **Massís d'Artà** – until, some 3km after the defile, a signposted turn signals the start of the strenuous part of the journey. Here, the track wriggles for 4km up and down the steep hillside before finally reaching the *ermita* at the end of a cypress-lined path.

Amongst the huddle of old stone buildings that comprise the hermitage, the **church** is perhaps the most interesting structure, its ponderous frame holding crude religious paintings on the walls and a poor-quality fresco on the ceiling. The *ermita's* only facility is a small shop (with uncertain opening hours) that sells religious trinkets and postcards, but there's more than enough compensation in the panoramic views down along the coast and across the Badía d'Alcúdia. A hiking trail leads down from the *ermita* to the bay, ending up on the road just to the east of Colònia de Sant Pere (see below), but this is a difficult hike and you'll need to be properly equipped.

EATING AND DRINKING

Sa Tafona de Son Fang Ctra. Ermita Betlem ☎ 971 82 95 91, ⓦ satafona.com. If you haven't taken your own picnic, make a pit-stop at the restaurant *Sa Tafona de Son Fang*, 3km or so out from Artà. In this galleried *finca*, which once housed an ancient oil press (*tafona*), you'll find a good range of Mallorcan dishes – they're particularly proud of their charcoal-grilled specialities. Daily except Wed 10am–4pm & 7–11.30pm.

Can Sion c/Cuitat 22 ☎ 971 82 92 75, ⓦ restaurante-cansion.com. Formerly called *Es Passeig*, this is a good-quality restaurant with a traditional menu featuring Mallorcan cooking in an up-to-the-minute setting. Main courses hover around €15. Daily 8am–3pm and 7–11.30pm.

La Calatrava c/Ses Roques 13 ☎ 971 83 66 63, ⓦ lacalatrava.com. Probably Artà's best place for fine dining, *La Calatrava* is situated in an expansive, beautifully decorated townhouse in the centre of town. Housing resident artists in the studios on the upper floors, *La Calatrava* exudes bohemian style. The food is excellent too. with main courses around €15–25. Daily from 7pm.

Mar de Vins c/Antoni Blanes 34 ☎ 662 03 04 60. Situated right in the pedestrianized centre of the town, *Mar de Vins* is a brightly coloured, friendly little bar ideal for midday tapas and a glass of wine. The small interior of the restaurant opens onto a large patio area that is perfect for whiling away a hot afternoon. Daily 9am–late.

Zezo and Gaudi Hotel Sant Salvador c/Castellet 7 ☎ 971 82 95 55, ⓦ santsalvador.com. Stylish twin restaurants in the *Hotel Sant Salvador* (see p.169), both of which serve great Mediterranean cuisine with a modern twist. *Zezo* offers gourmet dining, with meals around €55 a head, while *Gaudi* offers an equally enticing, but more economical, menu featuring main courses for around €10–15. *Gaudi* has tables indoors or outside on the terrace overlooking the swimming pool and gardens. Daily 1–3pm & 7.30–10pm.

Colònia de Sant Pere

COLÒNIA DE SANT PERE is a downbeat resort and one-time fishing village nestled beside the Badía d'Alcúdia, with the stern escarpments of the Massís d'Artà for a backdrop. Founded in 1881, the town is no more than a few blocks wide, its plain, low-rise modern buildings set behind a pocket-sized sandy beach, and although a flurry of recent building work has festooned the village with villa complexes, at least local planning laws prohibit the construction of houses more than two storeys high. Indeed, Colònia de Sant Pere is one of the only coastal

MARKET, SINEU (P.161) >

settlements in this part of Mallorca to have actively avoided mass development and tourism in recent decades. It's all very low-key and laid-back – perfect for families with young children – and this, along with the setting, is its charm as a day-trip destination or for a longer stay, though accommodation is thin on the ground unless you've booked a villa.

ACCOMMODATION AND EATING   COLÒNIA DE SANT PERE

Blau Mari Mari C/Es Viver 28 ☎971 58 94 07. On the seafront, one of the best choices for fresh fish is a long-established favourite, the *Blau Mari*. It specializes in seafood and paellas – and there's even a tank from which you can select your own live lobster. March–Oct daily 11am–4pm & 7–11.30pm.

Café & Restaurant Club Nautic Passeig de la Mar ☎971 58 90 09, ⓦdelnautico.com. On the seafront, with a terrace overlooking the harbour, the *Café & Restaurant Club Nautic* serves excellent paellas and *bacalao al ajo confitado* (salt cod with garlic confit). Main courses are quite pricey at €15–25. Daily 9am–11.30pm.

Es Vivers Paseo del Mar 25 ☎971 58 94 78, ⓦesvivers.com. At the low-key *Es Vivers* you can enjoy good-value salads, pastas and fresh seafood whilst sitting in the shade of tamarisk trees. It's also *the* place to go in the afternoons to sample the delicious home-made fruit flans (apple, lemon, apricot, strawberry) and cheesecakes. Feb & March daily 11am–6pm; April–Sept daily 11am–11.30pm; Oct daily except Tues 11am–10.30pm.

Hotel Rocamar c/Sant Mateu 9 ☎971 82 85 03, ⓦhotelrocamar.com. Colònia de Sant Pere is light on accommodation, with the only appealing central choice being the *Hotel Rocamar*, a bright, homely place with a rooftop terrace just in from the seashore. **€60**

Capdepera

Spied across the valley from the west or south, the crenellated walls dominating **CAPDEPERA**, a tiny village 8km east of Artà and 3km west of Cala Rajada, look too pristine to be true. Yet the triangular fortifications are genuine enough, built in the fourteenth century by the Mallorcan king Sancho to protect the coast from pirates. The village, snuggled below the walls, contains a pleasant medley of old houses, its slender main square, **Plaça de L'Orient**, acting as a prelude to the steep steps up to the lovely medieval fortress. The best time to visit is during the three-day **medieval market**, held in the third week of May. The locals dress up in medieval costumes and the entire town is jam-packed with people sampling local food, crafts and music.

Castell de Capdepera

Daily: April–Sept 9am–7.30pm; Oct–March 9am–4.45pm • €2

The steps that lead up from Capdepera's main square are the most pleasant way to reach the **Castell de Capdepera**, but you can also follow the signs and drive up narrow c/Major. Flowering cactuses give the fortress a special allure in late May and June, but it's a beguiling place at any time, with more than 400m of walls equipped with a parapet walkway and sheltering attractive terraced gardens. At the top of the fortress, **Nostra Senyora de la Esperança** (Our Lady of Good Hope) is the quaintest of Gothic churches, its aisle-less, vaulted frame furnished with outside steps that lead up behind the bell gable to a flat roof, from where the views are simply superb.

ARRIVAL AND INFORMATION   CAPDEPERA

By bus Plenty of buses pass through Capdepera, pulling in at c/Travessia Baltazar Coves.
Destinations Cala Rajada (Mon–Sat 8–17 daily, Sun 6–8 daily; 5min); Manacor train station (6–8 daily; 45min);

Palma (2–6 daily; 1hr 30min).
Tourist information The small but helpful tourist office is in the centre of town at Cuitat 22 (Mon–Fri 8am–3pm; ☎971 55 64 79).

ACCOMMODATION AND EATING

CAPDEPERA
La Fragua c/Es Pla d'en Coset 3 ☎971 56 50 50.

Capdepera has several excellent restaurants, the best being *La Fragua*, an intimate, romantic spot where they serve steak and other grilled specialities. It's located just off Plaça de L'Orient, on the way up towards the castle steps. Daily except Tues 11am–4pm & 7–11.30pm.

Pizzeria Kikinda Plaça de L'Orient ☎971 56 30 14 Several run-of-the-mill cafés line up on the town's main square – this is the best, serving good-value pizzas, pastas and salads at around €9–10. The outside seating provides an ideal spot for people-watching while you eat. Daily except Mon 2–11pm.

CALA MESQUIDA

★ **Son Barbassa** Cala Mesquida 07580 ☎971 56 57 76, ⊛sonbarbassa.com. There's nowhere to stay in Capdepera itself, but it's only about 3.5km north on the Cala Mesquida road to a first-rate *finca*, *Son Barbassa*, a carefully restored sixteenth-century rural estate complete with watchtower. There are twelve stylish rooms here as well as a pool with beautiful views over the valley and back across to Capdepera. They also have a very good restaurant that uses fresh vegetables from their own garden. €108

Cala Rajada

Awash with cafés, bars and hotels, vibrant **CALA RAJADA** lies on the southerly side of a stubby headland in the northeast corner of Mallorca. The town centre, an unassuming patchwork of low-rise modern buildings, is hardly prepossessing, but it is neat and trim, and around the town is a wild and rocky coastline, all backed by pine-clad hills and sheltering a series of delightful **beaches**.

Cala Rajada was once a fishing village, but there's little evidence of this today, and the **harbour** is now used by pleasure boats and overlooked by restaurants. From the harbour, **walkways** extend along the headland's south coast. To the southwest, past the busiest part of town, it takes about ten to fifteen minutes to stroll round to **Platja Son Moll**, a slender arc of sand overlooked by Goliath-like hotels.

4

Platja Cala Agulla

North of Cala Rajada, c/L'Agulla crosses the promontory to hit the north coast at **Platja Cala Agulla**. The approach road, some 2km of tourist tackiness, is of little appeal, but the beach, a vast curve of bright golden sand, is big enough to accommodate hundreds of bronzing pectorals with plenty of space to spare. The further you walk – and there are signed and shaded footpaths through the pine woods to assist you – the more privacy you'll get.

ARRIVAL AND INFORMATION   **CALA RAJADA**

By bus Most buses to Cala Rajada stop a short walk from the town centre, near the intersection of c/Juan Sebastian Elcano and c/Castellet. The town centre is easy to explore on foot, but for the outlying beaches you'll probably need a local bus. In summer useful services run from the bus stops along c/Castellet, a short distance north of Plaça dels Pins, to Cala Agulla, Platja de Canyamel and the Coves d'Artà. Destinations Artà (Mon–Sat 8–18 daily, Sun 6–8 daily; 15min); Capdepera (Mon–Sat 8–17 daily, Sun 6–8 daily;

5min); Coves d'Artà (May–Oct Mon–Sat 8 daily; 30min); Manacor train station (6–8 daily; 50min); Palma (2–6 daily; 1hr 35min); Platja de Canyamel (May–Oct Mon–Sat 12 daily; 15min).

By boat Cruceros Creuers (☎971 81 06 00, ⊛cruceroscreuers.com) offers a wide range of summer boat trips along the east coast, linking Cala Rajada with several resorts, but principally Porto Cristo (1–2 daily; €22 return).

THE ROUTE TO CALA GAT

It's a pleasant ten-minute stroll east from Cala Rajada harbour to **Cala Gat**, a narrow cove beach tucked tight up against the steep, wooded coastline. There's a beach bar, and at times it gets decidedly crowded – but it's an attractive spot all the same. Above the footpath to Cala Gat you can glimpse the gardens of the **Palau Joan March** (no public access), a lavish mansion built in 1916 for the eponymous tobacco baron (see p.57), who was to become the richest man in Franco's Spain. On the landward side of the gardens, c/Elíonor Servera, which begins in the town centre, twists steeply up through the pine woods to reach, after about 1km, the bony headlands and lighthouse of the **Cap de Capdepera**, Mallorca's most easterly point. The views out along the coast are a treat.

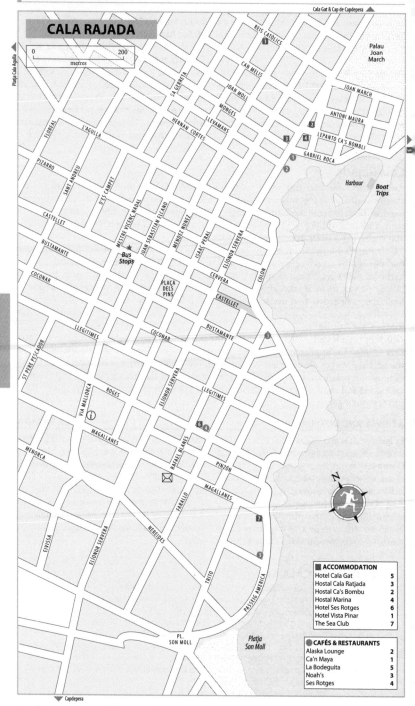

Cala Gat & Cap de Capdepera

CALA RAJADA

0   200
metres

REIS CATÒLICS
Palau
Joan
March
CAN MELIS
JOAN MOLL
MONGES
LLEVAMANS
S'A GERRETA
HERNAN CORTES
FLOREAL
L'AGULLA
JOAN MARCH
ANTONI MAURA
LEPANTO CA'S BOMBLI
GABRIEL ROCA
PIZARRO
SANT ANDREU
D'ES CAMPET
CASTELLET
BUSTAMANTE
MESTRE VICENÇ NADAL
JUAN SEBASTIAN ELCANO
MENDEZ NUÑEZ
ISAAC PERAL
ELIONOR SERVERA
COLON
CERVERA
CASTELLET
COCONAR
Bus
Stops
PLAÇA
DELS
PINS
LLEGITIMES
COCONAR
BUSTAMANTE
ST PERE PESCADOR
VIA MALLORCA
ROGES
ELIONOR SERVERA
LLEGITIMES
MAGALLANES
MENORCA
RAFAEL BLANES
PINZON
FARALLO
MAGALLANES
EIVISSA
ELIONOR SERVERA
NEREIDES
TRITO
PASSIG AMERICA
PL.
SON MOLL
Platja
Son Moll

Harbour
Boat
Trips

N

Platja Cala Agulla

Capdepera

■ ACCOMMODATION

Hotel Cala Gat	5
Hostal Cala Ratjada	3
Hostal Ca's Bombu	2
Hostal Marina	4
Hotel Ses Rotges	6
Hotel Vista Pinar	1
The Sea Club	7

● CAFÉS & RESTAURANTS

Alaska Lounge	2
Ca'n Maya	1
La Bodeguita	5
Noah's	3
Ses Rotges	4

Tourist information The tourist office is located at no. 36, Via Mallorca (Mon–Fri 9am–1.30pm & 2.30–5.30pm, Sat 9.30am–1.30pm; March–Oct also Sun 10am–1.30pm; ☎ 971 56 30 33), and can supply an excellent range of local information including restaurant lists, bus schedules, details of car and bicycle rental firms, and free town maps marked with all accommodation. They also sell a popular, though not very detailed, pamphlet on local hiking routes.

ACCOMMODATION

The only real problem with Cala Rajada is finding **accommodation**. The town is a favourite German package resort and in high season you'll be lucky to find a vacant room: the best place to try is among the *hostales* and hotels dotted around the busy commercial streets just up from the harbour. In the shoulder season, it's worth trying one of the popular hotels on the seafront. All the places listed here are closed between November and March.

Hotel Cala Gat Cala Gat s/n ☎ 971 56 31 66, ⓦ hotelcalagat.com. Unassuming, fairly traditional hotel in a secluded location in the pine woods above the beautiful beach of Cala Gat. Many rooms have sea-facing balconies. Closed Nov–March. €150

Hostal Cala Ratjada Corner of c/Monges at c/Elíonor Servera 79 ☎ 971 56 32 02, ⓦ hostalcalaratjada.com. Good-value family-run hostal, close to the port, set in a pleasant white-stucco building with rustic touches. The rooms may be minimal and small, but they are also some of the cheapest in town. Closed Nov–March. €38

Hostal Ca's Bombu c/Elíonor Servera 86 ☎ 971 56 32 03, ⓦ casbombu.com. Homely place kitted out in a rustic style with lots of dark wood, a pool and large bar. It's great value, too. Closed Nov–March. €40

Hostal Marina c/Elíonor Servera 96 ☎ 971 56 34 91, ⓦ hostalmarina.com. *Hostal Marina* is an economical and friendly choice. Popular with German tourists, it has spartan but clean and perfectly adequate budget rooms. The bar downstairs is always lively, and has free wi-fi. Closed Nov–March. €40

Hotel Ses Rotges c/Rafael Blanes 21 ☎ 971 56 31 08, ⓦ sesrotges.com. Delightful three-star establishment in an elegantly restored antique villa. With 23 rooms, it's in a good location just out of earshot of the main square. Closed Nov–March. €120

Hotel Vista Pinar c/Reis Catòlics 11 ☎ 971 56 37 51, ⓦ hotelvistapinar.com. Large, adequate and very affordable two-star hotel with ninety rooms – most with balconies – and its own swimming pool. The rooms are simple but comfortable, with all the usual facilities, and the hotel is just 300m from the beach at Cala Gat and 100m from the port. Closed Nov–March. €45

The Sea Club Avgda America, 27 ☎ 971 56 33 10 ⓦ theseaclub.es. Known affectionately as "little Gibraltar" or "Chelsea Arts Club sur Med", *The Sea Club* is a down-to-earth family-run resort popular with English visitors. One of the first hotel resorts on this stretch of the coast, *The Sea Club* has maintained a warm, relaxed family atmosphere, with guests dining en masse on the front veranda each evening before retiring to the convivial poolside bar to party. Book early, as repeat custom keeps the place full for the most of the high season. Closed Nov–March. €150

EATING AND DRINKING

Cala Rajada heaves with **restaurants**, **cafés and bars**, particularly on and around the seafront and c/Elíonor Servera, the main boulevard. Competition is fierce, but most restaurants have almost identical menus with something German – sauerkraut and sausages, for instance – plus a range of Spanish dishes. Naturally, seafood is a good option in the better restaurants around the port.

Alaska Lounge c/Elíonor Servera 74 ☎ 971 81 96 14. Right on the harbourfront, this modern restaurant-cum-bar offers great views from its terrace. Mains, using mainly organic ingredients, come in at around €18. Daily 2pm till late.

Ca'n Maya c/Elíonor Servera 80 ☎ 971 56 40 35, ⓦ canmaya.com. First choice for seafood, this upmarket place serves up superb main courses around €20–25 – try their first-rate paella and *arroz marinera*. Daily except Mon 11am–4pm & 7–11.30pm.

La Bodeguita Passeig America 14 ☎ 971 81 90 62. Inviting restaurant located in an old villa near the seashore on the southern side of the resort. Huge plates piled with meats, pastas and salads with prices ranging from €15–25. There's a leafy garden too. Daily 9am–midnight.

Noah's Passeig America 2 ☎ 971 81 81 25. Just beyond the main tourist traps, this café-bar serves up very decent mixed platters and is good for fresh pasta-salads; it also has the occasional DJ on the weekend. Happy hour lasts from 5–8pm, during which time you can enjoy one of Noah's signature premium gin and tonics. Daily 9am till late.

Ses Rotges c/Rafael Blanes 21 ☎ 971 56 31 08. A high-end, high-standard restaurant, serving a broadly French menu in immaculate surroundings; with main courses averaging about €30, though, it's very pricey. Mon–Sat 7–11pm.

Coves d'Artà

Daily: May–Oct 10am–6pm; Nov–April 10am–5pm; tours every 30min • €12 (free for children under 6) • ⓦ cuevasdearta.com • Buses (May–Oct Mon–Sat 8 daily) run to the caves from Cala Rajada (30min) and Capdepera (10min); daily boat trips run here from Font de Sa Cala (€12) and Cala Rajada (April–Oct; €12 not including admission)

The succession of coves, caves and beaches notching the seashore between Cala Rajada and Cala Millor begins promisingly with the memorable **Coves d'Artà** (often in Castilian "Cuevas de Artà"), reached along the first major turning off the main coastal road (here the Ma-4040) just south of Capdepera. This is the pick of the numerous cave systems of eastern Mallorca, its sequence of cavernous chambers, studded with stalagmites and stalactites, extending 450m into the rock face. Artificial lighting exaggerates the bizarre shapes of the caverns and their accretions, especially in the **Hall of Flags**, where stalactites up to 50m long hang in the shape of partly unfurled flags. Exiting the caves, you're greeted with a stunning view, courtesy of a majestic stairway that leads up to a yawning hole high in the cliffs above the bay. The place has had a chequered history. During the Reconquista, a thousand Moorish refugees from Artà were smoked out of the caves to be slaughtered by Catalan soldiers waiting outside. In the nineteenth century, touring the caves for their scientific interest became fashionable – Jules Verne was particularly impressed – and, today, tour guides give a complete geological description of the cave in several languages (including English) as you wander the illuminated abyss. Allow about an hour for the visit – more if there's a queue.

Platja de Canyamel

PLATJA DE CANYAMEL – not to be confused with the tedious Costa de Canyamel *urbanització* immediately to the south – is a cove resort whose smart modern villas are draped around a pine-backed sandy **beach** in sight of a pair of rocky headlands. The *platja* is situated about 1km south of the Coves d'Artà and makes an agreeable spot for a few hours' sunbathing. There are several inviting **restaurants** plus a number of **hotels**, though they're usually block-booked by German tour operators.

ARRIVAL AND DEPARTURE

PLATJA DE CANYAMEL

By bus From May to October, local buses link Platja de Canyamel with Cala Rajada and Capdepera (Mon–Sat 10 daily) and Artà (Mon–Sat 1–3 daily).

ACCOMMODATION AND EATING

Can Simoneta Carretera Artà-Canyamel Km 8 ☎ 971 81 61 10, ⓦ cansimoneta.com. Attractively sited on a cliff with incredible sea views, the deluxe, rural *Can Simoneta* is located between the *platja* and the *urbanització* – just follow signs from the main roundabout. This tranquil, luxurious hotel is divided between two nineteenth-century buildings and elegantly decorated in white and beige tints, with all the mod cons you could want. Adults only. **€370**

Laguna c/Costa Y Llobera 16 ☎ 971 84 11 50. Your only vague chance of finding a room on spec is at the *Laguna*, an attractive two-star hotel plonked right on the beach. Closed Nov–April. **€70**

Porto Cristo and around

Low-key **PORTO CRISTO** prospered in the early days of the tourist boom, sprouting a string of hotels and *hostales*, but it's since been eclipsed by larger nearby mega-resorts. Indeed, the jam of tourist buses clogging the town's streets are usually on their way to the nearby **Coves del Drac** (see p.178), and few of their occupants actually stay here. Consequently, this is one of the few places on the east coast where you're likely to find a room in July and August.

Porto Cristo's origins are uncertain, but it was definitely in existence by the thirteenth century, when it served as the fishing harbour and seaport of Manacor – it boasts one

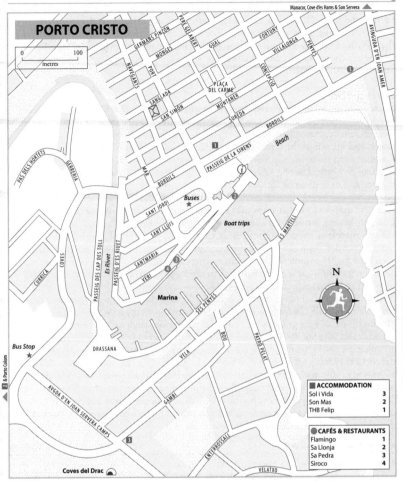

Manacor, Cove d'es Hams & Son Servera

PORTO CRISTO

ACCOMMODATION	
Sol i Vida	3
Son Mas	2
THB Felip	1

CAFÉS & RESTAURANTS	
Flamingo	1
Sa Llonja	2
Sa Pedra	3
Siroco	4

of the most sheltered harbours on the east coast. Nothing remains of the medieval settlement, however, and today the **town centre**, which climbs the hill behind the harbour, consists of high-sided terraced buildings mostly dating from the late nineteenth and early twentieth centuries. The town has its own **beach**, which is fine enough for sunbathing – though the swimming isn't great – and it's handily located

PORTO CRISTO'S REPUBLICAN LANDING

In August 1936, Porto Cristo was the site of a **Republican landing** designed to capture Mallorca from the Falangists. The campaign was a fiasco: the Republicans disembarked more than seven thousand men and quickly established a long and deep bridgehead, but their commanders, surprised by their initial success, didn't know what to do next. The Nationalists counterattacked and, supported by the Italian air force, soon had the Republicans dashing back to the coast. Barcelona Radio put on a brave face, announcing, "The heroic Catalan columns have returned from Mallorca after a magnificent action. Not a single man suffered from the effects of the embarkation."

right in the centre, tucked inside the **harbour**, a narrow V-shaped channel entered between a pair of rocky promontories. The harbour accommodates a marina and lies at the mouth of the oily-green River Es Rivet, which forms the town centre's southern perimeter. There's also a weekly **market** every Sunday (9am–1pm) at Passeig de la Sirena, next to the beach.

Coves del Drac

Daily: April–Oct 10am–5pm; Nov–March 10.45am–3.30pm; hour-long guided tours every hour or 90 min • €13.50 • W cuevasdeldrach
.com • Organized bus tours arrive directly at the Coves Del Drac, and there are four direct buses from Palma daily (1hr 10min); alternatively,
take a public bus to Porto Cristo (see below), then it's a 15min walk south across the river to the caves

Locals had known of the **Coves del Drac** ("Dragon's Caves" or "Cuevas del Drac" in Castilian, and sometimes spelled "Drach") for hundreds of years, but it was the Austrian archduke Ludwig Salvator (see p.107) who recruited French geologists to explore and map them in 1896. The French discovered four huge chambers that penetrated the coast's limestone cliffs for around 2km and were adorned with the eccentric shapes of myriad **stalactites and stalagmites**. As the leader of the French team, Edouard Martel, wrote, "On all sides, everywhere, in front and behind, as far as the eye can see, marble cascades, organ pipes, lace draperies, pendants of multi-faceted gems hang suspended from the walls and roof." Since the French exploration, the caves have been thoroughly commercialized, with a giant car park, ticket office and restaurant, behind which lurk the gardens that lead to the flight of steps down to the caves – be prepared to queue, especially at weekends.

Inside the caves, rainwater has dripped and drizzled through the soft limestone to create innumerable concretions of calcium carbonate – many of which are illuminated. The multilingual tour guides shunt you past formations such as "the Buddha", "the Pagoda" and "the Snowy Mountain" as well as magnificent icicle-like stalactites, some of which are snowy white, whilst others have picked up hints of orange and red from the rocks they hang off. The *tour de force* is the larger of the two **subterranean lakes**, at 177m long, 40m wide and 30m deep one of the largest underground lakes in the world. The lake's translucent waters flicker with reflected colours, while a small group of musicians drifts by in boats (performances usually begin on the hour). At the end of the tour, some visitors leave on foot, but you can also take a brief boat ride (included in the admission price) across part of the lake.

ARRIVAL AND DEPARTURE	**PORTO CRISTO AND AROUND**

By bus The main coastal road passes along Porto Cristo's seafront, and several long-distance buses, principally from Palma, terminate in the centre close to the harbour and the beach.

Destinations Arta (3 daily; 1hr); Cala Mondragó (3 daily; 40min); Inca (2 daily; 50min); Manacor train station (6–8 daily; 30min); Palma (May–Oct Mon–Sat 8 daily, Sun 3 daily; 1hr 10min).

INFORMATION AND ACTIVITIES

Tourist information The tourist office is close to the beach on c/Moll (Mon–Fri 9am–3pm; ☎971 81 51 03, W manacor.org), and can provide useful maps of the town and neighbouring resorts.

Boat trips Cruceros Creuers (☎971 81 06 00, W cruceroscreuers.com) organizes a wide range of

summer boat trips along the east coast, linking Porto Cristo with a string of resorts, including Cala Rajada (2 daily; €22 return). They also offer 90min scoots round Porto Cristo harbour in glass-bottomed boats from May to Oct (7 daily; €16).

ACCOMMODATION

Sol i Vida Avgda d'en Joan Servera Camps 11 ☎971 82 10 74, W solivida.es. A neat and trim two-star, family-run hotel in a pleasant wooded location on a residential street, metres from the Coves del Drac. It has twenty rooms with free wi-fi and a reasonable restaurant. **€70**

Son Mas Camí de Son Mas s/n ☎971 55 87 55, W sonmas.com. Owned by an architect and located in a cleverly renovated old farm, this seventeenth-century *finca* offers sixteen stylish suites, a climatized pool, sauna, spa and restaurant. To get there, follow the Ma-4014 towards

Porto Colom for 5km and turn right into the Camí de Son Mas de la Marina; the hotel is signposted from here. **€305**
THB Felip c/Bordils 41 📞 971 82 07 50, 🌐 thbhotels .com. Four-star chain hotel in a big old balconied

building overlooking the beach. The interior has been revamped in modern style and the rooms are neat and trim – ask for a harbour view. The lobby bar offers great views of the bay. **€100**

EATING AND DRINKING

Flamingo c/Bordils s/n 📞 971 82 22 59. Cream of the gastronomic crop, with excellent views over the town, beach and port, the *Flamingo* serves up delicious home-made paellas and seafood (especially the steamed mussels). The cartoon decor is odd but charming, and the owner, Pepe, is a gruff but affectionate giant of a man who welcomes you with open arms. Daily 10am–midnight.
Sa Llonja Passeig Moll 1 📞 971 82 28 59 or 📞 620 01 61 20. Right on the harbourfront near the tourist office, *Sa Llonja* is a second good choice if you can't get into *Flamingo*

and specializes in chargrilled seafood. Daily 9am–11.30pm.
Siroco c/Veri 📞 971 82 24 44. A highly recommended and inexpensive spot with a cosy terrace that abuts the harbour a few metres south of the beach. The service is very good, and the paella is as excellent as the tranquil seaview. Daily except Mon 9am–11pm.
Sa Pedra c/Veri 4 📞 971 82 09 32, 🌐 restaurantsapedra .com. An upmarket place that serves up delicious seafood on a terrace overlooking the harbour: a typical main course will set you back around €15–25. Daily noon–4pm & 7–11pm.

Porto Colom

PORTO COLOM is a burgeoning resort that straggles around a long and irregular bay some 20km south of Porto Cristo. Originally a fishing village supplying the needs of the neighbouring town of Felanitx, the port boomed throughout most of the nineteenth century thanks to the export trade in wine to France. The good times, however, ended when the phylloxera aphid wiped out the island's vines in the 1870s and the villagers returned to fishing – until, that is, the developers arrived in the 1990s, building villas by the street load. The seafront area of the town is, however, a pleasant enough place to wile away a few lazy hours.

ARRIVAL AND DEPARTURE   PORTO COLOM

By bus Porto Colom is easily reached by bus from Felanitx (May–Oct 5–7 daily; 30min) and Palma (May–Oct 3–6 daily; 1hr 30min).

Felanitx and around

The town of **FELANITX**, some 13km inland from Porto Colom, is an industrious place, producing wine, ceramics and pearls. Although hardly beautiful, it has a certain charm, its tangle of narrow streets lined by handsome old houses mostly dating from the eighteenth and nineteenth centuries. The finest building is the church of **Sant Miquel**, whose soaring, honey-gold facade boasts a dramatic statue of St Michael, shown triumphant with a cringing devil at his feet.
The church overlooks one of the town's main squares, **Plaça Sa Font**, where a wide and rather grand flight of stone steps digs down below street level to reach **Font de Santa Margalida**, once the municipal well and now a water fountain. The square is also home to a modern and distinctly macho **statue** of a muscular Balearic slinger in a loin cloth (see p.244): in classical times, the islanders were hired as slingers by any number of armies.
The best time to visit Felanitx is on Sunday morning, when a lively fresh produce and craft **market** takes over much of the town centre; there's also a very good covered market, the **mercat municipal** (Tues–Sun), just behind Sant Miquel on c/Esglesia. In particular, look out for the capers (Catalan *tapèras*; Castilian *alcaparras*), produced locally and sold by size; the smallest are the most flavoursome, either as *nonpareilles* (up to 7mm) or *surfines* (7–8mm).

Santuari de Sant Salvador

Puig de Sant Salvador • Daily 10am–5pm • Free • It's a 15min drive from Felanitx to the monastery: head east on the road to Porto Colom and after 2km take the signposted, 5km-long side road that weaves up the mountain

The best and most obvious attraction in the Serres de Llevant is the **Santuari de Sant Salvador**, whose assorted buildings stretch along a slender ridge at the top of the 509m-high Puig de Sant Salvador. The Santuari was founded in the fourteenth century in an attempt to stave off a further visitation of the Black Death, which had mauled Felanitx in 1348. It worked, but the original buildings were demolished long ago and the present structure, a strikingly handsome fortress-like complex perched on the edge of the ridge, dates from the early eighteenth century. Inside, beyond the strongly fortified gatehouse, ancient vaulted corridors lead to the **church**, which shelters a much-venerated image of the Virgin Mary. The other end of the ridge is dominated by a gargantuan **statue of Christ the King** on top of a massive plinth. Erected in 1934 and visible for miles around, it's possibly the island's ugliest landmark, though the views across Mallorca from the ridge are fabulous.

Castell de Santueri

Opening hours irregular • Small fee is sometimes charged

A pleasant footpath wends its way from the Santuari de Sant Salvador (the custodians here can point you towards the path) to the **Castell de Santueri**, about 4km away across the hills to the south. The ninety-minute walk is fairly easy-going, with the path meandering through a pretty landscape of dry-stone walls, flowering shrubs and copses of almond and carob trees. Plastered onto a rocky hilltop, the battered ramparts of the castle date from the fourteenth century, though it was the Moors who built the first stronghold here. Local legend insists that **Christopher Columbus** was conceived in the castle, the result of a coupling between a local servant girl, Margalida Colom, and an imprisoned baron, Prince Carl of Viana. Getting inside the ruins is pot luck: sometimes you can (in which case a small entry fee is levied at the main gate), but mostly you can't. If you don't fancy the walk, you can **drive** to a point below the castle along a 5km country lane, signed off the Felanitx–Santanyí road about 2km south of Felanitx.

ARRIVAL AND INFORMATION

FELANITX AND AROUND

By bus Felanitx is served by several routes, with buses stopping near the main square.
Destinations Palma (May–Oct Mon–Sat every 1–2hr, Sun 5 daily; 1hr); Porto Colom (May–Oct 5–7 daily; 30min);

Santanyí (May–Oct 1 daily; 1hr).
Tourist information There is no tourist office, and neither is there anywhere to stay except the nearby Santuari de Sant Salvador.

ACCOMMODATION AND EATING

SANTUARI DE SANT SALVADOR
★ **Petit Hotel Hostatgería Sant Salvador** Puig San Salvador Carretera, Felanitx ☎971 51 52 60, ⓦ santsalvadorhotel.com. Sant Salvador was Mallorca's final monastery to lose its monks – the last ones moved out in the early 1990s. Thereafter, visitors were lodged in the old cells, though a new wing has now been added that houses 24 sparse but comfortable, modern guest rooms, all en suite and most with stunning views. Breakfast is served in an ancient vaulted room. The monastery also has a café and a restaurant with an incredible terrace; but phone to check their opening times first or book online. The sanctuary makes an unusual, very tranquil and good-value base; you'll need a car. **€68**

Cala d'Or

South along the coast from Porto Colom, the pretty little fishing villages that once studded the quiet coves as far as Porto Petro have been replaced by interconnected resorts that are largely indistinguishable. This homogeneous strip of whitewashed, low-rise villas, hotels, restaurants and bars, mostly designed in a sort of *pueblo* style, is now lumped together under the title **CALA D'OR**, though this name in fact refers to one particular cove, which is also one of the smallest. The "Cala d'Or" we refer to in this account is the original cove and not the whole development. The main cove resorts are linked by **Avinguda Fernando Tarrago**, under its various designations, from Cala Esmeralda in the north to Cala Llonga in the south – about a twenty-minute walk from one end to the other.

To be fair, the pseudo-Andalucian style of the new resorts blends well with the ritzy *haciendas* left by a previous generation of sun-seekers. The latter are largely concentrated on the humpy little headland that separates the cove of **Cala d'Or** from its northerly neighbour, **Cala Gran**. Tucked between the cliffs along a wooded coastline, these two fetching little coves are the highlights of the area: although the narrow golden beaches are jam-packed throughout the season, the swimming is perfect.

ARRIVAL AND INFORMATION
CALA D'OR

By bus Buses from Palma (Mon–Sat 6 daily; Sun 3 daily; 1hr 10min) stop on Cala d'Or's crowded and charmless main drag, Avgda Fernando Tarrago, a 2min walk from the beach.

By tourist train From May to September, a tourist "train" on wheels, the *mini-tren* (May–Sept 9–11 daily; ☎ 971 58 33 20, ⓦ minitrenet.com), shuttles along the coast, linking Cala Esmerelda, Cala d'Or, Cala Llonga and Porto Petro (see below), stopping along the main street and beside all the beaches.

Tourist information The Cala d'Or tourist office (Mon–Fri 8.30am–2pm; May–Sept also Sat 9am–1pm; ☎ 971 65 74 63) is situated a few metres up from the Cala Llonga waterside at c/Perico Pomar 10. They can provide resort maps marked with all the hotels and *hostales*, though finding a place to stay is well-nigh impossible in the summer.

ACCOMMODATION AND EATING

★ **Hotel Cala d'Or** Avgda Bélgica ☎ 971 65 72 49, ⓦ hotelcalador.com. Cala d'Or's most appealing hotel is the four-star, family-run *Hotel Cala d'Or*, right above the beach. One of the first to be established hereabouts, the hotel has ninety-odd balconied bedrooms, each furnished in a modern style and most with sea views. It's secluded and peaceful despite the bars and tourist restaurants being only a short walk up the road, and the owners are very welcoming. It also has a picturesque beachside bar and restaurant. Advance reservations pretty much essential. **€150**

Hostal La Ceiba Avgda de Calonge 2 ☎ 971 65 75 07, ⓦ la-ceiba.com. Just 100m from the centre of Cala D'Or, *Hostal La Ceiba* has thirteen basic en-suite rooms and a pretty rooftop terrace. **€56**

4

Porto Petro

PORTO PETRO rambles round a twin-pronged cove a couple of kilometres south of Cala Llonga, its old and tiny centre perched on the headland above the marina, with a cluster of whitewashed houses recalling the days when it served as Santanyí's seaport. Although it's now all but swallowed up by the nearby Cala d'Or conurbation, Porto Petro still retains something of its original character: aside from a small artificial strip close to the *Blau* hotel, there's no beach, so development has been fairly restrained. Even though the old fishing harbour has been turned into a marina and villas dot the gentle, wooded hillsides, it remains a quiet and tranquil spot, with the only real activity being the promenade round the crystal-watered cove.

ARRIVAL AND DEPARTURE
PORTO PETRO

By bus Buses pull in right beside the harbour.
Destinations Cala d'Or (May–Oct 9 daily; 25min); Cala Mondragó (May–Oct Mon–Fri 9 daily; 10min); Felanitx (3 daily; 45min); Palma (May–Oct 3–6 daily; 1hr 15min); Santanyí (3–6 daily; 35min).

By tourist train An electric *mini-tren* (May–Sept 9–11 daily; ⓦ minitrenet.com) links Porto Petro with the resorts to the north and Cala Mondragó to the south.

ACCOMMODATION AND EATING

Ca'n Martina Paseo del Puerto 56 ☎ 971 65 75 17. Porto Petro has several very good, moderately priced, harbourside restaurants, of which the *Ca'n Martina*, by the main dock, is one: it's the place to go for a particularly delicious paella (€13 per person). Daily noon–4pm & 7–11.30pm.

Hostal Varadero C/Patrons Martina 3 ☎ 971 65 72 23, ⓦ hostalvaradero-portopetro.com. There's a reasonable chance of getting a room on spec at the two-star *Hostal Varadero*, a comfortable and neat little place occupying a three-storey modern block just above the main dock; the *hostal* also has its own outside pool, garden and rooftop sun terraces. Closed Nov–April. **€60**

Varadero C/Patrons Martina 3 ☏ 971 65 74 28. The

multi-level *Varadero* has the prettiest terrace, with comfortable sofas, a decent cocktail list and tasty seafood. This place is popular, so be sure to reserve ahead or arrive early. Daily 10am–11.30pm.

Mondragó Parc Natural

Fonts de n'Alis visitor centre Daily 9am–4pm · ☏ 971 18 10 22

Beginning about 3km south of Porto Petro, **Mondragó Parc Natural** protects a small but diverse slice of the east coast, around two thousand acres of wetland, farmland, beach, pine and scrub. There are two **car parks** to aim for, both signposted from the Ma-19 between Porto Petro and Santanyí: the better target is the **Fonts de n'Alis** car park, 100m from the tiny resort of Cala Mondragó (see below), which can also be reached direct from Porto Petro along a country road – just follow the signs. The other car park, **S'Amarador**, is on the low-lying headland south across the cove from Cala Mondragó. The park is latticed with footpaths and country lanes, and you can pick up a (rather poor) **map** from the Fonts de n'Alis **visitor centre**, at the Fonts de n'Alis car park. This shows the park's four hiking trails: all are easy loops, two of forty minutes, two of thirty, though the signposting is patchy. Amongst them, the blue route is pleasant enough giving good views of the bay and access to a small secluded beach: if you can't spot a sign, just keep the sea on your right-hand side and you shouldn't go far wrong.

Cala Mondragó

CALA MONDRAGÓ is one of Mallorca's prettiest resorts. There was some development here before the creation of the Mondragó Parc Natural in 1990, but it's all very low key and barely disturbs the cove's beauty, with low, pine-clad cliffs framing a pair of sandy beaches beside crystal-clear waters. Predictably, the cove's "unspoilt" reputation and safe bathing act as a magnet for sun-lovers from around, but you can escape the crowds by staying the night.

ARRIVAL AND DEPARTURE   CALA MONDRAGÓ

By bus Buses from Cala d'Or (May–Oct Mon–Fri 9 daily; 25min) and Porto Petro (May–Oct Mon–Fri 9 daily; 10min) pull in at the bottom of the hill, just next to the beach.

By tourist train Cala Mondragó is also the southern terminus of the summertime *mini-tren*, which runs north as far as Cala Esmerelda (May–Oct 9–11 daily).

ACCOMMODATION AND EATING

Hostal Condemar ☏ 971 65 77 56, ⊛ hostal condemar.com. An enticing and very economical *hostal* about 200m from the beach: most of the rooms have sea-view balconies and there's an outside pool. Closed Nov–April. **€35**

Hotel Playa Mondragó ☏ 971 65 77 52, ⊛ playa mondrago.com. A friendly, family-run modern block with simple but attractive rooms. It also has a reasonable restaurant located in a garden courtyard, adjacent to the swimming pool. Closed Nov–March. **€100**

Santanyí

Taking its name from a shortened version of 'Santi Annini' (the Lamb of God), the crossroads town of **SANTANYÍ**, about 10km west of Porto Petro, has long guarded the island's southeastern approaches, a role that has cost it dear. Corsairs ransacked the place time and time again, prompting a medieval German traveller to bemoan their fate – "The Saracens constantly arrive in their ships, carry away prisoners, torment them and use them as slaves or sell them for money." The townsfolk attempted to protect themselves by fortifying the town on several occasions and, although it didn't do them much good, one of the medieval gates, **Sa Porta**, has survived in good condition. Nonetheless, it's Santanyí's narrow alleys, squeezed between high-sided sandstone houses, that are the town's main appeal, along with **Sant Andreu Apòstol**, a bulky, eighteenth-century pile that incorporates a finely worked, early Gothic chapel, the **Capella del Roser**, a thirteenth-century survivor from the first church built on the site.

ARRIVAL AND DEPARTURE SANTANYÍ

By bus Buses pull in on Plaça Porta Murada.
Destinations Cala Figuera (May–Oct Mon–Sat 2 daily; 15min); Cala Santanyí (May–Oct Mon–Sat 1 daily; 10min); Colònia de Sant Jordi (May–Oct Mon–Sat 6–7 daily, Sun 3

daily; 25min); Felanitx (May–Oct 1 daily; 1hr); Manacor (2–4 daily; 50min); Palma (May–Oct Mon–Sat 6 daily, Sun 3 daily; 1hr); Porto Petro (3–6 daily; 35min).

ACCOMMODATION AND EATING

Es Cantonet Plaza Bernareggi 2 ☎971 16 34 07, ⓦes -cantonet.net. In a hundred-year-old townhouse, this traditional Mallorcan restaurant offers tasty main courses from €10–20. The menu changes seasonally and includes Majorcan dishes as well as other Mediterranean cuisine. Mon–Sat 6.30–11.30pm.

Es Coc c/Aljub 37 ☎971 64 16 31, ⓦrestaurantescoc .com. Owner Marc Vidal, has transformed his grandmother's old finca into a new upmarket restaurant, just outside the centre of Santanyi. It serves up gourmet Mallorcan dishes, with main courses from €15–25. Daily 1–4pm & 7pm–midnight.

Sa Botiga c/del Roser 2 ☎971 13 30 15, ⓦwww .sabotiga-santanyi. This petite and well-decorated,

German-run restaurant serves up tasty food for breakfast, lunch and dinner. Main courses cost approximately €10–15. Mon & Wed–Sat 9am–11.30pm, Sun & Tues noon–4pm.

Sa Cova 31 Plaça Major ⓦsacova.blogspirit.com. The pick of the cafés and bars on Santanyí's main square, *Sa Cova* is a groovy little place painted in cheerful, psychedelic colours and with a tiny stage hosting regular live music (Wed & Sat). Daily 10am till late.

Hotel Santanyí Plaça Constitució 7 ☎971 64 22 14, ⓦhotel-santanyi.com. In an old stone townhouse near the main square, *Hotel Santanyí* has seven pleasantly modern rooms and a roof terrace with views over the town. **€120**

Cala Figuera

CALA FIGUERA's ancient harbour sits beside a fjord-like inlet below the steepest of coastal cliffs. Local fishermen still land their catches and mend their nets here, but nowadays it's accompanied by scores of photo-snapping tourists. Up above, the pine-covered shoreline heaves with villas, hotels and *hostales*, although the absence of high-rise buildings means the development is never overbearing. There's no beach here: the nearest is 4km west at **Cala Santanyí**, a busy little resort with a medium-sized (and frequently crowded) **beach** at the end of a steep-sided, heavily wooded gulch. To get there, head back towards Santanyí for about 1.5km and follow the signs.

ARRIVAL AND DEPARTURE CALA FIGUERA

By bus Buses arrive at the corner of C/de Sant Pere and C/ de Bernareggi.

Destinations Palma (May–Oct Mon–Sat 1 daily; 2hr 5min); Santanyí (May–Oct Mon–Sat 1 daily; 15min).

ACCOMMODATION AND EATING

Cala Figuera is popular and there are precious few vacant **rooms** at its dozen or so hotels and *hostales*, even in the shoulder season. If you decide to chance your arm, the obvious place to start is on the steep pedestrianized ramp – c/Verge del Carmen – which leads up from the harbour.

Hostal Cala c/Verge del Carmen 50 ☎971 64 50 18. In a prime location, the unassuming *Hostal Cala* has twenty rooms above a restaurant. The rooms are pretty basic, but provide everything that you need for an inexpensive night's stay. Closed Nov–March. **€65**

La Marina c/Virgen del Carmen 64 ☎971 64 50 52. The most distinguished of Cala Figuera's restaurants are the seafood places lining c/Verge del Carmen, of which *La*

Marina is a good choice – it's first-rate, with good views and a decent selection of seafood. Daily noon–4pm & 7–11pm.

Hotel Villa Sirena c/Virgen del Carmen 37 ☎971 64 53 03, ⓦhotelvillasirena.com. The two-star *Hotel Villa Sirena* is a proficient modern hotel with its own swimming platforms above the water; it's located at the end of the promontory above the end of the cove. **€83**

Cap de Ses Salines

Mallorca's most southerly point, the wind-buffeted **Cap de Ses Salines** is a bleak, brush-covered headland surrounded by coastal pine woods. The stretch of coast between here and Palma has been hardly developed at all, since most of the shoreline is unenticingly spartan, a long and low rocky shelf with barely a decent beach in sight. That said, the landscape around the cape has an eerie sense of desolation – and some visitors find this barrenness strangely fascinating. Although Cap de Ses Salines' **lighthouse** is closed to the public, there are fine views out to sea: Thekla larks and stone curlews can often be seen, whilst gulls, terns and shearwaters glide about offshore, benefiting from the winds which, when they're up, can make the place intolerable. If the cape takes your fancy, then walk northwest along the seashore to the wide, shallow bay and deserted sandy beach of the **Platja des Caragol**: it's an easy walk of around thirty minutes each way.

Colònia de Sant Jordi

A smattering of modern resorts have gamely made the most of the disheartening landscape of the south coast and the pick of them is undoubtedly **COLÒNIA DE SANT JORDI**. It's a curious and most enjoyable amalgamation of tourist settlement and old seaport that thoroughly deserves an overnight visit. The town's wide streets lie 13km west of Santanyí and pattern a substantial and irregularly shaped headland that pokes its knobbly head out into the ocean.

The town

The main approach road to Colònia de Sant Jordi is **Avinguda Marquès del Palmer**, at the end of which – roughly in the middle of the headland – lies the principal square, the unremarkable **Plaça Constitució**. From here, Carrer Sa Solta and then Avinguda Primavera lead west to the *Hotel Marquès del Palmer*, which sits tight against the **Platja d'Estanys**, whose gleaming sands curve round a dune-edged cove. South of Avinguda Primavera is the surprisingly pleasant main tourist zone, whose domineering lines of flashy hotels are broken by low-rise villas and landscaped side streets. To the north are the **Salines de S'Avall**, the saltpans that once provided the town with its principal source of income.

The harbour

East of Plaça Constitució along c/Major, and then left (north) down c/Gabriel Roca, is the old **harbour**, the most diverting part of town. Framed by an attractive, early twentieth-century ensemble of balconied houses, the port makes the most of a handsome, horseshoe-shaped bay. There's nothing special to look at, but it's a relaxing spot with a handful of restaurants, fishing smacks, a marina and a pocket-sized beach, the **Platja Es Port**. It's also where you'll find the **kiosk** to book the boat to Cabrera (see p.189). From here, it's a five-minute walk along the footpath north round the bay to the slender, low-lying headland that accommodates the extensive sands of the **Platja d'es Dolç**.

Cabrera island visitor centre

c/Gabriel Roca s/n · Daily 10am–2.30pm & 3.30–6pm · Free

You can sample the island delights of Cabrera (see p.188) at the **Cabrera island visitor centre**, housed in a watchtower-like building at the north end of the harbour. The centre welcomes visitors with a short introductory film, after which you can view the impressive aquarium, displaying many species you're likely to find on local menus, as well as small sharks and rays. Upstairs is a less interesting section devoted to the island's terrestrial species.

CLOCKWISE FROM TOP CALA MONDRAGÓ (P.182); SEAFOOD; COLÒNIA DE ST JORDI (P.184) >

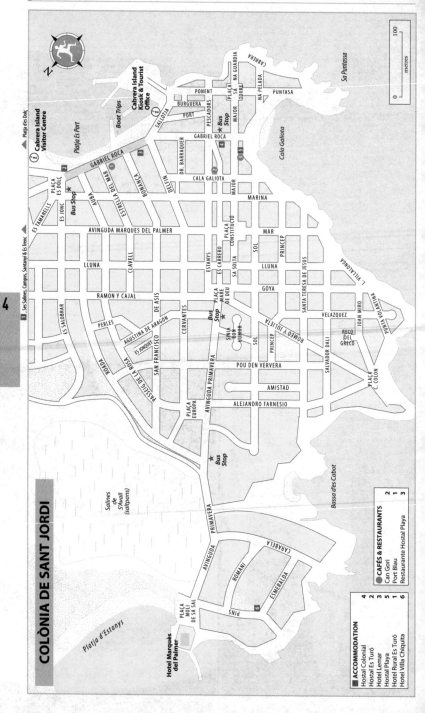

COLÒNIA DE SANT JORDI

ACCOMMODATION

Hostal Colonial	4
Hostal Es Turó	2
Hotel Lemar	3
Hostal Playa	5
Hotel Rural Es Turó	1
Hotel Villa Chiquita	6

● CAFÉS & RESTAURANTS

Can Gori	2
Port Blau	1
Restaurante Hostal Playa	3

ARRIVAL AND DEPARTURE

COLÒNIA DE SANT JORDI

By bus Buses to Colònia de Sant Jordi stop at several central locations, including the bus stop at the north end of the old harbour beside Plaça Es Dolç and again at the south end on c/Gabriel Roca. It's not an easy place to get to by bus from the south coast (connections are from Manacor or Santanyi), so if you are coming from this direction make sure that you plan ahead.

Destinations Manacor (2–4 daily; 1hr); Palma (May–Oct Mon–Sat 5–9 daily, Sun 3 daily; 1hr); Santanyí (May–Oct Mon–Sat 6–7 daily, Sun 3 daily; 10min).

GETTING AROUND AND INFORMATION

By train and taxi During the season, a toy-town *mini-tren* shuttles around town every hour or two, but if all else fails call a taxi (☎ 971 65 52 78).

By bike Cycling in the flatlands around the resort is a popular pastime: the tourist office has information on local bike rental shops.

Tourist information The tourist office is located next to the Cabrera kiosk right on the harbourfront (Mon–Fri 8am–2pm; ☎ 971 65 60 73, ⓦ www.mallorcainfo.com); they can supply free town maps and a comprehensive list of local accommodation.

ACCOMMODATION

The glossy modern hotels at the west end of the resort are very much package territory, but there is a good chance of a spare room on spec amongst the reasonably priced hotels and *hostales* in the vicinity of the old harbour.

Hostal Colonial c/Gabriel Roca 9 ☎ 971 65 61 82, ⓦ hostal-colonial.com. Very agreeable, family-run, one-star *hostal* with eight frugal but entirely adequate modern rooms, each of which has a small terrace or balcony. It's a short 50m walk to the sea, and about 500m to the centre of town, and there's a great ice-cream parlour downstairs. Closed Dec–Feb. **€35**

Hostal Es Turó Plaça Es Dolç s/n ☎ 971 65 50 57. Unassuming, clean and economical one-star *hostal* in a solid three-storey building plonked right on Es Port beach. There are eighteen guest rooms – those at the back look out over the beach. Closed Nov–April. **€30**

Hotel Lemar c/Gabriel Roca 55 ☎ 971 65 51 78, ⓦ hotellemar.com. Old but well-equipped, three-star balconied hotel overlooking the harbour. Some of the ninety-odd rooms give onto a side street – c/Bonança – so specify you want a room at the front. The hotel organizes good day trips and hiking in the surrounding countryside. Closed Nov to mid-April. **€56**

★ **Hostal Playa** c/Major 25 ☎ 971 65 52 56, ⓦ restauranteplaya.com. About a 5min walk from the main harbour, this appealing little family-run place has seven double rooms, four of which have a balcony overlooking the sea as it laps against the beach to the rear of the *hostal*. The rooms are pretty basic, but quite large, and the public area is delightfully old-fashioned with lots of wood, old photos and plates stuck on the walls. Breakfast is served on a pretty, sea-facing patio terrace, which doubles as a restaurant. **€40**

Hotel Rural Es Turó Camí de Cas Perets s/n ☎ 663 80 85 26, ⓦ esturo.com. A classic *finca*, which has been tastefully converted into an immaculate, luxury modern hotel, all bright-white walls, wood-beam ceilings and tiled floors. The hotel is located on a gentle hill 2.5km to the east of (and signposted from) the hamlet of Ses Salines, on the approach road to Colònia de Sant Jordi. **€85**

Hotel Villa Chiquita c/Esmeralda 14 ☎ 971 65 51 21, ⓦ hotelvillachiquita.com. This smart and well-tended hotel occupies a rambling, *pueblo*-style modern villa in the tourist zone at the west end of Avgda Primavera. It has a good-looking garden, with lots of exotic cactuses, and eighteen smartly decorated en-suite rooms. Closed Nov–Jan. **€90**

EATING AND DRINKING

A string of first-rate restaurants line up along the harbour, and although they are geared up for tourists, everything is pleasantly low-key and small-scale. Unsurprisingly in a town with its own fishing fleet, the big deal is seafood, and portions are substantial – you often get the whole fish rather than a slice. Things get busy from around 8pm, but close down early – by about 10.30pm.

Can Gori c/Estanys 21 ☎ 971 65 64 69. A favourite local hangout with cheap beer, tasty tapas – fried squid, green pepper, spicy sausages and so forth – plus very pleasant service. Not the place for an intimate dinner perhaps, but still a great spot for a quick bite and a lively slice of island life. Daily 8am–1am.

★ **Port Blau** c/Gabriel Roca 67 ☎ 971 65 65 55, ⓦ portblau.com. Smart harbourside restaurant that serves some of the town's top food, including big, beautifully presented portions of fresh fish, heaped salads and great bread. Mains around €25. Feb–Nov daily except Tues 11am–4pm & 7pm–midnight.

Restaurante Hostal Playa c/Major 25 ☎ 971 65 52 56. The restaurant of the *Hostal Playa* (see p.187) may lack a few frills, but there's no complaining about the food – fish and more fish prepared in the traditional Mallorcan manner. The restaurant occupies a very pleasant, sea-facing patio-terrace. Main courses average around €20–25. Tues–Sun noon–3.30pm & 7.30–10pm, Mon 7.30–10pm.

Es Trenc

A few kilometres west of Colònia de Sant Jordi's is **Es Trenc**, a 4km strip of sandy beach that extends as far as the eye can see. It's neither unknown nor unspoilt, but the crowds are easily absorbed except at the height of the season, and development is virtually non-existent. It's about 6km from Colònia de Sant Jordi: head north out of town for 0.5km and turn left at the roundabout towards Campos; after another 2.8km, take the signed left turn and follow the country lane leading across the salt pans and wetlands to the large car park (€7) at the east end of the beach. This end of the beach is far more appealing than the other, at **Ses Covetes**, which is blotched by improvised shacks and drinks stalls.

Several **footpaths** lead from Es Trenc beach into the saltpans, the **Salines de Llevant**, which are known for their birdlife (see box below). However, it's not a good area to explore on foot: the scenery is boring, it's smelly and for much of the year insects are a menace. It's much better to drive or cycle along the maze-like network of narrow country lanes that traverse the saltpans.

4 Cabrera National Park

The **Illa de Cabrera** ("Goat Island") is a bumpy, scrub- and tree-covered chunk of rock lying 18km offshore from Colònia de Sant Jordi. Largely bare, almost entirely uninhabited and no more than 7km wide and 5km long, it's the largest of a cluster of tiny islets that comprise the Cabrera archipelago. The only significant hint of Cabrera's eventful past is the protective **castle** above its supremely sheltered harbour. Pliny claimed the island to have been the birthplace of Hannibal; medieval pirates hunkered down here to plan future raids; and during the Napoleonic Wars, the Spanish stuck nine thousand French prisoners of war on the island and promptly forgot about them – two-thirds died from hunger and disease during their four-year captivity. More recently, the island was taken over by Franco's armed forces, subsequently winning protected status as the **Parc Nacional de l'Arxipèlag de Cabrera**.

The island

The seven- to eight-hour excursion (see opposite) starts with a one-hour voyage to the island. On the final stretch, the boat nudges round a hostile-looking headland to enter the harbour, **Es Port** – a narrow finger of calm water edged by hills and equipped with a tiny jetty. National Park personnel meet the boat to advise about what visitors can do and where – some parts of Cabrera are out of bounds – and there's a small park **information office** by the jetty too. The most popular excursion is the stiff, thirty-minute hoof up the path to the ruins of the fourteenth-century **castle**, which perches high up on Cabrera's west coast. The views from the fortress

---

BIRDLIFE OF THE SALTPANS

The saltpans backing the beach at Es Trenc – the **Salines de Llevant** – and the surrounding farm and scrubland support a wide variety of **birdlife**. Residents such as marsh harriers, kestrels, spotted crakes, fan-tailed warblers and hoopoes make a visit enjoyable at any time of year, but the best time to come is in spring when hundreds of migrants arrive from Africa. Commonly seen in spring are avocets, little ringed plovers, little egrets, common sandpipers, little stints, black-tailed godwits, collared pratincoles and black terns.

back to Mallorca are magnificent, and all sorts of **birds** can be seen gliding round the sea cliffs, including manx and cory's shearwaters and the rare Audouin's gulls, as well as peregrine falcons and shags. It is, however, the blue-underbellied **Lilford's wall lizard** that really steals the show: after you've completed the walk to the castle, have a drink down by the jetty, where you can tempt the Lilford's lizards out from the scrub with pieces of fruit.

As an alternative to the castle, it's an easy fifteen-minute walk round the harbour to **Sa Plageta beach**, or you can head inland to the sombre **memorial** commemorating the French dead: the path to the memorial begins at Sa Plageta and takes about twenty minutes to walk. Along the way you'll pass the **museum** (park staff can advise on its limited opening hours), in a former wine cellar and grain warehouse, which traces the history of Cabrera with a ragbag of archeological finds recovered from the island and its surrounding waters. On the return journey, the boat bobs across the bay to visit **Sa Cova Blava** (Blue Grotto), sailing right into the cave through the 50m wide entrance and on into the yawning chamber beyond. The grotto reaches a height of 160m and is suffused by the bluish light from which it gets its name; you can swim here too.

ARRIVAL AND DEPARTURE

By boat The harbourfront kiosk in Colònia de Sant Jordi (☎971 64 90 34, ⓦexcursionsacabrera.es) takes reservations for the daily boat to Cabrera island (March–Oct; 7–8hr; €35).
By speedboat If you don't want to spend the entire day venturing out to the island, a speedboat excursion

(March–Oct 6 daily; ☎622 57 48 06, ⓦmarcabrera.com; €40–50) will whisk you around all the highlights in two hours; Marcabrera, the company concerned, have their offices just back from the harbour at Gabriel Roca 20 (daily 9am–1pm & 4–8pm).

EATING AND DRINKING

There's just one **café** on Cabrera, just where the ferry docks, and it sells sandwiches and drinks. Alternatively, you can opt for the boat company's buffet (€7.50, with drinks an added extra).

Campos

Plonked down amongst the sun-baked flatlands of Es Pla, modest **CAMPOS**, 13km north of Colònia de Sant Jordi, isn't much to look at, but it does have two surprises up its sleeve: it's home to what many consider to be the best **patisserie** on the island, *Pastisserie Pomar*, in the main square at Plaça 20, while its church, **Sant Julià**, holds an especially fine painting of Christ by Bartolomé Esteban Murillo (1617–82), the first Spanish painter to achieve a Europe-wide reputation.

Llucmajor

Just 27km from central Palma, **LLUCMAJOR** has little to detain you, despite its significance in Mallorcan history, its medieval origins as a market town and its long association with the island's shoemakers. It was here in 1349, just outside the old city walls, that Jaume III, the last of the independent kings of Mallorca, was defeated and killed by Pedro IV of Aragon. The memorial to Jaume III on Passeig Jaume III, commemorates the event, while the mainly eighteenth-century Iglesia San Miguel, at Plaça Santa Catalina Tomàs, is also worth a look for its fine architecture.

EATING AND DRINKING   LLUCMAJOR

El Puerto II Costa I Llobera 1 ☎971 44 04 67. *El Puerto II* provides excellent food at reasonable prices. Classic Mallorcan dishes are a favourite in this unassuming local haunt – the lamb in particular is a specialty. Mains cost around €12–18. Daily 7–11.30pm.
Zaranda Sa Torre Camí de Sa Torre, km 8.7 ☎971 01

04 50, ⓦzaranda.es. Attached to the local *Hilton Sa Torre* and boasting a Michelin star, the restaurant *Zaranda* provides Mallorcan fine dining at its best. Prices reflect the quality of the culinary experience here, so be prepared for a large bill. Daily 7.30–11pm.

Menorca

196 Maó

206 Port de Maó

212 Southeast Menorca

214 Fornells and the northeast coast

219 Central Menorca

228 Ciutadella

237 Around Ciutadella

COVA D'EN XOROI

5

Menorca

Second largest of the Balearics, boomerang-shaped Menorca stretches west from the enormous natural harbour of Maó to the smaller port of Ciutadella. Just 45km apart, these two cities boast around seventy percent of the island's population, despite their diminutive size. Both have preserved much of their eighteenth- and early nineteenth-century appearance, though Ciutadella's labyrinthine centre, with its princely mansions and Gothic cathedral, maintains the edge over Maó's plainer, more mercantile architecture. Running through the rustic interior, the main Me-1 highway links the two ports via a trio of pocket-sized market towns – Alaior, Es Mercadal and Ferreries – with a sequence of side roads branching off the highway to the resorts and beaches of the north and south coasts.

The island's backbone, the **Me-1** acts as a rough dividing line between Menorca's two distinct geological areas. In the **north**, sandstone predominates, giving a red tint to the low hills that roll out towards the bare, surf-battered coastline, one of whose many coves and inlets shelters the lovely fishing village and mini-resort of **Fornells**. To the **south** all is limestone, with low-lying flatlands punctuated by bulging hills and fringed by a cove-studded coastline. Wooded ravines gash this southern zone, becoming deeper and more dramatic as you travel west – especially around **Cala Galdana**, a popular resort set beneath severe, pine-clad sea cliffs. Straddling the two zones, **Monte Toro**, Menorca's highest peak and the site of a quaint little church, offers panoramic views that reveal the topography of the island to dramatic effect.

The island's varied terrain is sprinkled with farmsteads, witnesses to an **agriculture** that had become, before much of it was killed off by urbanization/modernization, highly advanced. **A dry-stone wall** (*tanca*) protected every field – the island has no less than 15,000km of stone wall – and prevented the **Tramuntana**, the vicious north wind, from tearing away the topsoil. Even olive trees had their roots individually protected in little stone wells, while compact stone **ziggurats** sheltered cattle from both the wind and the blazing sun. Nowadays, apart from a few acres of rape and corn, many of the fields are barren, but the walls and ziggurats survive, as do many of the old twisted **gates** made from olive branches.

Tourism Menorca-style: reserves and conservation p.195
Maó Orientation p.196
Menorca's Talayotic sites p.202
Maó's mayonnaise mania p.204
Menorca's Top 5 restaurants p.205
Boat trips from Maó – and the islands of Port de Maó p.206
A coastal hike from Maó to Punta Prima p.208
Menorca's Top 5 fincas and agrotourismos p.213

Clubbing at the cliff-face: The Cova d'en Xoroi p.214
A day's hike: Es Grau to Sa Torreta p.216
Richard Kane and the Camí d'en Kane p.220
A day's hike: Es Migjorn Gran to the coast p.224
Coastal walks around Cala Galdana p.227
The Rissaga p.234
Top 5 island nightspots p.237

CAP DE FAVÀRITX

Highlights

❶ Maó The labyrinthine lanes and alleys of Menorca's engaging capital ramble along the top of a ridge, high above its deep and long harbour. **See p.196**

❷ Talatí de Dalt One of the most engaging of Menorca's many prehistoric remains, in a charming rustic setting just outside Maó. **See p.202**

❸ Cova d'en Xoroi Menorca's most outstanding place for a drink and a dance is this cliffside cave, with spectacular views over the sea. **See p.214**

❹ Cap de Favàritx Wind-stripped headland where a solitary black-and-white striped lighthouse shines out over a lunar-like landscape of tightly layered slate. **See p.216**

❺ Ciutadella The island's prettiest town, its compact centre an inordinately appealing maze of handsome stone buildings and waterside restaurants culminating in a pocket-sized Gothic cathedral. **See p.228**

❻ Cala Turqueta Menorca has a clutch of unspoilt cove beaches and this is one of the finest, with a band of fine white sand set between wooded limestone cliffs and crystal-clear waters. **See p.238**

HIGHLIGHTS ARE MARKED ON THE MAP ON P.194

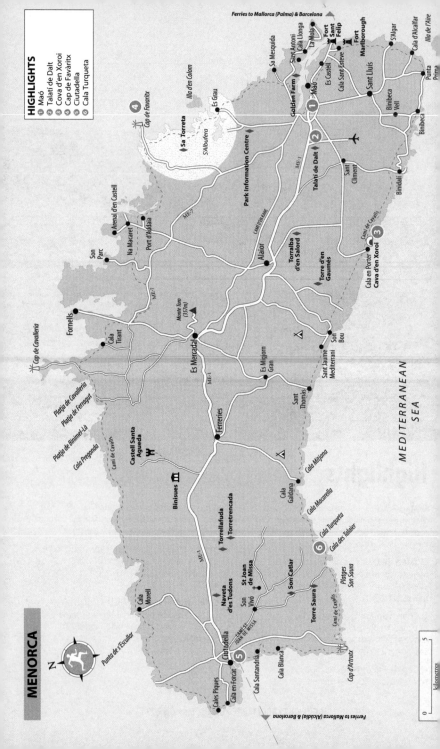

Brief history

Menorca's landscape is cluttered by scores of **prehistoric stone monuments**, mostly dating from the second millennium BC, though little is actually known of the island's early settlers. The most common remains are **talayots**, cone-shaped mounds made of stone that may or may not have been watchtowers. It's from these *talayots* that the prehistoric **Talayotic Period** is named, running from 1500 to 123 BC, when the Romans arrived. Four of the finest sites are **Talatí de Dalt**, just outside Maó; **Torre d'en Gaumés**, near Alaior; **Torrellafuda**, just off the Me-1; and the **Naveta d'es Tudons**, near Ciutadella.

In more recent times, Maó's long, deep-water port, the **Port de Maó**, promoted Menorca to an important position in European affairs. The **British** saw its potential as a **naval base** and captured the island in 1708 during the War of the Spanish Succession, confirming their conquest five years later under the terms of the Treaty of Utrecht. Spain regained possession in 1783, but with the threat of Napoleon in the Mediterranean, a new British base was temporarily established under admirals Nelson and Collingwood until Britain finally relinquished all claims to the island in 1802. The **British influence** on Menorca, especially its architecture, is still manifest: the sash windows so popular in Georgian design are even now sometimes referred to as *winders*, and locals often part with a fond *bye-bye*. The British also introduced the art of distilling juniper berries, and **Menorcan gin** (Xoriguer, Beltran or Nelson) is now world-renowned. Today, Menorca's economy is dependent on the **tourist industry**, which is mainly a niche affair focused on holiday homes and package tours with a strong sideline in activity holidays, from walking to diving.

ARRIVAL AND DEPARTURE

MENORCA

BY PLANE

Menorca airport Just 5km southwest of Maó, Menorca's international airport is a smart, compact affair with a handful of currency-exchange facilities and car-rental outlets.

Information The airport tourist information desk (May–Sept Mon 8am–3pm & 4–9.30pm, Tues 8am–3pm, Wed–Sun 8am–10.30am & 4–10pm; Oct–April closes Tues at 9.30am; ☎ 971 15 71 15) issues free island maps and has a good selection of free literature, including *Menorca Weekly*, a leaflet detailing forthcoming events, and a general information booklet, *Menorca Explorer*, which contains maps of every town on the island as well as all sorts of listings.

Buses There are regular buses from the airport to Maó bus station, which is handily located near the main square (May–Oct every 30min; Nov–April every 30min–1hr; €2.50). Alternatively, Shuttle Menorca (⚟ shuttlemenorca.com) offers affordable (around €12) minibus transfers between the airport and a range of destinations all across the island.

TOURISM MENORCA-STYLE: RESERVES AND CONSERVATION

Dominated by the British, who account for no less than sixty percent of the island's visitors, tourism in Menorca is a much quieter affair than in neighbouring Mallorca, and there are still many remote cove **beaches** with not a speck of concrete in sight – though access to them is usually along rough and dusty lanes. The island's development is largely confined to individual coves and bays, and only amongst the sprawling villa villages in the southeast of the island has it become at all overpowering. Neither is it likely to spread: determined to protect their island from the worst excesses of the tourist industry, the Menorcans have clearly demarcated **development zones** and have also created a chain of **conservation areas** that will eventually protect around forty percent of the island. It was this far-sighted plan that prompted UNESCO to declare Menorca a **Biosphere Reserve** in 1993. The islanders are especially keen to protect their undeveloped beaches, bringing both them and their immediate hinterland into public ownership as speedily as possible. To this end, the old mule and military track that encircles the entire island has been turned into a long-distance footpath, the **Camí de Cavalls**.

Despite this, the independent traveller is not especially well catered for. Only in Maó, Ciutadella and Fornells is there much chance of finding a **room on spec**, and tourism is very **seasonal**: outside May to October, many restaurants, cafés and hotels close and the **bus** network is reduced to a skeleton service.

5

Aiport taxi A taxi from the aiport to the centre of Maó will set you back €10–12.

BY FERRY

Most ferries and catamarans from Barcelona and Palma dock at Maó ferry terminal, a 5min walk from the town centre, but there's also a second, newly built ferry terminal at the other end of the island just south of Ciutadella (see p.234). For further details of ferries and catamarans to Menorca, turn to our Basics chapter (see p.22).

GETTING AROUND AND INFORMATION

By bus Island-wide bus timetables are available on Ⓦtmsa.es, with the exception of the northeast coast (Ⓦautosfornells.com) and the west coast resorts near Ciutadella (Ⓦe-torres.net).

By bike and scooter Anthony's Bikes, located 12km south of Maó in the resort of Cala en Porter, rents out various types of scooters and bicycles (Ⓣ971 37 77 56, Ⓦanthonysbikes.com). Prices for a 50cc moped begin at an affordable €35/day in high season, half that at other times of the year. Bicycles cost €10/day.

Website Menorca's official website is Ⓦmenorca.es.

Maó

Despite its status as island capital, **MAÓ** (in Castilian, Mahón) has a comfortable, small-town feel – the population is just 27,000 – and wandering around its ancient centre, with its long-established cafés and old-fashioned shops, is a relaxing and enjoyable way to pass a few hours. The town centre possesses two cultural highlights, the Churrigueresque chapel in the church of **St Francesc** and the historical paintings of the **Museu Hernández Sanz, Hernández Mora**, but all told it's much more the general flavour of the place that appeals rather than any individual sight. Outside the centre, you might enjoy visiting both the harbourside **Xoriguer gin distillery**, where you can sample as many of the island's liquors as you can brave, and the substantial Talayotic remains of **Talatí de Dalt**, just west of town along the Me-1.

Port it may be, but there's little seamy side to Maó. **Nightlife** is limited to a few bars and clubs near the ferry terminal, and the harbourfront's main draw is its long string of **restaurants and cafés** which attract tourists in their droves, though few stay the night, preferring the purpose-built resorts close by. As a result, Maó has surprisingly few *hostales* and hotels, which means that you can base yourself here and – if you avoid the waterfront – escape the tourist throngs with the greatest of ease. The lack of places to stay, however, means that **rooms** are in short supply in July and August, and **reserving** in advance during this period is strongly recommended.

MAÓ ORIENTATION

Thanks to its position beside the largest natural harbour in the Mediterranean, Maó has always been a **port**. Although today most visitors approach the town from its landward side, it's only from the water that the logic of the place becomes apparent, its centre crowding the crest of a steep ridge that stands tall against the south side of the harbour. From this angle, Maó is properly beautiful thanks to its striking and unusual **hybrid architecture**: tall, monumental Spanish mansions stand cheek-by-jowl with classical Georgian sash-windowed townhouses – elegant reminders of the British occupation – interrupted by fragments of the old city walls and the occasional church.

With its high-sided mansions and handsome churches, the oldest and most diverting part of Maó rolls along the **clifftop** above the harbour for roughly 1km. Behind, immediately to the south, the predominantly **nineteenth-century town** clambers upwards, its complicated pattern of tiny squares and short lanes bisected by the principal shopping street and pedestrianized main drag, which goes under various names, with **Costa de Sa Plaça** and **c/Moreres** being the longest individual strips. It takes five to ten minutes to walk from one end of the main street to the other and you emerge at **Plaça S'Esplanada**, the humdrum main square.

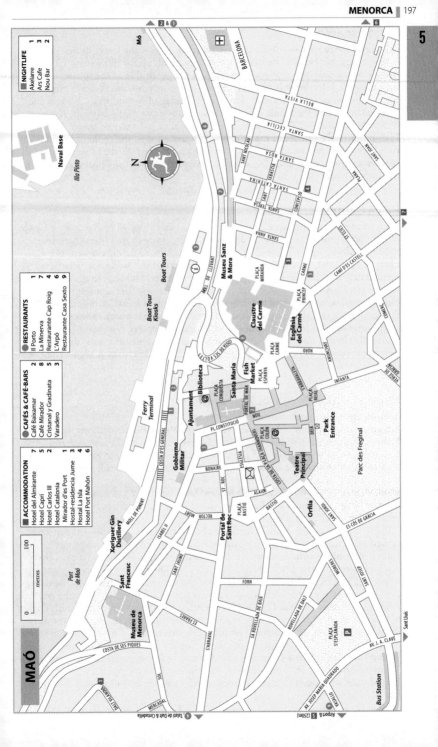

MAÓ

NIGHTLIFE
Akelarre	1
Ars Café	3
Nou Bar	2

RESTAURANTS
Il Porto	1
La Minerva	7
Restaurante Cap Roig	4
L'Arpó	6
Restaurante Casa Sexto	9

CAFÉS & CAFÉ-BARS
Café Baixamar	2
Café Mirador	8
Cristanal y Gradinata	5
Varadero	3

ACCOMMODATION
Hotel del Almirante	7
Hotel Capri	5
Hotel Carlos III	2
Hotel Catalonia	1
Mirador d'es Port	3
Hostal-residencia Jume	4
Hostal La Isla	4
Hotel Port Mahón	6

Naval Base

Illa Pinto

Port de Maó

Boat Tours

Boat Tour Kiosks

Ferry Terminal

Museu Sanz & Mora

Claustre del Carme

Església del Carme

Santa Maria

Fish Market

Biblioteca

Ajuntament

Gobierno Militar

Teatre Principal

Orfila

Portal de Sant Roc

Xoriguer Gin Distillery

Sant Francesc

Museu de Menorca

Park Entrance

Parc des Freginal

Bus Station

Sant Lluís

0 — 100 metres

MOLL DE LLEVANT
COSTA D'ES GENERAL
COSTA DE SES VOLTES
MOLL DE PONENT
ISABEL II
SANT JAUME
S'ARRAVAL
COSTA DE SES PIQUES
DALT VILANOVA
MERCADAL
SOL
COSTA DE SA PLAÇA
BONAIRE
ESGLÉSIA
PL. CONSTITUCIÓ
PLAÇA COLÓN
PORTAL DE MAR
PLAÇA CONQUISTA
PLAÇA ESPANYA
PLAÇA CARME
PLAÇA REIAL
INFANTA
NORD
CARME
NOU
DEIÀ
RECTOR MORT
ST. ROC
PLAÇA BASTIÓ
ALAIOR
BASTIÓ
SANT JORDI
MORERIES
FORN
FORC
ROVELLADA DE BAIX
ROVELLADA DE DALT
PLAÇA S'ESPLANADOM
AV. J. A. CLAVE
ES COS DE GRÀCIA
SANT JOSEP
JOSEP MARIA QUADRADO
MAÓLO
NORD
COMERÇ
CAMÍ D'ES CASTELL
SANT NICOLAU
BELLA VISTA
SANTA CECÍLIA
SANTA ROSA
SANTA SEBASTIÀ
SANT SEBASTIÀ
SANTA CATERINA
SANTA TERESA
CONCEPCIÓ
SANTA ANNA
PLAÇA MIRANDA
PLAÇA PRÍNCEP
SANT JOAN
PLAMA
ST. ELIES
VERGE DE GRÀCIA

Hotel de Dalt & Ciutadella

Airport & (250m)

N

M6

Boat Tours

Plaça Espanya

A graceful stone **stairway** and a narrow, twisting street – the Costa de Ses Voltes – tangle together behind the town port as they climb up the hill to emerge in the middle of the old town at **Plaça Espanya**. On the north side of the square, a sociable little **fish market** is plonked on top of a sturdy bastion that was originally part of the **Renaissance city wall**. This mighty zigzag of fortifications, bridges and gates once encased the whole city and replaced the city's medieval walls, sections of which also survive. Work on the new Renaissance walls started under the Habsburgs in the middle of the sixteenth century, though the chain of bastions took more than one hundred years to complete. On the right-hand side of the fish market a narrow, dead-end alley offers fine views down over the port and is home to the *Café Mirador* (see p.204).

Plaça Carme

Plaça Carme, just to the east of the fish market, is overshadowed by the massive facade of the eighteenth-century **Església del Carme**, a Carmelite church whose barn-like interior is almost entirely devoid of embellishment. The adjoining cloisters, the **Claustre del Carme**, were taken from the Carmelites in 1837 under a national edict confiscating church property and passing vast estates and buildings to the state in what was the largest redistribution of land since the Reconquista. Unsurprisingly, this was bitterly resented by the Church, but it caught the popular mood, with many small farmers hoping to buy the confiscated land from the state at knock-down prices. Later administrations did return some of the ecclesiastical property, but most of the land was lost to the Church for good. After l ong service as the municipal courts, the cloisters now house the town's fresh meat, fruit and vegetable **market** (daily 8.30am–9pm), with the stalls up against a set of vaulted arches.

Museu Hernández Sanz, Hernández Mora

Claustre del Carme, Plaza de la Miranda • Mon–Sat 10am–1pm • Free

On an upper floor of the Claustre del Carme, the **Museu Hernández Sanz, Hernández Mora** displays an idiosyncratic collection gathered together by the historian and connoisseur Hernández Sanz and gifted to the city by his son, **Joan Hernández Mora** (1902–84). It's not a large collection – it only fills half a dozen small rooms – but it begins smartly enough in the entrance hall with portraits of many of the leading figures from Menorca's history, including **Sir Richard Kane** (see p.220) and two pictures of **Admiral Byng**, one plump and bewigged, the other at his execution, by which time he seems to have lost a few pounds.

The first room proper holds several sketches of islanders in traditional costume as well as paintings of Hernández Sanz in his pomp. Then come two rooms stuffed with nineteenth-century paintings, marine-scapes for the most part, both oils and watercolours. The highlight here are **Joan Chiesa**'s five historical paintings recording, in precise detail, the comings and goings of the British army, including the final evacuation of Maó in 1802. Little is known of this Chiesa, but he was related to **Giuseppe Chiesa** (1720–89), one-time Spanish governor of the island and himself an artist with a penchant for painting historical scenes. The next room displays some rather dull canvases by one of the Mora family and then it's upstairs for a whole set of island maps. Look out too for the vitriolic British cartoon entitled *The English Lion Dismember'd*: Menorca had been returned to Spain by the Treaty of Amiens in 1802 and this clearly infuriated the cartoonist, who shows the English lion with one of his paws chopped off – and the offending paw is shaped like Menorca.

Plaça Conquesta

Just north of Plaça Espanya – and a short walk along the cobbled c/Alfons III from Plaça Constitució – the slender **Plaça Conquesta** is notable for its attractive Georgian facades. It is ill served, however, by a poorly crafted **statue of Alfonso III**, which was placed here by Franco in a typically nationalist gesture – this was the Aragonese king who expelled the Menorcan Moors.

Plaça Constitució

One of the central nerve centres of Maó, the narrow **Plaça Constitució** is where the horses and riders congregate during the *Mare de déu de Gràcia* fiesta every summer. It is, however, best known as the site Maó's town hall, or **Ajuntament**, on its northern edge, itself overshadowed by the grand **Església de Santa Maria**.

The Ajuntament

Plaça Constitució

The seventeenth-century **Ajuntament** (Town Hall) is characterized by genteel arcades, bull's-eye upper windows and wrought-iron grilles. This was all built by the Spanish, but subsequently occupied by the island's colonial governors, including Richard Kane (see box, p.220), who donated its distinctive clock. Kane also had portraits of King George III and Queen Charlotte hung in the entrance hall, but these were replaced long ago by portraits of three Spanish kings – Alfonso XIII (1886–1941), Carlos III (1716–88) and Carlos IV (1748–1819), the last two having the flamingo-like noses that centuries of inbreeding accentuated amongst the Spanish Habsburgs.

Església de Santa Maria

Plaça de la Constitució 3 • Daily 7.30am–1pm & 6–8.30pm • Free

The **Església de Santa Maria** is a heavy-duty pile founded in 1287 by Alfonso III to celebrate the island's reconquest. Rebuilt in the middle of the eighteenth century and remodelled on several subsequent occasions, the church's exterior is an enjoyable architectural hybrid, its Gothic features encased within later Neoclassical accretions. Inside, the **nave** is all Catalan Gothic, a hangar-like, aisle-less, single-vaulted construction designed to make the **high altar** visible to the entire congregation – and indeed there's no missing it, its larger-than-life Baroque excesses featuring the Virgin Triumphant with a flock of helpful cherubs. Unfortunately, the nave is also dark and gloomy, as most of the windows are bricked up in flat contradiction to the original design in which kaleidoscopic floods of light would have poured in through soaring, stained-glass windows.

In contrast to the clean lines of the nave, the truncated **transepts** sport intricate stuccowork, with another flock of cherubs peering out from a swirling, decorative undergrowth, but the church's pride and joy is really its Austrian-made **organ**, a monumental piece of woodwork from 1810 featuring trumpeting angels, four keyboards and three thousand pipes that fill the elevated gallery above the south entrance.

Carrer Isabel II

Running west from Plaça Constitució, long and slender **c/Isabel II** is distinguished by its Georgian architecture, all handsome wooden doors and fancy fanlights, sash windows, bay windows and ornate ironwork. This street was once the heart of the British administration, as recalled by today's military governor's house, the eighteenth-century **Gobierno Militar**, about halfway along, with its elaborate paintwork and shaded, colonial-style arcades.

5

There's a useful – and extremely pleasant – shortcut down to the harbour from c/ Isabel II: head down **Costa d'es General**, an alley at the foot of c/Rector Mort, which tunnels through the old city wall before snaking its way down the cliff to the waterside below.

The Església de St Francesc

Avgda Doctor Guardia • Daily 10am–12.30pm & 5–7pm • Free

The Baroque facade of the **Església de St Francesc** appears as a cliff-face of pale stone rising above the rounded, Romanesque-style arches of its doorway. The construction of the church was spread over the late seventeenth and eighteenth centuries following the razing of the town in 1535 by the piratical Hizir Barbarossa (c.1473–1547). The son of an Ottoman soldier, Barbarossa was well known for his attacks on Christian shipping, during which he would ransom his prisoners or sell them into slavery.

Inside the church, the strong lines of the Gothic **nave** are disturbed by some clumsy concrete panelling around the shallow side chapels, but there's aesthetic compensation in the pinkish tint of much of the stone and the unusual spiral decoration of the pillars. The roof vaulting is also very impressive and the flamboyant **high altar** is flanked by paintings depicting scenes from the lives of the Virgin Mary and St Francis, each and every one of them designed to edify the (illiterate) congregation. Tucked away off the north side of the nave, there's also the **Chapel of the Immaculate Conception**, an octagonal wonderland of clear white stone decorated with garlanded vines and roses in the full flourish of the Churrigueresque style. Completed in 1752, the chapel is attributed to Francesc Herrara, the painter, engraver and architect who trained in Rome and worked in Menorca before moving on to Palma in Mallorca.

Museu de Menorca

Avgda Doctor Guardia s/n • May, June & Oct Tues–Fri 10.30am–2pm; July–Sept Tues–Fri 10.30am–4.30pm; Nov–April Tues–Fri 9.30am–2pm, Sat & Sun 10am–2pm • €3

The old monastic buildings adjacent to the Església de St Francesc now house the **Museu de Menorca**, the island's largest museum. The collection is spread over **three floors**, with temporary exhibitions on the ground floor and the permanent collection above. The museum entrance is reached through the old Franciscan **cloister**, whose sturdy pillars and vaulted aisles, dating back to the early eighteenth century, illustrate the high point of the Menorcan Baroque.

The first floor

The **first floor** holds a wide range of prehistoric artefacts, beginning with bits and pieces left by the Neolithic pastoralists who were well established here by about 4000 BC. Then it's on to the **Talayotic period** (1500–123 BC), where the earlier items – household objects and the like – are pretty crude, unlike the later pieces, which exhibit considerable sophistication both in home-made goods and in the use of imported items. In particular, look out for the dainty, rather quizzical-looking **bronze bull**, probably of fifth-century Phoenician manufacture and found at Torralba d'en Salord (see p.221), and a small Egyptian bronze of **Imhotep** unearthed at Torre d'en Gaumés (see p.221). These key exhibits reflect the final flourishing of Talayotic culture when Menorca became a major port of call for ships sailing through the Mediterranean, particularly between Italy and Spain. The first floor is rounded off by an enjoyable sample of Roman pottery, including a number of notably large amphorae.

The second floor

The permanent collection continues on the **second floor**, where a series of displays gallops unconvincingly through the Moorish period up to 1900. Amongst the assorted

5

aristocratic portraits and paintings of Maó harbour, there's an interesting collection of majolica pottery, as well as a medieval stone cross retrieved from the Castell Santa Àgueda and three small displays on island crafts – costume jewellery, silver purses and shoes. Look out too for the whimsical wooden figurines (*vellons*) carved in the likeness of various island notables by two local carpenters, the scurrilous Monjo brothers, in the late nineteenth century.

Plaça Bastió

An attractive square not far from the Museu de Menorca, **Plaça Bastió** holds Maó's one remaining medieval gateway, the **Portal de Sant Roc**, a sturdy affair of roughly hewn stone comprising two turrets, a connecting arch and a projecting parapet. The gateway is named after St Roch, a fourteenth-century hermit who was popular hereabouts as a talisman to ward off the plague: Christian legend asserted that he both recovered from a bout of the plague and cured fellow sufferers, a good recommendation at a time when every city in Europe feared an outbreak.

Costa de Sa Plaça

Maó's steeply sloping main street is known as **Costa de Sa Plaça** (also signed as c/ Hannover), whose old-fashioned shops and tiny piazzas form the town's commercial centre. Another portion of the main drag is c/Moreres, where you'll spy a dinky bust-on-a-plinth of Maó's **Mateu Josep Orfila** (1787–1853), for all intents and purposes the founder of modern toxicology.

The quayside

Below the town centre stretches the 3km long **quayside**, in the middle of which is Maó's ferry terminal. To the west of the terminal, beyond a few bars and restaurants, the waterfront is occupied by the town's small fishing fleet and a mini-marina, and then comes an industrial area, that extends round the murky waters at the head of the inlet. To the east, it's a couple of hundred metres to the departure point for **boat tours** of Port de Maó (see box, p.206) and another short stroll to **Mô**, the pint-sized mermaid statue by local sculptor Leonardo Lucarini. Mô looks out at the town's **main marina**, an elongated affair where flashy chrome yachts face a string of restaurants, bars and cafés. By day, the half-hour stroll east along the quayside is tame verging on boring; at night, with tourists converging on the restaurants, it's slightly more animated.

Xoriguer gin distillery

Anden Pontiene 91 • June–Sept Mon–Fri 8am–7pm, Sat 9am–1pm; Oct–May Mon–Fri 9am–1pm & 4–7pm • Free • ⓦ xoriguer.es

A couple of minutes' walk west of Maó's ferry terminal is the showroom of the **Xoriguer gin distillery**, where you can help yourself to free samples of gin, various liqueurs and other spirits. Multilingual labels give details of all the different types, and there are some pretty obscure examples, such as **calent**, a sweet, brown liqueur with aniseed, wine, saffron and cinnamon, and **palo**, a liquorice-flavoured spirit supposedly of Phoenician provenance. The lime-green **hierbas**, a favourite local tipple, is a sweet and sticky liqueur, partly made from camomile collected on the headlands of La Mola (see p.212). In all its various guises, the main liquor is **gin** with *pomada*, a gin cocktail with lemonade, pretty much Menorca's national drink. British sailors first brought gin to Menorca in the late eighteenth century, but a local businessman, a certain Beltran, obtained the recipe in obscure circumstances and started making the stuff himself. Nowadays, Xoriguer is the most popular island brand, mostly sold in modern versions

5

of the earthenware bottles once used by British sailors and known locally as *canecas*. Here at the showroom, a litre of Xoriguer gin costs about €12.

Talatí de Dalt

4km west of Maó centre, just south off the Me-1 highway • May–Oct daily 10am–sunset; Nov–April open access • May–Oct €3; Nov–April free • If you're driving along the Me-1, watch for the sign and then follow the dusty track that reaches the site after 300m; there is no public transport

Of the several Talayotic sites in the vicinity of Maó, easily the pick is the rusticated remains of **Talatí de Dalt**. Partly enclosed by a Cyclopean wall, the site features an imposing *taula* set within a circular precinct. The *taula* here appears to be propped up by a second T-shaped pillar, though it's generally agreed that this is the result of an accidental fall, rather than by prehistoric design. Next to the *taula* are the heaped stones of the main **talayot** and just beyond are three **subterranean chambers** with columns and flagstones forming a rough roof. These three chambers, which date from the very end of the Talayotic period, abut an inner courtyard and are much more sophisticated in construction than the earlier prehistoric dwellings that dot the rest of the site. Their exact function is not known, but there's no doubt that the *taula* was the village centrepiece, and probably the focus of religious ceremonies too. The site's rural

MENORCA'S TALAYOTIC SITES

Menorca's **Talayotic sites** conform to a common pattern, though as you might expect there are marked differences in their state of repair. The tallest structure on each site is generally the *talayot* (from *atalaya*, Arabic for "watchtower"), a cone-shaped mound between 5m and 10m high, built of stone but without mortar or cement. Menorca is the site of dozens of ruined **talayots** and the detail of their original design varies from site to site: some are solid, others contain one or more chambers. Most are found in and around settlements, but there are solitary examples too. Such diversity has generated considerable academic debate about their original purpose, with scholars suggesting variously that they were built for defence, as dwellings for chieftains, as burial sites or as storehouses. Popular belief has it that they functioned as **watchtowers**, but it's a theory few experts accept: they have no interior stairway, for example, and only a handful are found along the coast. Even so, no one has come up with a more convincing explanation. The mystery of the *talayots*, which are also found on Mallorca, is compounded by their uniqueness. The only Mediterranean structures they vaguely resemble are the Nuragh towers on Sardinia, though a Sardinian kinship is but one of several options, with Egypt, Crete and Greece also posited as possible influences.

These *talayots* are often positioned a few metres from a **taula**, a T-shaped structure comprising two huge stones up to 4.5m high. Some sites may contain several *talayots*, but there's rarely more than one *taula*, and this almost always sits in the middle of a **circular enclosure** whose perimeter is (or was) marked by a low wall. Archeologists have unearthed objects in these enclosures and the remains of firepits have been found against the perimeter wall. These discoveries imply a **religious function**, though there is insufficient evidence to justify referring to the enclosures as "shrines". There's general agreement, however, that the *taula* and its enclosure formed the public part of the settlement, and on many sites the remains of family dwellings surround them. Finally, Menorca also holds a number of **navetas**, stone-slab constructions shaped like inverted loaf tins and dating from between 1400 and 800 BC. Many have false ceilings, and although you can stand up inside, they were clearly not living spaces, but rather communal tombs, or ossuaries. The prime example is the **Naveta d'es Tudons**, outside Ciutadella. *Navetas* are never found in the same place as the *talayots* and *taulas*.

Archeologists divide the **Talayotic period** into several different eras, but as far as the nonspecialist is concerned, the only significant difference between the various phases is the encircling, **perimeter wall**, a dry-stone affair often several metres high and made up of large stones. These Cyclopean walls were for defence and reflect an increase in piracy across the western Mediterranean: the earlier settlements lack them, while the later ones – from around 1000 BC – do. There's more on the Talayotic period, in Contexts (see p.242).

setting is also charming – olive and carob trees abound and a tribe of hogs roots around the undergrowth.

5

ARRIVAL AND DEPARTURE

BY BUS
Torres Autocars (☎902 07 50 66, ⊚e-torres.net) operates regular local buses to Maó from Menorca's airport (see p.195), 5km southwest of town. These buses run on a circular route, but they all drop by the bus station, off Avgda Josep Anselm Clavé, a couple of minutes' walk from Mao's main square, the leafy Plaça S'Esplanada. Torres Autocars also runs two other local bus services, both of which stop at the bus station before looping round Maó and travelling along the harbourfront past the ferry terminal. All island-wide buses arrive at – and depart from – the bus station too.

Destinations Alaior (Mon–Fri hourly, 6–8 on Sat, 6 on Sun; 10min); Cala Galdana (May–Oct 2 daily; Nov–April Mon–Sat 2 daily; 50min); Ciutadella (Mon–Fri hourly, 6–8 on Sat, 6 on Sun; 1hr); Es Castell (every 30–60 min; 10min); Es Grau (mid-June to mid-Sept 6–7 daily; 15min); Es Mercadal (Mon–Fri hourly, 6–8 on Sat, 6 on Sun; 25min); Es Migjorn Gran (May–Oct 4–6 daily; Nov–April Mon–Fri 6 daily, 3 on Sat; 30min); Ferreries (Mon–Fri hourly, 6–8 on Sat, 6 on Sun; 35min); Fornells (mid-June to mid-Sept Mon–Sat 8 daily, 3 on Sun; mid-Sept to mid-June 2–4 daily; 35min); Punta Prima (May–Oct hourly; 30min); Sant Tomàs (May–Oct 4–6 daily; 45min); Son Bou (May–Oct Mon–Sat hourly, 7 on Sun; 45min).

BY FERRY
From Barcelona and Palma Ferries sail up the Port de Maó to Maó harbour. The ferry terminal is located directly beneath the town centre, though sometimes ferries moor on the other side of the harbour, a 10- to 15min walk away. From the ferry terminal, it's a brief walk up the wide stone stairway of Costa de Ses Voltes to Plaça Espanya and the oldest part of town.

Car ferry and/or catamaran services. Three companies run between Maó and the Spanish mainland and/or Mallorca. They are Balearia (☎902 16 01 80, ⊚balearia.com); Acciona Trasmediterranea (☎902 45 46 45, ⊚trasmediterranea.es); and Iscomar (☎902 11 91 28, ⊚iscomar.com). Schedules, tariffs and tickets are available direct from the operators at the ferry terminal. There are more details of ferry and catamaran routes, as well as prices, in the Basics section (p.22).

BY CAR
Driving through the labyrinthine lanes of central Maó is well-nigh impossible and you're better off parking on the periphery. The easiest spot is the underground car park (Mon–Sat 8am–10pm; €2.40–2.60/hr) below Plaça S'Esplanada, though this is more expensive than on-street parking, which is metered during shopping hours (Mon–Fri 9am–2pm & 5.30–8.30pm, Sat 9am–2pm) with a maximum stay of two hours (€1.35). At other times, it's free – and there's more chance of a space. Note that if the time you've paid for overlaps into a free period, your ticket will be valid for the time you've got left when the next restricted period begins.

MAÓ

GETTING AROUND AND INFORMATION

Car rental Amongst many, there are branches of Europcar (☎971 36 64 00) and Centauro (☎971 35 58 88) at the airport. There are also lots of other, smaller downtown companies – the tourist office has the complete list.

Bike rental Bike Menorca, out on the ring road to the southeast of the centre at Avgda Francesc Femenies 44 (☎971 35 37 98, ⊚bikemenorca.com), rents out road and mountain bikes from €12/day.

Taxis There are taxi ranks on Plaça S'Esplanada and Plaça d'Espanya; alternatively, phone Radio Taxi Menorca on ☎971 36 71 11. Advance booking is recommended.

Tourist information There is a tourist information desk at the airport (see p.195) and another on Maó harbourfront, metres from the ferry terminal at Moll de Llevant 2 (May–Oct daily 8am–8.30pm; Nov–April Mon–Fri 10am–1pm & 5–7.30pm, Sat 10am–1pm; ☎971 35 59 52)There is also a third (larger) office in the city hall (Mon–Fri 10am–1.30pm & 5–8pm, Sat 10am–1.30pm). All will provide a free map of the island and leaflets on everything from beaches to bus timetables. They also sell the best Menorca road map on the market – the *Mapa Menorca* (1:60,000; €4.80), but they won't help you find accommodation. There's also a public transport information desk at the bus station.

ACCOMMODATION

Hotel del Almirante Carretera Maó ☎971 36 27 00, ⊚hoteldelalmirante.com. About 2km east of Maó beside the coastal road to Es Castell, this maroon and cream Georgian house was once the residence of British admiral Lord Collingwood. The delightful lobby is crammed with ancient bygones, and although the modern bedrooms beyond are modest, all are perfectly adequate. The garden terrace is especially attractive and there's an outside pool. Package-tour operators use the place, but there are often vacancies. From the town centre, take a taxi or the Es

5

Castell bus and ask to be dropped off. Closed Nov–April. **€110**

Hotel Capri c/Sant Esteve 8 ☎971 36 14 00, ⓦartiemhotels.com. Proficient three-star hotel in a modern block that's handily located near the old centre of Maó, just a couple of minutes' walk west of Plaça S'Esplanada. The pleasant, large-ish rooms have been given a splash of colour and style over the past few years, and most have balconies. The hotel also has a rooftop spa and pool. **€82**

★ **Hotel Carlos III** c/Carlos III ☎971 36 31 00, ⓦartiemhotels.com. Stellar three-star hotel with sleek, spacious rooms in white and grey, many with small balconies overlooking the pool and harbour. Lots of personality throughout, evident in unique touches such as lobby jazz on weekend evenings and printed recipes for organic Menorcan dishes left on your pillow during the day. **€78**

Hotel Catalonia Mirador d'es Port c/Dalt Vilanova 1 ☎971 36 00 16, ⓦhoteles-catalonia.com. This well-equipped, three-star chain hotel, with its own pool and gardens, occupies a modern block perched on a hill, about 10min walk west of Plaça Bastió. The interior is kitted out in brisk minimalist style and many of the bedrooms have balconies with wide harbour views. **€72**

Hostal-Residencia Jume c/Concepció 6 ☎971 36 32 66, ⓦhostaljume.com. Centrally located on a narrow side street, this large, old-fashioned, one-star *hostal* occupies a five-storey modern block and has 35 frugal, en-suite rooms. **€60**

Hostal La Isla c/Santa Caterina 4 ☎971 36 64 92, ⓦhostal-laisla.com. Rooms at this amenable one-star *hostal* may be on the small side, but they are reasonably attractive and comfortable, and all have private bathroom and TV. There's a bar and restaurant downstairs. **€60**

Hotel Port Mahón Avgda Port de Maó s/n ☎971 36 26 00, ⓦsethotels.com. Attractive, colonial-style, four-star hotel in a superb location overlooking the portside, with grand views down along the Maó inlet. There's an outside swimming pool and a patio café, plus each of the eighty-odd rooms is kitted out in smart, modern style with air conditioning. It takes about 20min to walk to the hotel from the town centre, but you can also get here by local city bus (see p.203); a flight of steps leads up to the hotel from the harbour. **€88**

EATING AND DRINKING

Traditional Menorcan food is hard to find these days, as most of Maó's **restaurants** specialize in Spanish, Catalan or Italian dishes. These tourist-oriented establishments are mainly spread out along the quayside – the Moll de Ponent west of the main stairway, the Moll de Llevant to the east. There's also a smattering of more economical **cafés** and **café-bars** in the town centre. Out of season, many places shut completely, while others close early depending on how business is doing.

CAFÉS AND CAFÉ-BARS

Café Baixamar Moll de Ponent 17. An attractively decorated little café-bar, with old-fashioned mirrors and pastel paintwork, serving tasty traditional Menorcan snacks – island cheese and sausage, for example, at very reasonable prices. Good wines too. Perfect for a snack before a trip on one of the sightseeing catamarans, which depart a few minutes' walk away. May–Oct 8am–2am; Nov–April noon–11.30pm.

Café Mirador Plaça Espanya 2. Located a few steps from the fish market – and just off the main stairway leading from the harbour to the town centre – this appealing little café-bar offers a good range of snacks and tapas, and has great views over the harbour from its terrace. Jazz is the favoured background music. Mon–Sat noon–1am.

Cristanal y Gradinata c/Isabel II, 1. Easy-going little café in the midst of the old town whose modern decor is enlivened by miscellaneous bygones, including several ancient radios. Good for drinks and snacks. Mon–Fri 8.30am–3pm & 7.30–11pm, Sat noon–3pm & 7.30–11pm. Closed Sept.

Varadero Moll de Llevant 4. Close to the ferry terminal – and adjacent to the Yellow Cats boat dock – this modern place has a restaurant on one side and a café-bar on the other. The café-bar is tasty a pleasant spot to nurse a drink and sample a small and range of tapas. Café-bar: Mon–Sat 9.30am–11pm, evenings only on Sun, and from noon in winter.

RESTAURANTS

Il Porto Moll de Llevant 225 ☎971 35 44 26. The cooks perform in full view here at this large and popular spot, turning out tasty fish and meat dishes from a wide-ranging

---

MAÓ'S MAYONNAISE MANIA

Maó has a curious place in culinary history as the birthplace of **mayonnaise** (*mahonesa*). Various legends, all of them involving the French, claim to identify its eighteenth-century inventor: take your pick from the chef of the French commander besieging Maó; a peasant woman dressing a salad for another French general; or a housekeeper disguising rancid meat from the taste buds of a French officer. The French also changed the way the Menorcans bake their bread, while the British started the dairy industry and encouraged the roasting of meat.

menu that features Italian dishes – the pizzas are particularly good (from €9.50). Popular with families. July & Aug daily 1am–4pm & 6.30pm–midnight; Sept & Oct & March–June daily 1–3.45pm & 7pm–midnight.

La Minerva Moll de Llevant 87 ☎ 971 35 19 95. This is one of the more polished restaurants in town, with smart furnishings and fittings, a pontoon-terrace, and a menu focused on seafood. It's also one of the most popular spots in town, which can be a bit of a problem – sometimes it feels more like a canteen than a restaurant. Nonetheless, many regular visitors swear by the paella and the main courses average a very affordable €15. Save room for the desserts – the vanilla custard boats in syrup speak (or even shout) for themselves. Reservations well-nigh essential at the height of the season. Daily 1.30–3.30pm & 8–11pm.

L'Arpó Moll de Llevant 124 ☎ 971 36 98 44. Unlike many of its quayside neighbours, this well-established restaurant has not jazzed itself up, but although the decor may be routinely modern, they serve an outstanding range of seafood – probably the widest selection in town. Attentive and friendly service too. Mains from €12.50. Daily noon–3pm & 7–10pm.

★ **Restaurante Cap Roig** C/Gran de Sa Mesquida, Sa Mesquida ☎ 971 18 83 83, ⓦ restaurantcaproig.com. Located 5km north of the city centre in the village of Sa

MENORCA'S TOP 5 RESTAURANTS

Restaurant Cap Roig Es Mesquida (Maó). See below

Sa Llagosta Fornells. See p.218

S'Engolidor Es Migjorn Gran. See p.223

Hotel Rural Morvedrà Nou Ciutadella. See p.236

La Guitarra Ciutadella. See p.236

Mesquida, this clifftop restaurant is well worth the trip. Ignore the uneventful interior and head straight for the catch of the day – they serve some of the best seafood on the island. Dinners can be romantic, but lunch is great too, since you really get to appreciate the views – this is when the locals really pack in. Daily 10am–midnight.

Restaurante Casa Sexto c/Vassallo 2 ☎ 971 36 84 07. First-rate Galician restaurant just off the main square. The interior is a little too dark for comfort and the service can lag, but there's a pavement gazebo and the food is reliably delicious, especially the seafood and the beef. Good wine cellar too. Mains average €18, whereas the *menú del día* is a snip at €9.90. Mon–Sat 12.30–3.30pm & 8–11pm, Sun 12.30–4pm.

BARS AND NIGHTLIFE

Nightlife isn't Maó's forte, and places come and go with remarkable speed, so the best advice is to follow the crowds. There are some fairly lively **bars** dotted along the harbourfront with one cluster just up from the ferry terminal and another towards the east end of the harbour on Moll de Llevant. These harbourfront bars open late – some not until midnight – and keep going until dawn at weekends, though they sometimes don't open at all in winter.

Akelarre Moll de Ponent 41 ☎ 971 36 85 20. Set down on the waterfront near the ferry terminal, this is probably the best – and certainly the most fashionable – bar in town, occupying an attractively renovated ground-floor vault with stone walls and a miniature garden-cum-terrace at the back, right at the foot of the old city walls. Jazz and smooth modern sounds form the backcloth, with occasional live acts. Daily 8pm till late, though sometimes closed in winter.

Ars Cafe Plaça Principe 12 ☎ 971 35 18 79 ⓦ arscafe

.wordpress.com. This cellar space has been retrofitted as a bar and small concert space that is very popular with twenty-somethings. They also do food, including seasonal, bistro-style meals, and great cocktails. June–Aug 11.30pm–6am.

Nou Bar c/Nou 1 ⓦ barnou.com. The ground-floor café, with its leather armchairs and gloomy lighting, is a dog-eared sort of place much favoured by locals. Standing-room only whenever there's a major festival – as there often is.

DIRECTORY

Banks Banks and ATMs are dotted along the main street between Plaça Espanya and Plaça S'Esplanada.

Email and internet access The public library, the Biblioteca Pública, on Plaça Conquesta, allows visitors one hour's free PC access (mid-June to mid-Sept Mon–Fri 9.30am–1.30pm; mid-Sept to mid-June Mon–Sat 9.30am–1.30pm & Mon–Fri 4.30–8.30pm).

Maps and books Llibrería Fundació, facing Plaça Colón at Costa de Sa Plaça 14 (Mon–Fri 9am–1.30pm & 5.30–8pm, Sat 9.30am–1.30pm & 5.30–8.30pm), stocks a

few English-language guidebooks and island birdwatching guides. It also sells Menorca road maps, though the main tourist offices (see p.203) have a much better range.

Market On Tuesdays and Saturdays (9am–2pm), there's a large open-air food and clothes market on Plaça S'Esplanada.

Parks Maó's main park, the Parc des Freginal (daily 8am–8pm; free), occupies a shallow gorge in the centre of town. The main entrance is on c/Deià.

5

BOAT TRIPS FROM MAÓ – AND THE ISLANDS OF PORT DE MAÓ

A boat trip from Maó is the easiest way to get close to the **three islets** that dot the inlet – four if you count tiny **Illa Pinto**, just opposite the dock, which is used by the navy and attached to the north shore by a causeway. The first of the islands to the east of Illa Pinto is the **Illa del Rei**, whose dilapidated buildings once accommodated a military hospital. This was also where Alfonso III landed at the start of his successful invasion of Muslim Menorca in 1287. Next comes pocket-sized **Illa Quarentena**, a pancake-flat islet that has been used variously as a quarantine station and a naval base. Finally, the larger **Illa del Llatzeret** is the site of a former hospital for infectious diseases, which remained in service until 1917. This islet is surrounded by imposing walls built of stone retrieved from Fort Sant Felip (see p.211): the Menorcans were convinced that contagion could be carried into town by the wind, so they built the walls to keep the germs inside. Internal walls separated patients suffering different diseases for precisely the same reason. Llatzeret was only separated from the mainland in 1900 when a canal was cut on its landward side to provide a more sheltered route to the daunting **La Mola** fortress (see p.212).

BOAT TRIPS TO THE ISLANDS

Departing from the dock near the foot of Costa de Ses Voltes, various companies run regular boat trips **along the Port de Maó**, with an hour-long scoot down and around the inlet costing €11 per person. Frequency depends on the season: from May to October there are departures every hour or so, whereas in January there are only a handful of sailings every week, if any at all. Almost all the boats have glass bottoms for underwater viewing. Of the three main companies, each of which has a harbourside ticket kiosk, **Yellow Cats** (☎639 67 63 51, ⓦyellowcatamarans.com) is as good as any. There is also a summer **water taxi** service (☎616 42 88 91, ⓦwatertaximenorca.com) down the inlet from Maó to the massive La Mola fortress, which costs €7.50 one way, and €10 return (see p.212), plus once-weekly guided tours of the decaying buildings of the Illa del Rei, though these start in Es Castell (see p.209); for more details, check out ⓦislahospitalmenorca.org or ask at Maó tourist office (see p.203).

BOAT TRIPS TO ES GRAU

In summer, longer boat trips head north and south along the coast with the most popular target being **Es Grau** (see p.215). Companies offering these longer trips include Rutas Marítimas de la Cruz (☎971 35 07 78, ⓦrutasmaritimasdelacruz.com) and Charter Menorca (☎655 75 38 08, ⓦchartermenorca.com). Prices vary enormously, but a day-long trip to Es Grau should cost around €20 per adult, including a stop for swimming and snorkelling.

Pharmacies Amongst several downtown pharmacies, there's one at c/S'Arravaleta 5 and another at c/Moreres 28 (Mon–Fri 9am–2pm & 5–8.30pm, Sat 9am–2pm).

Post Office The central *correu* is at c/Bonaire 15, just east of Plaça Bastió (Mon–Fri 8.30am–2pm; Sat 9.30am–2pm).

Port de Maó

Port de Maó, as Menorcans term the whole of the extended inlet that links Maó with the Mediterranean, is one of the finest natural harbours in the world. More than 5km long and up to 1km wide, the channel boasts the narrowest of deep-sea entrances, strategic blessings that have long made it an object of nautical desire. The high admiral of the Holy Roman Emperor Charles V quipped that "June, July, August and Mahon are the best ports in the Mediterranean", and after Barbarossa's destruction of Maó in 1535, the emperor finally took the hint and had the harbour fortified. Later, the British eyed up the port as both a forward base for Gibraltar and a lookout against the French naval squadron in Toulon, pouring vast resources into the harbour defences – fortifications which the Spanish have since updated and remodelled on several occasions.

A COASTAL HIKE FROM MAÓ TO PUNTA PRIMA

16km • 100m ascent • 5–6 hr • Easy • Trailhead GPS: +39° 53′ 20.29″, +4° 15′ 56.22″

Starting in the centre of **Maó**, this long but very varied walk winds around the southeastern corner of the island, initially following the **Port de Maó**, then detouring inland before rejoining the coast to finish at the resort of **Punta Prima**, from where there are regular buses back to Maó (May–Oct hourly; 30min). The coastal scenery is magnificent throughout, while the walk also gives a good impression of the successive layers of fortification that grew up to protect Maó's seaward approaches, as well as more recent tourist development.

THE HIKE

Beginning in Maó's **Plaça Espanya**, descend Costa de Ses Voltes and turn right along the waterfront, walking around the headland and the narrow inlet of **Cala Figuera** to reach, after 1.5km, the *Miramar* and *Rocamar hostales* (both shut-up and abandoned). About 200m beyond here, shortly before the road turns into a slipway and disappears under water, a flight of steps (leading up to no. 14) ascends to the right. Climb these and go through the gap in the wall at the top to reach an area of overgrown cliff-top scrub, divided into tiny fields by a lattice of stone walls. Follow the cliff-top path, from where there are expansive views across the Port de Maó: to the **Illa dei Rei** and its hospital buildings in the middle of the channel, with the striking salmon-pink Palladian villa known as the **Golden Farm** (see p.211) perched on a hilltop on the estuary's northern shore behind. Ahead in the distance, stacked up above the mouth of the port, are the sombre-looking bastions of **La Mola** (see p.212).

Continue along the cliffs to reach the edge of **Es Castell** (see p.209). You should come out at a large, dark-red apartment block. Keep left of this building, then continue straight on down c/Stuart for 150m to the junction with c/Cala Corb. Turn left here and walk down to the boat-filled *cala*, then up the steep flight of steps on your right. Carry on ahead down c/Cales Fonts to Es Castell's main square, also named **Plaça S'Esplanada**, then continue straight on to rejoin the waterfront above the cove of Cales Fonts. Head right here for 50m, go straight past the *Restaurante Irene* and take the second left (opposite the *Cafeteria Can Omi*) onto c/Llevant. Follow this road for 300m (straight ahead and over a crossroads) to reach the top of **Cala Padera**. Continue along this road and turn left down the paved steps which run in front of the *Sol Naciente* restaurant. These lead up to the Passeig Marítim, where you turn left and pass a block of memorably kitsch *pueblo*-style development. About 50m further on – just past a (nameless) *supermercat* and the *pueblo*-style *Sunrise Village* apartment block – a narrow and indistinct path heads left off the road. Take this path to walk along low cliff tops, with a line of holiday villas on the landward side; to reach open country.

Proceed along the waterfront, passing a walled enclosure containing a Civil War-era bunker. Beyond here, the path zigzags through the scattered outer remains of **Fort Sant Felip** (see p.211), Port de Maó's main defensive emplacement until Carlos III obligingly had it demolished, allowing the British to retake the island in 1798 without a single casualty. Continue 50m along the cliff top until you reach the high perimeter fence of the Fort Sant Felip army camp, part of the Es Castell complex. Then follow the path inland as it makes its way around the fence before bearing right across a field to reach the road leading to the army camp entrance, over which flies the Spanish flag. Turn right for 10m, then go left down the road with the dead-end sign

Both shores – as well as a trio of mid-channel islets (see box, p.206) – bear witness to all this military activity and are pockmarked by ruined fortifications, thick-walled affairs hugging the contours of the coast. The highlights of Port de Maó's **south shore** are the unusual subterranean fortress of **Fort Marlborough** and **Cala Sant Esteve**, the pretty fishing village where it is located. Of less interest is the former garrison town of **Es Castell**, purpose-built by the English in the 1770s. The **north shore** comprises a hilly promontory that nudges out into the ocean, protecting the channel from the insistent northerly wind, the Tramuntana. The promontory's steep terrain has deterred the islanders from settling here, and although recent development has spawned a pair of ritzy suburbs – Sant Antoni and Cala Llonga – the north shore's key feature is the

5

for 400m to reach a second dead-end sign, where a track heads off right – the solid-looking cobbles here are reputedly of Roman provenance, part of a road that once stretched back to Maó. Follow this track down to reach the sequestered inlet of **Cala Sant Esteve** (see p.211), then rejoin the road and turn right, heading round the *cala* for 300m and past the subterranean entrance to **Fort Marlborough** (see p.211).

When the road ends, head up through a tiny gap in the clump of trees on your left in front of house number 128 and scramble up to the top to reach a huge well. Then continue around the cliff top through further decaying military remains and innumerable crumbling dry-stone walls, aiming for the fort's most notable surviving structure, the imposing **Torre d'en Penyat** ("The Hanging Tower"). Built by the British in 1798 at the beginning of their third and final occupation of the island, the tower subsequently acquired a rather lurid reputation as a place in which local miscreants were executed – you can climb a small ladder up into the tower to enjoy its eerily echoing acoustics.

The route now heads inland. From here, go round the right-hand side of the tower, following the small path that heads inland to reach an old donkey trail between high stone walls – the **Camí de Cavalls**, for many centuries a major agricultural and military thoroughfare that ran right round Menorca's coast. Recently restored, the *camí* is open to hikers once more, but this particular stretch is distinctly overgrown. Turn left onto the *camí* and after about 400m you will reach the entranceway to Villa Eugenia. Continue over this and after a further 750m you will emerge onto a large track. Turn right here and follow the track as it curves round to the left until it meets a tarmac road. This road leads to the nearby **Binissaida de Devant** farm with its handsome farm buildings. The word *bini* is a Moorish legacy, meaning "sons" in Arabic and a common component of many place names hereabouts. If you wish to view the farm, turn right along the tarmac road. If not, turn left along the tarmac road where after about 30m a path signed Camí de Cavalls turns off to the right.

Follow this path until you reach the entrance to Son Vidal farm, where the path meets a much larger farm access road. Continue on this larger road for 300m to a T-junction and the gate to **Rafalet Nou** farm, which is to your left. If the gate is locked, circumnavigate it by carefully climbing onto the stone wall that flanks the farm access road. Then head on to the farmhouse a further 750m beyond and continue straight on through another gate. After 150m there's a gateway (currently minus its gate) where a small path heads off to the right. Follow this path for 200m to a T-junction. Turn right and continue along it for 400m where you cross a cattle grid. Go on past the drab outlying buildings of **S'Algar** for a further 600m (ignoring all side roads off on the left) until you reach a tarmac road. Head straight across for 500m to reach a second road. Turn left, then right, following signs down to the tiny **Xuroy beach**.

Walk to the top of the beach, then go left through the gap in the wall and up around the cliff top, heading to the right of the large **Torre d'Alcalfar Vell** (tower), constructed by the Spanish in 1787 and restored in the 1990s. The final 2km to Punta Prima is along magnificently unspoilt coast. The path here is waymarked by wooden posts denoting the "Camí de Cavalls" and clearly visible is the Illa de l'Aire lighthouse just offshore. Once in **Punta Prima**, a standard-issue modern resort with a wide and windy cove beach with safe swimming (and windsurfing), **buses** back to Maó can be picked up from the bus stop just west of the beach on c/Xaloc, beside the *Hotel Xaloc*.

nineteenth-century fortress of **La Mola**, which sprawls over the headland at its very tip, some 7km from Maó.

Es Castell

Tucked in tight against Port de Maó's south shore just 3km from Maó, the gridiron streets of **ES CASTELL** have a militaristic and very English air. Originally called Georgetown, the town is ranged around **Plaça S'Esplanada**, the old parade ground-cum-plaza, whose elongated barracks and Georgian-style town hall, with its stumpy, toy-town clock tower, bear witness to the British influence. Elsewhere, sash windows,

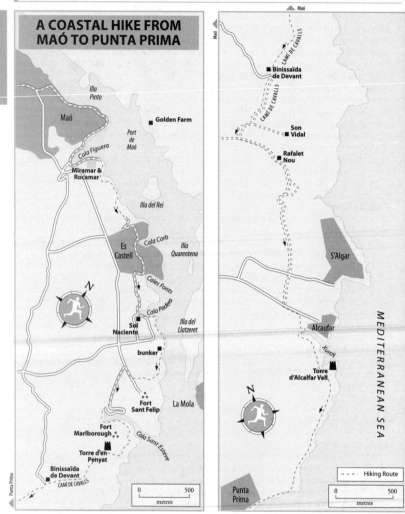

A COASTAL HIKE FROM MAÓ TO PUNTA PRIMA

Illa Pinto

Maó

Port de Maó

■ Golden Farm

Cala Figuera

Miramar & Rocamar

Illa del Rei

Es Castell

Cala Corb

Illa Quarentena

Cales Fonts

Cala Padera

Illa del Llatzeret

Sol Naciente

bunker ■

N

Fort Sant Felip

La Mola

Fort Marlborough

Cala Sant Esteve

Torre d'en Penyat

Binissaïda de Devant

CAMÍ DE CAVALLS

Punta Prima

0 — 500
metres

Maó

■ **Binissaïda de Devant**

CAMÍ DE CAVALLS

CAMÍ DE CAVALLS

■ **Son Vidal**

Rafalet Nou ■

S'Algar

Alcaufar

Xuroy

Torre d'Alcalfar Vell ■

N

M E D I T E R R A N E A N   S E A

Punta Prima

- - - - Hiking Route

0 — 500
metres

doors with glass fanlights, and wrought-iron grilles adorn many of the older houses, though nowadays the centre looks somewhat bedraggled: as a garrison town, the fortunes of Es Castell have always been tied to those of the military, and, with Franco gone, the army no longer has the same prestige.

Nevertheless, Es Castell is still worth a brief wander, beginning on the Plaça S'Esplanada, where one of the old barracks is home to a modest **military museum**, equipped with a motley collection of old rifles and uniforms (June–Aug Mon–Fri & first Sun in the month 10am–1pm; Sept–May Mon, Wed, Fri & first Sun in the month 10am–1pm; €3). From the plaza, it's a couple of minutes' walk east down c/Stuart to the harbour, a pleasant spot occupying the thumb-shaped cove of **Cales Fonts**. Stroll north along the waterside from here and you'll pass a string of **restaurants** before you reach the sullen **bastion** at the end of the harbour that is all that remains of the town's fortifications. Beyond, c/Bellavista leads west back towards the main square – hang a left at either c/Sant Ignasi or c/Victori. Buses from Maó stop on c/Gran, just steps away from the main square along c/Victori.

Fort Sant Felip

Guided tours only: June–Sept Thurs & Sun 10am; Oct, Nov & March–May Sat 10am • €5 • ☎ 971 36 21 00

The main coastal road continues beyond Es Castell down towards the mouth of the Port de Maó before veering right for Sant Lluís (see p.213). Keeping straight, you soon pass the turning for Cala Sant Esteve (see below), from where it's a further 300m or so to the gates of a *zona militar*. This restricted military area sprawls over the inlet's most southerly headland, where the Emperor Charles V built an imposing star-shaped fortress in the 1550s, naming it **Fort Sant Felip** after his son, later Philip II. Once Menorca's greatest stronghold, the fort was adapted by the British, who controlled the seaway from the multitude of subterranean gun batteries they and their predecessors had carved in the soft sandstone. Unfortunately, this irritated the Spanish so much that once Menorca was returned to them in 1782 they promptly destroyed the fort in a fit of pique – a rather misguided move since the lack of defences allowed the British to recapture the island with the greatest of ease just a few years later. Today, next to nothing survives save the most fragmentary of ruins above ground with several old Spanish and British gun galleries and tunnels down below.

Fort Marlborough

Cala Sant Esteve • Currently closed for restoration; check with Maó tourist office (see p.203) for latest opening details

In the extraordinarily picturesque little village of **CALA SANT ESTEVE**, where old fishermen's houses necklace a slender cove with a turquoise sea lapping against crumbly cliffs, a tunnel burrows into the hillside to enter what was once **Fort Marlborough**. This intricate, largely subterranean stronghold was built by the British to guard the southern approach to Fort Sant Felip between 1710 and 1726 and substantially reinforced sixty years later. The fort, which was named after one of Britain's most talented generals, Sir John Churchill, the Duke of Marlborough, was besieged twice – by the French in 1756 and the Spanish in 1781 – and although it was captured on both occasions, it was only after a prolonged battle. One of the advantages of this type of fortress was that it could tie up a large enemy force for weeks and yet require a minuscule garrison – the British put just sixty men here.

Golden Farm

Ctra. La Mola Km3 • No public access • ☎ 971 59 51 52, ⓦ sanantoniomenorca.com

From the traffic island at the west end of Maó's harbour, a byroad soon leaves the city behind, threading its way over leafy hills to pass, after 3km or so, the **Golden Farm**, a fine old mansion in the British colonial style, perched on the hillside on the northern shore of the Port de Maó. The house is actually seen to best advantage when approached from the east and only then can you spy its grand portico, whose two arcaded galleries dominate the south (Maó) side of the house. The upper gallery – the balcony – is equipped with a delicate balustrade and classical deities decorate the tympanum, a trio of languorous figures in vaguely erotic poses.

The mansion may well have been **Admiral Nelson**'s headquarters, albeit briefly, during the island's third British occupation (1798–1802), and there's all sorts of folkloric tittle-tattle alluding to romantic trysts here between Nelson and his mistress, **Emma Hamilton**. In fact, Nelson was much too concerned with events in Naples, where the Hamiltons were ensconced, and did his best to avoid visiting Menorca at all – he only came here once or twice for a couple of days apiece – despite it being crucial for

5

Britain's naval control of the Mediterranean. In July 1799, his superior, Lord Keith, mustered his fleet at Port de Maó to resist a possible French attack and ordered Nelson to join him. Nelson refused point blank, writing to the Admiralty, "I am fully aware of the act I have committed, but, sensible of my loyal intentions, I am prepared for any fate which may await my disobedience." The Admiralty let it go, and Keith ranted and raved in vain.

La Mola

May–June & Sept daily 10am–8pm; July & Aug daily 10am–9pm; Oct–April Tues–Sun 10am–2pm • €8 • ☎ 971 36 40 40, Ⓦ fortalesalamola.com

Beyond Golden Farm, the road along Port de Maó's northern shore weaves over a stretch of wind-raked heathland before passing close to the severe stone walls of the **Illa del Llatzeret** (see box, p.206) as it approaches the causeway over to the imposing fortifications of **La Mola**. Visitors proceed over the causeway, carrying on for another 600m or so until they reach the car park in sight of the main gate, the **Porta de la Reina** (Queen's Gate), named after **Queen Isabel II** of Spain, during whose turbulent reign the fortress was constructed.

Well worth a few hours' visit, La Mola is one of the most imposing fortresses in the Mediterranean, its assorted stone walls and gun emplacements dominating the spatulate headland that rears up at the end of the Port de Maó. It was built to protect Spain's Mediterranean coast from the French and British, with construction beginning on the fortress in 1850 and continuing for 25 years. Most of the effort went into the remarkable **landward defences**, whose tiers of complementary bastions, ditches and subterranean gun batteries were designed to resist the most intensive of artillery bombardments. In the event, it was hardly put to use: La Mola was built on the assumption that naval guns had a limited elevation, but when the British, amongst others, armed their ships with guns that could be elevated (and therefore lob shells over the walls) the fortress became immediately obsolete. Luckily, though, this meant that no one ever bothered to attack it and it's been kept in a good state of repair.

ARRIVAL AND DEPARTURE   LA MOLA

By bus Buses to La Mola (mid-May to mid-June Mon, Wed & Fri 1 daily; mid-June to mid-Sept Mon–Sat 1 daily) leave from the ticket office on Maó's waterfront, at the foot of Costa de Ses Voltes: reservations advised.

By water taxi Alternatively, water taxis also leave from the ticket office on Maó's waterfront, at the foot of Costa

de Ses Voltes (mid-May to mid-June Tues, Thurs & Sat 1 daily; mid-June to mid-Sept 1 daily; €17 including fortress admission fee). Reservations (which can also be made at the ticket office) should be made at least 24hr in advance.

Southeast Menorca

The southeast corner of Menorca, bounded by the road between Maó and Cala en Porter, consists of a low-lying limestone plateau fringed by a rocky shoreline with a string of craggy coves. In recent years, resorts have mushroomed along the coast hereabouts – not the high-rise resorts of the 1960s, but low-rise villa-villages that have gobbled up large chunks of land. It's difficult to be enthusiastic, especially in **Cala en Porter**, the biggest and perhaps the ugliest *urbanització* of the lot, though earlier developments, such as the attractive resort of **Cala d'Alcalfar**, which fringes a particularly picturesque cove, are more appealing. Away from the coast, the interior is dotted with holiday homes, but it's all very discreet and for the most part this remains an agricultural landscape crisscrossed by country lanes and dotted with tiny villages, plus one town – the mildly diverting **Sant Lluís**.

5

MENORCA'S TOP 5 FINCAS AND AGROTOURISMOS

Alcaufar Vell Cala d'Alcalfar. See p.214
Biniarroca Sant Lluís. See below
Binigaus Vell Es Migjor Gran. See p.225
Ca Na Xini Ferreries. See p.226
Hotel Rural Morvedrà Nou Ciutadella. See p.236

GETTING AROUND   SOUTHEAST MENORCA

By bus From May to October, getting around by bus is fairly straightforward, with hourly services from Maó to Sant Lluís and Punta Prima, as well as regular services to Cala d'Alcalfar. In winter, there's a good bus service from Maó to Sant Lluís, but little else. Bear in mind also that, with the exception of Cala d'Alcalfar and Punta Prima, most of the resorts hereabouts spread for miles, and if you've rented a villa you could face a long trek from the nearest bus stop.

By taxi If you don't have your own transport, you may need to ring for a taxi – try Radio Taxis on ☏ 971 36 71 11.

ACCOMMODATION

Holiday homes and **package-tour operators** rule the local roost, so there are only lean pickings for the independent traveller. Nevertheless, there is a reasonable chance of finding a **room** here and there amongst the southeast's scattering of hotels and *hostales*, and there are also a couple of lovely renovated *fincas* in the region.

Sant Lluís

Just 4km south from Maó along the Me-8, **SANT LLUÍS** is a trim, one-square, one-church town of brightly whitewashed terraced houses. As at Es Castell, the town's gridiron street plan betrays its colonial origins: on this occasion, it was a French commander, the Duc de Richelieu, who built Sant Lluís to house his Breton sailors in the 1750s, naming the new settlement after the thirteenth-century King Louis IX, who was beatified for his part in the Crusades. The French connection is further recalled by the three coats of arms carved on the west front of the large, whitewashed **church** – those of the royal household and two French governors.

ARRIVAL AND DEPARTURE   SANT LLUÍS

By bus Buses from Maó pull in at the north end of Sant Llius beside Plaça Nova.

ACCOMMODATION

★ **Biniarroca Hotel** Camí Vell 57, Sant Lluís ☏ 971 15 00 59, ⓦ biniarroca.com. A lavishly renovated old *finca*, just to the northeast of Sant Lluís. Run by a charming British landscape painter and her partner, this deluxe hotel comes with eighteen plush guest rooms decorated in pleasant retro style. There's also an outside pool and gardens with lovely classical sculptures, and a first-rate restaurant (reservations required), where the menu features home- and island-grown ingredients. Closed mid-Oct to April. **€170**

Cala d'Alcalfar

A pretty little resort 5km southeast of Sant Lluís, **CALA D'ALCALFAR** consists of little more than a smattering of holiday homes and old fishermen's cottages set beside an inlet of flat-topped cliffs and a turquoise sea. Here development is restrained, and you can enjoy the sandy beach, then stroll out across the surrounding headlands, one of which has its own Martello tower. To get here, keep on the main road (the Me-8) from Sant Lluís, then take the fork which does not lead to S'Algar, whose rank upon rank of suburban-looking villas sprawl along the coast.

ARRIVAL AND DEPARTURE   CALA D'ALCALFAR

By bus Buses from Maó arrive in the centre of Cala d'Alcaufar, about 200m from the *Hostal Xuroy*.

5

CLUBBING AT THE CLIFF-FACE: THE COVA D'EN XOROI

Sprawling **CALA EN PORTER** may be an unappetizing *urbanització*, but it does possess one of the island's most popular attractions, the **Cova d'en Xoroi**, a large cave set in the cliff-face high above the ocean with a dramatic stairway leading to the entrance from the clifftop up above. During the day, the cave is open to visitors (May–Oct daily 11.30am–9pm; €8, including one drink; ☎971 37 72 36, ⍟covadenxoroi.com), but at night it really comes into its own as a **nightclub** (May–Oct Fri–Sun from 11pm) showcasing some big-name DJs; check the website or give them a call to see who is on when. A taxi from Maó to the *cova* should cost around €25.

The cave is also the subject of one of the island's best-known **folk tales**. Legend has it that a shipwrecked Moor named **Xoroi** (literally, "One Ear") hid out here, raiding local farms for food. Bored and lonely, he then kidnapped a local virgin – the so-called "Flower of Alaior" – and imprisoned her in his cave. Eventually, Xoroi's refuge was discovered when locals picked up his tracks back to the cave after a freak snowstorm. Cornered, Xoroi committed suicide by throwing himself into the ocean, while the girl (and the children she'd borne) were taken back to Alaior.

ACCOMMODATION

★ **Alcaufar Vell** Carretera Alcalfar, Sant Lluís ☎971 15 18 74, ⍟www.alcaufarvell.com. This delightful, charming fifteenth-century stone farmhouse, 1.5km from the coast at Cala Alcalfar, has been boutique-ified to become one of Menorca's most atmospheric hotels. The 21 rooms are simple, awash with whitewashed stone and adobe-coloured tile, and some of them have pitched roofs and beamed ceilings, but all have jacuzzi-style baths. The restaurant is highly recommended, as is the staff. **€278**

Hostal Xuroy ☎971 15 18 20, ⍟xuroymenorca.com. The main footpath down to Cala Alcalfar's beach runs through the family-run *Hostal Xuroy*, a pleasant two-star establishment with forty-odd, spick-and-span (but basic) modern rooms, the pick of which have sea-facing balconies; it's a popular spot, so advance reservations are advised. Closed Nov–April. **€60**

Fornells and the northeast coast

Stretching out between Es Grau and the Cap de Cavalleria, Menorca's **northeast coast** holds some of the island's prettiest scenery, its craggy coves, islets and headlands rarely rattled by developers as the harsh prevailing wind – the Tramuntana – makes life too blustery for sun-seeking packagers. There are developed coves, for sure, but most of this stretch of coast remains delightfully pristine.

Much of the northeast coast is readily reached via the enjoyable, 25km-long **Me-7**, linking Maó and Fornells. This runs alongside cultivated fields protected by great stands of trees, with the low hills that form the backbone of the interior in the distance. The first turning takes you to **Es Grau**, the starting point for a delightful two- to three-hour hike along the coast or a shorter stroll along the marshy shores of **S'Albufera**, a freshwater lake noted for its birdlife. The next major turning – just beyond the Camí d'en Kane (see p.220) – clips north to the windy bleakness of the **Cap de Favàritx**, and the two turnings after that head north again for the four big villa resorts hereabouts – Port d'Addaia, Na Macaret, Arenal d'en Castell and Son Parc – though you're unlikely to want to stop at any of these. More rewarding is the bayside **Fornells**, one of the most appealing resorts on the island. Although there's no **beach** at Fornells itself, it makes a good base for visiting some of the more remote cove beaches nearby, such as **Platja de Cavalleria** and Platja de Ferragut.

GETTING AROUND

FORNELLS AND THE NORTHEAST COAST

By bus From mid-June to mid-September, there's a good bus service from Maó to both Fornells and Es Grau, but nothing to Cap de Favàritx. In the same months, there is also a goodish bus service from Maó to Arenal d'en Castell and Son Parc. Out of season, there's a skeleton service from Maó to Fornells, but nothing much else. All these buses are operated by Autos Fornells (⍟autosfornells.com).

5

Es Grau

A neat, trim little village overlooking a horseshoe-shaped bay, **ES GRAU** sees scrub and sand dunes fringing a vaguely unenticing arc of greyish sand. The shallow waters here are, however, ideal for children, and at weekends the handful of bars and restaurants that dot the main street are crowded with holidaying Mahonese. It is reached by taking the first right turn off the Maó–Fornells road, then threading your way up through some lovely wooded hills.

EATING AND DRINKING   ES GRAU

Bar Es Grau Plaça des Mestre Jaume 13 ☎971 35 94 16. The most popular place to eat is the *Bar Es Grau*, whose shaded terrace perches on the water's edge at the start of the village, though you'd be well advised to stick to their salads rather than the pizzas.

Tamarindos Paso Des Tamarell 14 ☎971 35 94 20. Along the waterfront, *Tamarindos* is a smart place, where they serve a good range of seafood with main courses averaging €15–20. May–Oct daily 7–9pm; June–Aug daily noon–4pm & 7–10.30pm.

Parc Natural S'Albufera des Grau

Park information centre May–Sept Mon, Tues, Sat & Sun 9am–3pm, Wed–Fri 9am–7pm • ☎ 971 35 63 03

The scrub-covered dunes behind Es Grau's beach form the eastern periphery of an expanse of dunes encircling the **freshwater lagoon** of S'Albufera des Grau. Only 2km from east to west and a couple of hundred metres wide, the lagoon has just one outlet, the faint stream – La Gola – that trickles out into the bay beside Es Grau. The lake was once fished for bass, grey mullet and eels – a real island delicacy – but fishing and hunting have been banned since the creation of the **Parc Natural S'Albufera des Grau** in the 1990s. The park boasts a varied terrain, including dunes (which are glued together by a combination of Aleppo pine, marram grass and beach thistle), and wetland, concentrated at the west end of the lake and containing patches of saltworts and rushes. Not surprisingly, the lagoon and its surroundings are rich in birdlife, attracting thousands of migrant birds in spring and autumn. For more on Menorca's birds, see Contexts (pp.262–263 & pp.265–266).

The **access road** into the park begins 2.5km back from Es Grau on the road to Maó. Just 1.5km long, it skims past a scattering of villas before reaching the **park information centre**. Beyond here, veer left at the fork and keep going until you reach the dirt **car park**,

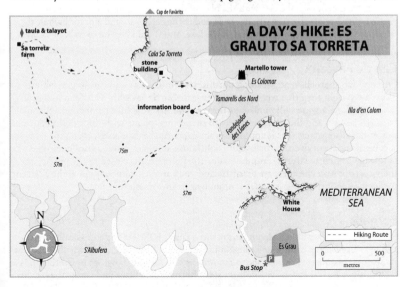

A DAY'S HIKE: ES GRAU TO SA TORRETA

5

A DAY'S HIKE: ES GRAU TO SA TORRETA

Circular • 9km • 150m ascent • 3hr–3hr 30min • Easy • Trailhead GPS: +39° 56′ 56.99″, +4° 16′ 3.26″

This **coastal walk** takes you from the small resort of Es Grau along one of the wildest sections of the Menorcan seaboard, with a circular detour inland past the S'Albufera lagoon to visit the Talayotic complex of Sa Torreta, one of the remotest prehistoric sites on the island. The going is mainly easy and largely along well-marked tracks, with only one modest ascent towards the highest point of the walk at Sa Torreta farm. Note that some of the gates on the route are inscribed "Propriedad Privato" (Private Property): you can safely ignore these signs, but make sure that you keep to the tracks.

THE HIKE

Starting at the tarmac car park (and bus stop) at the entrance to **Es Grau**, walk round the large sandy beach and follow the path on the far side as it climbs up onto the low cliffs. At the top, ignore the well-defined track that heads off left and continue straight on, descending very sharply, then follow the path as it bears right until you see a solitary white house ahead.

About 50m before you reach the house, a path branches off uphill to the left. Follow this to the top of the hill, with the low-slung **Illa d'en Colom** (island) off the coast directly ahead, after which the path swings left, giving expansive views of the rugged coast beyond, without a single sign of human habitation to be seen until, about 50m further on, the **lighthouse** on Cap de Favàritx hoves into view. As soon as you see the lighthouse, watch out for the path that descends to your right. Clamber down this path, past a curious little stone shelter built into the cliff side, then continue leftwards along the coast, which is clothed in wild maquis, comprising low, convoluted clumps of mastic and wild olive dotted with spiky pin-cushions of *Launaea cervicornis* (try not to sit on them). Aim about 45 degrees left of the Martello tower ahead, keeping left of the bare, rocky headland to your right and follow any of the various paths that cross the maquis to reach the small bay of **Fondejador des Llanes**, a tiny, driftwood-covered cove, plus a longer, sandier inlet immediately beyond.

Follow the path directly above the beach, which is waymarked with posts inscribed "Camí de Cavalls", to a wall with a gap. Twenty metres beyond this is a small sandy clearing that accommodates a large information board relating to Cala Tamarells, a neighbouring beach. Bear

from where clearly marked paths run along the lake's southern shore. It's easy walking and the scenery is gentle on the eye, with the blue of the lake set against the rolling greens and yellows of the dunes. Birders – both casual and enthusiasts – should aim for **Es Prat**, the large patch of wetland at the west end of the lake, and should be sure to pack binoculars.

Cap de Favàritx

On the Maó–Fornells road, heading northwest from the Es Grau turning, it's about 7km to the right turn that weaves its way over to **Cap de Favàritx**. This 8km long side road cuts along a wide valley and slips through dumpy little hills before the landscape becomes barer – and the grass gives way to succulents (plants with thick fleshy leaves or stems that store water) – as it approaches the cape. At the cape itself, even the succulents can't survive and the solitary **lighthouse** shines out over a bare lunar-like landscape of tightly layered, crumbly slate. The lighthouse is closed to the public, but the views out over the coast are dramatic and you can pick your way along the adjacent rocks, though if the wind is up (as it often is) this isn't much fun.

Fornells

Set roughly midway along Menorca's northern coast, **FORNELLS** is a classically pretty fishing village at the mouth of a long and chubby bay. The place is known above all for its **seafood restaurants**, whose speciality, *caldereta de llagosta* (langosta in Castilian), is a fabulously tasty – if expensive – lobster stew. Beyond the village and across the bay lie

left at the end of the clearing, following a path for a few more metres to reach a wide track (remember this point carefully for later on). Turn left and follow the track inland as it climbs up and then downhill through a beautifully secluded valley. After 750m the track gradually swings right and you have your first proper view of the **S'Albufera lagoon** (see p.215) to your left, one of Menorca's richest ornithological sites (with binoculars you may be able to see some of its bird life). The track slaloms right and gradually ascends for 1km, climbing steadily uphill (ignore the couple of subsidiary paths which head off to the left). The island's highest point, **Monte Toro** (see p.222), now becomes visible in the distance as you ascend, while near the top to your left there's an overgrown and impassable walled track, typical of many of the island's abandoned donkey trails.

Go through a Menorcan-style gate to reach a T-junction, then go left to arrive at the farmhouse of **Sa Torreta**. Go through another gate, then turn right and walk 100m to a second T-junction. Go left here through a third gate. After 25m you'll pass a large circular threshing floor on your left, with the Sa Torreta's **taula and talayot** now visible ahead. Just past the threshing floor, go through the gap in the wall on your right and cross the field to reach the walled Talayotic enclosure, one of the least-visited prehistoric sites on Menorca, and one of the few on the northern side of the island. The fine 4m *taula* and partly collapsed *talayot* here are proof of the longevity of Menorca's megalithic culture, postdating earlier examples by as much as a thousand years.

You're now at the highest point of the walk, with grand views down to the coast below. Retrace your steps past the threshing floor and back to the (third) gate, then turn left, continuing on along the main track for 1km downhill (ignoring a prominent left turn just before you rejoin the seafront) through a Menorcan style gate to reach **Cala Sa Torreta**, a remote, scrub-covered beach littered with dried seaweed and sea-borne rubbish – not much good for swimming, though the clump of Aleppo pines behind the beach is a pleasant spot for a picnic and some birdwatching.

The track continues behind the beach to reach a fork. Go left here and past a small stone building, then across a small headland back towards the small bay of **Tamarells des Nord** and the Martello tower which you saw earlier. Here the path swings away from the shore. Walk inland on the track and continue for about 500m until you reach the narrow path on your left leading back to the sandy clearing with the Cala Tamarells information board. From this point retrace your steps back to Es Grau.

austere rocky headlands, where winter storms and ocean spray keep vegetation to a minimum. This bleak terrain envelops various fortifications – evidence of the harbour's past importance – of which two are easy to reach: the battered remains of **Castell de Sant Antoni** (open access; free), in Fornells itself, and a circular watchtower, the **Torre de Fornells** (April–Oct Tues–Fri 10am–3.30pm, Sat & Sun 10am–3pm; €2.40), which is approached up a wide walkway at the northern end of the village. The short haul up to the watchtower is worth the effort as the views over the coast are simply fantastic.

Fornells picked up its first **fortifications** in the late seventeenth century to ward against the threat of Arab and Turkish corsairs, but the British went further, constructing a string of mini-forts here, including the Torre de Fornells, and then posting a garrison. One of the British commanders here exceeded his military brief, turning a local chapel into a tavern and incurring the disapproval of fellow officer John Armstrong: "In the Temple of Bacchus, no bounds are set to their [the soldiers'] Debauches and such a quantity of Wine is daily swallowed down, as would stagger Credulity itself."

ARRIVAL AND INFORMATION   FORNELLS

By bus Fornells' de facto bus station is right on the waterfront in front of the main restaurant strip, metres from the minuscule main square, Plaça S'Algaret. There is regular service to Maó (mid-June to mid-Sept Mon–Sat 8 daily, 3 on Sun; mid-Sept to mid-June 2–4 daily; 35min).

Tourist information There is a tourist information office

inside the Torre de Fornells which can offer information about the area (May–Oct Mon–Fri 9.30am–3pm, Sat & Sun 10am–2pm).

By car Parking can be a pain: the long approach road leading into Fornells is often jam packed, but there's nearly always space on the waste ground just behind – and west of – the main square.

5

ACTIVITIES

The village's sweeping inlet provides ideal conditions for **scuba diving** – the coastline around here offers easily the best diving in Menorca – and **windsurfing**, as evidenced by the flocks of windsurfers scooting across the calm waters at the southern end of the bay as you approach Fornells.

Aventura Náutica Passeig Marítim 68 ☎ 689 02 28 86, ⓦ aventuranauticamenorca.com. Aventura Náutica, just south of the centre along the waterfront, organizes speedboat excursions round the north coast with snorkelling and swimming part of the deal. Prices start from €60, which includes refreshments and snorkelling equipment hire.

Diving Center Fornells ☎ 971 37 64 31, ⓦ divingfornells.com. The Diving Center Fornells, on the waterfront at the south end of the village, rents out equipment and organizes diving courses for both novice

and experienced divers. Dives including full equipment rental start from €60 in high season; open-water diving courses cost €450 in high season. Advance reservations for courses and equipment are strongly advised, though 24hr is usually enough except in the height of the season.

Wind Fornells ☎ 971 18 81 50, ⓦ windfornells.com. Wind Fornells, located just beyond the southern edge of the village, offers windsurfing tuition to both novices and more experienced hands, and teaches sailing skills too. Four-hour courses start from €136.

ACCOMMODATION

Fornells has a few reasonably priced and comfortable **hostales** that don't get block-booked by package-tour operators, so there's a fair chance of a vacancy even in high season – but it's best to book ahead just in case.

Hostal La Palma Plaça S'Algaret 3 ☎ 971 37 66 34, ⓦ hostallapalma.com. Bang in the centre of Fornells on the main square, this two-star *hostal* is a neat little place, with simple, but cheerfully bright and colourful, en-suite rooms. There's also an outside pool, and they have larger apartments for longer stays. Closed Nov–March. **€95**

Hostal S'Algaret Plaça S'Algaret 7 ☎ 971 37 65 52, ⓦ hostal-salgaret.com. Straightforward two-star *hostal* right on a small square with some thirty guest rooms, all en suite and decorated in brisk modern style, plus a small outside pool. Closed Jan. **€90**

EATING AND DRINKING

Fornells is renowned for its excellent **restaurants** that populate the centre of the village: such is their reputation that many islanders phone up days in advance to book a table or place an order.

Es Cranc c/Escoles 31 ☎ 971 37 64 42. A 5min walk north of Plaça S'Algaret, along the pedestrianized main street and just past the church, this popular and very informal restaurant offers a wide variety of fish dishes, with the signature *caldereta de llagosta* going for €68. April to mid-Nov Mon, Tues & Thurs–Sun 1–3pm & 7.30–10.30pm.

Es Port c/Riera 5 ☎ 971 37 64 03. On the waterfront, just south of Plaça S'Algaret, this relaxed and easygoing restaurant specializes in a magnificent *caldereta de llagosta* (€64). April–Oct Sat–Thurs 1–4pm & 7.30–11pm.

★ **Sa Llagosta** c/Gabriel Gelabert 12 ☎ 971 37 65 66. This cosy little restaurant, in a sympathetically converted old fisherman's house just along the waterfront from Plaça

S'Algarete, has a small but select menu with the emphasis on local dishes and ingredients. The portions may be petite, but the flavours are delicious with each dish carefully prepared and presented. Main courses average around €20, though the *caldereta de llagosta* will cost you €69. April–Sept daily 11am–3pm & 6–10.30pm.

Sa Nansa c/Vivers 5. Just out of the main restaurant scrum, a short walk north along the waterfront from the centre of the village, this café-restaurant may be short on decorative charm, but its menu is competitively priced and it covers all the Menorcan classics as well as pizzas and *bocadillos from* €10. Eat inside or on the small pavement terrace. April–Oct daily 11am–4pm & 6–11pm.

Cap de Cavalleria

About 3km south of Fornells, the roads from Maó and Es Mercadal meet at a staggered crossroads. From here, a signposted turning leads west down a pretty country lane through a charming landscape of old stone walls and scattered farmsteads. After about 3km, keep straight on at the intersection and proceed for another kilometre or so to the signposted right turning that leads north (along an asphalted byroad) to the **Cap de Cavalleria**, Menorca's northernmost point, named after the *cavalleries* – baronial estates – into which the island was divided after the Reconquista. Amid dramatic coastal scenery, the Cap itself is a bleak and wind-buffeted hunk of rock with 90m-high sea cliffs, topped by a lonely **lighthouse** (*far*; no access). If you're lucky you'll glimpse some of the Balearic shearwaters that congregate here – a recent environmental project to restore their habitat has boosted their numbers.

The beaches

Around 2km beyond the Cap de Cavalleria turn-off, at the bend in the road, roadside parking marks the start of the 700m-long footpath that leads across the dunes to **Platja de Ferragut**, an arc of sand sheltered to the west by a jutting promontory. It's another 1km to the car park for the delightful **Platja de Cavalleria**, a slightly longer and wider beach next door to Platja de Ferragut: the walk to the beach only takes a few minutes, but there are no facilities so bring your own food and drink. Other more secluded coves can be reached from these two beaches along the Camí de Cavalls coastal footpath, the two obvious targets being the **Platja de Binimel-Là**, a shale beach where the waters are clear and good for swimming and snorkelling, though seaweed can be a problem, and, further to the west, **Cala Pregonda**, a seastack-studded bay with a wide sandy beach.

Ecomuseu Cap de Cavalleria

Camí de Sa Cavalleria Apartado 68 • Daily: April–June & Oct 10am–7pm; July–Sept 10am–8.30pm • €3 • ⓦ ecomuseodecavalleria.com

About 1km beyond the Platja de Cavalleria car park, a short side road leads up to the **Ecomuseu Cap de Cavalleria**, an excellently curated little museum located in an old farmstead perched on a hillock with wide views over the cape beyond. This area was settled by the Romans in 123 BC, a connection that convinced the European Union to fund the Ecomuseu and a number of archeological digs around here. The museum runs a summertime archaeological field school for students, some of whose Roman and Talayotic finds end up on display in the museum.

Clearly visible from the Ecomuseu, about 500m north of the museum turning, is the site of the Roman settlement of **Sanisera**. The Romans built the town and port of Sanisera on the ruins of an earlier Phoenician settlement, beside a long and sheltered inlet, the **Port de Sanitja** – though almost nothing survives from either period. Archeologists have explored the site of the Roman settlement – there's a small collection of their finds in the Ecomuseu – and you can spot the scant results of their endeavours beside the road, but the main historical artefact hereabouts is the **Martello tower** – the **Torre de Sanitja** – built at the very mouth of the inlet by the British at the end of the eighteenth century.

Central Menorca

A traditional region, **Central Menorca** is the agricultural heart of the island, its rippling hills and rolling plains speckled with scores of whitewashed farmsteads. The land still carries the myriad marks of past agrarian endeavours in its dry-stone walls and stone **ziggurats** (*barraques*), which were built to shelter cattle from wind and sun, and there are scores of **Talayotic sites** in various states of repair. Neither have the four little towns of the interior – **Alaior**, **Es Mercadal**, **Ferreries** and **Es Migjorn Gran** – been much modernized, and each contains a comely ensemble of old houses dating from the eighteenth century, sometimes olds. All four towns are readily reached via the Me-1, which runs the 45km across the island from Maó to Ciutadella.

5

RICHARD KANE AND THE CAMÍ D'EN KANE

In 1712, during the first British occupation of the island, **Sir Richard Kane** (1662–1736) was appointed **Lieutenant-Governor of Menorca**, a post he held – with one or two brief interruptions – until the year of his death. When Kane first arrived in Menorca he found a dispirited and impoverished population, so set about improving the island's woefully inadequate **food supply**. He drained swampland near Maó and introduced new and improved strains of seed corn. The governor also had livestock imported from England – hence the Friesian cattle that remain the mainstay of the island's cheese-making industry. Meanwhile, a tax on alcohol provided cash to improve the port facilities at Maó and build the first **road** right across the island. Much of this road, the **Camí d'en Kane**, has since disappeared beneath newer versions, but part of it – from just north of Maó to Es Mercadal – has survived and now serves as a scenic alternative to the Me-1.

Kane's innovations were not approved of by the Menorcan aristocracy, who were offended when he arranged for the capital to be moved from Ciutadella to Maó. They bombarded London with complaints, eventually inducing a formal governmental response in an open letter to the islanders entitled "A Vindication of Colonel Kane". In addition, the governor caused offence by holding Protestant services for his troops in Catholic churches. Despite this, however, most Menorcans welcomed Kane's benevolent administration, and by the time of his death, Kane was a widely respected figure on the island.

GETTING AROUND CENTRAL MENORCA

By bus Fast and frequent buses ply the Me-1, with supplementary summertime services running from Maó to Sant Tomàs, Son Bou, and Cala Galdana plus destinations in between. Es Migjorn Gran and Cala Galdana are also reachable by bus from both Maó and Ciutadella.

ACCOMMODATION

Accommodation for the independent traveller in this region is sparse. The resorts are dominated by the package-tourist industry, though you can, of course, take pot luck. Of the four inland towns, Ferreries, Es Mercadal and Es Migjorn Gran have one or two recommendable hotels or *hostales* each, but there's nowhere to stay in Alaior.

Alaior and around

ALAIOR, an old market town some 12km from Maó, has long been a nucleus of the island's dairy industry, but in recent years it has also become something of a manufacturing centre, its tangle of new buildings spreading formlessly across the flat land north of the Me-1. This modern part of town is uninspiring, but beyond, about 1km up a steep hill, is the more appealing **old centre**, whose rabbit-warren of narrow lanes and alleys surround the imposing parish church of **Santa Eulàlia**. This magnificent edifice of fortress-like proportions was built between 1674 and 1690: its main doorway is a Baroque extravagance whose exuberant scrollwork drips with fruits and fronds, while the facade above accommodates a rose window and a pair of balustrades. Beyond the church – just up the hill to the northwest along the L-shaped c/Moli de l'Angel – a mini-watchtower is plonked on top of the **Munt de l'Angel**, a hill from where you can look out over the countryside. From the end of c/Moli de l'Angel, it's a few metres north to the old town's main square, **Plaça Nova**, an attractive piazza flanked by pastel-painted civic buildings of considerable age.

The best time to be in Alaior is the second weekend of August, when the town lets loose with the **Festa de Sant Llorenç**, a drunken knees-up with displays of horsemanship. As its climax, a procession of horses tears through the packed town square, bucking and rearing, with their riders clinging on for dear life. Although no one seems to get hurt, you might enjoy the spectacle more from the safety of a balcony.

Torralba d'en Salord

3km southeast of Alaior beside the road to Cala en Porter • June–Sept Mon–Sat 10am–8pm; April, May & Oct Mon–Sat 10am–6pm; Nov–March Mon–Fri 10am–2pm • €3.50

One of the island's more extensive Talayotic settlements, **Torralba d'en Salord** is a confusing site, sliced through by the old (and disused) Cala en Porter road, with modern stone walls built alongside both the old and new roads. From the car park, signs direct you around the remains of a **talayot** just beyond which is the **taula**, one of the best preserved on the island. The rectangular enclosure surrounding it is also in good condition, and has been the subject of much conjecture by archeologists, who discovered that several of the recesses contained large fire pits, that may well have been used for the ritual slaughter of animals. It was, however, the unearthing of a tiny **bronze bull**, now in Maó's Museu de Menorca (see p.200), that really got the experts going. The theory was that the Menorcans (in common with several other prehistoric Mediterranean peoples) venerated the bull, with the *taula* being a stylized representation of a bull's head. Beyond the *taula*, the signed trail circumnavigates the remainder of the site, which contains a confusion of stone remains, none of them especially revealing. The most noteworthy are the battered remains of a second **talayot** just next to the *taula* and an underground chamber roofed with stone slabs.

Torre d'en Gaumés

3.5km southwest of Alaior • Mid-March to mid-April Tues–Sun 9.30–3pm; mid-April to Oct Tues–Sat 9.30am-8pm, Sun 9.30am–3pm; Nov–mid-March open access • Mid-March to Oct €3; Nov to mid-March free • To get to the ruins, take the Son Bou turning off the Me-1 west of Alaior; after about 2km, turn left at the signposted fork

A rambling Talayotic settlement, **Torre d'en Gaumés** is fronted by a small **visitor information centre**, though its two short films on Talayotic life are eminently missable and you're better off pressing on the extra 1km to the site itself. The higher part of Torre d'en Gaumés – the part near the entrance – possesses three **talayots**, the largest of which is next to a broken-down **taula** in the centre of a walled, horseshoe-shaped enclosure. Together, the *taula* and the enclosure form what is presumed to have been the public part of the village, and it was here that archeologists unearthed a little bronze figure of the Egyptian god of knowledge, **Imhotep**, now in the Museu de Menorca in Maó (see p.200), a discovery that reinforced the theory that these enclosures possessed religious significance. In the lower part of the settlement, there are the scant remains of several more houses, another walled enclosure and a comparatively sophisticated storage chamber – the subterranean *Sala Hipostila*. Here also are the clearly discernible remains of a **water collection system** in which rainwater was channelled down the hillside between a series of shallow, artificial indentations to end up in underground cisterns and a cave, that had previously served as a funerary chamber – the site was inhabited and continually modified well into Roman times.

ARRIVAL AND ACCOMMODATION

ALAIOR AND AROUND

By bus Buses to Alaior pull in on c/St Joan Baptista, from where it's a steep 500m haul northwest to the old centre – and the church of Santa Eulàlia.

Accommodation As there is nowhere of note to stay in town, you're best off bedding down either west in Es Migjorn Gran (see p.223) or east in Maó (see p.203).

Son Bou and Sant Jaume Mediterrani

Located roughly 7km southwest of Alaior, the coastal resort of **SON BOU** boasts an extensive **cave complex**, cut into the cliff-face above the final part of the approach road. There are also the foundations of an early **Christian basilica**, set behind the beach at the east end of the resort, but these pale in comparison to the **beach**, a whopping pale-gold strand some 3km long and 40m wide. This is Menorca's longest beach, and behind it has mushroomed a massive tourist complex of skyscraper hotels and villa-villages that spreads

5

west into the twin resort of **SANT JAUME MEDITERRANI**. The sand shelves gently into the sea, but the bathing isn't quite as safe as it appears: ocean currents are hazardous, particularly when the wind picks up, and you should watch for the green and red flags. The beach accommodates several bars, and **watersports equipment** is widely available – everything from jet-skis, snorkels and windsurfing boards down to sunloungers and pedalos. The development is at its crassest – and crowds at their worst – towards the east end of the beach, while bathing is much better to the west: here a strip of dune-fringed, marshy scrubland runs behind the strand, providing the shoreline with some much-needed protection and pushing the villa developments 1km or so inland.

ACCOMMODATION   SON BOU AND SANT JAUME MEDITERRANI

Sol Milanos/Sol Pingüinos Playa de Son Bou ☎ 971 37 12 00, ⓦ solmelia.com. Alongside each other, these two high-rise hotels boast 600 rooms between them and share facilities, including sun terraces, trampolines, outside pools, bars and restaurants. Neither has the most fashionable rooms – the *Sol Milanos* displays a curious Flintstones motif in parts – and they tend to have bland white bathrooms, but they're acceptable at a pinch, and half the rooms have small balconies with sea views, so ask for one of these. *Sol Milanos* closed mid-Oct to April; *Sol*

Pingüinos closed mid-Sept to May. **€190**

Son Bou Ctra. de St Jaume-Torre Solí, Km 3.5 ☎ 971 37 27 27, ⓦ campingsonbou.com. One of Menorca's rare campsites, the *Son Bou* is located 3.5km inland on the more westerly access road linking the Me-1 with Sant Jaume Mediterrani. This well-equipped campsite has several hundred pitches in amongst the pine woods, as well as its own swimming pool, sports area, laundry, supermarket and restaurant. Closed Oct–March. Tent **€8.95**, plus **€8.10** per person; cabin **€77.50**

Es Mercadal

ES MERCADAL, 9km northwest of Alaior along the Me-1, sits amongst the hills at the very centre of the island. Another old market town, it's an amiable little place whose antique centre of whitewashed houses and trim allotments is now flanked by modern houses of a neat and trim demeanour. At the heart of the town, the minuscule main square, **Plaça Constitució**, has a couple of sleepy cafés and is a few paces from the Ruritanian **Ajuntament** (Town Hall), at c/Major 16. That's just about it for sights unless, that is, you count the rain-catching water reservoir – the **Aljub** – which was built on the orders of Richard Kane (see p.220); it's located on the edge of town, a short walk northwest of c/Major off c/Sol.

ARRIVAL AND DEPARTURE   ES MERCADAL

By bus Buses to and from Es Mercadal congregate along Avgda Mestre Gari, just off the Me-1 on the southern edge of town, a 5min walk from Plaça Constitució: to get there, walk straight down Avgda Mestre Gari and its

continuation c/Nou.

Destinations Ciutadella (Mon–Fri hourly, 8 on Sat, 6 on Sun; 35min); Maó (Mon–Fri hourly, 8 on Sat, 6 on Sun; 25min).

ACCOMMODATION

Hostal Jeni c/Mirada del Toro 81 ☎ 971 37 50 59, ⓦ hostaljeni.com. Set within a brightly decorated modern building, this *hostal* has fifty-odd, spick-and-span, modern

en-suite bedrooms, as well as a swimming pool and sauna; it's situated on the south side of town one block east of Avgda Mestre Gari. **€112**

Monte Toro

Es Mercadal is the starting point for the ascent of **MONTE TORO**, a steep 3.2km climb along a serpentine but easily driveable road. At 357m, the summit is the island's highest point and offers wonderful views: on a good day you can see almost the whole island; in inclement weather, you can still see at least as far as Fornells. From this lofty vantage point, Menorca's **geological division** becomes apparent: to the north, Devonian rock (mostly reddish sandstone) supports a hilly, sparsely populated landscape edged by a fretted coastline; to the south, limestone predominates in a rippling, wooded plain that boasts the island's best farmland and, as it approaches the south coast, its deepest wooded gorges (*barrancs*).

It's likely that the **name of the hill** is derived from the Moorish al-Thor ("high point"), though medieval Christians claimed that villagers spotted a mysterious light on the mountain and, on closer investigation, were confronted by a bull (*toro*), which led them to a miracle-making statue of the Virgin. Whatever the truth, a statue of the Virgin – the Verge del Toro – was installed in a crude but long departed shrine in the thirteenth century and Monte Toro has been a place of pilgrimage ever since. The ceremonial highlight is on the first Sunday of May, when the **Festa de la Verge del Toro** (Festival of the Virgin of the Bull) begins with a special mass at the Monte Toro church and continues with a knees-up down in Es Mercadal.

The monastery

The Augustinians plonked a monastery on the summit in the seventeenth century, but fearful islanders soon interrupted their monkish reveries by building a small fortress here against the threat of an Ottoman invasion. Bits of both the monastery and the fort survive, the former incorporated within the present **monastery** – though the monks left long ago – the latter in a square stone **tower** that now stands forlorn and neglected. High above both stands a **statue of Christ** erected in honour of those Menorcans who died in a grubby colonial war launched by Spain in Morocco in the 1920s.

The church

The tower and much of the monastery is out of bounds, but the **public area**, approached across a handsome courtyard with a dinky little well, is still large enough to accommodate a couple of gift shops, a terrace café, a restaurant, and a charming **church**, entered through a low and deep stone porch that is decorated with flowers and shrubs. Inside, the barrel-vaulted nave is a modest, truncated affair dating from 1595, its gloominess partly dispelled by a central dome. The most prominent feature is the gaudy, 1940s high altarpiece, whose fancy woodwork swarms with cherubs and frames the much-venerated **Verge del Toro**, depicting the crowned Virgin holding Jesus in her arms with the enterprising bull of folkloric fame at her feet. The statue is typical of the so-called black Catalan Madonnas, made either from black-stained wood or dark stone.

Es Migjorn Gran

Trailing along a low ridge amidst intricate terraced fields, **ES MIGJORN GRAN** ("great southerly wind"), is a sleepy little town that lies some 7km southwest of Es Mercadel. One of several settlements founded on the island in the eighteenth century, it is the only one not to have been laid out by foreigners. Consequently, the gridiron streets of the likes of Es Castell are replaced by a more organic layout, the houses of the old agricultural workers straggling along the elongated main street, **c/Major**, as it curves through town. While the village hardly sets the pulse racing, it is the starting point for an excellent hike (see pp.224–225).

ARRIVAL AND DEPARTURE

ES MIGJORN GRAN

By bus Buses pull in beside the bypass on the southeast side of Es Migjorn Gran, a short walk from c/Major.
Destinations Ciutadella (May–Oct 4–6 daily; Nov–April Mon–Fri 4 daily; 40min); Ferreries (May–Oct 4–6 daily; Nov–April Mon–Sat 1 daily; 10min); Maó (May–Oct 4–6 daily; Nov–April 6 daily, 1 on Sat; 30min); Sant Tomàs (May–Sept daily roughly hourly; Oct Mon–Sat 7 daily).

ACCOMMODATION AND EATING

★ **Fonda S'Engolidor** c/Major 3 ☎971 37 01 93, ⊛ sengolidor.com. Easily the most agreeable of the two options in the town centre, this small family-run spot has five extremely cosy guest rooms in a cheerfully restored

5

A DAY'S HIKE: ES MIGJORN GRAN TO THE COAST

Circular • 8km • 150m ascent • 3hr–3hr 30min • Moderate • Trailhead GPS: +39° 56' 58.42", +4° 3' 2.57"

Despite its modest dimensions, Menorca packs a surprising diversity into its landscape. One of the island's most unexpected – and best hidden – topographical features are the dramatic limestone gorges, or *barrancs*, which score the southern coast, running from the hills inland down to the sea. Starting in the inland village of **Es Migjorn Gran**, this walk follows one of these gorges, the **Barranc de Binigaus**, down to the coast near Sant Tomàs, passing through an area rich in **Talayotic** remains and impressive natural limestone formations.

The walk starts on the edge of Es Migjorn Gran at the **car park** outside the municipal sports stadium (Camp Municipal D'Esports), by the town's main roundabout. From here, walk along the right-hand side of the main road (Avgda del Mar) in the direction of Sant Tomàs as far as the **Bar S'Auba**. Turn right up the hill along Avgda David Russell and continue to the T-junction with Escola Publica in front of you and turn left – a distance of about 450m.

The first half of the walk follows the road that you are now on, after a short while; it becomes a stony track, meandering slowly downhill towards the coast. The road starts by running picturesquely between limestone walls flanked by handsome old Aleppo pines, an old enclosure housing the substantial remains of two *talayots*, and a cemetery. Some 200m further on you'll pass another *talayot* on your right, followed by an attractive ensemble of white houses and Menorcan-style gates. Continue for a further 1km, passing enclosures littered with limestone boulders, until you reach the attractive old whitewashed farmstead of *Binigaus Vell* (see opposite).

Just past here you'll have your first sight of the sea. The path continues for a further 750m, with the dramatic limestone formations of the **Barranc de Binigaus** coming into view on your left. Beyond here, the track passes through an intricate but overgrown system of terraces and enclosures before climbing past a potholed limestone outcrop to reach the brow of the hill. Two more *talayots* are now visible to your left – the land hereabouts holds an incredible jumble of natural, prehistoric and more recent agricultural stone-working, with the Barranc de Binigaus issuing into the sea via a narrow defile – your eventual goal – far ahead and below.

Descend through a Menorcan-style gate to the farmhouse of **Binigaus Nou**, a striking baronial-looking structure. About 50m before a second farm gate, turn right off the track onto a narrow path signed **Cova-y-Platja**. This leads to an unusual (but strangely unsigned) Talayotic **hypostyle chamber** and a fine view of the limestone cliffs of a secondary arm of the *barranc* behind. From the chamber continue along the path to rejoin the track. From here, the track hairpins down into the *barranc* beneath high walls of limestone and then proceeds past further wildly overgrown agricultural terracing before reaching the bottom of the hill at a Menorcan-style gate opposite a path signposted to the **Cova dels Coloms**.

The route continues along this path to the *cova* (cave). If you want to make the brief **detour to the coast**, walk through the gate ahead and continue straight on for 150m to reach the sea next to an old gun emplacement buried in the dunes and covered in windswept vegetation. If you're in need of refreshment, detour left here and walk along the beach for 750m to reach the resort of **Sant Tomàs** (see p.225). Back on the main route, head along the path signposted to the **Cova dels Coloms**. This path gradually ascends back into the *barranc* for 1km through woodland before reaching a large dry stone wall and a fork. Head right here, along the narrowing gorge and beneath increasingly impressive limestone cliffs, scored with caves, until, after a further 750m, you reach a gap in another large wall marked with a splash of red paint. Pass through the gap and then bear left – ignoring the path going straight ahead – up a narrow path through thick woodland for about 500m, where you need to look out for a narrow side path joining acutely from the right. Take this side path and follow it uphill for 20m and then turn left up a zigzagging stone terrace to reach the Cova dels Coloms – a huge, impressively large natural cave.

Retrace your steps to the main path and turn right. After a few metres the path climbs to the left and becomes boulder strewn. It then zigzags up out of the gorge and returns you to the original track that you came down on at a point between Binigaus Vell and Binigaus Nou. Turn right and retrace your steps uphill to **Es Migjorn Gran** (see p.223).

eighteenth-century house towards the west (Ferreries) end of town. It's also home to an excellent restaurant with an outdoor terrace at the back (see below). Closed Nov–April. **€70**

★ **Hotel Rural Binigaus Vell** c/Camí de sa Mala Garba ☎971 05 40 50, ⓦbinigausvell.com. Possibly the sleekest place to stay on the entire island – and definitely worthy of the term boutique – this whitewashed *hotel rural* stands out as a modern-rustic gem. Rooms here have very high ceilings and spacious baths, and the best ones are built into the stone that once made up the *finca*'s stables. The medium-sized infinity pool helps with finding some bliss. **€229**

★ **S'Engolidor** c/Major 3 ☎971 37 01 93, ⓦsengolidor.com. On the ground floor of the *Fonda*, this is a smashing little restaurant, where the emphasis is on traditional Menorcan cuisine with mains around €17. The restaurant has a charming, (summer-only) courtyard garden with views over a wooded gorge; reservations are strongly advised. Tues–Fri 7–11pm, Sat & Sun 1–4pm & 7–11pm.

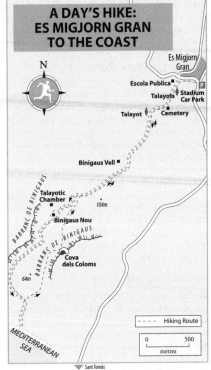

A DAY'S HIKE: ES MIGJORN GRAN TO THE COAST

Sant Tomàs

South of Es Migjorn Gran, the road shuttles along a wooded ravine that leads down to the south coast – and the crass hotel and apartment buildings of **SANT TOMÀS**. The resort's saving grace is its inviting 3km-long sandy **beach**, very similar to that of Son Bou, a couple of headlands away to the east. The road reaches the shore halfway along the beach, which is called **Platja Sant Adeodat** to the west and **Platja Sant Tomàs** to the east. The latter is easily the more congested, and it's here you'll find the resort's high-rise hotels, as well as your choice of **watersports** facilities, including windsurfing boards, jet-skis and pedalos.

ACCOMMODATION   **SANT TOMÀS**

Santo Tomàs Playa de Santo Tomás, s/n ☎971 37 00 25, ⓦsethotels.com. Set right on the beach, this air-conditioned, high-rise hotel dates from the 1980s, and has 85 rooms featuring faux marble bathrooms. It also has two pools (one indoor, one out), two restaurants and night-time entertainment in the form of a small bar.

Closed Nov–March. **€240**

Sol Menorca Playa de Santo Tomás, s/n ☎971 37 00 50, ⓦsolmelia.com. Spiffy modern high-rise whose acceptable chain-like rooms boast a modicum of charm. There's a small pool, and – unusually for Menorca – it's adults-only. Closed Nov–April. **€227**

Ferreries

The old centre of **FERRERIES**, a modest little town on the Me-1 some 8km west of Es Mercadal, is tucked into a hollow beneath a steep hill, its narrow, sloping streets framed by ancient whitewashed houses. A surprise here is the pagoda-like piece of modern sculpture in the main square, the **Plaça Espanya**, while just up the hill at the back of the *plaça* – along c/Fred – stands the neatly shuttered **Ajuntament**, primly facing the parish church of **Sant Bartomeu**, a largely eighteenth-century edifice with an 1884-vintage belfry tacked onto the top. The liveliest time to be here is on Saturday morning

5

(9am–1pm), when a small food and crafts **market** is held on Plaça Espanya. For further retail therapy, the large **Jaime Mascaró factory shoe and leather outlet** (Mon–Sat 9.30am–8.30pm, Sun 11am–2pm; ⊕mascaro.com), lies 1km or so east of town along the Me-1.

Hort de Sant Patrici cheese farm

Camí de Sant Patrici s/n • May–Oct Mon–Sat 9am–1.30pm & 4.30–8pm; Oct–April Mon–Fri 9am–1pm & 4–6pm, Sat 9am–1pm • Free; guided tour at 10am includes a cheese and wine tasting (€6; reservations recommended) • ⊕ santpatrici.com • It's 1.2km from the Me-1 roundabout on the eastern edge of Ferreries: take the unsigned northern exit by the Meubles Allés store, then drive for a couple of minutes through the industrial estate (*polígon industrial*) then along a country lane

In a pleasant rural setting, an assortment of farm buildings surround a good-looking old *hacienda* with attractive gardens at the **Hort de Sant Patrici cheese farm**. Known generically as Queso Mahon, after the island capital, from where it was traditionally exported, **Menorcan cheese** is a richly textured, white, semi-fat cheese made from pasteurized cow's milk with a touch of ewe's milk added for extra flavour. The cheese is sold at four different stages of maturity, either *tierno* (young), *semi-curado* (semi-mature), *curado* (mature) or *añejo* (very mature). Hort de San Patrici is the most enjoyable of Central Menorca's cheese-making plants (the tourist office in Maó has a full list): it's well set up for visitors and you can watch cheese being made, buy it at the shop, stroll the gardens and visit the cheese museum.

ARRIVAL AND DEPARTURE | FERRERIES

By bus Buses stop in front of *Vimpi*, a 4min walk from Plaça Espanya, straight up Avgda Verge del Toro.

Destinations Alaior (Mon–Fri hourly, 6–8 on Sat, 6 on Sun; 25min); Cala Galdana (hourly; 15min); Ciutadella (Mon–Fri hourly, 6–8 on Sat, 6 on Sun; 25min); Es Mercadal (Mon–Fri hourly, 6–8 on Sat, 6 on Sun; 10min); Es Migjorn Gran (May–Oct 4–6 daily; Nov–April Mon–Sat 1 daily; 10min); Maó (Mon–Fri hourly, 6–8 on Sat, 6 on Sun; 35min).

ACCOMMODATION

Ca Na Xini Camí de Sant Antoni de Ruma ☎971 37 45 12, ⊕canaxini.com. The only spot with any atmosphere to stay around laconic Ferreries, the eight spacious and modern rooms in this old estate house are run by the same family who operate the Sant Patrici cheese plant. A great place if you want to stay central and stylish – exposed beams, flat screens, minimalist white interior – but well away from the resorts. Located roughly 1.5km north along the Cami de Sant Patrici from the centre of Ferreries. Two-night minimum. **€254**

EATING AND DRINKING

Vimpi Plaça Joan Carles, beside the Me-1. This café-bar serves tasty tapas for €3–8 and has a large terrace at the front located alongside where the buses that traverse the island stop. Daily 6am–11am.

Cala Galdana

Once a much-loved beauty spot, the resort of **CALA GALDANA**, on Menorca's south coast, roughly midway between Sant Tomás and Tamarinda, is now cluttered with high-rises and low-rises alike and a rash of development. Despite the concrete, there's no denying the beauty of the setting, and the curving sandy **beach**, framed by wooded, limestone cliffs and flanked by a pint-sized rocky promontory set alongside a narrow river, is positively beguiling. Early in the morning or out of season is the best time to appreciate the scene – or you can escape the crowds by hiking west or east along the coast to more secluded coves. It's possible to hire out all sorts of **watersports** equipment in Cala Galdana, from pedalos and water scooters to windsurfing boards and snorkelling tackle, and there are a couple of **car hire** outlets, too. The resort is reached via the fast, 8km road that cuts south off the Me-1 from just to the west of Ferreries.

5

COASTAL WALKS AROUND CALA GALDANA

There are several exquisite **cove beaches** within easy walking distance of Cala Galdana, the most obvious choice being **Cala Mitjana**, just 1km to the east, a broad strip of sand (no facilities) set at the back of a chubby little cove with wooded cliffs to either side. One favourite sport here is jumping into the crystal-clear water from the surrounding cliffs. It is reached via a 30min walk along a footpath that begins at the Plaça Na Gran car park, near the main entrance to the *Hotel Sol Gavilanes* (see below).

Heading west, it's approximately a 50min walk from Cala Galdana to **Cala Macarella** (and neighbouring **Cala Macarelleta**), whose severe, partly wooded limestone cliffs surround a band of white sand great for swimming that shelves gently into the Med. To reach here, take the footpath steps alongside the large and lumpy *Hotel Audax*, which stands near the beach at the west end of the resort. Continuing west along the coast from Cala Macarella, it takes about 2hr to walk to the next major beach, **Cala Turqueta** (see p.238), via the Camí de Cavalls long-distance footpath.

ARRIVAL AND DEPARTURE · CALA GALDANA

By bus From May to October, there are regular buses to Cala Galdana from Maó (approx every 30min; 40min), Ferreries (2–4 daily; 10min) and Ciutadella (2–4 daily; 30min); buses stop in the centre of the resort, a brief walk from the beach. There is also a bus stop outside the campsite, but be sure to let the driver know you want to get off here, otherwise you will go whizzing by.

ACCOMODATION

S'Atalaia campsite ● 971 37 42 32, ⓦ campingsatalaia .com. Located about 3km back down the road towards Ferreries, the *S'Atalaia campsite* has pine trees shading much of the site, with an outdoor swimming pool, a supermarket and a restaurant-bar; it's not a large campsite and it is popular, so advance reservations are strongly advised. There'a an extra charge for cars (€2.15), and there is a small supplementary charge for electrical hook-ups. Closed Oct–March. Tents €4–9, plus €6.90 per adult.

Sol Gavilanes ● 971 15 45 45, ⓦ solmelia.com. The resort has four large chain hotels, easily the pick of which is the four-star *Sol Gavilanes*, set in its own verdant grounds and built against the cliffs that frame the beach. The hotel has every facility, from air-conditioning and swimming pools to satellite TV, and most of the attractive, modern guest rooms have sea-facing balconies. Closed Nov–March. €251

Torrellafuda

Heading west out of Ferreries, the Me-1 soon leaves the central hills behind for the flatlands that precede Ciutadella. These flatlands are dotted with some of the island's more important prehistoric sites, the first one of real significance being **Torrellafuda** (open access; free), whose car park is reached down a clearly signed, 800m-long dirt road on the south side of the Me-1. From the car park, it's a brief walk to the site, where a particularly well-preserved *talayot* stands close to the *taula*, which is hidden away in a little wooded dell. The rustic setting is delightful – it's a perfect spot for a picnic.

Naveta d'es Tudons

Just off the Me-1, almost 3km from the Torrellafuda turning · Mid-March to mid-April Tues–Sun 9.30am–3pm; mid-April to Oct Tues–Sat 9am–8pm, Sun 9am–7pm, Mon 9am–3pm; Nov to mid-March open access · mid-March–Oct €2; Nov to mid-March free

Standing in a field a short stroll from the main Me-1, the **Naveta d'es Tudons** is easily the best-preserved *naveta* on the island. Seven metres high and 14m long, it consists of massive stone blocks slotted together using a sophisticated dry-stone technique. The narrow entrance on the west side leads into a small antechamber, which was once sealed off by a stone slab; beyond lies the main chamber where the bones of the dead were stashed away after the flesh had been removed. Folkloric memories of the *navetas'* original purpose survived into modern times – Menorcans were loath to go near these odd-looking and solitary monuments until well into the nineteenth century.

5

Lithica Pedreres de S'hostal

Camí Vell s/n • June–Sept Mon–Sat 9.30am–2.30pm & 4.30pm–dusk, Sun 9.30am–2.30pm; March–May, Oct& Nov daily 9.30am–2.30pm • €4 • Ⓦ lithica.es

One of the island's most unusual sights, the **Lithica Pedreres de S'hostal**, lies just to the south of the main Me-1, a couple of kilometres east of Ciutadella. Stone has been quarried here for centuries and the old workings have recently been opened to the public. From the ticket office, you descend to the old quarry floor, where you can wander amongst a labyrinth of giant stone stacks cut to all sorts of fanciful shapes. It was long the custom for the quarry men to plant gardens in some of their old workings and there's a lovely verdant garden here today, shaded by orange and almond trees, as well as an open-air theatre, which is used for live performances, and a stone maze.

Ciutadella

Like Maó, **CIUTADELLA** sits high above its harbour, though the narrow channel here is too slender for all but the smallest of cargo ships. Ciutadella was the island's capital until the eighteenth century, and despite its many invaders, its **architecture** has remained decidedly Spanish: the narrow, cobbled streets boast fine old palaces, hidden away behind high walls, and a set of Baroque and Gothic churches very much in the Castilian tradition.

The city's key attractions are clustered in the **town centre**, a dense cobweb of narrow lanes and alleys flanked by old mansions and handsome churches. Most of the centre is pedestrianized, but it only takes a few minutes to walk from one side to the other, and keeping your bearings is fairly straightforward – the main square and pleasure harbour are on the west of the centre, the inner ring road to the east. The commercial harbour, where all ferries now arrive and depart, is located 4km south of town in a newly built complex at Son Blanc.

Essentially, it's the whole ensemble, centred on stately **Plaça d'es Born**, that gives Ciutadella its appeal, though the mostly Gothic **cathedral** is a delight, as is the eclectic **Museu Diocesà de Menorca**. An ambitious renovation programme has further enhanced the town, restoring most of the old stone facades to their honey-coloured best. Added to this are some excellent **restaurants** and a reasonably adequate supply of *hostales* and **hotels**. All in all, it's a lovely place to stay, and nothing else on Menorca rivals the evening *passeig* (promenade), when the townsfolk amble the narrow streets of the centre, dropping in on pavement cafés as the sun sets. Allow at least a couple of days, more if you seek out one of the beguiling **cove beaches** within easy striking distance of town. There are several wonderful spots to choose from, but **Cala Turqueta** is probably the pick of the bunch. Save time also for the prehistoric sites hereabouts, most pertinently the **Naveta d'es Tudons** (see p.227) and **Son Catlar**.

Brief history

Ciutadella is a unique settlement originally chosen by the Romans, adopted by the Moors (as Medina Minurka), then flattened and rebuilt by the Catalans during the Reconquista. It was razed again by the Turks in 1558, when the **Turkish corsairs** carted off some three thousand captives – around eighty percent of the population – to the slave markets of Istanbul. As news spread of the disaster, the pope organized a European whip-round, and an intrepid Menorcan doctor, one Marcos Martí, ventured east to buy the slaves back. Martí was remarkably successful and the returning hostages, together with the survivors of the assault, determinedly **rebuilt Ciutadella** in grand style. They refortified the town's compact centre and then, reassured, set about adorning it with fine stone churches and sweeping mansions.

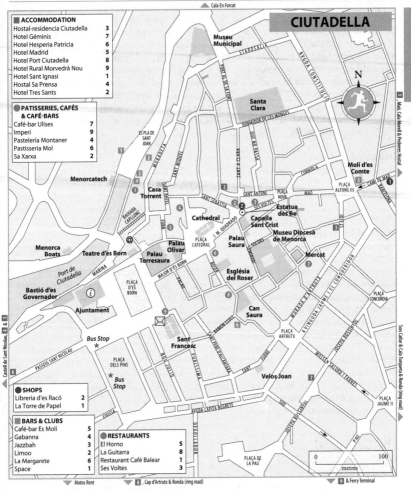

ACCOMMODATION

Hostal-residencia Ciutadella	3
Hotel Géminis	7
Hotel Hesperia Patricia	6
Hotel Madrid	5
Hotel Port Ciutadella	8
Hotel Rural Morvedrà Nou	9
Hotel Sant Ignasi	1
Hostal Sa Prensa	4
Hotel Tres Sants	2

PATISSERIES, CAFÉS & CAFÉ-BARS

Café-bar Ulises	7
Imperi	9
Pastelería Montaner	4
Pastissería Mol	6
Sa Xarxa	2

SHOPS

Librería d'es Racó	2
La Torre de Papel	1

BARS & CLUBS

Café-bar Es Molí	5
Gabanna	4
Jazzbah	3
Limoo	2
La Margarete	6
Space	1

RESTAURANTS

El Horno	5
La Guitarra	8
Restaurant Café Balear	1
Ses Voltes	3

Throughout the seventeenth century, Menorca's leading **landowners** hung out in Ciutadella, confident of their position and power. They were, however, in for a shock: the colonial powers of the eighteenth century had little time for the town's feeble port when compared with Maó's magnificent inlet, and the **British** simply – and abruptly – moved the capital to Maó in 1722. Thereafter, Maó flourished as a trading centre, while Ciutadella stagnated – a long-lasting economic reverie that has, by coincidence, preserved the town's old and beautiful centre as if in aspic.

Plaça d'es Born

Primarily a nineteenth-century creation, **Plaça d'es Born** is easily the finest main square in the Balearic islands. In the middle soars an **obelisk** commemorating the futile defence against the Turks in 1558, a brutal episode that was actually something of an accident. The Ottomans had dispatched 15,000 soldiers and 150 warships west to assist their French allies against the Habsburgs. With no particular place to go, the Turks rolled around the Mediterranean for a few weeks and, after deciding Maó wasn't worth

5

the candle, they happened on Ciutadella, where the garrison numbered just forty. For the locals, the results were cataclysmic. The one-sided siege ended with the destruction of the town and the enslavement of its population – there was so much damage that when the new Spanish governor arrived, he was forced to live in a cave. The obelisk's original Latin inscription, penned by the mid-nineteenth-century politician and historian **Josep Quadrado**, reads, "Here we fought until death for our religion and our country in the year 1558." Such grandiose nationalism was typical of Quadrado, then the region's most prominent politician and leader of the reactionary Catholic Union, which bombarded Madrid with complaints and petitions whenever the local governor did anything progressive.

The buildings

The Plaça is surrounded by a handful of interesting buildings: on its western side is the **Ajuntament** (Town Hall), whose early nineteenth-century arches and crenellations mimic Moorish style, purposely recalling the time when the site was occupied by the Wali's *alcázar* (palace). On the square's north side, the **Teatre d'es Born** is a neat, late nineteenth-century structure built to salvage some municipal pride: the merchants of Maó had just completed their opera house, so the oligarchs of Ciutadella promptly followed suit – though they weren't quite as energetic when it came to getting people to perform here and the building lay neglected for years.

Built in the nineteenth century but looking far older, the **Palau Torresaura** is the grandest of several aristocratic mansions that edge the Plaça, its sweeping lines dominating the northeast corner. Embellished by two handsome loggias, its frontage proclaims the family coat of arms above a large wooden door leading into a spacious coutryard. The antique interior, however, is off limits – like most of its neighbours, the house is still owner-occupied. Finally, the **Església de St Francesc** sits in the southeast corner of the square, a clean-lined, unpretentious structure whose hybrid architecture reflects the island's ups and downs – it was first built shortly after the Reconquista, levelled by the Turks in 1558, rebuilt to the original specifications in the 1590s, then ransacked again by the Republicans during the Civil War. Take a look inside the Baroque side door at some of the embellishments and the motley crew of polychromatic saints.

The Cathedral

Plaça de la Catedral 1 • Daily 9am–1pm & 6–9pm • Free

The town's **cathedral** is a good-looking structure built by Jaume II at the beginning of the fourteenth century on the site of the chief mosque, but remodelled after the Turkish onslaught of 1558. During the rebuilding, the flying buttresses of the original were partly encased within a thick stone wall to guard against future attack, a modification that gives the cathedral its distinctive appearance. The Gothic **side door** – on the south side of the church – was, however, left intact, its arching columns decorated with strange-looking beasts and the coats of arms of Aragón and Ciutadella, all surmounted by a delicate carving of the Magi honouring the infant Christ. Another survivor was the set of fierce-looking **gargoyles** that decorates the buttresses at roof level. The principal (west) **entrance** was added much later, in 1813, its flashy Neoclassical portico contrasting with the rest of the church and the intricate rose window above.

The interior

Inside, light filters through the stained glass of the narrow, lofty windows to bathe the high altar in an ethereal glow. There's also a sequence of glitzy Baroque side chapels, though these look very mediocre when compared with the beautifully carved stonework of the chapel just off the top left-hand corner of the nave. The wall behind the high altar carries a medieval **panel painting**, *The Purification of the Virgin*, but most of the church's old furnishings and fittings were destroyed when the Republicans took control of Menorca during the Civil War. Although the British had made Maó the island's capital in 1722, Ciutadella remained Menorca's ecclesiastical centre and, almost without exception, its resident Catholic hierarchy were rich and reactionary in equal measure. The priesthood enthusiastically proclaimed its support for the officers of the Maó garrison when the latter declared for Franco in July 1936, but this turned out to be a major gaffe. The bulk of the garrison stayed loyal to the Republic, and, allied with local left-wing groups, they captured the rebels, shot their leaders and ransacked Ciutadella's main churches as retribution.

Palau Olivar

Plaça de la Catedral s/n • No access

Directly opposite the cathedral's main entrance is the **Palau Olivar**, whose stern, eighteenth-century facade is partly relieved by a pair of miniature balconies fronted by wrought-iron grilles. In 1707, the house witnessed one of the town's crueller episodes, when a reclusive mother and daughter who worked and lived here were accused of witchcraft. Found guilty on palpably potty charges, the older woman was sent to prison for life, and the younger was executed – by any standard, a heavy price to pay for not joining in the town's social life.

Església del Roser

c/Roser • Mon–Sat 11am–1pm & 6–9pm • Free

Dating from the seventeenth century, the diminutive **Església del Roser** is fronted by a hulking Churrigueresque facade, its quartet of pillars festooned with intricate tracery. The church was the subject of bitter controversy when the British governor Richard Kane (see p.220) commandeered it for Church of England services, which greatly displeased the Dominican friars who owned the place. Now deconsecrated, the church's interior has been covered in cream paint and is used for temporary exhibitions of contemporary, mostly local, art and crafts.

Carrer Seminari

The top end of the **Carrer Seminari** is dominated by the flamboyant facade of the **Capella del Sant Crist**, a Baroque extravaganza with garlands of fruit and a pair of gargoyle-like faces. Inside, the intimate nave supports an octagonal stone dome and is also home to an unattributed medieval panel painting depicting three local saints of obscure significance. The skeletal crucified Christ above the high altar is supposed to have dripped with sweat in 1661 and remains a popular object of devotion. Just around the corner, a few metres north of the chapel on c/J.M. Quadrado, the **Estatua des Be** is a reminder of Ciutadella's biggest shindig, the Festa de Sant Joan (see p.33): symbolizing the Lamb of God, this perky bronze statue of a lamb carries a flag bearing the cross of St John the Baptist. Just south of the Capella is the savings bank that occupies part of the **Palau Saura**, built in grand style by the British for a Menorcan aristocrat, Joan Miquel Saura, in return for his help in planning their successful invasion of 1708.

Museu Diocesà de Menorca

c/Seminari • May, June & Oct Mon–Sat 10.30am–2pm; July–Sept Mon–Sat 10.30am–4.30pm • €3.50

The mildly enjoyable **Museu Diocesà de Menorca** (Diocesan Museum) occupies an old convent and its church. Before entering the museum, take a look at the convent's elongated **perimeter wall**, a sober affair interrupted by two doorways – one for the

5

cloisters and the museum, the other for the church, though this is now closed off. This old church doorway is surmounted by the most bizarre of sculpted cameos, depicting the **Virgin Mary**, armed with a cudgel and standing menacingly over a cringing, cat-like dragon-devil.

The collection

Inside, the **museum collection** is distributed amongst the tiny rooms that flank the immaculately preserved Baroque **cloister**, whose vaulted aisles sport coats of arms and religious motifs. The first two rooms – to either side of the entrance – hold a hotchpotch of Talayotic and early classical archeological finds, notably a superbly crafted, miniature bull and a similarly exquisite little mermaid (*sirena*), almost certainly Greek bronzes dating from the fifth century BC. On the left-hand side of the cloister is the domed and single-aisled **Església dels Socors**, whose standard-issue Baroque decoration culminates in an extraordinarily artless high altar. The vaulted **refectory** displays some dreadful eighteenth-century religious paintings and some much more fetching Impressionist-style still-lifes, landscapes and village scenes by local artist **Pere Daura** (1896–1976). Born in Ciutadella, the one-time Communist and Republican soldier fled Spain for France and the USA after Franco seized power.

The market

Plaça Francesc Netto & Plaça Llibertat • Mon–Sat 9am–2pm

Ciutadella's **market** (*mercat*) rambles over two miniature squares, Plaça Francesc Netto and Plaça Llibertat. This is another delightful corner of the old town, where fresh fruit, vegetable, meat and fish stalls mingle with lively and inexpensive cafés selling the freshest of *ensaimadas*. The fish stalls occupy a dinky little structure of 1895; the rest fill out a slender arcaded gallery that was constructed thirty years before as part of a municipal drive to clean up the town's food supply.

The Convent of Santa Clara

C/Santa Clara • Free

Directly opposite the top of c/Seminari, a long, straight street – **c/Santa Clara** – shoots off north, hemmed in by the walls of old aristocratic palaces. At the top is the **Convent of Santa Clara**, a mundanely modern incarnation of a centuries-old foundation. In 1749, this was the site of a scandal when three young women escaped from the convent into the protection of their British boyfriends, who they wanted to marry – turning Protestant at the same time. In this delicate situation, **Governor Blakeney** had the room where the women were staying sealed up by a priest every night. But he refused to send them back to the convent and allowed the weddings to go ahead, thereby compounding a religious animosity that had begun in the days of Richard Kane.

Museu Municipal

c/Portal de Sa Font • May–Sept Tues–Sat 10am–2pm & 6–9pm; Oct–April Tues–Sat 10am–2pm • €2.46, but free on Wed • Ⓦ ajciutadella.org

The **Museu Municipal** occupies part of the old municipal fortifications, a massive bastion overlooking a slender ravine that once had, until it was redirected, a river running along its base and on into the harbour. The museum consists of a long vaulted chamber that is mostly given over to a wide range of archeological artefacts, primarily a substantial collection of **Talayotic remains**, featuring finds garnered from all over the island. Each cabinet is clearly labelled, though the displays are not chronological: the

FORNELLS (P.216) >

5

small introductory section attempts an overview, but sadly only serves to confuse the chronology further. A leaflet detailing the exhibits in English is available free at reception.

The **earlier pieces**, dating from around 1500 to 700 BC, include many examples of crudely crafted beakers and tumblers as well as a set of **five skulls**, which appear to have been subjected to some form of brain surgery, though no one is sure quite how or why. **Later work** – from around 700 BC – reveals a far greater degree of sophistication, both in terms of kitchenware, with bowls and tumblers particularly common, and bronze weaponry. From this later period, which ended with the arrival of the Romans in 123 BC, comes most of the (imported) jewellery, whose fine detail and miniature size suggests a Carthaginian origin.

Carrer Sa Muradeta

Running more or less parallel to the waterfront from the Museu Municipal to Plaça d'es Born, **Carrer Sa Muradeta** provides pleasant views down the ravine to the harbour. As you near Plaça d'es Born, a wide flight of steps – the **Baixada Capllonc** – cuts down to the harbour, where yachts and fishing smacks bob around in front of a series of waterside restaurants, with the old town walls forming a scenic background.

Casa Museu Torrent

Sant Rafel 11 • Currently closed: check opening hours at the tourist office • Free • ⓦ menorcaweb.net/pintortorrent

The **Casa Museu Torrent** displays around a hundred paintings in the old home of Ciutadella's own **José Roberto Torrent** (1904–90). The son of a cobbler, Torrent is usually regarded as the town's finest painter, a prolific and versatile artist who began with deftly coloured Menorcan landscapes in the Realist tradition. Later, in the 1960s, his paintings became more expressionistic, rendering island scenes in striking colours and shapes, but perhaps his most evocative work was produced in his old age with paintings of infirmity, loneliness and isolation.

ARRIVAL AND DEPARTURE   CIUTADELLA

By bus Buses from Maó and points east halt at the bus stops on the west side of Plaça dels Pins; those from the tourist resorts of the west coast stop on the north side. From Plaça dels Pins, it's only a couple of minutes' walk into the town centre.

Destinations Alaior (Mon–Fri hourly, 6–8 on Sat, 6 on Sun; 50min); Cala Galdana (May–Sept 3–4 daily; Oct Mon–Sat 4 daily; 30min); Cala Morell (May–Oct 3 daily; 25min); Cala Santandria (May–Oct 1–2 hourly; Nov–April 2–4 daily; 15min); Es Mercadal (Mon–Fri hourly, 6–8 daily on Sat, 6 on Sun; 35min); Es Migjorn Gran (May–Oct 4–6 daily; Nov–April Mon–Fri 4 daily; 40min); Ferreries (Mon–Fri hourly, 6–8 daily on Sat, 6 on Sun; 25min); Maó (Mon–Fri

hourly, 6–8 daily on Sat, 6 on Sun; 1hr); Sant Tomàs (May–Oct 4–6 daily; 45min).

By ferry Car ferries and catamarans dock beside the terminal building at the new €85 million, three-quay harbour at Son Blanc, located near the ring road about 4km south of the centre: regular buses link Son Blanc with the centre of Ciutadella (May–Sept 8 daily; 10min; Oct–April 4 daily; 10min); a taxi will only cost around €7. Three companies offer car ferry and/or catamaran services between Ciutadella and the Spanish mainland and/or Mallorca: Balearia (☎902 16 01 80, ⓦ balearia.com); Acciona Trasmediterranea (☎902 45 46 45, ⓦ trasmediterranea.es); and Iscomar (☎902 11 91 28,

THE RISSAGA

Almost all the time, Ciutadella's long and slender harbour is as flat as a mill-pond, but every so often, for reasons that remain obscure, it is subjected to a violent disturbance, the **Rissaga**. This begins with sudden changes to the sea level and is followed by a dramatic rush of water into the harbour before normality returns. The last great Rissaga took place in 1984 and submerged the harbourside beneath two metres of water.

ⓦiscomar.com). Schedules, tariffs and tickets (see p.22) are available direct from the operators at the ferry terminal. Note that Menorca's car rental firms do not allow their vehicles to leave the island.

By car If you're driving into Ciutadella, there's no missing the inner ring road, which, under various names – principally Avgda Jaume I El Conqueridor and Avgda Capità Negrete – encircles the old town. Approaching from the east, turn left when you hit it at the T-junction and keep going until you reach its conclusion beside the Plaça dels Pins. If you can't find a parking spot actually on this square, turn left at the top and drive down Passeig Sant Nicolau, where there's always space. Driving east out of Ciutadella is more difficult as the last stretch of the Me-1 is westbound only; the solution is to use the outer ring road (*the ronda*).

By taxi There's a taxi stand on Plaça dels Pins(ⓣ 971 48 22 22). The approximate fare between Ciutadella and Maó airport is €50.

GETTING AROUND

Bicycle and moped rental Motos Rent, Plaza de Menorca (daily 9am–2pm, 5pm–8pm; ⓣ669 11 32 88, ⓦmotosrent.com), rents out dozens of new Honda scooters from €30/day, while Velos Joan, c/Sant Isidre 34, near Plaça Artrutx (Mon–Fri 8am–1.30pm & 4–8.30pm, plus mid-May to mid-Oct Sat 10am–1pm & 7–8.30pm, Sun 10.30am–noon; ⓣ971 38 15 76, ⓦvelosjoan.com) has bikes from €10/day, and electric bikes for €18/day.

Car rental One centrally located car rental company is Europcar Menorca, on the ring road at Avgda Jaume I El Conqueridor 59 (ⓣ 971 38 29 98).

INFORMATION AND ACTIVITIES

Tourist information The main tourist office on Plaza de Born in the Ajuntament, just above the port (May–Oct Mon–Fri 9.30am–8.30pm, Sat 9.30am–3.30pm; Nov–April Mon–Fri 9am–2pm & 4–8pm, Sat 9.30am–1.30pm; ⓣ971 48 14 12). It has a good range of information on Menorca as a whole and Ciutadella in particular, including bus timetables, ferry schedules, lists of *hostales* and hotels and free maps, but doesn't help with finding accommodation.

Diving Menorcatech, Es Pla de Sant Joan 10 (ⓣ971 38 60 30 or ⓣ628 130 487, ⓦmenorcatech.com) organizes a wide range of deep-sea diving trips out along the west coast.

Boat hire Menorca Boats, down on the harbour near the bridge, rents out all manner of speed boats (ⓣ971 48 42 81, ⓦmenorcaboats.com). Prices begin at a hefty €430/day in high season, €230 in low.

ACCOMMODATION

By Menorcan standards at least, Ciutadella has a good supply of non-package **hotels** and *hostales*, and nearly all of them are either in or within easy walking distance of the town centre. In addition, there are also a few more inviting (if somewhat pricier) options to be found a few minutes' drive outside of town.

IN THE CENTRE

Hostal-Residencia Ciutadella c/Sant Eloi 10 ⓣ971 38 34 62, ⓦalojarseenmenorca.com. Well-maintained, two-star *hostal* in a pleasantly updated older building on a side street off Plaça Alfons III. Has seventeen small and modest but comfortable rooms, each decorated in shades of yellow and brown. There's also an affordable, solid restaurant on ground floor. Open all year. **€90**

Hotel Géminis c/Josepa Rossinyol 4 ⓣ971 38 46 44, ⓦhotelgeminismenorca.com. Distinctively painted in pink and white, this well-tended, comfortable two-star hotel has thirty rooms, each decorated in bright if somewhat frugal modern style. The rooms at the front have Art Deco-style balconies and overlook a quiet suburban street; those at the back overlook the small pool and courtyard. Popular with backpackers and easy-going older couples. To get there on foot, walk a few paces down c/ Mossèn J. Salord i Farnés from the ring road and watch for the archway on the right; go through the arch and the hotel's on the right. Closed Oct–March. **€98**

Hotel Hesperia Patricia Passeig Sant Nicolau 90 ⓣ971 38 55 11, ⓦhesperia.com. Smart, modern three-star hotel popular with business folk and in a great location, a few minutes' walk from the town centre. The comfortable, well-appointed rooms come with all facilities, the only downer being the lack of a sea view – though the best rooms have rooftop balconies with wide vistas over the town centre. There's also an outside swimming pool. **€95**

Hotel Madrid c/Madrid 60 ⓣ971 38 03 28, ⓦhotelmadridmenorca.com. Located near the ocean, a 15min walk west of the town centre, *Madrid* comprises fourteen quite comfortable rooms in a run-of-the-mill, villa-style, two-star hotel with its own ground-floor café-bar. There's an outside pool, too. To get there, follow Passeig Sant Nicolau from the Plaça dels Pins, take the third turning on the left (c/Saragossa) and you'll hit c/Madrid just east of the hotel at the second intersection. Closed Nov–April. **€65**

Hotel Port Ciutadella Passeig Marítim 36 ⓣ971 38 25 20, ⓦsethotels.com. A 15min walk southwest of Plaça dels Pins, this slick and ultra-modern four-star hotel flaunts a cleverly designed outside pool and 94 brightly decorated

5

bedrooms with all mod cons – and wooden floors. To get there head south on c/Mallorca and at the end turn left at the roundabout. **€170**

Hostal Sa Prensa c/Madrid 70 ☎971 38 26 98, ⓦsaprensa.com. Close to the rocky seashore at the end of c/Madrid, a 15min walk west of the centre, this neat and trim, villa-like, one-star *hostal* offers seven spartan bedrooms, three of which have balconies and sea views. To get there, follow Passeig Sant Nicolau from the Plaça dels Pins, take the fourth turning on the left (c/Joan Ramis i Ramis) and you'll hit c/Madrid just beside the *hostal* (sited above a café-bar) at the first major intersection. **€85**

★ **Hotel Tres Sants** c/Sant Cristòfol 2 70 ☎971 48 22 08 or ☎626 05 35 36, ⓦgrupelcarme.com. This boutique hotel has been the talk of the island since it opened several years ago. Set in an eighteenth-century manor house built over the remains of what is thought to be the island's first Christian church, the eight rooms here are spacious, airy and done up completely in white, with four poster beds bedecked with draped netting. There are excellent views from the terrace, too. **€210**

OUT OF THE CITY

★ **Hotel Rural Morvedrà Nou** Camí Sant Joan de Misa, 6km from Ciutadella ☎971 35 95 21, ⓦmorvedranou.es. This wonderfully placed, sympathetically converted stone farmhouse is one of the most handsome and alluring on the island. The seventeen air-conditioned guest rooms are set a few metres away from a lovely pool. Great staff, too, and an excellent restaurant that makes it worth making a trip out here for dinner alone. April–Oct. **€215**

Hotel Sant Ignasi Carretera Cala Morell s/n ☎971 38 55 75, ⓦsantignasi.com. This elegant nineteenth-century manor house has been tastefully converted into an immaculate hotel. Each of the twenty bedrooms is individually decorated in a style that blends with the original building, and there are gardens and an outside pool too. It's sited about 4km northeast of the centre of Ciutadella and clearly signposted (down a very narrow 1.5km-long lane) from the road to Cala Morell. While the countryside location is peaceful, the surrounding farmland is nevertheless flat and dull. Closed Oct–March. **€285**

EATING AND DRINKING

For an early **breakfast** the best place to go is the market (*mercat*) on Plaça Llibertat, where a couple of simple cafés serve coffee and fresh pastries. Later in the day, around **lunchtime**, aim for c/J.M. Quadrado, Plaça Nova and Plaça Alfons III, which together hold a good selection of inexpensive café-bars offering tapas and light meals. In the **evening**, most tourists make a beeline for the **restaurants** that line up along the harbourside, but – with the odd exception – you're better off seeking out the good-value establishments amongst the side streets near Plaça d'es Born. Whilst the outside terraces on the harbourside restaurants look enticing, the nautical activity along the waterfront can be deafening, especially when the ferries sail. Restaurants are likely to close for one day a week and those down on the harbour mostly close altogether during the winter.

PATISSERIES, CAFÉS AND CAFÉ-BARS

Café-Bar Ulises Plaça Llibertat s/n. This easy-going café-bar, in the heart of the city market, has loads of atmosphere (white plank wooden flooring, cabinets of old ceramics and books, for example) and is popular with a youngish local clientele. Offers a tasty range of pastries and tortillas in the morning, with lots of drinks and (turned-down) house music/jazz at night – as well as the occasional live concert by a local or Catalunian music group. Mon–Sat 8am–late.

Imperi Plaça d'es Born 6. Green-shuttered, neatly turned out café offering good (Illy) coffee, snacks and cakes. Giving onto the main square, its tiny terrace is a smashing spot to watch the milling crowd. Daily 7am–1am.

Pastelería Montaner c/Bisbe 11. Near the cathedral, this is the oldest pastry shop in town and sells what many locals argue are the tastiest *ensaimadas* on the island, baked in their ancient ovens. Mon–Sat 9.30am–5pm.

Pastisseria Mol c/Roser 2. Across the square from the cathedral, this first-rate bakery sells excellent take-away pizza slices, filled bread rolls and mouthwatering cakes. Mon–Sat 8.30am–2pm & 5.30–8pm.

Sa Xarxa c/Sebastià 1. Agreeable café serving a good line in tapas and snacks, all at inexpensive prices. Its terrace is just set off the main drag, which means it's a good place to watch the evening *paseo*. Summer daily 10am–10pm; winter Mon–Sat 9am–midnight.

RESTAURANTS

El Horno c/Forn 12 ☎971 38 07 67. Neat and trim cellar restaurant near the northeast corner of Plaça d'es Born featuring a canny combination of Menorcan and French dishes. Try the rabbit or the mussels and don't miss out on the fish soup. Mains average €13. Daily 7–11pm.

★ **La Guitarra** c/Nostra Senyora dels Dolors 1 ☎971 38 13 55. Located a short walk from the cathedral, this is arguably the best restaurant in town, a family-run affair featuring the very best of Menorcan cuisine with main courses – anything from seafood and lamb to rabbit and pigs' trotters – averaging an extremely reasonable €15. The restaurant occupies an old cellar, whose stone walls sport a scattering of agricultural antiques. Mon–Sat noon–3.30pm & 7.15–11pm.

★ **Restaurant Café Balear** Es Pla de Sant Joan 15 📞971 38 00 05, 🌐cafe-balear.com. Justifiably popular, this attractively decorated restaurant sits at the back of the harbour by the bridge – at a safe distance from the ferries and the moored boats. The waterside terrace is the best place to eat, but there are tables inside too. The food is first rate, with shellfish and fish the big deals – go for the swordfish carpaccio if it's available – though the steaks are good too: main courses average around €20. Reservations advised. Mon–Sat 12.30–4pm & 7.30–11.30pm, but may operate more restricted hours in winter.

Ses Voltes Ses Voltes 16 📞971 38 14 90, 🌐recibaria .com. This casual, modern café-restaurant serves tapas,

salads, baguettes and pizzas – try the delicious Menorquina, with mozzarella, Emmental, tomatoes, local sausage and honey (€4.30). Set across two floors, it has comfy benches and funky art on the walls, and just about everything on the menu is under €5. Daily 9am–midnight.

NIGHTLIFE

People don't come to Ciutadella for the **nightlife**, but there is a small complement of **late-night bars** dotted round the old town with the liveliest places in the ravine at the head of the port, on Es Pla de Sant Joan. Ciutadella is also one of the few places in the Balearics where the evening **paseo** (promenade) has survived in fine fettle, with families wandering up and down the main street taking the evening air as they have done for generations.

BARS AND CLUBS

Café-Bar Es Molí Camí de Maó 1. Housed in the Moli d'es Comte, the old windmill across the street from Plaça Alfons III, this is a noisy and gritty café-bar, with a (very) young Menorcan crowd at night crowding around the pool table, and old timers during the day. Street seating looks right onto the square. Sun–Thurs 6am–midnight, Fri & Sat 6am–3am.

Gabanna Es Pla de Sant Joan s/n 📞 971 38 18 01. Cool and groovy bar-cum-club with a chill-out terrace and alternative jazz, house, rock and world music scene. June–Aug daily 11pm–4am.

Jazzbah Es Pla de Sant Joan 3 📞609 70 06 49, 🌐jazzbah.es. This cool indoor/outdoor bar is one of Menorca's best places for a night out. It has several individual spaces with live music – and wild DJs when the bands have the night off. A large dance space means lots of regular parties. Fri & Sat 11pm–6am.

Limoo Es Pla de Sant Joan s/n. Swishest place in town, a three-floor disco extravaganza with one floor devoted to house, a second to retro and a third holding a cocktail bar. June–Aug daily 11pm–4am.

La Margarete Sant Juan Baptista 6 🌐lamargarete .com. This cute garden bar is a real hidden gem, with a young clientele and regular DJs playing outside. It stays open late, so tends to be one of the last stops for nights out. May–Aug 8pm–3am.

Space Pla de Sant Juan 15, 🌐spacemenorca.com. Opened in 2012, this portside copy of the renowned Ibiza club brings high-powered sound systems, fancy lighting and great DJ bookings to Menorca. There is a terrace with lounge seating upstairs from the main dance floor. Summer daily midnight–6am.

DIRECTORY

Banks ATMs are dotted all over the centre and there's one at the Banca March, Plaça d'es Born 10.
Maps and books Libreria d'es Racó, c/J.M. Quadrado 40, stocks a limited range of island road maps, while La Torre de Papel, Camí de Maó 46, has an excellent selection of used books.
Pharmacies Amongst several downtown options, there's a pharmacy at Plaça Nova 2.
Post Office The main *correu* is handily located at Plaça d'es Born 8 (Mon–Fri 8.30am–2pm, Sat 9.30am–1pm).

Around Ciutadella

The diverse attractions of west Menorca are all within easy striking distance of Ciutadella, beginning with the pristine **cove beaches** that notch the island's **southern shore** just a few kilometres away. There are several delightful beaches to choose from here, the most memorable being **Cala Turqueta**, plus the prehistoric settlement of **Son Catlar**. All the south coast beaches are accessed via the cross-country **Camí de Sant Joan**

5

de Missa that runs southeast from Ciutadella for about 3km to the farmhouse of **Son Vivó**, where the road branches into two: each (signposted) fork leads to several south-coast beaches, the nearest of which are a further 6km away. Both roads are in fairly good condition, and the signs are easy to follow.

North of Ciutadella, the coast is wild and almost completely undeveloped, but there is one resort here, the smart villa-village of **Cala Morell**, which occupies a bleak and barren cove with a gritty beach.

The **west coast** is different again with a flat and mostly treeless coastal plain slicing down to a string of resorts that dot the coast to either side of Ciutadella from Cales Piques in the north to Cap d'Artrutx, 15km away to the south. Most of these resorts have little to recommend them, comprising long lines of modern villas built in a sort of pan-Hispanic style, but here and there the villas bunch round narrow coves to form lovely little resorts, the pick of which is undoubtedly **Cala Santandria**.

GETTING AROUND   **AROUND CIUTADELLA**

By bus From May to October, regular buses run from Ciutadella's Plaça dels Pins to Cala Santandria (hourly; 15–30min) and the other tourist settlements of the west coast. There are also buses to Cala Morell (June–Sept 4–5 daily; 15min), but none to the beaches southeast of town, including Cala Turqueta. In winter, from November to April, there is a limited bus service to most, but not all of the area's resorts; all these bus services are operated by Torres Autocars (☎ 902 07 50 66, ⓦ e-torres.net).

Cala Turqueta

If you take the more easterly road from the Son Vivó fork, it's about 1.5km futher to the **Ermita de St Joan de Missa**, a squat, brightly whitewashed church with a dinky little bell tower. There's a fork here too, but the signposting is clear and you keep straight, with the road slicing across the countryside, before you swing past the **Marjal Vella farmhouse**. Shortly afterwards, about 4.3km from the church, you turn at the sign, going through the gateway to cross the 500m-long dirt road that brings you to the car park for **Cala Turqueta**, a lovely cove flanked by wooded limestone cliffs. The beach consists of a sheltered horseshoe of white sand sloping gently into the sea, making it ideal for bathing, and because there are limited facilities it's unusual to find a crowd.

Son Catlar

Take the westerly road from the Son Vivó fork, and it's 3km to **Son Catlar** (open access; free), the largest prehistoric settlement on Menorca and one which was still expanding when the Romans arrived in force in 123 BC. The most impressive feature of this sprawling Talayotic village is its extraordinary stone wall, originally 3m high and made of massive blocks – the square towers were added later. Inside the walls, however, all is confusion. The widely scattered remains are largely incomprehensible and only the *taula* compound and the five battered *talayots* make much sense.

Platges Son Saura

About 1.2km beyond Son Catlar, the asphalt stops at the ornate gateway of the **Torre Saura farmhouse**. To the left of the gateway, a 2km-long dirt road bumps its way down to the parking lot behind a wide horseshoe-shaped cove whose two beaches make up the **Platges Son Saura**. The west side of the cove is more exposed and is often sticky with seaweed, so aim for the more sheltered eastern side, where a wide arc of white sand is fringed by pines. There are more facilities here than at most of its neighbours, including a summer beach bar.

Cala Morell

Signposted from the Me-1 on the eastern outskirts of Ciutadella, a well-surfaced country lane cuts northeast across a pastoral landscape bound for the smallish tourist settlement of **CALA MORELL**, just 8km north of town. This is one of the island's more refined *urbanitzaciós*, its *pueblo*-style villas – on streets named in Latin after the constellations – hugging a steep and rocky, dog-legged bay. There's swimming off the gritty beach here, and you can also visit some of the old **caves** for which Cala Morell is noted, visible beside the road as you drive down into the resort. Dating from the late Bronze and Iron Ages, the caves form one of the largest prehistoric necropolises known in Europe, and are surprisingly sophisticated, with central pillars supporting the roofs, and, in some instances, windows cut into the rock and classical designs carved in relief. No one owns the caves, so there's unlimited access – just scramble up from the road – but if you're after more than just a quick glimpse, bring your own torch.

From the car park at the end of the main access road, a rough footpath leads north out along the bare and rocky promontory that protects the west side of the bay, but only the truly adventurous will attempt the very difficult hike west to the **Punta de S'Escullar** headland, the site of one of the largest colonies of Cory's shearwaters in the western Mediterranean, with thousands of birds returning to their cliffside burrows in the late afternoon throughout the summer.

Cala Santandria

Heading south from Ciutadella, the main road stays within earshot of the coast, where a string of resorts cluster around the dinky little coves that lie just beyond the edge of town. Perhaps the prettiest is **CALA SANTANDRIA**, a former fishing village whose narrow slit of a rocky cove backs onto a small, gently shelving sandy beach with safe swimming. Despite its small size, there are ample facilities here, including toilets, a sailing club, and sun loungers, pedalos and banana boats for hire.

ARRIVAL AND DEPARTURE   CALA SANTANDRIA

By bus The Ciutadella bus pulls in just 200m from the beach.

EATING AND DRINKING

Café del Sol c/del Signe Leo. Smack on the beach, this small spot serves up the freshest of salads and snacks, and they have a daily set menu meal (€14) that's a sure bet. The best (and one of the few) places to eat around this low-key beach. June to mid-Sept daily 10am–6pm.

WILD FLOWERS IN SPRING, MALLORCA

Contexts

241 History

259 Flora and fauna

267 Books

271 Language

280 Glossary

History

Mallorca and Menorca share similar but quite distinct histories: the Romans and the Moors coveted and conquered them both, but the British were only interested in Maó's splendid harbour and the government in Madrid rarely gave two hoots about either. What the two islands do share is a long history of political and economic domination by a landowning elite, who were all too often absentees. Until the twentieth century, this caste presided over what was, to a large extent, a backward-looking, priest-ridden society and many hated them for it: look at any old rural manor house, especially in Mallorca, and it will almost invariably be heavily fortified not so much from fear of invasion – though that was an issue – but more to keep the peasantry at bay.

Earliest peoples

The earliest inhabitants of the Balearics seem to have reached the islands from the Iberian peninsula, and carbon-dating of remains indicates that human occupation was well established by 2800/2600 BC in Mallorca, 2300 in Menorca. The discovery of pottery, flints and animal horns fashioned into tools suggests that these early people were **Neolithic pastoralists**, who supplemented their food supplies by hunting. A key part of their diet appears to have been *Myotragus balearicus*, a species of diminutive mountain goat unique to the islands and now extinct. Hundreds of these animals' skulls have been discovered and several are exhibited in the islands' larger museums. The frequency of these finds has encouraged some experts to assert that the *Myotragus* was actually domesticated, the principal evidence being the supposed remains of crude corrals on the coast of Mallorca near Deià, though this assertion is now largely discredited.

Cave dwellers

Why, or how, the earliest of these Neolithic peoples moved to the Balearic islands is unknown. Indeed, the first landfall may have been entirely accidental, made by early seafarers travelling along the shores of the Mediterranean – and part of a great wave of migration that is known to have taken place in the Neolithic period. Many of the oldest archeological finds have been discovered in natural **caves**, where it seems likely that these early settlers first sought shelter. Later, cave complexes were dug out of the soft limestone that occurs on both islands, comprising living quarters, usually circular and sometimes with a domed ceiling, as well as longer, straighter funerary chambers. These complexes represent the flourishing of what is commonly called the **Balearic cave culture** – one good (and readily accessible) example is at the resort of **Cala Morell**, on Menorca (see p.239).

2700 BC	2500 BC	1500 BC
Neolithic pastoralists established across Mallorca, colonizing Menorca about four centuries later	The Balearics' native goat, the diminutive *Myotragus balearicus*, becomes extinct possibly through over-hunting	The islanders learn how to work bronze; the beginning of the Talayotic period

The Beaker people

The archeological evidence indicates that Balearic cave dwellers soon came into regular contact with other cultures: the Mediterranean, with its relatively calm and tide-free waters, has always acted as a ready conduit. One of the earliest of these outside influences was the **Beaker people**, whose artefacts have been found right across Western Europe. Named after their practice of burying their dead with pottery beakers, their presence on the Balearics has been indicated by the discovery of Beaker ware at Deià. The Beaker people also had knowledge of the use of **bronze**, an alloy of copper and tin, and they exported their bronze-working skills into the Balearics around 1500 BC. This technological revolution marked the end of the cave culture and the beginning of the Talayotic period.

The Talayotic period

The megalithic remains of the **Talayotic period**, which lasted until the arrival of the Romans in 123 BC, are strewn all over Mallorca and Menorca – though, surprisingly, there's no evidence of them on Ibiza. The structure that gives its name to the period is the **talayot**, a cone-shaped tower with a circular base between 5m and 10m in height. These *talayots* are commonly thought of as watchtowers, but this is unlikely and their actual function is unknown. What is clear is that by 1000 BC a relatively sophisticated, largely pastoral society had developed on both Mallorca and Menorca, with at least some of the islanders occupying the walled settlements that still dot the interior. The three best examples are all in Menorca; **Torre d'en Gaumés** (see p.221), near Alaior, where you can still inspect three *talayots* and the remains of several houses; **Ses Païsses** (see p.167), a well-protected settlement of impressive proportions outside Artà; and **Son Catlar** (see p.238), not far from Ciutadella. All three were occupied well into the Roman period.

Menorca's taulas and hypostyles

Talayotic culture reached dizzying heights on Menorca, and it's here you'll find the most enigmatic remains of the period. These are the **taulas** ("tables" in Catalan), T-shaped structures standing as high as 4m and consisting of two massive dressed stones. Their purpose is unknown, though many theories have been advanced. One early nineteenth-century writer believed that they were altars used for human sacrifice, but the height of most *taulas* makes this very unlikely – unless the islanders were on stilts. More intriguingly, some academics have argued that the "T" was a **stylized head of a bull**, an animal that was much venerated in many parts of the ancient Mediterranean, most notably in Minoan Crete. True or not, it seems probable that the enclosures that surround every *taula* had religious significance. This was confirmed during excavations at **Torralba d'en Salord** (see p.221), where archeologists discovered animal remains and pottery in side recesses of fireplaces, and concluded that these must have been ritual offerings. They also found a bronze sculpture of a bull, suggesting that cattle were, indeed, worshipped. Torralba d'en Salord is one of the many places where *taulas* and *talayots* stand cheek by jowl. Often the remains are too broken down to be of much interest, but three other good spots are **Torrellafuda** (see p.227), **Torre d'en Gaumés** (see p.221) and **Talatí de Dalt** (see p.202), which incorporates a *talayot*, a *taula* and several columned chambers or **hypostyles**. Partly dug out of the ground and roofed

1000 BC	900 BC	800 BC	700 BC
Pirate attacks encourage the Talayotic people to move into walled settlements	Phoenicians use the Balearics as a trading station, bringing greater security to the islands	Greeks displace the Phoenicians as the dominant power in the Balearics	Carthaginians begin to colonize the Balearics

with massive slabs of stone, these hypostyles must have taken considerable effort to build, and may have been used for important gatherings, possibly of communal leaders.

Menorca's navetas

The other distinctive structure to be found on Menorca is the **naveta**, made of roughly dressed, dry-stone blocks and looking like an inverted bread tin. Dating from the beginning of the Talayotic period, the **Naveta d'es Tudons**, near Ciutadella (see p.227), is the finest example, but there are around 35 others sprinkled across the island. They were collective tombs, or, more correctly, ossuaries, where, after the flesh had been removed, the bones of the dead were placed along with some personal possessions such as jewellery, pottery and bone buttons. Curiously, long after their original purpose was forgotten, the Menorcans gave the *navetas* a wide berth right up until the early twentieth century.

Phoenicians

Fearful of attack from the sea, the Talayotic people built their walled settlements a few kilometres inland. This pattern was, however, modified from around 900 BC, when the Balearics became a staging post for the **Phoenicians**, maritime traders from the eastern Mediterranean whose long voyages reached as far as Cornwall in southwest England: the Phoenicians made the islands safer and more secure and the Talayotic peoples were able to venture out from their walled settlements. According to the Roman historian Pliny, the Phoenicians established a large settlement at **Sanisera** on Menorca's north coast (see p.219), and archeologists have also discovered Phoenician artefacts at **Alcúdia** on Mallorca (see p.144). In general, however, very few Phoenician remains have been found on the Balearics – just a handful of bronze items, jewellery and pieces of coloured glass.

Greeks

The **Greeks** displaced the Phoenicians around 800 BC, as several city-states explored the western Mediterranean in search of trade and potential colonies. Like the Phoenicians, the Greeks appear to have used the Balearics primarily as a staging post, for no Greek buildings have survived on either Mallorca or Menorca. The absence of metal apparently made the islands unsuitable for long-term colonization, and the belligerence of the native population may have played a part too: the Greeks coined the islands' name, the "**Balearics**", which they derived from *ballein*, meaning "to throw from a sling". The islanders were adept at this form of warfare, and many early visitors were repelled with showers of polished sling-stones – though some historians dispute this theory, claiming rather that the name comes from the Baleri tribe of Sardinia.

The Carthaginian Empire

The Greeks were also discouraged from colonization by the growth of the **Carthaginian Empire** across the western Mediterranean. The Phoenicians had established Carthage on the North African coast in 814 BC, and from this base they gradually extended their authority across the western Mediterranean. They began to colonize the Balearics in the seventh century BC and the islands were firmly under their control by the

3rd–2nd century BC	247 BC	146 BC	123 BC
Carthage and Rome wrestle for control of the Iberian peninsula in three Punic Wars. Rome wins all three and mainland Spain is incorporated into the Roman Empire	Birth of Hannibal, the brilliant Carthaginian commander, possibly on Ibiza	Final defeat of the Carthaginians by Rome	Rome seizes and then colonizes the Balearics

beginning of the third century BC, if not earlier. Little is known of the Carthaginian occupation except that they established several new settlements. It is also claimed that the Carthaginian general, **Hannibal**, was born on Cabrera island off Mallorca, though Ibiza and Malta claim this honour too.

In the third century BC, the expansion of the Carthaginian Empire up into the Iberian Peninsula triggered two **Punic Wars** with Rome. In both of these wars the Balearics proved extremely valuable, first as stepping stones from the North African coast to the European mainland and second as a source of mercenaries. **Balearic slingers** (see box below) were highly valued and accompanied Hannibal and his elephants across the Alps in the Second Punic War, when (for reasons that remain obscure) the islanders refused gold and demanded payment in wine and women instead. After Hannibal's defeat by the Romans at the battle of Zama in 202 BC, Carthaginian power began to wane and they withdrew from Mallorca and Menorca, although they continued to have some influence over Ibiza for at least another seventy years.

The Romans

As the Carthaginians retreated so the **Romans** advanced, incorporating Ibiza within their empire after the final victory over Carthage in 146 BC. On Mallorca and Menorca, the islanders took advantage of the prolonged military chaos to profit from piracy, until finally, in 123 BC, the Romans, led by the consul Quintus Metellus, restored maritime order by occupying both islands. These victories earned Metellus the title "Balearico" from the Roman senate and two of the islands were given new names, Balearis Major (Mallorca) and Balearis Minor (Menorca).

For the next five hundred years all the Balearic islands were part of the Roman Empire. Amongst many developments, Roman colonists introduced viticulture, turning the Balearics into a wine-exporting area, and initiated olive-oil production from newly planted groves. As was their custom, the Romans consolidated their control

---

BALEARIC SLINGERS

Quintus Metellus, the Roman commander who invaded Mallorca in 123 BC, had a healthy respect for the warlike qualities of the islanders in general and their skill with the **stone-throwing sling** in particular. He had good reason. The Carthaginians had been using Balearic mercenaries for many decades and the islanders had inflicted heavy casualties on the Roman legions throughout the Punic Wars. Consequently, Metellus went to great trouble to protect his men by erecting mammoth shields of hide along the decks of all his ships – a stratagem that worked extremely well.

Male islanders were trained to use the sling in childhood and they could propel a stone with great accuracy and force sufficient to crush most shields and helmets. The slinger had three slings of different lengths, one held in his hand, another wrapped round his stomach and a third tied round his head. According to the historian **Diodorus Siculus** (90–30 BC) these **slingers** were a particularly disagreeable bunch. They often went naked, covering their bodies in a mixture of pig fat and olive oil; were inordinately fond of wine; were keen on female slaves; and rounded off their weddings with all the male guests having congress with the bride in descending order of age – before passing her over to the groom.

5th century AD	425 AD	711
Roman Empire collapses and the Visigoths become Spain's dominant military force	The Germanic Vandals pour over the Balearics destroying everything in their way	Islamic Moors (Arabs and Berbers from North Africa) conquer almost all of mainland Spain

of the islands by building roads and establishing towns. On Mallorca, they founded Pollentia (Alcúdia) in the north and Palmaria on the south coast, near the site of modern Palma, whilst on Menorca they developed Port Magonum (Maó) as an administrative centre with Sanisera – previously the site of a Phoenician trading post – becoming an important port. Initially, the Balearics were part of the Roman province of Tarraconensis (Tarragona), but in 404 AD the islands became a province in their own right with the name **Balearica**.

The Vandals and Byzantines

By the fifth century the Roman Empire was in decline, its defences unable to resist the westward-moving tribes of central Asia. The **Vandals**, one of these tribes, moved in on the Balearics in around 425 AD, ending Roman rule at a stroke. So thoroughgoing was the destruction they wrought that Roman remains are at a premium, the only significant ruins being those of Pollentia at **Alcúdia** (see p.146). One of the reasons for the ferocity of the attack was religious. The Vandals had been Christianized long before they reached the Mediterranean, but they were followers of the **Arian sect**. This interpretation of Christianity, founded by Arius, an Alexandrian priest, insisted that Christ the Son and God the Father were two distinct figures, not elements of the Trinity. To orthodox Christians, this seemed dangerously close to the pagan belief in a multiplicity of gods and, by the end of the fourth century AD, Arianism had been forcibly extirpated within the Roman Empire. However, the sect continued to flourish amongst the Germanic peoples of the Rhine, including the Vandals, who, armed with their "heretical" beliefs, had no religious truck with their new Balearic subjects, persecuting them with vim and gusto.

In 533 the Vandals were defeated in North Africa by the Byzantine general Count Belisarius – who was later to be the subject of a novel by one of Mallorca's adopted sons, Robert Graves. This brought the Balearics under **Byzantine** rule and, for a time, restored prosperity and stability. Nonetheless, the islands were too far removed from Constantinople to be of much imperial importance and, when the empire was threatened from the east at the end of the seventh century, they were abandoned in all but name.

The Moors

As the influence of Byzantium receded, so militarized Islam moved in to fill the vacuum. In 707–8 the **Moors** of North Africa conducted an extended raid against Mallorca, destroying its entire fleet and carrying away slaves and booty, and by 716 the Balearics' position had become even more vulnerable with the completion of the Moorish conquest of Spain. In 798 the Balearics were again sacked by the Moors – who were still more interested in plunder than settlement – and in desperation the islanders appealed for help to **Charlemagne**, the Frankish Holy Roman Emperor. As emperor, Charlemagne was the military leader of Western Christendom (the pope was the spiritual leader), so the appeal signified the final severance of the Balearics' links with Byzantium and the East.

Charlemagne's attempt to protect the islands from the Moors met with some success, but the respite was only temporary. By the middle of the ninth century, the Christian

756	859	902–905
Abd ar-Rahman I proclaims the Emirate of Córdoba, confirming Moorish control over most of Spain	The Vikings raid the Balearics in force	The Moors conquer the Balearics. They introduce many new crops including the orange, lemon, peach, apricot and fig

position had deteriorated so badly that the Balearics were compelled to enter a non-aggression pact with the Moors, and, to add to the islanders' woes, the Balearics suffered a full-scale **Viking** raid in 859. Finally, at the beginning of the tenth century, the **emir of Córdoba** conquered both Menorca and Mallorca. Moorish rule lasted more than three hundred years, though internal political divisions among the Muslims meant that the islands experienced several different regimes. In the early eleventh century, the emirate of Córdoba collapsed and control passed to the *wali* (governor) of Denia, on the Spanish mainland. This administration allowed the Christians – who were known as **Mozarabs** – to practise their faith, and the islands prospered from their position at the heart of the trade routes between North Africa and Islamic Spain.

The Amortadhas

In 1085 the Balearics became an independent emirate with a new dynasty of *walis*, from **Amortadha** in North Africa. The Amortadhas pursued a more aggressive foreign and domestic policy, raiding the towns of Catalonia and persecuting their Christian citizens. These actions blighted trade and thereby enraged the emergent city-states of Italy at a time when Christendom was fired by crusading zeal. Anticipating retaliation, the Amortadhas fortified Palma, which was known at this time as Medina Mayurka, and several mountain strongholds. The Christian attack came in 1114 when a grand Italian fleet – led by the ships of Pisa and supported by the pope as a mini-crusade – landed an army of 70,000 Catalan and Italian soldiers on Ibiza. The island was soon captured, but Mallorca, the crusaders' next target, proved a much more difficult proposition. Palma's coastal defences proved impregnable, so the Christians assaulted the landward defences instead, the concentric lines of the fortifications forcing them into a long series of bloody engagements. When the city finally fell, the invaders took a bitter revenge, slaughtering most of the surviving Muslim population. Yet, despite their victory, the Christians had neither the will nor the resources to consolidate their position and, loading their vessels with freed slaves and loot, they returned home.

The Almoravides

It took the Moors just two years to re-establish themselves on the islands, this time under the leadership of the **Almoravides**, a North African Berber tribe who had previously controlled southern Spain. The Almoravides proved to be tolerant and progressive rulers, and the Balearics prospered: agriculture improved, particularly through the development of irrigation, and trade expanded as commercial agreements were struck with the Italian cities of Genoa and Pisa. The Pisans – crusaders earlier in the century – defied a papal ban on trade with Muslims to finalize the deal; consciences could, it seems, be flexible even in the "devout" Middle Ages when access to the precious goods of the east (silks, carpets and spices) was the prize.

Jaume I and the Reconquista

In 1203 the Almoravides were supplanted by the **Almohad** dynasty, who attempted to forcibly convert the islands' Christian population to Islam. They also started raiding the mainland, but this was an extraordinary miscalculation as the kingdoms of Aragón and Catalunya had recently been united, thereby strengthening the Christian position in

11th century	**1162**	**1229**
Moorish Spain disintegrates into squabbling *taifas*, or petty fiefdoms	Alfonso II unites the kingdoms of Aragón and Catalunya; the Reconquista (the re-conquest of Spain by Christians) picks up speed	Jaume I of Aragón and Catalunya captures Mallorca from the Moors; a bloodbath follows

this part of Spain. The unification was a major step in the changing balance of power: with their forces combined, the Christians were able to launch the **Reconquista**, which was eventually to drive the Moors from the entire Iberian peninsula. Part of the Christian jigsaw was the Balearics and, in 1228, the emir of Mallorca imprudently antagonized the young **King Jaume I of Aragón and Catalunya** by seizing a couple of his ships. The king's advisers, with their eyes firmly fixed on the islands' wealth, determined to capitalize on the offence. They organized the first Balearic publicity evening, a feast at which the king was presented with a multitude of island delicacies and Catalan sailors told of the archipelago's prosperity. And so, insulted by the emir and persuaded by his nobility, Jaume I committed himself to a full-scale invasion.

The invasion of Mallorca

Jaume's expedition of 150 ships, 16,000 men and 1500 horses set sail for **Mallorca** in September 1229. The king had originally planned to land at Pollença, but adverse weather conditions forced the fleet further south and it eventually anchored off Sant Elm, where it must have given the solitary shepherd who lived there a terrific shock. The following day, the Catalans defeated the Moorish forces sent to oppose the landing and Jaume promptly pushed east, laying siege to Medina Mayurka. It took three months to breach the walls, but on December 31 the city finally fell and Jaume was hailed as "**El Conqueridor**".

The invasion of Ibiza

The cost of launching an invasion on this scale placed an enormous strain on the resources of a medieval monarch. With this in mind, Jaume subcontracted the capture of **Ibiza**, entering into an agreement in 1231 with the Crown Prince of Portugal, Don Pedro, and the count of Roussillon. In return for the capture of the island, the count and the prince were to be allowed to divide Ibiza between themselves, provided they acknowledged the suzerainty of Jaume. This project initially faltered, but was revived with the addition of the archbishop of Tarragona. The three allies captured Ibiza in 1235 and divided the spoils, although Don Pedro waived his rights and his share passed to Jaume.

The capture of Menorca

In the meantime, Jaume had acquired the overlordship of **Menorca**. Unable to afford another full-scale invasion, the king devised a cunning ruse. In 1232 he returned to Mallorca with just three galleys, which he dispatched to Menorca carrying envoys, while he camped out in the mountains above Capdepera on Mallorca. As night fell and his envoys negotiated with the enemy, Jaume ordered the lighting of as many bonfires as possible to illuminate the sky and give the impression of a vast army. The stratagem worked and the next day, mindful of the bloodbath following the invasion of Mallorca, the Menorcan Moors capitulated. According to the king's own account, they informed his envoys that "they gave great thanks to God and to me for the message I had sent them for they knew well they could not long defend themselves against me".

The terms of the Reconquista

In Menorca, Jaume's terms were generous: the Moors handed over Ciutadella, their principal settlement, and a number of other strong points, but the new king

1232	1298	1311	1324
Jaume I seizes Menorca from the Moors	Accession of Jaume II as king of Mallorca and Menorca	Death of Jaume II; accession of Sancho	Death of Sancho and accession of Jaume III as king of Mallorca and Menorca

acknowledged the Muslims as his subjects and appointed one of their leaders as his *rais* (governor). The retention of Moorish government in Menorca, albeit under the suzerainty of the king, was, however, in marked contrast to events on Mallorca. Here, the land was divided into eight blocs, with four passing to the king and the rest to his most trusted followers, who leased their holdings in the feudal fashion, granting land to tenants in return for military service. In 1230 Jaume consolidated his position in Mallorca by issuing the **Carta de Població** (People's Charter), guaranteeing equality before the law, an extremely progressive precept for the period. Furthermore, Mallorca was exempted from taxation to encourage Catalan immigration, and special rights were given to Jews resident on the island, a measure designed to stimulate trade. Twenty years later, Jaume also initiated a distinctive form of government for Mallorca, with a governing body of six **jurats** (adjudicators) – one from the nobility, two knights, two merchants and one peasant. At the end of each year the *jurats* elected their successors. This form of government remained in place until the sixteenth century.

The Balearic Kingdom in the thirteenth century

Jaume I died at Valencia in 1276. In his will he divided his kingdom between his two sons: **Pedro** received Catalunya, Aragón and Valencia, whilst **Jaume II** was bequeathed Montpellier, Roussillon and the Balearics. Jaume II was crowned in Mallorca on September 12, 1276, but the division infuriated **Pedro**, as the Balearics stood astride the shipping route between Catalunya and Sicily, where his wife was queen. He forced his brother to become his vassal, but in response Jaume II secretly schemed with the French. Predictably enough, Pedro soon discovered his brother's treachery and promptly set about planning a full-blooded invasion. However, Pedro died before the assault could begin and it was left to his son, **Alfonso III**, to carry out his father's plans. Late in 1285, Alfonso's army captured Palma without too much trouble, which was just as well for its inhabitants: wherever Alfonso met with resistance – as he did later in the campaign at the castle of Alaró – he extracted a brutal revenge. Indeed, even by the standards of thirteenth-century Spain, Alfonso was considered excessively violent and the pope excommunicated him for his atrocities – but not for long.

Alfonso invades Menorca

With Mallorca secured and Jaume deposed, Alfonso turned his attention to Menorca, where he suspected the loyalty of the Moorish governor – the *rais* was allegedly in conspiratorial contact with the Moors of North Africa. Alfonso's army landed on Menorca in January 1287 and decisively defeated the Moors just outside Maó. The Moors retreated to the hilltop fortress of Santa Agueda, but their resistance didn't amount to much and the whole island was Alfonso's within a few days. The king's treatment of the vanquished islanders was savage: those Muslims who were unable to buy their freedom were enslaved, and those who couldn't work as slaves – the old, the sick and the very young – were taken to sea and thrown overboard. Alfonso rewarded the nobles who had accompanied him with grants of land and brought in hundreds of Catalan settlers. The capital, Medina Minurka, was renamed **Ciutadella**, and the island's mosques were temporarily converted to Christian usage, before being demolished and replaced.

1349	1479	1492
Aragon invades the Balearics; death of Jaume III; end of independence for Mallorca and Menorca	Castile and Aragón, the two pre-eminent Christian kingdoms, are united under Isabella I and Fernando V (*Los Reyes Católicos*)	The fall of Granada, the last Moorish kingdom; Columbus reaches the Americas

The Balearic Kingdom in the fourteenth century

Alfonso's violent career was cut short by his death in 1291 at the age of 25. His successor was his brother, Jaume, also the king of Sicily. A more temperate man, Jaume conducted negotiations through the papacy that eventually led, in 1298, to the restoration of the partition envisaged by Jaume I: he himself presided over Catalunya, Aragón and Valencia, while his exiled uncle, **Jaume II**, ruled as king of Mallorca and Menorca, Montpellier and Roussillon. Restored to the Crown, Jaume II devoted a great deal of time to improving the commerce and administration of the Balearics. To stimulate trade, he established a weekly market in Palma, reissued the currency in gold and silver, and founded a string of inland towns, including Manacor, Felanitx, Llucmajor and Binissalem on Mallorca and Alaior and Es Mercadal on Menorca. Jaume II attended to God as well as Mammon, and his reign saw the building of many churches and monasteries. In the same vein, the king also patronized **Ramon Llull** (see p.62), the Mallorcan poet, scholar and Franciscan friar, providing him with the finance to establish a monastic school near Valldemossa. Perhaps his most important act, though, was to grant Menorca its own **Carta de Població**, which bestowed the same legal rights as the Mallorcans already enjoyed.

King Sancho

On his death in 1311, Jaume was succeeded by **Sancho**, his asthmatic son, who spent most of his time in his palace at Valldemossa, where the mountain air was to his liking. Nonetheless, Sancho did his job well, continuing the successful economic policies of his father and strengthening his fleet to protect his territories from North African pirates. Mallorca and Menorca boomed: Mallorca in particular had long served as the entrepôt between North Africa and Europe, its warehouses crammed with iron, figs, salt, oil and slaves, but in the early fourteenth century its industries – primarily shipbuilding and textiles – flourished. In 1325, the traveller Ramón Muntaner praised Palma as an "honoured city of greater wealth than any with the most businesslike inhabitants ... of any city in the world". He may have been exaggerating, but not by much, and Palma's merchants were certainly inventive: spotting a gap in the market they went into **crossbow-making** and by 1380 they were exporting them by the boat load.

The end of independence

Internationally, Sancho worked hard to avoid entanglement in the growing antagonism between Aragón and France, but the islands' future still looked decidedly shaky when he died without issue in 1324. Theoretically, the islands should have passed to Aragón, but the local nobility moved fast to crown Sancho's ten-year-old nephew as **Jaume III**. Hoping to forestall Aragonese hostility, they then had him betrothed to the king of Aragón's five-year-old daughter, though in the long term this marriage did the new king little good. After he came of age, Jaume III's relations with his brother-in-law, **Pedro IV of Aragón**, soured and Pedro successfully invaded the Balearics in response to an alleged plot against him. Jaume fled to his mainland possessions and sold Montpellier to the French to raise money for an invasion. He landed on Mallorca in 1349, but was no match for Pedro, who defeated and killed him on the outskirts of Llucmajor. His son, the uncrowned **Jaume IV**, was also captured and although he eventually escaped, he was never able to drum up sufficient support to threaten the Aragonese.

1494	16th century	1519
The Treaty of Tordesillas divides the New World between Spain and Portugal	Spain emerges as a single political entity, with the Inquisition acting as a unifying force; economic decline in the Balearics	Cortés lands in Mexico, seizing its capital two years later

Unification with Spain

For a diversity of reasons the **unification** of the Balearics with Aragón – and their subsequent incorporation within Spain – proved a disaster for the islanders. In particular, the mainland connection meant the archipelago's nobility soon gravitated towards the Aragonese court, regarding their local estates as little more than sources of income to sustain their expensive lifestyles. More fundamentally, general economic trends moved firmly against the Balearics. After the fall of Constantinople to the Turks in 1453, the lucrative overland trade routes from the Mediterranean to the Far East were blocked and, just as bad, the Portuguese discovered the nautical route round the Cape of Good Hope to the Indies.

In 1479, **Fernando V of Aragón** married **Isabella I of Castile**, thereby uniting the two largest kingdoms in Spain, but yet again this was bad news for the islanders. The union brought mainland preoccupations and a centralized bureaucracy, which rendered the islands a provincial backwater – even more so when, following Columbus's reaching the Americas in 1492, the focus of European trade moved from the Mediterranean to the Atlantic seaboard almost at a stroke. The last commercial straw was the royal decree that forbade Catalunya and the Balearics from trading with the New World. By the start of the sixteenth century, the Balearics were starved of foreign currency and the islands' merchants had begun to leave, signalling a period of long-term economic decline.

Sixteenth-century decline

Political and economic difficulties destabilized the islands' social structures throughout the sixteenth century. The **Jews**, as useful scapegoats, focused some of the swirling antagonisms that perturbed the islands, but there were many other signs of discontent. The aristocracy was divided into warring factions, the country districts were set against the towns, and perhaps most destabilizing of all were high taxes and an unreliable grain supply. In Mallorca, this turbulence coalesced in an **armed uprising** of peasants and artisans in 1521. Organized in a **Germania**, or armed brotherhood, the insurrectionists

---

HARSH TREATMENT: MALLORCA'S JEWS

For several centuries, Mallorca's large **Jewish** community, concentrated in Palma and Inca, played a crucial role in maintaining the island's money supply and sustaining trade with North Africa. In return, they were treated in that strangely contradictory manner that was common across most of medieval Europe, alternately courted and discriminated against. They were, for instance, expected to live in their own ghettos and wear a distinctive type of dress, but were also allowed (unlike their Christian neighbours) to divorce and re-marry. Predictably, they were often blamed for things over which they had no control, from famine to plague, and were intermittently subjected to **pogroms** like the ones in Palma in 1391 and again in 1435 (see p.61). They were also subject to the attentions of the **Holy Office of the Inquisition**, which set up shop in Palma in 1484 determined to impose orthodoxy on all of the island's citizenry. The Inquisitors bore down on the Jews, most of whom either left or chose the course of least resistance and converted to Christianity, though a small percentage were burnt to death. As late as the 1970s, the descendants of these converts still formed a distinct group of Palma gold- and silversmiths, but no such enclave exists today.

1532	1556	1588
Pizarro "discovers" Peru, capturing Cuzco the following year	Felipe II (Philip II), becomes king of Spain and wages unsuccessful war against Europe's Protestants	The English defeat Felipe II's Armada, eliminating Spain as a major sea power

seized control of Palma, whose nobles beat a hasty retreat to the safety of either Palma's Castell de Bellver or the Alcúdia citadel – those who didn't move fast enough were slaughtered in the streets. The rebels soon captured the Bellver, and polished off the blue-bloods who had sought protection there, but Alcúdia held out until relieved. It was a long wait: only in 1523 did the forces of authority return under the command of **Emperor Charles V**, king of Spain, Habsburg Holy Roman Emperor and the grandson of Fernando and Isabella. Charles negotiated generous terms for the surrender of Palma, but once in possession of the city, promptly broke the agreement and ordered the execution of five hundred rebels, who were duly hung, drawn and quartered.

Pirate attacks

The Balearics witnessed other sixteenth-century horrors with the renewal of large-scale **naval raids** from North Africa. This upsurge of piratical activity was partly stimulated by the final expulsion of the Moors from Spain in 1492, and partly by the emergence of the Ottoman Turks as a Mediterranean superpower. Amongst many attacks, Muslim raiders ransacked Pollença (1531 and 1550), Alcúdia (1551), Valldemossa (1552), Andratx (1553) and Sóller (1561), whilst **Hizir Barbarossa** ravaged Menorca's Maó after a three-day siege in 1535. Hundreds of Menorcans were enslaved and carted off, prompting Charles V to construct the fort of Sant Felip to guard Maó harbour. Two decades later, the Turks returned and sacked Ciutadella, taking a further three thousand prisoners – about eighty percent of the city's population. Muslim incursions continued until the seventeenth century, but declined in frequency and intensity after a combined Italian and Spanish force destroyed the Turkish fleet at **Lepanto** in 1571.

The arrival of the British

The Balearics' woes continued throughout the **seventeenth century**. Trade remained stagnant, landowners failed to invest in their estates, and the population declined, a sorry state of affairs that was exacerbated by continued internal tensions. Palma, in particular, was plagued by **vendettas** between its aristocratic families, with the Canavall and Canavant factions regularly involved in street battles and assassinations. By the 1630s the population problem had become so critical that Philip IV exempted the islands from the levies that raised men for Spain's armies, though this gain was offset by the loss of 15,000 Mallorcans to the **plague** in 1652.

A new development was the regular appearance of **British** vessels in the Mediterranean, a corollary of Britain's increasing share of the region's seaborne trade and the Royal Navy's commitment to protect its merchantmen from Algerian pirates. The British didn't have much use for Mallorca, and largely ignored it, but they were impressed by **Maó's splendid harbour**, a secure and sheltered deep-water anchorage where they first put in to take on water in 1621. Forty years later, Charles II of England formalized matters by instructing his ambassador to Spain to "request immediate permission for British ships to use Balearic ports and particularly Port Mahon" – and the Spanish king granted the request.

The British seize Menorca

For a time the British were simply content to "borrow" Maó, but their expanding commercial interests prompted a yearning for a more permanent arrangement. It was

1598	17th century	1701–14
Felipe II dies. His legacy is an enormous but bankrupt empire	Spain enters a period of precipitate military, economic and political decline. Cervantes publishes *Don Quixote* in 1605	Europe's nation states slug it out in the War of the Spanish Succession; Britain takes Menorca and Gibraltar

the dynastic **War of the Spanish Succession** (1701–14), fought over the vacant throne of Spain, which gave them their opportunity. A **British force invaded Menorca** in 1708 and, meeting tepid resistance, captured the island in a fortnight. Apart from the benefits of Maó harbour, Menorca was also an ideal spot from which to blockade the French naval base at Toulon, thereby preventing the union of the French Atlantic and Mediterranean fleets. In fact, Menorca was so useful to the British that they negotiated its retention at the **Treaty of Utrecht**, which both rounded off the war and formalized the island's **first period of British occupation**, which was to last from 1708 to 1756.

The occupation of Menorca

Sir Richard Kane, Menorca's first significant British governor, was an energetic and capable man who strengthened the island as a military base and worked hard at improving its administration, facilities and economy. He built the first **road** across the island from Maó to Ciutadella and introduced improved strains of seed and livestock. Indeed, such were the benefits of British rule that during the first forty years of the occupation the production of wine, vegetables and chickens increased by five hundred percent. Relations between the occupying power and the islanders were generally good – though the Catholic clergy no doubt found it difficult to stomach the instruction to "pray for His Britannic Majesty".

The French interlude

The first phase of British domination ended when the **French** captured Menorca in 1756 at the start of the **Seven Years War**. Admiral Byng was dispatched to assist the beleaguered British garrison, but, after a lacklustre encounter with a French squadron, he withdrew, leaving the British force with no option but to surrender. Byng's indifferent performance cost him his life: he was court-martialled and executed for cowardice, prompting Voltaire's famous aphorism that the English shoot their admirals "pour encourager les autres". The new French governor built the township of **Sant Lluís** (see p.213) to house his Breton sailors and, once again, the Menorcans adjusted to the occupying power without too much difficulty. In 1763, Britain regained Menorca in exchange for the Philippines and Cuba, which it had captured from France during the Seven Years War.

The second British occupation of Menorca

The **second period of British occupation** (1763–82) proved far less successful than the first. None of the governors were as adept as Kane and their tendency to ignore the islanders undermined the Menorcans' trust in the British. The crunch came in 1781, when, with Britain at war with both Spain and France, the Duc de Crillon landed on

1804	1805	1808–14
Napoleon crowned Emperor of France; Spain assists him in his war against England	The British navy, under Nelson, destroys the Franco-Spanish fleet at the Battle of Trafalgar	Napoleon arrests the Spanish king and occupies Spain; this starts the War of Independence (or Peninsular War), pitting the French against the Spanish and their new-found allies, the British

the island with eight thousand soldiers. In command of a much smaller force, the British governor, John Murray, withdrew to Fort Sant Felip, where he was promptly besieged. Crucially, the Menorcans decided to succour Crillon's Franco-Spanish army and, with this material support, they were able to starve the British into submission after eight long months; thereafter, Menorca temporarily reverted to Spain.

The third British occupation of Menorca

The **third and final period of British rule over Menorca** ran from 1798 to 1802, when the island was occupied for its value as a naval base in the Napoleonic Wars. Landing at Port d'Addaia, the British took just nine days – and suffered no casualties – in recapturing the island, helped in no small measure by the foolhardy destruction of Fort Sant Felip by the Spaniards in the mid-1780s. It seems that the Spanish high command did not believe they could defend the fortress, so they simply flattened it, thereby denying it to any colonial power – and, of course, making the island vulnerable in the process. The British finally relinquished all claims to Menorca in favour of Spain under the terms of the Treaty of Amiens in 1802.

Eighteenth-century Mallorca

Meanwhile **Mallorca**, lacking a harbour of any strategic significance, was having a much quieter time, though the islanders did choose the wrong side in the War of the Spanish Succession (1701–14). Most of Spain favoured the French candidate, Philip of Anjou, but Catalunya and Mallorca preferred the Austrian Habsburg Charles III, who was supported by Britain and the Netherlands. Philip won, and promptly proceeded to strip the island of its title of kingdom and remove many of its historic rights. Otherwise, Mallorca was left pretty much untouched by the European conflicts that rippled around it, but even so it did not prosper. Instead it turned in on itself, becoming a caste- and priest-ridden backwater preoccupied with its own internal feuds. By the 1740s, however, this reactionary introspection was ruffled by more progressive elements, who introduced liberal and rationalist ideas into island society under the banner of the **Enlightenment**. Oddly enough, the ideological conflict between Conservatives and Liberals focused on Ramón Llull (see p.62), with the former keen to have him beatified, the latter eager to denigrate his complex mysticism. The traditionalists won, but the bitterness of the dispute combined with its length (1749–77) divided the middle class into hostile camps.

One other major change was Madrid's edict pronouncing **Castilian** as the official language of the Balearics in place of the local dialect of Catalan.

The early nineteenth century

For both Mallorca and Menorca, the **nineteenth century** brought difficult times. Neglected and impoverished outposts, they were subject to droughts, famines and epidemics of cholera, bubonic plague and yellow fever. Consequently, the islanders became preoccupied with the art of survival rather than politics, and generally stayed out of the **Carlist** wars that raged between the Liberals and the Conservatives on the Spanish mainland. Nevertheless, the islanders were obliged to implement a Liberal decree of 1836, which suppressed all of Spain's larger convents and monasteries – hence

1811 onwards	**19th century**	**1923**
The South American colonies assert their independence, detaching themselves from Spain one by one	Further Spanish decline – protracted conflict between the liberals and the monarchists	General Primo de Rivera organizes a right-wing military coup and seizes control of Spain

George Sand and Frédéric Chopin's extended stay in a monk-free Valldemossa monastery (see p.109). The leading political figure of the period was the historian **Josep Quadrado**, who led the reactionary Catholic Union, which bombarded Madrid with petitions and greeted every Conservative success with enthusiastic demonstrations. Otherwise, many islanders emigrated, some to Algeria after it was acquired by the French in 1830, others to Florida and California.

Into the twentieth century

Matters began to improve towards the end of the nineteenth century, when **agriculture**, particularly almond cultivation, revived. Modern services, like gas and electricity, began to be installed and a regular steam-packet link was established between Mallorca and the mainland. Menorca also developed a thriving export industry in **footwear** thanks to the entrepreneurial Don Jeronimo Cabrisas, a Menorcan who had made his fortune in Cuba and later supplied many of the boots worn by the troops in World War I. Around this time too, a **revival of Catalan culture**, led by the middle classes of Barcelona, stirred the Balearic bourgeoisie. In Palma in particular, Catalunyan novelists and poets were lauded, Catalan political groupings were formed, and the town was adorned with a series of splendid *Modernista* buildings.

By 1900, Balearic politics had become polarized between Conservative and Liberal groupings. The failure to create a political discourse between rival factions mirrored developments in the rest of Spain, and both here and on the mainland chronic instability was to be the harbinger of the **military coup** that ushered in the right-wing dictatorship of General Primo de Rivera, who seized power on the Spanish mainland in 1923.

The Balearics in the Civil War

During the **Spanish Civil War** (1936–39), Mallorca and Menorca supported opposing sides. General Goded made Mallorca an important base for the Fascists, but when

---

THE SPANISH CIVIL WAR AND ITS AFTERMATH

With Spain in political turmoil, **General Francisco Franco** (1892–1975), who was the commander of the Spanish army in Africa, took the opportunity to lead a right-wing military rebellion against the Republican government in Madrid. His **Nationalists** received substantial support from Hitler and Mussolini, whilst the **Republicans** secured only sporadic help from the Soviet Union, though they were also assisted by thousands of politically active volunteers, organized in the **International Brigades**. The Civil War was vicious and bloody, but the Nationalists eventually prevailed and Franco became the head of a **Fascist dictatorship**; Pope Pius XII congratulated him on his "Catholic victory". Not a man to show much mercy, Franco took bloody reprisals against his enemies and although no one knows for sure how many people died, it was certainly many thousands. After the death of Franco, no effort was made to hunt down his murderous thugs – part of an accommodation between left and right designed to stop Spain from degenerating into a cycle of political revenge. This accommodation is still in place, though there are periodic attempts to get the issues re-opened and establish exactly who did what to whom, where and when.

1930	**1936–39**
Rivera dies and one of his key supporters, the Spanish king Alfonso XIII, abdicates the following year; the Republicans take control and Spain polarizes to the political left and right	Spanish Civil War. General Francisco Franco and his Fascists win and extract a terrible revenge

General Bosch attempted to do the same on Menorca, his NCOs and men mutinied and, with the support of the civilian population, declared their support for the Republic. In the event – apart from a few bombing raids and an attempted Republican landing at Porto Cristo (see p.176) – the Balearics saw very little fighting. Nevertheless, the Menorcans were dangerously exposed towards the end of the war, when they were marooned as the last Republican stronghold. A peaceful conclusion was reached largely through the intervention of the British, who brokered the surrender of the island aboard *HMS Devonshire*. Franco's troops occupied Menorca in April 1939 and the *Devonshire* left with 450 Menorcan exiles.

The fledgling tourist industry

The rich and famous discovered Mallorca's charms in the late nineteenth century – Jules Vernes, for one, liked to visit and both Edward VII and the German Kaiser regularly cruised its waters. The high-water mark of this elitist tourist trade was reached in the 1930s when a wealthy Argentinian, Adan Diehl, opened the *Hotel Formentor* (see p.144). Never knowingly outdone, Diehl advertised the hotel in lights on the Eiffel Tower and attracted guests such as Edward VIII, the Aga Khan and Winston Churchill – no mean guest list by any standard.

From such small and privileged beginnings, the Balearics' **tourist industry** mushroomed at an extraordinary rate after World War II. In 1950, Mallorca had just one hundred registered hotels and boarding houses, but by 1972 the total had risen to more than 1600, and similarly the number of visitors to Menorca rose from 1500 in 1961 to half a million in 1973. It was an extraordinary phenomenon greatly assisted by the Franco regime's indifference to planning controls and regulations.

The late twentieth century

After the **death of Franco** in 1975, the prodigious pace of development accelerated across the Balearics, thereby further strengthening the local economy. One twist, however, was the relative price of real estate: traditionally, island landowners with coastal estates had given their younger children the poorer agricultural land near the seashore, but it was this land the developers wanted – and so younger siblings found their prospects transformed almost at a stroke. In more general terms, the burgeoning tourist economy pumped huge quantities of money into the Balearics and, by 1990, the archipelago had one of the highest per capita incomes in Spain, four times that of Extremadura for instance, and well above the EU average. There was also the small matter of **sex**: the Franco regime had attempted to enforce a strict moral code in which Spanish girls kept their bodies to themselves until they were married. Many of the arriving tourists had no such inhibitions – much to the delight of a legion of local men – and it took a couple of decades for Spanish women to re-focus their sights – and their mores.

The Autonomous Communities

The Balearics also benefited from the political restructuring of Spain following the death of Franco. In 1978, the Spanish parliament, the Cortes, passed a new **constitution**, which reorganized the country on a federal basis and allowed for the

1939–75	1975	1976–82
Franco establishes a one-party state, backed up by stringent censorship and a vigorous secret police	Death of Franco; Juan Carlos, the grandson of Alfonso XIII and Franco's appointed successor, becomes king	Juan Carlos helps steer the country towards democracy, but there are to be no trials of Franco's thugs

establishment of regional Autonomous Communities – in theory if not altogether in practice. Four years later, Felipe González's Socialist Workers' Party – the **PSOE** – was elected to office with a huge majority and the promise of change and progress. The PSOE did not fulfil all its objectives, but it did make a serious attempt to deal with Spain's deep-seated separatist tendencies by negotiating a large degree of regional autonomy. In the Balearics, the upshot was the creation of the **Comunidad Autónoma de las Islas Baleares** in 1983 and although the demarcation of responsibilities between central and regional governments has proved immensely problematic, the islanders have used their new-found independence to good effect, asserting the primacy of their native Catalan language – now the main language of education – and exercising greater control of their economy.

Tourism: a new direction

In 1996, the PSOE was defeated in the Spanish **general election**, but although the new Conservative regime – led by the **Partido Popular (PP)** – had strong centralizing credentials, it was also reliant on the regionalists for its parliamentary majority. Consequently, the trend towards **decentralization** continued with most government expenditure now coming under the control of the Autonomous Communities. In particular, the Balearic administration used these regionalized resources to upgrade a string of holiday resorts and modernize much of the archipelago's infrastructure. In part this reflected a particular concern with Ibiza and Mallorca's somewhat tacky image and was accompanied by the imposition of **stricter building controls**, a number of environmental schemes and the spending of millions of pesetas on refurbishing the older, historical parts of Palma. On Menorca, the money also paid for the creation of a Parc Natural, protecting the wetlands of S'Albufera d'es Grau along with the adjacent coastline.

The Conservatives, in power in the Balearics since the elections of 1991, also made moves to curb tourist development, but in this they failed to keep pace with public sentiment – as exemplified by a string of large-scale **demonstrations** held during 1998 and 1999. The demonstrations focused on four primary and inter-related concerns: the spiralling cost of real estate, foreign ownership of land (some twenty percent of Mallorca was in foreign hands), untrammelled development and loutish behaviour in the budget resorts. This failure to keep abreast of popular feeling resulted in the defeat of the Conservatives in the **1999 regional elections**.

The twenty-first century

The Balearics' Conservative administration was replaced by an **unwieldy alliance** of regionalists, socialists and greens committed to halting further tourist development in its tracks. As one of its spokesmen said: "We need to dignify the tourist sector, not promote it as the cheapest in Europe with the idea that you can come here and do whatever you like." Faced with an annual influx of around eleven million holidaymakers, few islanders disagreed, and the coalition made significant progress, though they came unstuck when the tourist industry hit (comparatively) hard times in 2002 with an eight percent drop in the number of visitors. The main reason for the decline was the economic travails of Germany, but Balearic anxieties focused on the

1981	1986	1999	2002
Colonel Tejero and a group of Guardia Civil officers loyal to Franco's memory storm parliament, but the putsch soon collapses	Rafael Nadal born in Manacor, Mallorca; Spain joins the EU	Spanish economy enters a nine-year boom	Spain adopts the euro; peseta abandoned

THE SPANISH ELECTION 2004

At the start of 2004, Spanish opinion polls showed solid public support for the **Partido Popular (PP)** government, suggesting that the **general election** scheduled for March would return them to office. Then, on March 11, three days before polling day, a series of bombs exploded on Madrid's commuter trains, killing 192 people and injuring almost two thousand more. Rashly, the PP leadership blamed the Basque terrorist/separatist group ETA for the explosions, believing, so it would seem, that this false accusation would deflect attention away from the real reason for the attack – Spain's support for the Iraq war (ninety percent of Spaniards had been against it) – just long enough for the votes to be counted. It didn't wash and by the time the polls opened, many had come to believe that – as was subsequently proved to be the case – Islamic terrorists had blown up the trains. The voters vented their political spleen against the PP, giving the **PSOE** an unexpected victory; the new regime's first act was to announce the immediate withdrawal of Spanish troops from Iraq.

so-called **tourist tax** imposed by the regional government in May 2002. The idea was to impose a modest tax on every visitor over twelve years of age and spend the money – potentially about thirty million euros a year – on **environmental improvements**. However, the tourist industry created a huge hullabaloo that undermined the Balearic administration, and the Conservatives, who had pledged to rescind the tax, were (just) returned to office in the **regional elections of 2003**. This was a major setback for the environmentalist cause at a time when Spain's regionalists were already losing ground to Madrid – the Conservatives had won a second **general election in 2000**, but this time with an overall majority in the Cortes, thus firmly sidelining the regionalists.

The environment: a step back

After their 2003 election victory, the Conservative-led Balearic administration proved remarkably gung-ho when it came to **development**, ignoring environmental concerns by embarking, for example, on a large-scale road-building programme in the belief that more roads create better motoring – never mind the disfiguring of agricultural land that this involved. Indeed, they even became quite evangelical in their desire for development, most notably supporting a mass demonstration in favour of the expansion of port facilities at Ciutadella – an expansion that Menorca's PSOE-led council strongly opposed. The PP Mayor of Andratx, one **Eugenio Hidalgo**, joined in the development bonanza, but in his case there were **shady dealings** involving illegal construction permits – amongst much else – and in 2008, two years after the scandal broke, Hidalgo was sent to prison for four years. This was all very depressing, but nevertheless the PP still managed to garner more votes than any other party in the Balearic **regional elections of 2007**. The catch was that they didn't quite secure an overall majority and their opponents united to form a new ruling PSOE-led coalition.

Recession and depression

In 2007, the new PSOE-led, Balearic administration, under the leadership of **Francesc Antich**, put the brakes on the helter-skelter development of its predecessor, but its priorities were soon muddied and modified by the worldwide recession: in 2009, Spain's housing market took a nose dive and unemployment began to rise, whilst in the

2003	2004	2005
The Conservative (PP) government commits to the invasion of Iraq; huge protests	Islamic terrorists bomb Madrid; Socialists win the general election and pull Spanish troops out of Iraq	Same-sex marriage made legal in Spain; Catholic priests in a huff

Balearics the number of tourists dropped by about ten percent, bringing many hotels to the point of bankruptcy. Antich and his colleagues were obliged to consider all sorts of stimulus packages and then, as if things weren't bad enough, ETA, the Basque separatist group, exploded a number of **bombs** on Mallorca in the summer of the same year.

For the next two years, Antich and his colleagues did their best to keep the Balearics afloat, but in 2011 grumpy islanders ejected the administration in favour of the Conservatives with the PP securing an overall majority under the leadership of **José Ramón Bauzà**, who remains in power at time of writing. Along with many other European politicians, Bauzà appears unable to do very much in the face of the islands' continued woes: the building industry is at a standstill; tourist numbers have dipped, but fortunately not dived; and in the autumn of 2012, unemployment hit a staggering 28 percent. These travails are paralleled at the national level, where Spain's government, under PP control again since 2011, will almost certainly be forced to seek a bail-out from the EU – and no one can be sure if this will finally start to solve the country's underlying economic problems or not. Also in the autumn of 2012, Madrid cut its regional subsidy to the Balearics by 48 percent; Bauzà immediately hit the airwaves to protest, but since fellow PP politicians run the national government, few were convinced or impressed.

2008	2009	2012
Spanish economy hits the buffers	Car bomb explodes in Palma Nova, the work of Basque separatists; no one killed	Austerity and recession – but where is the king? Answer: he's hunting elephants in Botswana. Much derision follows

Flora and fauna

Despite their reputation as overdeveloped, package-holiday hotspots, Menorca and more especially Mallorca have much to offer birders and botanists alike. Separated from the Iberian peninsula some fifty million years ago, the Balearic archipelago has evolved (at least in part) its own distinctive flora and fauna, with further variations between each of the islands. Among the wildlife, it's the raptors inhabiting the mountains of northwest Mallorca – particularly the black vulture – that attract much of the attention, but there are other pleasures too, especially the migratory birds that gather on the islands' saltpans and marshes in April and May and from mid-September to early October. The islands are also justifiably famous for their fabulous range of wild flowers and flowering shrubs.

The account below serves as a general introduction, and includes mention of several important birding sites, cross-referenced to the descriptions given throughout the Guide. For more specialist information, we have also listed some recommended **field guides** (p.268).

Habitats

The Balearic islands are a continuation of the Andalucian mountains of the Iberian peninsula, from which they are separated by a submarine trench never less than 80km wide and up to 1500m deep. **Mallorca** comprises three distinct geographical areas with two ranges of predominantly limestone mountains/hills falling either side of a central plain, **Es Pla**. The **Serra de Tramuntana** dominates Mallorca's northwest coast and comprises a slim, 90km range of wooded hills and rocky peaks, all fringed by tiny coves and precipitous sea cliffs; it reaches its highest point at Puig Major (1447m). Also edged by sea cliffs is the **Serres de Llevant**, a range of more modest hills that runs parallel to the island's east shore and rises to 509m at the Santuari de Sant Salvador.

Menorca has less topographical diversity, dividing into two distinct but not dramatically different zones. The **northern half** of the island comprises rolling sandstone uplands punctuated by wide, shallow valleys and occasional peaks, the highest of which is Monte Toro at 357m. To the **south** lie undulating limestone lowlands and deeper valleys. Steep sea cliffs and scores of rocky coves trim the island's north and south shores.

Mallorca and Menorca share a temperate Mediterranean **climate**, with winter frosts a rarity, but there are significant differences between the two. The Serra de Tramuntana protects the rest of Mallorca from the prevailing winds that blow from the north and also catches most of the rain. Menorca, on the other hand, has no mountain barrier to

---

GOB – A VOICE FOR PRESERVATION

The threat to the islands' flora and fauna from developers has spawned an influential conservation group, **GOB** (Grup Balear d'Ornitologia i Defensa de la Naturalesa; ⓦ gobmallorca .com), which has launched several successful campaigns in recent years. It helped save the S'Albufera wetlands from further development; played a leading role in the black vulture re-establishment programme; successfully lobbied to increase the penalties for shooting protected birds; and won its fight to protect and preserve Cabrera island.

protect it from the cold dry wind (the Tramuntana) that buffets the island from the north, giving much of the island's vegetation a wind-blown look, and obliging farmers to protect their crops with stone walls.

Mallorcan flora

The characteristic terrain of Mallorca up to around 700m is **garrigue**, partly forested open scrubland where the island's native trees – Aleppo pines, wild olives, holm oaks, carobs and dwarf palms – intermingle with imported species like ash, elm and poplar. Between 700m and 950m, the *garrigue* gives way to **maquis**, a scrubland of rosemary, laurel, myrtle and broom interspersed with swaths of bracken. Higher still is a rocky terrain that can only support the sparsest of vegetation, such as an assortment of hardy grasses and low-growth rosemary.

Across much of the island, this indigenous vegetation has been destroyed by cultivation. However, the **Aleppo pine** and the evergreen **holm oak** – which traditionally supplied acorns for pigs, wood for charcoal and bark for tanning – are still common, as is the **carob tree**, which prefers the hottest and driest parts of the island. Arguably the archipelago's most handsome tree, the carob boasts leaves of varying greenness and bears conspicuous fruits – large pods that start green, but ripen to black-brown. The **dwarf palm**, with its sharp lance-like foliage, is concentrated around Pollença, Alcúdia and Andratx. The **wild olive** is comparatively rare (and may not be indigenous), but the cultivated variety, which boasts silver-grey foliage and can grow up to 10m in height, is endemic and was long a mainstay of the local economy. There are also **orange** and **lemon** orchards around Sóller and innumerable almond trees, whose pink and white blossoms adorn much of the island in late January and early February.

Mallorca has a wonderful variety of **flowering shrubs**. There are too many to list here in any detail, but look out for the deep blue flowers of the **rosemary**; the reddish bloom of the **lentisk** (or mastic tree); the bright yellow broom which begins blossoming in March; the many types of **tree heather**; and the autumn-flowering **strawberry tree**, found especially around Ca'n Picafort. **Rockroses** are also widely distributed, the most common members of the group being the spring-flowering, grey-leafed cistus, with its velvety leaves and pink flowers, and the narrow-leafed cistus whose bloom is white.

Wild flowers and plants

In spring and autumn the fields, verges, woods and cliffs of Mallorca brim with **wild flowers**. There are several hundred species and only in the depths of winter – from November to January – are all of them dormant. Well-known flowers include marigolds, daisies, violets, yellow primroses, gladioli, poppies, hyacinths, several kinds of cyclamen, the resinous St John's wort with its crinkled deep-green leaves and, abundant in the pine woods near the sea and in the mountains, many types of orchid. Two common mountain plants are the pampas-like grass **Ampelodesmos mauritanica**, giant clumps of which cover the hillsides, and a local variety of the sarsaparilla, **Smilax balearica**, which flourishes in limestone crevices where its sharp thorns are something of a hazard for walkers. Other common and prominent plants are the giant-sized **agave** (century plant), an imported amaryllid with huge spear-shaped, leathery leaves of blue-grey coloration, which produces a massive flower spike after ten years (just before it dies). There's also the distinctive **asphodel**, whose tall spikes sport clusters of pink or white flowers from April to June. The asphodel grows on overgrazed or infertile land and shoemakers once used its starch-rich tubers to make glue. Another common sight is the **prickly pear**, traditionally grown behind peasants' houses as a windbreak and toilet wall. A versatile plant, the prickly pear has a smell that deflects insects (hence its use around toilets) and its fruit is easy to make into pig food or jam.

Finally, many islanders maintain splendid **gardens** and here you'll see species that flourish throughout the Mediterranean, most famously bougainvilleas, oleanders, geraniums and hibiscus.

Mallorcan birds

Mallorca's diverse **birdlife** has attracted ornithologists for decades. The island boasts a whole batch of resident Mediterranean specialists and these are supplemented by migrating flocks of North European birds that descend on the island in their thousands during the spring and autumn.

The limestone **Serra de Tramuntana** mountains crimping the northwest coast are a haven for birds of prey. The massive **black vulture** is the real star here. This rare and impressive resident raptor, with its near 3m wingspan, breeds in small numbers, but its size means there's a reasonable chance of a sighting. The Puig Roig area (see p.131) is an excellent place to see this vulture, but note that during late spring and summer there are sometimes access restrictions to the bird's active sea cliff nesting areas. The booted eagle is another mountain highlight, and there's a supporting cast of ospreys, red kites, Eleonora's falcons, kestrels and peregrines.

The **Embassament de Cúber**, or Cúber Reservoir, (see p.128), just west of Lluc, provides a natural amphitheatre from where up to ten species of bird of prey can be seen, including ospreys and red-footed falcons hunting over the water itself. The colourful rock thrush breeds in the quarry just west of the reservoir dam and on the nearby crags.

Seabirds

The **sea cliffs** of the western coast are the breeding grounds of shearwaters, Mediterranean shag, storm petrels and Audouin's gulls. The most impressive seabird colonies are in the **Parc Natural de Sa Dragonera**, an island fastness off Sant Elm (see p.119), which is home to all these birds as well as several dozen pairs of Eleonora's falcons. The district's seabirds may also be viewed from **La Trapa**, a small headland nature reserve of pristine coastal *garrigue*. The reserve is about an hour's walk north of Sant Elm, but the going is fairly tough. A similarly good spot for seabirds is the **Cap de Formentor** (see p.142), at the other end of the island, from where a wide range of birds wander the neighbouring bays of Pollença and Alcúdia.

Scrubland birds

Characteristic birds of the island's **scrubland** can also be found around the Embalse de Cúber, including a variety of warblers and small songbirds, such as nightingales, larks, pipits and chats. Another area of rich scrubland is the **Vall de Bóquer** (see p.141), near Pollença. Thoughtless development has harmed the olive groves and almond orchards at the base of the valley, but the Bóquer remains a migration hotspot, its pine avenues and denser wooded slopes hosting firecrests and crossbills among more familiar woodland birds like tits and woodpigeons. If you venture to the north end of the valley, you should be rewarded with the colourful delights of Marmora's warbler and the blue rock thrush. In spring, hundreds of bee-eaters can be heard and seen in and around the valley, as these stunning birds move through to breed elsewhere in the Mediterranean.

Wetland birds

Wetlands are a magnet for birds in the arid climate of the Mediterranean. Mallorca boasts the most important birdwatching spot in the whole of the Balearics in the marshes of the **Parc Natural de S'Albufera** (see p.152). Here, resident species are augmented by hundreds of migrating birds, who visit to find fresh water after their long journey north or south. Amongst scores of species, the shorter grasses shelter moorhens, coots, crakes and the re-introduced purple gallinule, while the reeds hide

SELECTED BIRDS OF MALLORCA AND MENORCA

The list below describes many of the most distinctive **birds** to be found on Mallorca and/or Menorca. We have given the English name, followed in italics by the Latin, a useful cross-reference for those without a British field guide.

Serin (*Serinus serinus*). Menorca. Winter visitor. Tiny, green-and-yellow canary-like bird of the finch family, with characteristic buoyant flight. Seen in almost any habitat.

Fan-tailed warbler (*Cisticola juncidis*). Mallorca & Menorca. Very common breeding resident. Typical small brown bird, but with very distinctive "zit-zit-zit" song, usually uttered in flight. Prefers wetland areas.

Nightingale (*Luscinia megarhynchos*). Mallorca & Menorca. Common breeding summer visitor. Rich-brown-coloured, robin-like bird with rich, vigorous and varied song. Prefers to sing from deep inside small bushes, often out of sight.

Wryneck (*Jynx torquilla*). Mallorca & Menorca. Mallorca: breeding resident. Menorca: spring, autumn and winter visitor. Medium-sized with a complex pattern of brown, grey and lilac plumage. A member of the woodpecker family. Favours olive groves.

Hoopoe (*Upupa epops*). Mallorca & Menorca. Common breeding resident. Pigeon-sized, pinky-brown bird with black head-crest. It is named after its distinctive "upupu upupu" call. Its wings sport a complex black and white barring, creating a striking sight when in flight. Favours open areas with some trees nearby for nesting.

Black vulture (*Aegypius monachus*). Mallorca. Breeding resident only in the northern mountains. Massive, dark, powerful and solitary raptor with a wingspan approaching 3m. The most distinctive of the islands' birds. Faced extinction in the 1980s, but a concerted conservation effort has raised the population considerably.

Booted eagle (*Hieraaetus pennatus*). Mallorca & Menorca. Resident breeder. A small and very agile eagle, similar in size to a buzzard. Prefers the mountains, but happily hunts over scrub and grasslands too.

Eleonora's falcon (*Falco eleonorae*). Mallorca & Menorca. Mallorca: fairly common breeding summer visitor. Menorca: spring and autumn migrant. Dark, slim, elegant falcon. Hunts small birds and large insects with fantastic speed and agility. Often seen hunting insects near water.

Rock thrush (*Monticola saxatilis*). Mallorca & Menorca. Mallorca: breeding summer visitor. Menorca: spring and autumn migrant. Beautifully coloured rock- and quarry-loving thrush. Males have a pale blue head and orangey-red breast and tail. Females are a less distinctive brown and cream.

Blue rock thrush (*Monticola solitarius*). Mallorca & Menorca. Common breeding resident. Blue-coloured thrush, recalling a deep-blue starling. Can be found in any rugged, rocky areas at any time of year.

Firecrest (*Regulus ignicapillus*). Mallorca & Menorca. Common breeding resident. The smallest bird on the islands. This tiny pale green bird is named after its vivid orange-and-yellow crown. Abundant in any woodland.

Crossbill (*Loxia curvirostra*). Mallorca. Abundant breeding resident. The vivid red males and the lemon-green females of this bulky finch have an unusual crossed bill and a distinctive parrot-like appearance. The bill is adapted to extract seeds from pine cones.

Marmora's warbler (*Sylvia sarda*). Mallorca. Common breeding resident. A small blue-ish grey warbler with a long, often-upright tail and distinctive red eye-ring. Prefers the bushy cover of the coastal lowlands.

Purple gallinule (*Porphyrio porphyrio*). Mallorca. Breeding resident only at Mallorca's S'Albufera. This purple-blue oddity was re-introduced to its marshland habitat at S'Albufera in 1991. It is now well established. Its incredibly long feet and swollen red bill make this hen-like bird very distinctive.

Little bittern (*Ixobrychus minutes*). Menorca. Spring and autumn visitor. Secretive wetland specialist. This is the smallest member of the heron family breeding in Europe at little more than 30cm tall. The male is an attractive pink-cream colour with contrasting black wings and cap. Males advertise themselves with a far-carrying gruff basal note, repeated regularly.

Purple heron (*Ardea purpurea*). Mallorca. Breeding summer visitor. Large, slender heron fond of reed beds. The male plumage has beautiful purple and rich-brown tones. Despite its size it can be rather elusive, hiding deep inside the reeds.

Black-winged stilt (*Himantopus himantopus*). Mallorca & Menorca. Mallorca: common breeding resident; Menorca: summer visitor. Incredibly long-legged black-and-white wader. Its medium size is somewhat extended by its long, straight, fine, red bill. Can appear anywhere there is mud, but particularly common on saltpans.

Kentish plover (*Charadrius alexandrinus*). Mallorca & Menorca. Mallorca: common breeding resident. Menorca: spring and autumn visitor. Small, delicate wader of saltpans and marshes. Its pale-brown upper body contrasts with its gleaming white head-collar and underparts.

Cetti's warbler (*Cettia cetti*). Mallorca & Menorca. Very common breeding resident. This rather nondescript, chunky, wren-like warbler prefers dense thickets close to water. It possesses an astonishingly loud explosive song: "chet-chet-chet-chetchetchet".

Scops owl (*Otus scops*). Mallorca & Menorca. Common breeding resident. This tiny owl (just 20cm tall) is stubbornly nocturnal. At night, its plaintive "tyoo" note is repeated every few seconds often for long (monotonous) periods. Groves, plantations, small clumps of trees, conifer woodland and gardens can host this bird.

Greater flamingo (*Phoenicopterus ruber*). Mallorca & Menorca. Winter/spring visitor in small numbers. The unmistakable silhouette of this leggy wader with roseate wings, bill and legs can be seen on any wetland in spring. In winter, it's confined to the southern reaches of Mallorca – especially the S'Albufera wetland.

Great white egret (*Egretta alba*). Mallorca & Menorca. Winter visitor. This marshland specialist is really just a large version of the commoner little egret – an all-white, tall, elegant heron.

Audouin's gull (*Larus audouinii*). Mallorca & Menorca. Resident breeder. This rare gull favours the rocky coastline of both islands. It's the size and light-grey colour of a typical "seagull" but boasts a splendid red bill. Unfortunately it takes three years for birds to reach this adult plumage and prior to this they are much less distinctive.

Bee-eater (*Merops apiaster*). Mallorca & Menorca. Mallorca: common spring visitor, rare summer breeder. Menorca: breeding summer visitor. A brightly coloured, medium-sized bird, with a slim body, long pointed wings and slightly de-curved bill. It has a distinctive green, orange, yellow and blue plumage, and an instantly recognizable bubbling "pruuk" call. It prefers open, relatively flat, rugged countryside.

Egyptian vulture (*Neophron percnopterus*). Mallorca & Menorca. Mallorca: rare migrant. Menorca: breeding resident. Medium-sized raptor with small, rather pointed protruding head and featherless face. Wings held flat when soaring.

Stone curlew (*Burhinus oedicnemus*). Mallorca & Menorca. Resident breeder, more common in summer. Thick-set wader that prefers dry rolling countryside to mud. Has a large, yellow, almost reptilian eye. Largely dull brown with some darker streaking, but with distinctive, long yellow legs. When in flight, its striking black-and-white wings become apparent.

< HOOPOE

healthy numbers of several species of heron, bittern and egret as well as the occasional flamingo. A wide variety of small wading birds visit the marsh too, including the distinctively long-legged black-winged stilt and the abundant Kentish plover. The open water is popular with ducks, while in spring large numbers of terns may be seen. In winter the variety of duck species increases and kingfishers are common.

This rich birdlife attracts birds of prey and this is as good a place as any to see ospreys and marsh harriers. In addition, more than one hundred Eleonora's falcons have been seen together over the marsh in spring. Among the smaller birds, the spring dusk and dawn choruses provided by wetland warblers such as Cetti's, moustached and great reed are unforgettable. Neither is the sound of birds restricted to the daytime. At night, listen for the plaintive single note of the scops owl against a backdrop of warblers, crakes and crickets. The scops owl can also be heard in the south of the island, usually preferring almond groves and olive clumps.

Birds of the saltpan

Generally speaking, the south of Mallorca is not as rich in birdlife as other parts of the island, the main exception being the **saltpan** habitat of the **Salines de Llevant**, near Colònia de Sant Jordi (see p.184). Here, a wide variety of migrant wading birds, wintering duck and small flocks of wintering flamingoes and cranes can be seen. The site also has a breeding flock of more than a hundred black-winged stilts in summer and the abundance of prey attracts raptors, most frequently marsh harriers, kestrels and ospreys. The pans also host terns and Audouin's gulls: this red-billed gull is a Mediterranean specialist and although favouring the southern saltpans, can be chanced upon at many coastal spots.

Birds of the central plain

The country lanes that lattice Mallorca's **central plain**, Es Pla, have their own distinctive birdlife. In spring and summer, the calls and songs of small birds like serins, corn buntings and Sardinian warblers and the ubiquitous fan-tailed warbler create a busy backdrop to hot, lazy afternoons. Nightingales seem to be everywhere and their rich song leaves a lasting impression. In the shade of the abundant olive groves, the subtly plumaged wryneck can be found all year, often sharing this ancient landscape with the striking hoopoe.

Other Mallorcan fauna

Mallorca's surviving **mammals** are an uninspiring bunch. The wild boar and red fox were eliminated early in the twentieth century, leaving a motley crew of mountain goats, wild sheep, pine martens, genets, weasels and feral cats, as well as commonplace smaller mammals such as hedgehogs, rabbits, hares and shrews.

As far as **reptiles** go, there are four types of snake – all hard to see – and two species of gecko (or broad-toed lizard): the lowland-living wall gecko and the mountain-dwelling disc-fingered version. With any luck, you'll spot them as they heat up in the sun, but they move fast since warm gecko is a tasty morsel for many a bird. Off the south coast of Mallorca, the island of Cabrera (see p.188) has a large concentration of another lizard, the rare, blue-bellied **Lilford's wall lizard**.

Among **amphibians**, Mallorca has a healthy frog population, concentrated in its marshlands but also surviving in its mountain pools (up to around 800m). There are also three types of toad, of which the **Mallorcan midwife toad**, hanging on in the northern corner of the island, is the rarest and strangest. With no natural predators, its evolution involved a reduction in fecundity (it produces only a quarter of the number of eggs laid by its mainland relative) and the loss of its poison glands. This was fair enough until someone introduced the viperine snake to the island and, in the ensuing slaughter, the midwife toads were all but wiped out – only about five hundred pairs remain.

Common **insects** include grasshoppers and cicadas, whose summertime chirping is so evocative of warm Mediterranean nights, as well as more than two hundred species of moth and around thirty types of **butterfly**. Some of the more striking butterflies are red admirals, which are seen in winter, and the clouded yellows and painted ladies of spring. One of the more unusual species is the two-tailed pasha, a splendidly marked gold-and-bronze butterfly that flits around the coast in spring and late summer, especially in the vicinity of strawberry trees.

Menorcan flora

The indigenous vegetation in Menorca, which is far flatter than its neighbour, is almost all **garrigue** (partly forested scrubland), though intensive cultivation has reduced the original forest cover to a fraction of its former size – nowadays only about fifteen percent of the island is wooded. Native trees are the holm oak, the dwarf palm, the carob and, commonest of all, the **Aleppo pine**, which has bright green spines, silvery twigs and ruddy-brown cones. Olive trees are endemic and illustrate the effects of the prevailing Tramuntana, with grove upon grove almost bent double under the force of the wind.

Menorca's soils nourish a superb range of **flowering shrubs** and **wild flowers**. There is less variety than on Mallorca, but the islands have many species in common. In addition, Menorca boasts a handful of species entirely to itself, the most distinguished of them being the dwarf shrub **Daphne rodriquezii**, a purple-flowering evergreen, present on the cliffs of the northeast coast. In addition, the cliffs of much of the coast have a flora uniquely adapted to the combination of limestone yet saline soils. Here, **aromatic inula**, a shrubby perennial with clusters of yellow flowers, grows beside the **common caper**, with its red pods and purple seeds, and the **sea aster**.

Menorcan birds

The varied **birdlife** of Menorca includes birds of prey, wetland specialists, seabirds, waders and characteristic Mediterranean warblers, larks and pipits, but perhaps the most striking feature is the tameness of many of the birds – presumably because shooting birds is less popular here than in almost any other part of the Mediterranean.

There are several ornithological hotspots, but wherever you are **birds of prey** should be evident. Of these, the Egyptian vulture is the most impressive; there are around a hundred of them, the only resident population in Europe. Red kites, booted eagles and ospreys can also be seen year round, and they are joined by marsh and hen harriers in winter. Peregrines, kestrels and, in winter, sparrowhawks complete the more reliable raptors, although in spring and autumn several others – such as the honey buzzard and black kite – may appear. **Monte Toro** (see p.222), the highest point on Menorca, is as good a vantage point for birds of prey as any.

Birds of S'Albufera lake

Menorca's **best birdwatching spot** is the marshland, reeds and *garrigue* fringing **S'Albufera** lake near Es Grau (see p.215), which is itself part of the larger Parc Natural S'Albufera des Grau that extends north to Cap de Favaritx. The lake and its environs are popular with herons and egrets, the most elegant of wetland birds. Over the course of a year, little and cattle egrets, and purple, grey, night and squacco herons can all be seen too. Booted eagles are also common, flying over the area, while the muddy parts of the marsh attract many smaller waders in spring and the leggy black-winged stilt in summer. The lake itself hosts several thousand ducks in winter. The nearby pine woodland, next to the beach at Es Grau, is used by night herons that rest high in the trees by day and then move onto the marsh at dusk. Also at dusk, listen out for the plaintive single note of the scops owl against a backdrop of warblers, crakes and crickets; and, most strikingly, the rich-toned song of the nightingale. The tiny firecrest is common in the woodland, and in the spring this whole area comes alive with hundreds of migrants.

Birds of Cala Tirant and Son Bou

There are smaller marshes elsewhere on Menorca and those at Cala Tirant in the north and Son Bou in the south are very good for birds. The wetland at **Son Bou** (see p.221) holds the island's largest reed-bed and the characteristic species of such a rich habitat are the noisy great reed warbler, moustached warbler and Cetti's warbler. The wetland at **Cala Tirant**, near Fornells, can be just as prolific and the sandy area just inland of the beach is a first-rate place to see the spectacular bee-eater, which breeds in several small colonies on the island.

Birds of the Cap de Cavalleria

The **Cap de Cavalleria** (see p.218), at the northern tip of Menorca, attracts the curious-looking stone curlew, and several larks and pipits; and ospreys can often be seen fishing in the cape's **Port de Sanitja** (see p.219). Another special Balearic bird is the distinctive red-billed Audouin's gull, one of the world's rarest. A good place to see these is just off the coast by the lighthouse at the end of Cap de Cavalleria, where Mediterranean shags and shearwaters are also regularly seen.

Birds of the Algendar Gorge

The lush vegetation in the bottom of the **Algendar Gorge**, just inland of **Cala Galdana** (see p.226), is a magnet for small birds and a perfect setting to hear nightingales and the short explosive song of Cetti's warbler. Above the gorge, booted eagles, Egyptian vultures and Alpine swifts nest. The ravine also attracts a wonderful array of butterflies.

Birds of the Punta de S'Escullar

The barren, stony landscape of the northwest coast may seem an unpromising environment, but **Punta de S'Escullar** is the site of one of the largest colonies of Cory's shearwaters in the western Mediterranean. Thousands return to their cliffside burrows in the late afternoon throughout the summer. This rugged terrain also hosts the attractive blue rock thrush and migrant chats, wheatears and black redstarts. Pallid swifts and crag martins also breed on the cliffs.

Other Menorcan fauna

Menorca's **mammals** are a low-key bunch, an undistinguished assortment of weasels, feral cats, hedgehogs, rabbits, hares, mice and shrews. The one highlight is the island's **reptiles**. Of the four species of Balearic lizard, Menorca has three. There are two types of **wall lizard** – a green, black and blue version of Lilford's, and the olive-green and black-striped Italian lizard – as well as the Moroccan rock lizard, with olive skin or reticulated blue-green coloration.

Common **insects** include grasshoppers and cicadas as well as more than a hundred species of moth and around thirty types of **butterfly**. Three of the more striking butterflies are red admirals, which are seen in winter, and the clouded yellows and painted ladies, seen in spring.

Books

Most of the books listed below are in print and in paperback, and those that are out of print (o/p) should be easy to track down either in secondhand bookshops or through Amazon's used and secondhand book service (ⓦamazon.co.uk or ⓦamazon.com). Two excellent specialist sources of books about Spain are Books4Spain (ⓦbooks4spain.com) and Paul Orssich, (ⓦorssich.com), who focuses on rare, used and out of print books. Titles marked with the ★ symbol are especially recommended.

ART AND ARCHITECTURE

Barbara Catoir *Miró on Mallorca* (o/p). Lavishly illustrated book covering Miró's lengthy residence in Cala Major, just outside Palma (see p.80). There's discussion of the work Miró produced in this period and of his thoughts on the island as a whole. A little too hagiographical for some tastes, perhaps – and could do with an update (it was published in 1995).

Gijs van Hensbergen *Gaudí: the Biography*. A worthy biography of one of the world's most distinctive architects with Van Hensbergen putting substantial flesh on the man while placing his work firmly in context.

Janis Mink *Miró*. Recently reprinted, this beautifully illustrated book tracks through the artist's life and times. The text is perhaps a tad ponderous, but there are lots of interesting quotations and, at 96 pages, you're not drowned in detail.

CONTEMPORARY EX-PAT TALES

Elena Davis *Witches, Oranges and Slingers: Half a Century on Mallorca*. Some ex-pats may breeze in and out, but not Elena Davis, a New Yorker who first visited the island in 1955 – and stayed after falling in love with Sóller. The long perspective makes this 200-page memoir particularly engaging.

Peter Kerr *Snowball Oranges: One Mallorcan Winter*. Scottish farmer moves to a farmhouse in Mallorca – and loves it. In fact, he loves it so much that he goes on to write *Manana, Manana: One Mallorcan Summer; Viva Mallorca! One Mallorcan Autumn*; and *A Basketful of Snowflakes: One Mallorcan Spring*.

Chuck Maisel *Majorca, Paradise Not Lost: Living the Dream on a Spanish Island*. More tales of ex-pat lives and rural idylls – this time one is a painter, the other a writer.

Anna Nicholas *A Lizard in my Luggage*. Racy tale of the author's breathless escape from PR hell in Mayfair to sun-kissed evenings in rural Mallorca. The first of a quartet – *Goats from a Small Island; Donkeys on My Doorstep*; and *Cat on a Hot Tiled Roof* are the other three – all ploughing a similar furrow. In 2012, Nicholas added a fifth title, *A Bull on the Beach*, in which she and her family attempt to be as self-sufficient as possible, discussing the whys and wherefores with local cheese makers, shepherds and honey makers. Full marks to Nicholas for getting to know the island and its inhabitants so well.

FICTION

Agatha Christie *Problem at Pollensa Bay*. Amongst her many attributes, Agatha Christie (1890–1976) was a pioneering world traveller, who spent long periods of time in the Middle East working on archeological digs alongside her husband Max Mallowan. Christie visited Mallorca on several occasions and the tale that gives this collection of short stories its title is redolent of the days when only well-heeled visited the island.

Ernest Hemingway *The Sun Also Rises* and *For Whom the Bell Tolls*. Hemingway remains a big part of the American myth of Spain – *The Sun Also Rises* contains some lyrically beautiful writing, while the latter – set in the Civil War – is a good deal more laboured. Hemingway also published two books on bullfighting, the better of which is the enthusiastic *Death in the Afternoon* (1932).

Roderic Jeffries *Sun, Sea and Murder*. Jeffries has turned out a number of murder mysteries set in Mallorca with Inspector Alvarez as his protagonist cop. Other novels in the Alvarez series that are currently in print and in paperback include *The Ambiguity of Murder* and *Murder, Majorcan Style*.

Sian Mackay *Rafael's Wings*. Mackay knows contemporary Mallorca like the back of her hand and, although the drama at the centre of the book doesn't work too well, there's all sorts of interesting stuff on the island, its customs and predicaments.

Javier Marias *Tomorrow in the Battle Think on Me*. There are many who rate Marias as Spain's finest contemporary novelist – and the evidence is here in this searching, psychological thriller with its study of the human capacity for concealment and confession. Several other Marias novels are also available in English translation, including *A Heart So White* and *All Souls*.

★ **Manuel Vázquez Montalbán** *Murder in the Central Committee; An Olympic Death; The Angst-ridden Executive; Off Side*. Original and wonderfully entertaining tales by the man who was, until his untimely death in 2003, Spain's most popular crime thriller writer. A long-time member of the Communist Party and Barcelona resident, Montalbán became a well-known journalist in post-Franco Spain. His great creation was the gourmand private detective Pepe Carvalho. If this quartet of titles whets your appetite, move on to *Southern Seas* and a world of disillusioned Communists, tawdry sex and nouvelle cuisine – Montalbán's trademark ingredients – but don't bother with his very disappointing *The Man of My Life*.

Llorenç Villalonga *The Dolls' Room* (o/p). Subtle if somewhat laboured portrait of nobility in decline in nineteenth-century Mallorca. Villalonga (1897–1980) was Mallorca's most prominent writer for several decades, but none of his books is currently in print in English. The author's old house in Binissalem is now a museum (see p.159).

Carlos Ruiz Zafón *The Angel's Game*. One of the fastest-selling books in Spanish publishing history, this lengthy novel is an idiosyncratic mix of supernatural thriller-chiller and murder mystery. It's set in the backstreets of Barcelona in the early twentieth century.

FLORA AND FAUNA

Anthony Bonner *Plants of the Balearic Islands*. The only book on this subject currently in print.

Michael Eppinger *Field Guide to the Wild Flowers of Britain and Europe*. Published in 2006, this is the most recent field guide on this subject.

Dave Gosney *Finding Birds in Mallorca: the New Book* (2012). A detailed guide to the best birding sites on Mallorca with supplementary DVD and smartphone app, the latter providing the most up-to-date information regarding bird sitings. Needs to be used with a field guide for bird identification.

Christopher Grey-Wilson, et al *Wild Flowers of the Mediterranean*. Excellent, comprehensive field guide.

Enric Ramos *The Birds of Menorca* (2000). More of a bird report than a field guide, this details the status of all bird species known on the island. It is aimed at the enthusiast, but still provides useful information about what to spot and where.

Maties Rebassa, et al *A Birding Tourist's Guide to Majorca* (2009). Written by local birders, this provides a guide to the island's best birding sites and detailed information about more than 200 birds including photos of the 80 most coveted sitings.

Lars Svensson et al *Collins Bird Guide: The Most Complete Field Guide to the Birds of Britain and Europe* (2nd edition, 2010). The definitive European birding field guide. Published in US as *Birds of Europe*.

FOOD AND DRINK

Vicky Bennison *The Taste of a Place – Mallorca*. Enjoyable, well-illustrated book giving the lowdown on Mallorcan food and wine – not so much where to eat it, but more what it is like and where to buy it. Recipes too. Published in 2003, it could, however, do with an update.

Tomás Graves *Bread & Oil: Majorcan Culture's Last Stand*. Written by a son of Robert Graves, this intriguing and entertaining book explores Mallorca via its palate, with sections on what the islanders eat and how the ingredients end up where they do. Adopting a similar approach, but with music in mind, is the same author's *Tuning up at Dawn: A Memoir of Music and Majorca*.

Jan Read *Wines of Spain*. Encyclopedic but still pocketable guide to the classic and emerging wines of Spain by a leading authority. Includes maps, vintages and vineyards and has a eight-page chapter devoted to the Balearic and Canary islands. First published in 1983, it was last updated in 2005.

GENERAL BACKGROUND

Phil Ball *Morbo: The Story of Spanish Football*. Excellent account of the history of Spanish football from its nineteenth-century beginnings with the British workers at the mines of Río Tinto in Huelva. Has sections on the golden years of Real Madrid; the dark days of Franco; and the stunning World and European Cup victories of recent years. Ever-present as a backdrop is the ferocious rivalry or *morbo* – political, historical, regional and linguistic – which has driven the Spanish game since its birth. Essential reading for every football aficionado visiting (or even thinking about visiting) Spain.

★ **R. J. Buswell** *Mallorca and Tourism: History, Economy and Environment (Aspects of Tourism)*. One of a series investigating the effects of tourism on particular areas/regions, this intriguing and scholarly book is well argued and well researched with pieces on just about everything you can think of – from the growth of mass tourism through to golf and hiking. The only catch is the price – even the paperback version is quite expensive.

★ **Brian Dendle & Shelby Thacker** *British Travellers in Mallorca in the Nineteenth Century: An Anthology of Texts*. There are perhaps no outstanding contributors in this anthology, but the overall picture is intriguing and informative in equal measure: the engineer E.G. Bartholomew took a liking to stewed hedgehog ("dainty fat little joints") and the aristocrat Sir John Carr raved about the Jardins d'Alfàbia (see p.99) and was welcomed in style by the grandees of La Granja (see p.112).

★ **Lucia Graves** *A Woman Unknown: Voices from a Spanish Life*. This moving memoir, by Robert Graves's daughter, is a succinct and thoughtful exploration of a life in between cultures – English and Mallorcan/Spanish. No one has explored the deadening psychological weight of Franco's regime better.

William Graves *Wild Olives: Life in Mallorca with Robert Graves*. Another son of Robert Graves, William was born in 1940 and spent much of his childhood in Palma and Deià, sufficient inspiration for these mildly diverting accounts of his Mallorcan contemporaries. The book's real focus, however, is his troubled family life and his difficult relationship with his father.

★ **John Hooper** *The New Spaniards*. This excellent, authoritative portrait of post-Franco Spain was first written by *The Guardian*'s former Spanish correspondent in the 1980s and published in a revised edition in 2006. It is one of the best possible introductions to contemporary Spain.

George Orwell *Homage to Catalonia*. Stirring account of Orwell's participation in – and early enthusiasm for – leftist revolution in Barcelona, followed by his growing disillusionment with the factional fighting that divided the Republican forces during the Civil War.

Miranda Seymour *Robert Graves: Life on the Edge*. Lengthy account of Robert Graves's personal life with lacklustre commentary on his poetry and novels. Includes much detail on Graves's long-time residence in Deià.

Giles Tremlett *Ghosts of Spain: Travels Through a Country's Hidden Past*. Tremlett (*The Guardian*'s Madrid correspondent) digs into the untold story of Spain's Civil War dead and the collective conspiracy of silence surrounding the war's terrors; he then goes on to peel away the layers of the post-Franco era to present an enthralling and often disturbing study of contemporary Spain – warts and all.

HISTORY

Michael Baigent & Richard Leigh *The Inquisition*. Trenchant trawl through the history of this infamous institution – from medieval beginnings to gradual collapse. Particularly good on the Inquisition's relationship with the papacy.

Antony Beevor *The Battle for Spain: The Spanish Civil War*. Long before Beevor hit the headlines with *Stalingrad*, he was ploughing an historical furrow – and this competent synopsis of the Civil War, running to more than six hundred pages and published in 2007, had its genesis in the 1980s.

Roger Collins *The Arab Conquest of Spain 710–97* (o/p). Much lauded, enjoyably concise study documenting the Moorish invasion of Spain and the significant influence the conquered Visigoths had on early Muslim rule. Published in 1994, it's currently out of print, as is its companion title, Collins's *Visigothic Spain 409–711*. However, the same author's *Caliphs and Kings: Spain, 796–1031* is in print and it contains an intriguing insight into what is an oft-neglected corner of Spanish history.

★ **J.H. Elliott** *Imperial Spain 1469–1716*. The best introduction to Spain's "golden age" – academically respected as well as being a gripping yarn. Also see his erudite *The Revolt of the Catalans: A Study in the Decline of Spain 1598–1640* (o/p), though this comes in at a whopping 648 pages.

★ **Henry Kamen** *The Spanish Inquisition: An Historical Revision*. A highly respected examination of the Inquisition and the long shadow it cast across Spanish history. Kamen's *Philip of Spain* was the first full biography of Felipe II, the ruler most closely associated with the Inquisition, and there's also his intriguing *Imagining Spain: Historical Myth and National Identity*.

Bruce Laurie *Life of Richard Kane: Britain's First Lieutenant Governor of Minorca* (o/p). Detailed (290-page) historical biography that provides a fascinating insight into eighteenth-century Menorca.

★ **Geoffrey Parker** *The Army of Flanders and the Spanish Road (1567–1659)*. Sounds dry and academic, but this fascinating book gives a marvellous insight into the morals, manners and organization of the Spanish army, at the time the most feared in Europe.

Paul Preston *Franco: A Biography* and *The Spanish Civil War: Reaction, Revolution and Revenge*. A penetrating – and monumental – biography of Franco and his regime, which provides as clear a picture as any of how he won the Civil War and survived in power so long. The same author's *Spanish Civil War* is a compelling introduction to the subject and is also more accessible for the general reader than Hugh Thomas's work (see below). Preston has also written a similarly authoritative account of the life and times of the Spanish king entitled *Juan Carlos: Steering Spain from Dictatorship to Democracy*, exploring in depth how Carlos helped move the country from beneath the long shadow of Franco. In 2012, Preston returned to similar themes in his *The Spanish Holocaust: Inquisition and Extermination in Twentieth-Century Spain*. Making use of newly available material, Preston demonstrates that terror on an industrial scale was a key part of Franco's policy.

Hugh Thomas *The Spanish Civil War*. Exhaustively researched and brilliantly detailed account of both the war and the complex political manoeuvrings surrounding it. Includes a small section on Mallorca. First published in 1961, it remains the classic text on the subject.

RELIGION AND FOLKLORE

Anthony Bonner (ed.) *Doctor Illuminatus: A Ramon Llull Reader*. A selection from the lengthy and heavy-going treatises on mysticism and Christian zeal written by Llull, the thirteenth-century Mallorcan scholar and philosopher (see p.62). Llull's works were some of the first to be written in Catalan, but are not for the faint-hearted. A more manageable introduction to Llull is provided by Henry Carrigan (see below).

Henry Carrigan Jr (ed.) *Romancing God: Contemplating the Beloved* (o/p). Billed as a "Christian Classic", this 120-page book serves as a useful introduction to the collected

thoughts of Mallorca's own Ramon Llull (see box, p.62).

David Huelin (ed.) *Folk Tales of Mallorca* (o/p). The nineteenth-century priest and academic Mossèn Antoni Alcover spent decades collecting Mallorcan folk tales and this is a wide selection of them, running to almost 400 pages. They range from the intensely religious through to parable and proverb, but many reveal an unpleasant edge to rural island life, both vindictive and mean-spirited. Makes for intriguing background material, but unfortunately particular places on the island are never mentioned or described.

SPECIALIST HIKING GUIDES

Discovery Walking Guides (ⓦ walking.demon.co.uk). This British company produces four relevant hiking guides – *Walk! Menorca*; *Walk! Mallorca (North & Mountains)*; *GR221: Mallorca's Dry Stone Way*; *Walk! Mallorca West*. All four come with a complete set of GPS waypoints (available as downloadable files from the website), which allows for route inputting directly into a navigation device. The guides are supplemented by clear 1:40,000 maps. These

publications are the best on the market, but they are almost impossible to find on Mallorca or Menorca, so get them beforehand (see p.34).

June Parker *Walking in Mallorca*. Refreshed in 2006, this popular, long-established hiking guide covers all the island's classic walks and has a GR221-specific companion guide, *Trekking through Mallorca* by Paddy Dillon. Both are published by Cicerone (ⓦ cicerone.co.uk).

TRAVELOGUES

Sir John Carr *Descriptive Travels in the Southern and Eastern Parts of Spain and the Balearic Islands* (o/p). Written in 1811, and very much a period piece, Carr's detailed description of Mallorca is both well written and entertaining, though his anti-Semitism – the British consul in Palma was Jewish – is hard to bear.

Lucy McCauley (ed) *Travelers' Tales Spain: True Stories*. It would be hard to better this anthology of writing on Spain, which gathers its short stories and journalism from the 1980s and 1990s – the book was published in 2002. Featured authors include Gabriel García Márquez, Colm Tóibín and Louis de Bernières, whose "Seeing Red", on the tomato-throwing festival of Buñol, is worth the purchase price alone, and there's also the striking "In a Majorcan Garden" by Jill Burberry.

George Sand *A Winter in Majorca*. Accompanied by her lover, Frédéric Chopin, Sand spent the winter of 1838–39 on Mallorca, holed up in the monastery of Valldemossa. These are her recollections, often barbed and sharp-tongued – and very critical of the islanders (see p.110). Always available at Valldemossa monastery (see p.109).

Gordon West *Jogging Round Majorca*. (o/p). This gentle, humorous account of an extended journey around Mallorca by Gordon and Mary West in the 1920s vividly portrays the island's pre-tourist life and times. The trip had nothing to do with running; "jogging" here refers to their leisurely progress. West's book lay forgotten for decades until a BBC radio presenter, Leonard Pearcey, stumbled across it in a secondhand bookshop and subsequently read extracts on air.

Language

In recent decades the Balearics have attracted thousands of migrants from the rest of western Europe and today German, English, Catalan and Spanish are all widely spoken. Traditionally, the islanders are bilingual, speaking Castilian (Spanish) and their local dialect of the Catalan language – *Mallorquín* or *Menorquín* – with equal facility. *Català* (Catalan) has been the islanders' everyday language since the absorption of the Balearics into the medieval Kingdom of Aragón and Catalunya in the thirteenth century; Castilian, on the other hand, was imposed much later as the official language of government and business at the instigation of Madrid – and with special rigour by Franco. Almost inevitably, therefore, Spain's recent move towards regional autonomy has been accompanied by the islanders' re-assertion of Catalan as their official language. The most obvious sign of this has been the change of all the old Castilian town and street names into their Catalan equivalents.

On paper, **Catalan** looks like a cross between French and Spanish and is generally easy to understand if you know these two languages, although when it is spoken it has a very harsh sound and is surprisingly hard to come to grips with. To assist, there's currently one **Catalan-English/English-Catalan dictionary and phrasebook** on the market and it's published by Hippocrene books (ⓦhippocrenebooks.com). **Spanish phrasebooks and dictionaries** are, by comparison, fairly commonplace with the most user-friendly being Rough Guides' *Spanish Dictionary Phrasebook*.

Introduction

When **Franco** came to power in 1939, *Català* publishing houses, bookshops and libraries were raided and their books destroyed. Furthermore, throughout his dictatorship Franco excluded Catalan from the radio, TV, daily press and, most importantly, the schools, which is why many older people cannot read or write *Català* even if they speak it all the time. Since Franco's death in 1975, however, the Balearic islanders have reasserted the primacy of Catalan as their language of choice, though the emigration of thousands of mainland Spaniards to the islands means that Castilian is the dominant language in around forty percent of Balearic households.

   Català is a Romance language, stemming from Latin and more directly from medieval Provençal, and is spoken by more than six million people in the Balearics, Catalunya, part of Aragón, most of Valencia, Andorra and parts of the French Pyrenees; it is thus much more widely used than several better-known languages such as Danish, Finnish and Norwegian. While Spaniards in the rest of the country often belittle it by saying that to get a *Català* word you just cut a Castilian one in half (which is often true), in fact the grammar is much more complicated than Castilian and there are eight vowel sounds, three more than in Castilian.

Getting by in Mallorca and Menorca

Although Catalan is the preferred **language** of most islanders, you'll almost always get by perfectly well if you speak Castilian (Spanish), as long as you're aware of the use of

Catalan in timetables and so forth. Once you get into it, Castilian is one of the easiest languages there is, the rules of pronunciation pretty straightforward and strictly observed. You'll find some basic pronunciation rules below for both Catalan and Castilian, and a selection of words and phrases in both languages. Castilian is certainly easier to pronounce, but don't be afraid to try Catalan, especially in the more out-of-the-way places – you'll generally get a good reception if you at least try communicating in the local language.

Castilian (Spanish): a few rules

Unless there's an accent, words ending in d, l, r, and z are **stressed** on the last syllable, all others on the second to last. All **vowels** are pure and short; combinations have predictable results.

A somewhere between back and father.

E as in get.

I as in police.

O as in hot.

U as in rule.

C is lisped before E and I, hard otherwise: cerca is pronounced "thairka".

CH is pronounced as in English.

G is a guttural H sound (like the ch in loch) before E or I, a hard G elsewhere: gigante is pronounced "higante".

H is always silent.

J is the same sound as a guttural G: jamón is pronounced "hamon".

LL sounds like an English Y: tortilla is pronounced "torteeya".

N as in English, unless it has a tilde (ñ) over it, when it becomes NY: mañana sounds like "man-yaana".

QU is pronounced like an English K.

R is rolled, **RR** doubly so.

V sounds more like B, vino becoming "beano".

X has an S sound before consonants, a KS sound before vowels.

Z is the same as a soft C, so cerveza is pronounced "thairvaitha".

Catalan: a few rules

With *Català*, don't be tempted to use the few rules of Castilian pronunciation you may know – in particular the soft Spanish Z and C don't apply, so unlike in the rest of Spain it's not "Barthelona" but "Barcelona", as in English.

A as in hat if stressed, as in alone when unstressed.

E varies, but usually as in get.

I as in police.

IG sounds like the "**tch**" in the English scratch: lleig (ugly) is pronounced "yeah-tch".

O varies, but usually as in hot.

U lies somewhere between put and rule.

Ç sounds like an English S: plaça is pronounced "plassa".

C followed by an E or I is soft; otherwise hard.

G followed by E or I is like the "zh" in Zhivago; otherwise hard.

H is always silent.

J as in the French "Jean".

LL sounds like an English Y or LY, like the "yuh" sound in "million".

N as in English, though before F or V it sometimes sounds like an M.

NY replaces the Castilian Ñ.

QU before E or I sounds like K; before A or O as in "quit".

R is rolled, but only at the start of a word; at the end it's often silent.

T is pronounced as in English, though sometimes it sounds like a D, as in viatge or dotze.

TX is like the English CH.

V at the start of a word sounds like B; in all other positions it's a soft F sound.

W is pronounced like a B/V.

X is like SH in most words, though in some, like exit, it sounds like an X.

Z is like the English Z.

Useful words and phrases

BASICS

ENGLISH	CASTILIAN	CATALAN
Yes, No, OK	Sí, No, Vale	*Si, No, Val*
Please, Thank you	Por favor, Gracias	*Per favor, Gràcies*
Where, When	Dónde, Cuándo	*On, Quan*
What, How much	Qué, Cuánto	*Què, Quant*
Here, There	Aquí, Allí, Allá	*Aquí, Allí, Allà*
This, That	Esto, Eso	*Això, Allò*
Now, Later	Ahora, Más tarde	*Ara, Més tard*
Open, Closed	Abierto/a, Cerrado/a	*Obert, Tancat*
With, Without	Con, Sin	*Amb, Sense*
Good, Bad	Buen(o)/a, Mal(o)/a	*Bo(na), Dolent(a)*
Big, Small	Gran(de), Pequeño/a	*Gran, Petit(a)*
Cheap, Expensive	Barato/a, Caro/a	*Barat(a), Car(a)*
Hot, Cold	Caliente, Frío/a	*Calent(a), Fred(a)*
More, Less	Más, Menos	*Més, Menys*
Today, Tomorrow	Hoy, Mañana	*Avui, Demà*
Yesterday	Ayer	*Ahir*
Day before yesterday	Anteayer	*Abans-d'ahir*
Next week	La semana que viene	*La setmana que ve*
Next month	El mes que viene	*El mes que ve*

GREETINGS AND RESPONSES

ENGLISH	CASTILIAN	CATALAN
Hello, Goodbye	Hola, Adiós	*Hola, Adéu*
Good morning	Buenos días	*Bon dia*
Good afternoon/night	Buenas tardes/noches	*Bona tarda/nit*
See you later	Hasta luego	*Fins després*
Sorry	Lo siento/discúlpeme	*Ho sento*
Excuse me	Con permiso/perdón	*Perdoni*
How are you?	¿Cómo está (usted)?	*Com va?*
I (don't) understand	(No) Entiendo	*(No) Ho entenc*
Not at all/You're welcome	De nada	*De res*
Do you speak English?	¿Habla (usted) inglés?	*Parla anglès?*
I (don't) speak	(No) Hablo Español	*(No) Parlo Català*
My name is...	Me llamo...	*Em dic...*
What's your name?	¿Cómo se llama usted?	*Com es diu?*
I am English	Soy inglés/esa	*Sóc anglès/esa*
Scottish	escocés/esa	*escocès/esa*
Australian	australiano/a	*australià/ana*
Canadian	canadiense/a	*canadenc(a)*
American	americano/a	*americà/ana*
Irish	irlandés/esa	*irlandès/esa*
Welsh	galés/esa	*gallès/esa*

HOTELS AND TRANSPORT

ENGLISH	CASTILIAN	CATALAN
I want	Quiero	*Vull (pronounced "fwee")*
I'd like	Quisiera	*Voldria*
Do you know...?	¿Sabe...?	*Vostès saben ?*
I don't know	No sé	*No sé*
There is (is there?)	(¿)Hay(?)	*Hi ha(?)*

Give me...	Deme...	*Doneu-me...*
Do you have...?	¿Tiene...?	*Té...?*
...the time	...la hora	*...l'hora*
...a room	...una habitación	*...alguna habitació*
...with two beds/double bed	...con dos camas/cama matrimonial	*...amb dos llits/llit per dues persones*
...with shower/bath	...con ducha/baño	*...amb dutxa/bany*
for one person (two people)	para una persona (dos personas)	*per a una persona (dues persones)*
for one night (one week)	para una noche (una semana)	*per una nit (una setmana)*
It's fine, how much is it?	Está bien, ¿cuánto es?	*Esta bé, quant és?*
It's too expensive	Es demasiado caro	*És massa car*
Don't you have anything cheaper?	¿No tiene algo más barato?	*En té de més bon preu?*
Can one...?	¿Se puede...?	*Es pot...?*
...camp (near) here?	¿...acampar aquí (cerca)?	*...acampar a la vora?*
It's not very far	No es muy lejos	*No és gaire lluny*
How do I get to...?	¿Por dónde se va a...?	*Per anar a...?*
Left, right, straight on	Izquierda, derecha, todo recto	*A l'esquerra, a la dreta, tot recte*
Where is...?	¿Dónde está...?	*On és...?*
...the bus station	...la estación de autobuses	*...l'estació de autobuses*
...the bus stop	...la parada	*...la parada*
...the railway station	...la estación de ferrocarril	*...l'estació*
...the nearest bank	...el banco más cercano	*...el banc més a prop*
...the post office	...el correo/la oficina de correos	*...l'oficina de correus*
...the toilet	...el baño/aseo/servicio	*...la toaleta*
Where does the bus to... leave from?	¿De dónde sale el autobús para...?	*De on surt el autobús a... ?*
Is this the train for Barcelona?	¿Es este el tren para Barcelona?	*Aquest tren va a Barcelona?*
I'd like a (return) ticket to...	Quisiera un billete (de ida y... vuelta) para	*Voldria un bitllet (d'anar i tornar) a...*
What time does it leave (arrive in...)?	¿A qué hora sale (llega a...)?	*A quina hora surt (arriba a...)?*
What is there to eat?	¿Qué hay para comer?	*Què hi ha per menjar?*
What's that?	¿Qué es eso?	*Què és això?*

DAYS OF THE WEEK

ENGLISH	CASTILIAN	CATALAN
Monday	lunes	*dilluns*
Tuesday	martes	*dimarts*
Wednesday	miércoles	*dimecres*
Thursday	jueves	*dijous*
Friday	viernes	*divendres*
Saturday	sábado	*dissabte*
Sunday	domingo	*diumenge*

MONTHS OF THE YEAR

ENGLISH	CASTILIAN	CATALAN
January	enero	*gener*
February	febrero	*febrer*
March	marzo	*març*
April	abril	*abril*
May	mayo	*maig*
June	junio	*juny*
July	julio	*juliol*
August	agosto	*agost*
September	septiembre	*setembre*
October	octubre	*octubre*

November	noviembre	*novembre*
December	diciembre	*desembre*

NUMBERS

ENGLISH	CASTILIAN	CATALAN
1	un/uno/una	*un(a)*
2	dos	*dos (dues)*
3	tres	*tres*
4	cuatro	*quatre*
5	cinco	*cinc*
6	seis	*sis*
7	siete	*set*
8	ocho	*vuit*
9	nueve	*nou*
10	diez	*deu*
11	once	*onze*
12	doce	*dotze*
13	trece	*tretze*
14	catorce	*catorze*
15	quince	*quinze*
16	dieciséis	*setze*
17	diecisiete	*disset*
18	dieciocho	*divuit*
19	diecinueve	*dinou*
20	veinte	*vint*
21	veintiuno	*vint-i-un*
30	treinta	*trenta*
40	cuarenta	*quaranta*
50	cincuenta	*cinquanta*
60	sesenta	*seixanta*
70	setenta	*setanta*
80	ochenta	*vuitanta*
90	noventa	*novanta*
100	cien(to)	*cent*
101	ciento uno	*cent un*
102	ciento dos	*cent dos (dues)*
200	doscientos	*dos-cents (dues-centes)*
500	quinientos	*cinc-cents*
1000	mil	*mil*
2000	dos mil	*dos mil*

Food and drink

In this section we have provided a reasonably extensive **Castilian and Catalan menu reader**, though most restaurants, cafés and bars have **multilingual menus**, with English, Catalan and Castilian almost always three of the options. The main exceptions are out in the countryside, where there may only be a Catalan menu or maybe no menu at all, in which case the waiter will rattle off the day's dishes in Catalan or sometimes Castilian.

BASICS

ENGLISH	CASTILIAN	CATALAN
Bread	Pan	*Pa*
Butter	Mantequilla	*Mantega*
Cheese	Queso	*Formatge*

English	Castilian	Catalan
Eggs	Huevos	*Ous*
Fruit	Fruta	*Fruita*
Garlic	Ajo	*All*
Oil	Aceite	*Oli*
Pepper	Pimienta	*Pebre*
Rice	Arroz	*Arròs*
Salt	Sal	*Sal*
Sugar	Azúcar	*Sucre*
Vinegar	Vinagre	*Vinagre*
Vegetables	Verduras/Legumbres	*Verdures/Llegumes*
To have breakfast	Desayunar	*Esmorzar*
To have lunch	Almorzar	*Dinar*
To have dinner	Sopar	*Cenar*
Menu	Carta	*Menú*
Bottle	Botella	*Ampolla*
Glass	Vaso	*Got*
Fork	Tenedor	*Forquilla*
Knife	Cuchillo	*Ganivet*
Spoon	Cuchara	*Cullera*
Table	Mesa	*Taula*
The bill/check	La cuenta	*El compte*
Grilled	A la brasa	*A la planxa*
Fried	Frit	*Fregit*
Stuffed/rolled	Relleno	*Farcit*
Casserole	Guisado	*Guisat*
Roast	Asado	*Rostit*

FRUIT (FRUITA) AND VEGETABLES (VERDURES/LLEGUMES)

ENGLISH	CASTILIAN	CATALAN
Apple	Manzana	*Poma*
Asparagus	Espárragos	*Espàrrecs*
Aubergine/eggplant	Berenjenas	*Albergínies*
Banana	Plátano	*Plàtan*
Carrots	Zanahorias	*Pastanagues*
Cucumber	Pepino	*Concombre*
Grapes	Uvas	*Raïm*
Melon	Melón	*Meló*
Mushrooms	Champiñones	*Xampinyons (also bolets, setes)*
Onions	Cebollas	*Cebes*
Orange	Naranja	*Taronja*
Peach	Melocotón	*Préssec*
Pear	Pera	*Pera*
Peas	Arvejas	*Pèsols*
Pineapple	Piña	*Pinya*
Potatoes	Patatas	*Patates*
Strawberries	Fresas	*Maduixes*
Tomatoes	Tomates	*Tomàquets*

BOCADILLOS (SANDWICH) FILLINGS

ENGLISH	CASTILIAN	CATALAN
Catalan sausage	Butifarra	*Butifarra*
Cheese	Queso	*Formatge*
Cooked ham	Jamón York	*Cuixot dolç*

Cured ham	Jamón serrano	*Pernil salat*
Loin of pork	Lomo	*Llom*
Omelette	Tortilla	*Truita*
Salami	Salami	*Salami*
Sausage	Salchichón	*Salxitxó*
Spicy sausage	Chorizo	*Xoriç*
Tuna	Atún	*Tonyina*

TAPAS AND RACIONES

ENGLISH	CASTILIAN	CATALAN
Anchovies	Boquerones	*Anxoves*
Stew	Cocido	*Bollit*
Squid, usually deep- fried in rings	Calamares	*Calamars*
Squid in ink	Calamares en su tinta	*Calamars amb tinta*
Snails, often served in a spicy/ curry sauce	Caracoles	*Cargols*
Cockles (shellfish)	Berberechos	*Cargols de mar*
Whole baby squid	Chipirones	*Calamarins*
Meat in tomato sauce	Carne en salsa	*Carn amb salsa*
Fish or chicken croquette	Croqueta	*Croqueta*
Fish or meat pasty	Empanadilla	*Empanada petita*
Russian salad (diced vegetables in mayonnaise)	Ensaladilla	*Ensalada russa*
Aubergine (eggplant) and pepper salad	Escalibada	*Escalibada*
Broad beans	Habas	*Faves*
Beans with ham	Habas con jamón	*Faves amb cuixot*
Liver	Hígado	*Fetge*
Prawns	Gambas	*Gambes*
Mussels (either steamed, or served with diced tomatoes and onion)	Mejillones	*Musclos*
Razor clams	Navajas	*Navallas*
Olives	Aceitunas	*Olives*
Hard-boiled egg	Huevo cocido	*Ou bollit*
Bread, rubbed with tomato and oil	Pan con tomate	*Pa amb tomàquet*
Potatoes in garlic mayonnaise	Patatas alioli	*Patates amb all i oli*
Fried potato cubes with spicy sauce and mayonnaise	Patatas bravas	*Patates cohentes*
Meatballs, usually in sauce	Albóndigas	*Pilotes*
Kebab	Pincho moruno	*Pinxo*
Octopus	Pulpo	*Pop*
Sweet (bell) peppers	Pimientos	*Prebes*
Kidneys in sherry	Riñones al jerez	*Ronyons amb xeres*
Sardines	Sardinas	*Sardines*
Cuttlefish	Sepia	*Sípia*
Tripe	Callos	*Tripa*
Potato omelette	Tortilla española	*Truita espanyola*
Plain omelette	Tortilla francesa	*Truita francesa*
Pepper, potato, pumpkin and aubergine (eggplant) stew with tomato purée	Tumbet	*Tumbet*
Mushrooms, usually fried in garlic	Champiñones	*Xampinyons*
Spicy sausage	Chorizo	*Xoriç*

SELECTED BALEARIC DISHES AND SPECIALITIES

Many of the specialities that follow come from the Balearics' shared history with Catalunya. The more elaborate fish and meat dishes are usually limited to the fancier restaurants.

SAUCES

Allioli	Garlic mayonnaise
Salsa mahonesa	Mayonnaise
Salsa romesco	Spicy tomato and wine sauce to accompany fish (from Tarragona)

SOUPS (SOPA), STARTERS AND SALADS (AMANIDA)

Amanida catalana	Salad with sliced meat and cheese
Carn d'olla	Mixed meat soup
Entremesos	Starter of mixed meat and cheese
Escalivada	Aubergine/eggplant, pepper and onion salad
Escudella	Mixed vegetable soup
Espinacs a la Catalana	Spinach with raisins and pine nuts
Esqueixada	Dried cod salad with peppers, tomatoes, onions and olives
Fideus a la cassola	Baked vermicelli with meat
Llenties guisades	Stewed lentils
Pa amb oli	Bread rubbed with olive oil, eaten with ham, cheese or fruit
Samfaina	Ratatouille-like stew of onions, peppers, aubergine/eggplant and tomato
Sopa d'all	Garlic soup
Sopas mallorquínas	Vegetable soup, sometimes with meat and chickpeas (garbanzos)
Truita (d'alls tendres; de xampinyons; de patates)	Omelette/tortilla (with garlic; with mushrooms; with potato). Be sure you're ordering omelette (tortilla), not trout (truita).

RICE DISHES

Arròs a banda	Rice with seafood, the rice served separately
Arròs a la marinera	Paella: rice with seafood and saffron
Arròs negre	"Black rice", cooked with squid ink
Paella a la Catalana	Mixed meat and seafood paella, sometimes distinguished from a seafood paella by being called Paella a Valencia

MEAT (CARN)

Albergínies en es forn	Aubergines/eggplants stuffed with grilled meat
Botifarra amb mongetes	Spicy blood sausage with white beans
Conill (all i oli)	Rabbit (with garlic mayonnaise)
Escaldum	Chicken and potato stew in an almond sauce
Estofat de vedella	Veal stew
Fetge	Liver
Fricandó	Veal casserole
Frito mallorquín	Pigs' offal, potatoes and onions cooked with oil
Mandonguilles	Meatballs, usually in a sauce with peas
Perdius a la vinagreta	Partridge in vinegar gravy
Pollastre (farcit; amb gambas; al cava)	Chicken (stuffed; with prawns; cooked in sparkling wine)
Porc (rostit)	Pork (roast)
Sobrasada	Finely minced pork sausage, flavoured with paprika

FISH (PEIX) AND SHELLFISH (MARISC)

Bacallà (amb samfaina)	Dried cod (with ratatouille)
Caldereta de llagosta	Lobster stew
Cloïsses	Clams, often steamed
Espinagada de Sa Pobla	Turnover filled with spinach and eel

Greixonera de peix	Menorcan fish stew, cooked in an earthenware casserole
Guisat de peix	Fish and shellfish stew
Llagosta (amb pollastre)	Lobster (with chicken in a rich sauce)
Lluç	Hake, either fried or grilled
Musclos al vapor	Steamed mussels
Pop	Octopus
Rap a l'all cremat	Monkfish with creamed garlic sauce
Sarsuela	Fish and shellfish stew
Suquet	Fish casserole
Truita	Trout (sometimes stuffed with ham, a la Navarre)

DESSERTS (POSTRES) AND PASTRIES (PASTAS)

Cocaroll	Pastry containing vegetables and fish
Crema Catalana	Crème caramel, with caramelized sugar topping
Ensaimada	Flaky spiral pastry, often with fillings such as cabello de ángel (sweetened citron rind)
Mel i mató	Curd cheese and honey
Postres de músic	Cake of dried fruit and nuts
Turrón	Almond fudge
Xurros	Deep-fried doughnut sticks (served with hot chocolate)

DRINKING

ENGLISH	CASTILIAN	CATALAN
Water	Agua	*Aigua*
Mineral water	Agua mineral	*Aigua mineral*
(sparkling)	(con gas)	*(amb gas)*
(still)	(sin gas)	*(sense gas)*
Milk	Leche	*Llet*
Juice	Zumo	*Suc*
Tiger nut drink	Horchata	*Orxata*
Coffee	Café	*Café*
Espresso	Café solo	*Café sol*
White coffee	Café con leche	*Café amb llet*
Decaff	Descafeinado	*Descafeinat*
Tea	Té	*Te*
Drinking chocolate	Chocolate	*Xocolata*
Beer	Cerveza	*Cervesa*
Wine	Vino	*Vi*
Champagne/Sparkling wine	Champán/Cava	*Xampan/Cava*

Glossary

GLOSSARY OF CATALAN TERMS

Ajuntament Town Hall
Albufera Lagoon (and surrounding wetlands)
Altar major High altar
Aparcament Parking
Avinguda (Avgda) Avenue
Badía Bay
Barranc Ravine
Barroc Baroque
Basílica Catholic church with honorific privileges
Cala Small bay, cove
Camí Way or road
Ca'n At the house of (contraction of casa and en)
Capella Chapel
Carrer (c/) Street
Carretera Road, highway
Castell Castle
Celler Cellar, or a bar in a cellar
Claustre Cloister
Coll Col, mountain pass
Convent Convent, nunnery or monastery
Correu Post office
Coves Caves
Església Church
Estany Small lake
Festa Festival
Finca Estate or farmhouse
Font Water fountain or spring
Gòtic Gothic
Illa Island
Jardí Garden
Llac Lake
Mercat Market
Mirador Watchtower or viewpoint
Modernisme Literally "modernism", the Catalan form of Art Nouveau, whose most famous exponent was Antoni Gaudí; adjective *"Modernista"*.
Monestir Monastery
Mozarabe A Christian subject of a medieval Moorish ruler; hence **Mozarabic**, a colourful building style that reveals both Christian and Moorish influences.
Mudéjar A Moorish subject of a medieval Christian ruler. Also a style of architecture developed by Moorish craftsmen working for Christians,

characterized by painted woodwork with strong colours and complex geometrical patterns; revived between the 1890s and 1930s and blended with Art Nouveau.
Museu Museum
Nostra Senyora The Virgin Mary ("Our Lady")
Oficina d'Informació Turística Tourist office
Palau Palace, mansion or manor house
Parc Park
Passeig Boulevard; the evening stroll along it
Pic Summit
Plaça Square
Platja Beach
Pont Bridge
Port Harbour, port
Porta Door, gate
Puig Hill, mountain
Rambla Avenue or boulevard
Reconquista The Christian Reconquest of Spain from the Moors beginning in the ninth century and culminating in the capture of Granada in 1492.
Rei King
Reial Royal
Reina Queen
Reixa Iron screen or grille, usually in front of a window
Renaixença Rebirth, often used to describe the Catalan cultural revival at the end of the nineteenth and beginning of the twentieth centuries. Architecturally, this was expressed as Modernisme.
Retaule Retable, a wooden ornamental panel behind an altar
Riu River
Romeria Pilgrimage or gathering at a shrine
Salinas Saltpans
Santuari Sanctuary
Sant/a Saint
Serra Mountain range
Talayot Cone-shaped prehistoric tower
Taula T-shaped prehistoric megalithic structure
Torrent Stream or river (usually dry in summer)
Urbanització Modern estate development
Vall Valley

GLOSSARY OF ENGLISH ART AND ARCHITECTURAL TERMS

Ambulatory Interior covered passage around the outer edge of the choir in the chancel of a church.

Apse Semi-circular protrusion (usually) at the east end of a church.

Art Deco Geometrical style of art and architecture popular in the 1930s.

Art Nouveau Style of art, architecture and design based on highly stylized vegetal forms. Particularly popular in Mallorca in the early part of the twentieth century – where it is normally referred to as Modernisme (see opposite).

Balustrade An ornamental rail, running, almost invariably, along the top of a building.

Baroque The art and architecture of the Counter-Reformation, dating from around 1600 onwards. Distinguished by its ornate exuberance and (at its best) complex but harmonious spatial arrangement of interiors. Some elements – particularly its gaudiness – remained popular in the Balearics well into the twentieth century.

Caryatid A sculptured female figure used as a column.

Chancel The eastern part of a church, often separated from the nave by a screen; contains the choir and ambulatory.

Churrigueresque Fancifully ornate form of Baroque named after its leading exponents, the Spaniard José Churriguera (1650–1723) and his extended family.

Classical Architectural style incorporating Greek and Roman elements – pillars, domes, colonnades and so on – at its height in the seventeenth century and revived, as Neoclassical, in the eighteenth.

Clerestory Upper storey of a church, incorporating the windows.

Cyclopean Prehistoric style of dry-stone masonry comprising boulders of irregular form.

Fresco Wall painting – durable through application to wet plaster.

Gothic Architectural style of the thirteenth to sixteenth centuries, characterized by pointed arches, rib vaulting, flying buttresses and a general emphasis on verticality.

Majolica A type of glazed pottery (see p.130).

Nave Main body of a church.

Neoclassical Architectural style derived from Greek and Roman elements – pillars, domes, colonnades and so on – that was popular in the late eighteenth and nineteenth centuries.

Plateresque Elaborately decorative Renaissance architectural style, named for its resemblance to silversmiths' work (*platería*).

Renaissance That period of European history – beginning in Italy in the fourteenth century – that marks the end of the medieval and the beginning of the early modern era. It is defined, amongst many criteria, by an increase in classical scholarship, geographical discovery, the rise of secular values and the growth of individualism; the term is also applied to the art and architecture of the period.

Retable Altarpiece.

Romanesque Early medieval architecture distinguished by squat forms, rounded arches and naive sculpture.

Stucco Marble-based plaster used to embellish ceilings, etc.

Transept Arms of a cross-shaped church, placed at ninety degrees to nave and chancel.

Triptych Carved or painted work on three panels.

Tympanum Sculpted, usually recessed, panel above a door.

Vault An arched ceiling or roof.

Small print and index

283 Small print

284 About the author

285 Index

291 Map symbols

A ROUGH GUIDE TO ROUGH GUIDES

Published in 1982, the first Rough Guide – to Greece – was a student scheme that became a publishing phenomenon. Mark Ellingham, a recent graduate in English from Bristol University, had been travelling in Greece the previous summer and couldn't find the right guidebook. With a small group of friends he wrote his own guide, combining a highly contemporary, journalistic style with a thoroughly practical approach to travellers' needs.

The immediate success of the book spawned a series that rapidly covered dozens of destinations. And, in addition to impecunious backpackers, Rough Guides soon acquired a much broader readership that relished the guides' wit and inquisitiveness as much as their enthusiastic, critical approach and value-for-money ethos.

These days, Rough Guides include recommendations from budget to luxury and cover more than 200 destinations around the globe, as well as producing an ever-growing range of eBooks and apps.

Visit **roughguides.com** to see our latest publications.

Rough Guide credits

Editor: Amanda Tomlin
Layout: Anita Singh
Cartography: Swati Handoo
Picture editor: Sarah Cummins
Proofreader: Samantha Cook
Managing editor: Monica Woods
Assistant editor: Dipika Dasgupta
Production: Charlotte Cade
Cover design: Nicole Newman, Anita Singh

Editorial assistant: Olivia Rawes
Senior pre-press designer: Dan May
Design director: Scott Stickland
Travel publisher: Joanna Kirby
Digital travel publisher: Peter Buckley
Operations coordinator: Helen Blount
Publishing director (Travel): Clare Currie
Commercial manager: Gino Magnotta
Managing director: John Duhigg

Publishing information

This sixth edition published May 2013 by
Rough Guides Ltd,
80 Strand, London WC2R 0RL
11, Community Centre, Panchsheel Park,
New Delhi 110017, India
Distributed by the Penguin Group
Penguin Books Ltd,
80 Strand, London WC2R 0RL
Penguin Group (USA)
345 Hudson Street, NY 10014, USA
Penguin Group (Australia)
250 Camberwell Road, Camberwell,
Victoria 3124, Australia
Penguin Group (NZ)
67 Apollo Drive, Mairangi Bay, Auckland 1310,
New Zealand
Penguin Group (South Africa)
Block D, Rosebank Office Park, 181 Jan Smuts Avenue,
Parktown North, Gauteng, South Africa 2193
Rough Guides is represented in Canada by Tourmaline
Editions Inc. 662 King Street West, Suite 304, Toronto,
Ontario M5V 1M7
Printed in Italy by L.E.G.O. S.p.A., Lavis (TN)

© Phil Lee, 2013
Maps © Rough Guides
No part of this book may be reproduced in any form
without permission from the publisher except for the
quotation of brief passages in reviews.
296pp includes index
A catalogue record for this book is available from the
British Library
ISBN: 978-1-40936-380-4
The publishers and authors have done their best to
ensure the accuracy and currency of all the information
in **The Rough Guide to Mallorca & Menorca**, however,
they can accept no responsibility for any loss, injury, or
inconvenience sustained by any traveller as a result of
information or advice contained in the guide.
3 5 7 9 8 6 4 2

MIX
Paper from
responsible sources
FSC™ C018179
www.fsc.org

Help us update

We've gone to a lot of effort to ensure that the sixth
edition of **The Rough Guide to Mallorca & Menorca** is
accurate and up-to-date. However, things change – places
get "discovered", opening hours are notoriously fickle,
restaurants and rooms raise prices or lower standards. If
you feel we've got it wrong or left something out, we'd like
to know, and if you can remember the address, the price,
the hours, the phone number, so much the better.

Please send your comments with the subject line
"**Rough Guide Mallorca & Menorca Update**" to ✉ mail
@uk.roughguides.com. We'll credit all contributions and
send a copy of the next edition (or any other Rough Guide
if you prefer) for the very best emails.

Find more travel information, connect with fellow
travellers and book your trip on ⓦ roughguides.com

ABOUT THE AUTHOR

Phil Lee has been writing for Rough Guides for well over twenty years. His other books in the series include Canada, Norway, Belgium & Luxembourg, Norfolk & Suffolk, and England. He lives in Nottingham, where he was born and raised.

Acknowledgements

Phil Lee would like to thank his editor, Amanda Tomlin, for her help in the preparation of this new edition of Mallorca & Menorca. Special thanks also to Roger Norum – sterling stuff as ever – and Patrick Alexander for their help with the update; Maria Peterson for her translation skills in sorting out lots of bits and pieces; Jane Stanbury for her tips and tweaks; Ferran of the *Hotel Dalt Murada* for his excellent advice, hospitality and assistance in Palma; Antonia Pascual for her hospitality in Estellencs; Richard Strutt, hiking guide extraordinaire, for his opinions and advice; James Hiscock for his hospitality and help with the wine recommendations (I could not have done it without him); Dave Robson for his Port de Sóller tips and hints; and the author Anna Nicholas for pointing me in the right direction in Sóller and for her enjoyable conversation.

Roger Norum Grand *gràcies* go to Phil Lee for think-ing of me in the first place, to Monica Woods for her organisational acumen, to Amanda Tomlin for being such a thorough and generous editor, and to Patrick Alexander for contributory companionship both pre- and post-field. On the islands, my gratitude goes to Lindsay Mullen, Victoria Bendito, Pere Sales, Lana Johnson, Laura Ruiz and Javier Homs for their hospitality, as well as Sam Mejias, Laura Gost and Alejandro and Lourdes Reig for insights into island society, culture, kayaking and olives.

Patrick Alexander Many thanks to Phil Lee, and to Monica Woods and Amanda Tomlin for their gracious and generous editorial support. A special thanks to Roger E. Norum for his literary and anthropological insights. Many humble thanks to all the hospitable and talkative souls in Mallorca who made the research and writing process a pleasure. Finally, a special thanks to my wonderful wife Laura.

Readers' letters

Thanks to all the readers who have taken the time to write in with comments and suggestions (and apologies if we've inadvertently omitted or misspelt anyone's name):

Jim Ainsworth; Roger Berkley; Peter Bettess; Joan B. Bonnín; Christopher Bowers; Derek Brampton; Philip Burnard; Tom Coley; Stephan Conradi; Malcolm Curtis; Rosie Davies; Padraig & Barbara Doyle; William J. Drake; Diana Godden; Jackie Herbst; Carl Jackson; Coloma Jaume; Mike Kerr; Thomas Leppard; Leticia Lope; Carmela Lo Presti; Yvonne McFarlane; M. J. D. Mackenzie; Richard McLellan; Judy Mallett; S. F. A. Martin; Eric Milesi; Andy Mitter; Jean Mountfield; Clive Paul; Andy & Carol Pead; Tom Pritchard; Karolina Roziecka; Jacopo Rumi; Alan & Claire Russell; Peter Tasker; David Taylor; Judy Taylor; Ronald Turnbull; Judith Weller; Paul Westlake; Claire Woodward-Nutt.

Photo credits

All photos © Rough Guides except the following:
(Key: t-top; c-centre; b-bottom; l-left; r-right)

p.1 Alamy: Robert Harding World Images
p.2 Corbis: AWL
p.4 Alamy: LOOK Die Bildagentur der Fotografen GmbH (c); Corbis: AWL (r)
p.7 Alamy: Greg Balfour Evans (tr); Corbis: SOPA (b)
p.8 Alamy: Robert Harding World Imagery
p.9 Alamy: LOOK Die Bildagentur der Fotografen GmbH
p.11 Alamy: Ed Holt
p.12 Alamy: LOOK Die Bildagentur der Fotografen GmbH
p.13 Getty Images: LOOK (tl); Alamy: Avatra Images (c); Alamy: Stephen French (b)
p.14 Alamy: Robert Harding World Imagery (b)
p.15 Alamy: Travel Division Images (tl); Jon Arnold Images Ltd (tr); Corbis: O. Alamany & E. Vicens (bl); AWL (br)
p.16 Alamy: Eric James (t); Corbis: Douglas Pearson (b)
p.17 Alamy: AWL (tl); Robert John (tr)
p.18 Alamy: Novarc Images (tl).
p.20 Alamy: Novarc Images
p.42 Corbis: Jon Hicks
p.45 Alamy: Peter Barritt
p.63 Corbis: JAI (tr); Alamy: Jon Arnold Images (br)

p.79 Alamy: Greg Balfour Evans
p.113 Alamy: Avatra Images
p.122 Corbis: SOPA
p.25 Corbis: Robert Harding
p.143 Corbis: Douglas Pearson
p.154 Corbis: Robert Harding
p.157 Alamy: LOOK Die Bildagentur der Fotografen GmbH
p.171 Alamy: Blickwinkel
p.185 Alamy: LOOK Die Bildagentur der Fotografen Gmb (t); Alamy: Bon Appetit (br)
p.190 Corbis: AWL Images
p.233 Alamy: Greg Balfour
p.240 Corbis: Robert Harding Images
p.262 Corbis: Minden Pictures

Front cover Calò des Moro, Mallorca © Massimo Ripani/SIME/4Corners
Back cover Almudaina Palace and Cathedral of Palma de Mallorca © Paul Thompson/Corbis (t); Soller © Hemis/Alamy; Es Calo des Marmols beach © Pep Roig/Alamy

Index

Maps are marked in grey

A

accommodation...............25–27
accommodation prices.............27
agrotourism.................................27
airport, Mallorca.........................69
airport, Menorca.......................195
Alaior..220
Alaró...102
Albarca valley............................131
Alcúdia.......................................144
Alcúdia...................................... 145
Alcúdia, Badía d'......................144
Alcúdia peninsula........147–149
Alfàbia, Jardins d'.......................99
Alfonso III.................................248
Almohads, the...........................246
Almoravides, the......................246
Amortadhas, the......................246
Andratx.......................................118
Anglada Camarasa, Hermen....66
Antich, Francesc.......................257
Aqualand.....................................85
aquarium, Palma........................84
Archduke Ludwig Salvator....107, 108
Arenal d'en Castell...................214
Art Centre, Andratx.................118
Artà................................ 167–170
Artà.. 168
Artà caves..................................176
artificial pearls.........................166
ATMs...39
Autonomous Communities, creation of..............................255

B

Badía d'Alcúdia.........................144
Badía de Palma.................78–85
Balearic cuisine.........................278
banks...39
Banyalbufar................................116
Barbarossa, Hizir......................251
Bardolet, José Coll....................130
Barranc de Biniaraix...................98
Barranc de Binigaus.................224
Bauzà, José Ramón..................258
beach sports................................33
beaches...............................11, 78
Beaker People............................242
beer...31
Benàssar, Dionis.......................134

Betlem, Ermita de.....................170
bibliography................267–270
bicycle rental...............................25
Biniaraix.......................................98
Binibona.....................................132
Binigaus, Barranc de................224
Binissalem.................... 159–160
Binissalem................................ 160
birdlife (Mallorca).........261–265
birdlife (Menorca)....... 262–263, 265–266
birdwatching (Mallorca)
....261–265
birdwatching (Menorca)
.............................262–263, 265–266
birdwatching books.................268
black pig, Mallorcan..................77
black vulture.......6, 141, 261, 262
boat trips, Port de Maó...........206
bocadillos.....................................28
Bodega José Luis Ferrer..........160
bodegas...29
Bonaire......................................147
Bonany, Ermita de Nostra Senyora de..............................162
books...........................267–270
Bóquer valley.............................141
botanical gardens........93, 99, 131
brandy...31
breakdown, vehicle....................24
British occupation of Menorca
....251–253
Bunyola................................91, 100
buses......................................23, 70
Byng, Admiral John..................198
Byzantine rule..........................245

C

Ca N'Alluny...............................104
Ca'n Pastilla................................84
Ca'n Picafort.................... 144, 150
Cabrera, Illa de 188
boats to..................................189
visitor centre........................184
Cabrera National Park............188
Cala Agulla................................173
Cala Banyalbufar......................117
Cala Bóquer..............................141
Cala d'Alcalfar..........................213
Cala Deià....................................105
Cala d'Or....................................180
Cala en Porter................. 212, 214
Cala Esmerelda.........................181

Cala Estellencs..........................118
Cala Figuera (Mallorca)...........183
Cala Figuera (Menorca) 208
Cala Fornells...............................83
Cala Galdana.............................226
Cala Gat............................ 173, 175
Cala Gran...................................181
Cala Llonga................................181
Cala Macarella..........................227
Cala Macarelleta.......................227
Cala Major........................... 80, 83
Cala Mesquida...........................173
Cala Mitjana.............................227
Cala Mondragó.........................182
Cala Morell...............................239
Cala Padera...............................208
Cala Pregonda...........................219
Cala Rajada 173–175
Cala Rajada.............................. 174
Cala Sa Torreta..........................217
Cala Sant Esteve.......................211
Cala Sant Vicenç.......................137
Cala Sant Vicenç..................... 137
Cala Santandria.........................239
Cala Santanyí.............................183
Cala Tuent..................................128
Cala Turqueta............................238
Calderers de Sant Joan, Els
....165
calent...201
Cales Fonts................................210
Calvià..82
Camí d'en Kane.........................220
Camí de Cavalls.........34, 195, 209
Camp de Mar...............................83
camping..............................27, 28
Campos.......................................189
Can Prohom.................................92
Can Prunera Museu Modernista
....93
Canyamel, Platja de.................176
canyoning....................................33
Cap de Capdepera.....................173
Cap de Cavalleria......................218
Cap de Favàritx.........................216
Cap de Formentor....................142
Cap de Ses Salines....................184
Capdepera..................................172
Capdepera, Cap de...................173
car and ferry travel from the UK
....22
car rental......................................24
Caragol, Platja des....................184
Carlists.......................................253
Carthaginians, the....................243

casas de huéspedes 26
Castell d'Alaró 102
Castell de Santueri 180
Castilian 271, 272
Castilian menu reader
.... **275–279**
Catalan 271, 272
Catalan menu reader... 275–279
catamaran companies 22
  between Mallorca and Menorca ...22
  from Ibiza 22
  from mainland Spain 22
  inter-island 203
  to Menorca 234
cava 29
Cavalleria, Cap de 218
Cavalls, Camí de 34
cave culture, Balearic 241
caves
  Artà 176
  Cala Morell 239
  Drac 178
  Son Bou 221
  Xoroi 214
CCA Andratx 118
cell phones...................................... 40
cellers.................................... 29, 31
cervesa.. 31
Charlemagne 245
Charles V, Emperor 251
cheese, Menorcan 226
cheese-making plant, Ferreries
....226
chemists.. 38
Chiesa, Giuseppe 198
Chiesa, Joan 198
child-minding 41
children, travelling with............ 41
Chopin, Frédéric............... 109, 110
Ciutadella 228–237
Ciutadella 229
Civil War, Spanish.......................254
climate... 36
climate change............................... 21
clothing sizes................................. 35
Cocons, Torrent des 170
coffee 31
cognac... 31
Coll de Sóller 93
Colom, Illa d'en..............................216
Colònia de Sant Jordi
.... **184–188**
Colònia de Sant Jordi 186
Colònia de Sant Pere...............170
Columbus, Christopher 180
condoms... 38
Convent de Sant Vicenç Ferrer
....166
Cornadors, Es 98
costs, average 36
Cova Blava, Sa 189
Cova d'en Xoroi 214

Cova dels Coloms 224
Coves d'Artà 176
Coves del Drac...............................178
Covetes, Ses 188
credit cards 39
crime 36
crossbow-making 249
Cúber Reservoir............................128
cuisine 278
Cura, Santuari de Nostra
  Senyora de 164
currency exchange 39
cycling 25
Cyclopean walls 202

D

Davallament, the 32, 135
debit cards 39
Deià 103–107
Deià 103
Deià Archeological Museum... 105
Despuig, Cardinal Antonio...... 69,
  100
dictionaries 271
disabilities, travellers with........ 41
diving, scuba 34
doctors 38
Dolors, Església Nostra Senyora
  Verge dels 166
Douglas, Michael 107
Drac caves 178
Dragonera, Parc Natural de Sa
....119
drinks 29–31
driving 24
  licences 24
  rules 24
  to the Balearics from the UK........ 22
Dry-stone Route (GR221).........34,
  90, 127

E

eating and drinking 28–31
EEA reciprocal health
  arrangements 38
EHIC 38
El Encinar 169
electricity.. 37
Els Calderers de Sant Joan 165
email... 38
Embassament de Cúber..........128
embassies, Spanish.....................37
emergency numbers.................. 37
Encinar, El 169
ensaimada 28
entry requirements.................... 36
Ermita de Betlem......................170

Ermita de la Victòria 147
Ermita de Nostra Senyora de
  Bonany 162
Ermita de Nostra Senyora del
  Puig, Pollença............... 135, 136
Ermita de St Joan de Missa....238
Es Castell 209
Es Cornadors 98
Es Grau 215, 216
Es Mercadal....................................222
Es Migjorn Gran 223
Es Pla 156
Es Portixol 84
Es Prat 216
Es Trenc 188
Escorca 129
Església Nostra Senyora Verge
  dels Dolors 166
Esporles 116
Estellencs 117
ETA..258
EU reciprocal health
  arrangements 38
euro, the.. 39
Eurotunnel 22
exchange rate 39
exchange, currency 39

F

fauna, flora and....259–266, 268
Favàritx, Cap de...........................216
Felanitx 179
Fernando V....................................250
Ferrer, Bodega José Luis..........160
Ferrer, José 30
Ferreries 225
ferries
  between Mallorca and Menorca
....22
  from Ibiza 22
  from mainland Spain....................22
  in Alcúdia (to Menorca)...............151
  inter-island 151, 203
ferry companies 22
ferry terminal, Palma.................70
ferry terminals, Menorca........203,
  234
ferry travel, car and, from the UK
....22
festivals...............................32–33
field guides (fauna and flora)
....268
fincas 10, 27
flights
  between Mallorca and Menorca
....22
  from Australia.............................. 21
  from Canada.................................. 21
  from Ibiza 22
  from Ireland.................................. 21

from mainland Spain.........................22
from New Zealand............................21
from South Africa............................21
from the UK.....................................21
from the USA....................................21
flora and fauna............ 259–266, 268
flowers, wild 260
fondas 26
Fondejador des Llanes 216
food and drink menu reader
....**275–279**
Foradada, Sa.................................108
Formentor Hotel...........................144
Formentor peninsula 142
Formentor, Cap de 142
Fornalutx 98
Fornells 216–218
Fort Marlborough.........................211
Fort Sant Felip..............................211
Franco 254, 255
Franja Roja 30
French occupation of Menorca
....252
Fundació Pilar i Joan Miró 80
Fundació Yannick i Ben Jakober
....147
Fuster, Joan....................................111

G

gardens
  Alfàbia..99
  La Granja..112
  Lluc..131
  Raixa..100
  Sóller...93
gas...24
Gaudí, Antoni..................................51
gay and lesbian travellers 37
Germania...250
gin...31
gin distillery (Xoriguer), Maó
....201
glossary
  architectural terms.....................280
  art terms..280
  Catalan terms...............................280
GOB (Grup Balear d'Ornitologia i
  Defensa de la Naturalesa)
....259
Golden Farm..................................211
Gordiola glassworks 163
Gorg Blau.......................................127
GR221........................ 34, 90, 127
  Biniaraix..98
  Gorg Blau.......................................128
  Sant Elm...119
Grau, Parc Natural S'Albufera des
....215
Graves, Robert..............................104

Greeks, the 243
Grup Balear d'Ornitologia i
  Defensa de la Naturalesa
  (GOB)...259
guides, hiking 90

H

Hannibal 244
health...37
Hidalgo, Eugenio 257
Hidropark 151
hierbas 201
hikes
  Alcúdia peninsula.........................148
  Alcúdia peninsula 149
  Barranc de Biniaraix 98
  Es Cornadors....................................98
  Es Grau to Sa Torreta.............216–217
  Es Grau to Sa Torreta 215
  Es Migjorn Gran to the coast.......224
  Es Migjorn Gran to the coast
  ....**225**
  La Trapa..119
  Maó to Punta Prima 208–209
  Maó to Punta Prima 210
  Port de Pollença to Cala Bóquer
 141
  Port de Pollença to Cala Bóquer
  ....**139**
  Serra de Tramuntana 90, 127
  Valldemossa to Puig d'es Teix
 114–115
  Valldemossa to Puig d'es Teix
  ....**114**
hikers' hostels....... 27, 90, 97, 102,
  106, 127, 128, 131
hiking 33–34
  books, specialist 270
  guides 90
  guidebooks and maps 34
history 241–258
holidays, public..............................39
Homar, Catalina............................107
horseriding 33
Hort de Sant Patrici cheese
  plant, Menorca 226
hospital treatment 37
hostales...26
hostal-residencias...........................26
hotel-residencias.............................26
hotels..26
hotels d'interior 26
hypostyles.....................................242

I

Illa d'en Colom...........................216
Illa de Cabrera.............................188
Illa del Llatzeret.................206, 212
Illa del Rei 206, 208

Illa Pinto 206
Illa Quarentena............................206
Illetes...81, 83
Inca..160
Inquisition, Spanish 250
insurance, travel...........................38
inter-island ferries 22
inter-island flights 22
internet access..............................38
Isabella I..250
itineraries..18
IVA tax......................................29, 36

J

Jaime Mascaró shop.................226
Jakober, Fundació Yannick i Ben
....147
Jardí Botànic (Sóller)..................93
Jardins d'Alfàbia 99
Jaume I 246–248
Jaume II................................248, 249
Jaume III...249
Jaume IV...249
Jews, the 61, 250
José Ferrer 30

K

Kane, Camí d'en...........................220
Kane, Richard 198, 220, 252
Knights Templar............................62

L

La Granja...112
La Mola..212
La Trapa..119
language 271–279
lesbian travellers, gay and........37
Lilfords wall lizard...........189, 264
Lithica Pedreres de S'hostal
....228
Llenaire (Hotel Llenaire)..........140
Llevant, Serres de ...156, 167, 170
Lluc monastery..............................129
Llucalcari (Hotel Costa d'Or)
....106
Llucmajor.......................................189
Llull, Ramon................62, 164, 249

M

Magaluf 82
magazines...31
Mahon ....see Maó

mail 38
majolica 130
Mallorca airport 69
Mallorcan cuisine 278
Mallorcan Primitives (painters)
   Alcúdia 146
   Palma 50–51, 55–56, 59
   Pollença 134
Manacor 165–167
Maó 196–205
Maó 197
Maó, Port de 206–212
maps
   hiking 34
   road 39
Maravelles, Ses 84
March, Joan 56, 57
March, Palau Joan (Cala Rajada)
   173
Marineland 81
Marivent, Palacio de 80
markets, open-air 36
Marlborough, Fort 211
Mascaró, Jaime, shop 226
Massanella, Puig de 128
Massís d' Artà 170
Maura, Antoni 64
mayonnaise, origins of 204
media, the 31
medical treatment 37
Menorca 192–239
Menorca 194
   airport 195
   ferry terminals (Maó) 203
Menorca, Museu de 200
Menorcan cuisine 278–279
menú del día 29
menu reader 275–279
mercats (open-air markets) 36
Migjorn Gran, Es 223
Miquel Oliver 31
Miramar 108
Miró, Joan 66, 91
Miró, Joan (Fundació) 80
mobile phones 40
Modernista, Can Prunera Museu
   93
Mola, General 66
Mola, La 212
monastery accommodation ... 26
   Alcúdia peninsula 147
   Lluc 131
   near Felanitx 180
   near Petra 163
   Pollença 136
   Puig Randa 165
Mondragó Parc Natural 182
Monestir de Lluc 129
Monestir de Nostra Senyora de
   Lluc 129
Monte Toro 222
Moors, the 245

Mora, Juan Hernández 198
mountain refuges (Mallorca)
   27
Mozarabs, the 246
Muro 152
Museu de Menorca 200
Myotragus balearicus 105

N

Na Macaret 214
Naveta d'es Tudons 227
navetas 202, 243
Nelson, Admiral Horatio 211
Newman, Philip 134
newspapers 31
Northern Mallorca 122–153
Northern Mallorca 126

O

Oliver, Antoni Ribas 130
Oliver, Miquel 31
Orfila, Mateu Josep 201
Orient 100

P

pa amb oli 28
Països, Ses 167
Palacio de Marivent 80
Palau Joan March (Cala Rajada)
   173
Palma 44–78
Palma 48–49
Palma and around 46
Palma, Central 52–53
   accommodation 71–73
   airport 69
   Ajuntament 64
   Antoni Maura, Avinguda d' 64
   Arc de L'Almudaina 60
   Argentina, Avinguda 65
   arrival 69
   Avinguda d'Antoni Maura 64
   Avinguda Jaume III 65
   Baluard, Es 66
   Banys Àrabs 58
   bars, late-night 75
   bars, tapas 73
   Basílica de Sant Francesc 61
   beaches 78
   bicycles 71
   bike rental 71
   books 77
   bus station 70
   buses 70
   cafés 73
   Caixa Forum art gallery 66
   Can Alomar 65

Can Balaguer 66
Can Bordils 60
Can Moner 65
Can Oleza 60
Can Pavesi 65
Can Rei 67
Can Solleric 65
Can Vivot 61
car rental 71
carriage, horse and 71
Castell de Bellver 66
Cathedral 47–54
chemists 78
city tours 71
clubs 76
Consolat de Mar 68
consulates 78
Corte Inglés, El 65, 77
crafts, shopping 77
directory 78
drink, shopping 77
driving 70
eating and drinking 73–75
El Corte Inglés 65, 77
El Puig de Sant Pere 65
Es Baluard museu d'art 66
Feixina, La 65
ferry terminal 70
food, shopping 77
football 76
Gaudí, Antoni (Palma) 51
Gran Hotel 66
guided tours 71
harbourfront 68
horse and carriage 71
hotels 71–73
Jaume III, Avinguda 65
L'Àguila 67
La Feixina 65
La Ruta Martiana 75
libraries 78
Llotja, Sa 68
Llull, Ramon 62
mansions in Palma 60
maps 77
March, Joan 57
markets 78
Martiana, La Ruta 75
Museu de la Catedral 50
Museu de Mallorca 58
Museu Diocesà 55
Museu Fundació Juan March 67
nightclubs 76
old town 58
orientation 47
Palau de l'Almudaina 54–55
Palau March 56
Palma 44–78
Parc de la Mar 58
Parc Quarentena 68
parking 70
Passeig d'es Born 64
Passeig Mallorca 65
performing arts 76
pharmacies 78
Plaça Cort 64
Plaça de la Reina 64
Plaça Major 67

Plaça Marquès del Palmer 67
Plaça Mercat 66
Plaça Weyler 66
Poble Espanyol 68
Portella gateway 58
post office..78
Primitives, Mallorcan (painters)
............................50–51, 55–56, 59
railways..70
Ramon Llull 62
restaurants..74
Ruta Martiana, La 75
Sa Llotja..68
Sant Francesc, Basilica de 61
Sant Jeroni, church of 62
Sant Miquel, church of 67
Sant Pere, El Puig de 65
Santa Eulalia, church of 60
shopping.......................................76–78
tapas bars 73
taxis...71
Teatre Principal 76
Templar chapel 62
theatres...76
tourist offices 71
tours, guided 71
train station 70
trains..70
transport, city 70
Unió, Carrer 66
walls, city.......................................56–58
Palma Aquarium 84
Palma Nova.......................................82
palo...201
Parc Natural de Sa Dragonera
....119
Parc Natural de S'Albufera......152
Parc Natural S'Albufera des Grau
....215
Parc Natural, Mondragó..........182
Park, Cabrera National.............188
parks, regional and national
....34
passports...37
pearls, artificial 166
Pedra en Sec, Ruta de 34, 90, 127
Pedreres de S'hostal, Lithica
....228
Pedro IV...249
Pedro, King......................................248
Peguera..82
Península de Formentor 142
pensions 26
Perlas Majorica pearl factory
....166
Petra 162
petrol 24
pharmacies 38
Phoenicians, the 243
phones 40
phrasebooks.....................................271
phylloxera..30
Picasso, Pablo.............................66, 91

pinxtos 29
Platges Son Saura......................238
Platja Cala Comtesa 81
Platja de Binimel-Là.....................219
Platja de Canyamel 176
Platja de Cavalleria....................219
Platja de Ferragut.....................219
Platja de Formentor...................142
Platja de Palma...............................84
Platja des Caragol......................184
Platja Sant Adeodat....................225
Platja Sant Tomàs 225
police, the..37
Pollença 132–136
Pollença 133
Pollentia...146
pomada...201
Port d'Addaia..................................214
Port d'Andratx 120–121
Port d'Andratx......................121
Port d'Alcúdia..................................149
Port d'Alcúdia 150
Port de Maó....................................206
Port de Maó boat trips 206
Port de Pollença...........138–141
Port de Pollença....................139
Port de Sanitja 219
Port de Sóller....................95–98
Port de Sóller 96
Port de Sóller tram......................91, 93
Port de Valldemossa.......................112
Portals Nous 81, 84
Portixol, Es..84
Porto Colom 179
Porto Cristo.................176–179
Porto Cristo.........................177
Porto Petro......................................181
post..38
prickly pear 260
Primitives, Mallorcan (painters)
    Alcúdia.....................................146
    Palma................50–51, 55–56, 59
Pollença..134
Prohom, Can.....................................92
public holidays 39
Puig d'es Teix..................................115
Puig de l'Àguila..............................137
Puig de Massanella 128
Puig Major.......................127, 128
Puig Randa......................................164
Puig Roig...131
Punic Wars.....................................244
Punta de S'Escullar........................239
Punta Prima....................................209

Q

Quadrado, Josep..............230, 254
Queso Mahon 226

R

racions...29
radio 32
Rafalet Nou 209
rail contacts 24
rainfall...36
Raixa..100
Ramís, Juli (in Valldemossa)...111
Ramon Llull................62, 164, 249
Randa................................164, 165
Reconquista 246–248
refugi (hikers' hostels)........27, 90, 97, 102, 106, 127, 128, 131
Rissaga, The 234
Roman remains (Alcúdia) 146
Romans, the....................................244
romerias 32
Rubió, Joan 92
Ruta de Pedra en Sec 34, 90, 127

S

S'Albufera, Parc Natural de.....152
S'Albufera des Grau, Parc Natural
....215
S'Algar...209
S'Arenal..84
S'Arracó...119
S'Atalaia campsite 227
S'Estaca...107
Sa Calobra 128
Sa Dragonera, Parc Natural de
....119
Sa Foradada...................................108
Sa Torreta.......................................217
safety, personal 36
Sagrera, Guillermo 68
Salines de Llevant 188
Salvator, Ludwig 107, 108
Sancho, King....................................249
Sand, George 109, 110, 270
Sanisera.............................219, 243
Sanitja, Port de 219
Sant Elm...119
Sant Felip, Fort..............................211
Sant Jaume Mediterrani..........222
Sant Joan de Missa, Ermita de
....238
Sant Lluís 213
Sant Salvador, Santuari de (Artà)
....167
Sant Tomàs.....................................225
Sant Vicenç Ferrer, Convent de
....166
Santa Catalina Thomàs...........111
Santa Ponça....................................82
Santanyí...182

Santuari de Gràcia......................164
Santuari de Nostra Senyora de Cura 164
Santuari de Sant Honorat.......164
Santuari de Sant Salvador (Puig de Sant Salvador) 180
Santuari de Sant Salvador (Artà) 167
Santueri, Castell de 180
sausages, Mallorcan 77
scuba diving 34, 218
Selva 132
Serra de Tramuntana.........88, 124
Serra, Junipero...................61, 162
Serres de Llevant 156, 167, 170
Sert, Josep Maria 56
Ses Covetes................................188
Ses Maravelles 84
Ses Països....................................167
Ses Salines, Cap de 184
sherry 31
shoe sizes 35
shopping 35
Sineu 161
siurells 77
slingers, Balearic 244
smoking (regulations)................40
Sóller **91–95**
Sóller 92
Sóller train 91, 93
Sóller tunnel 93
Sometimes 84
Son Amer....................................131
Son Bou......................................221
Son Catlar...................................238
Son Marroig................................107
Son Parc 214
Southern Mallorca 156–189
Southern Mallorca 158
Spanish (language).........271, 272
Spanish Civil War 254
Spanish embassies.......................37
Spanish Inquisition 250
Spanish menu reader... 275–279
sparkling wine, Spanish 29
speed limits 24
spirits..31
sports..33
St James the Greater...............159

T

Tafona de Son Fang, Sa 170
Talatí de Dalt 202
Talayotic period, Menorca....200, 202, 232, 242
Talayotic sites, Menorca 202
talayots 195, 202, 242
Tamarells des Nord 217

tapas...29
taulas 202, 242
tavernas 29
taxes, local (IVA) 29, 36
taxis 25
tea 31
Teix, Puig d'es............................115
telephones 40
television 32
temperatures 36
Templar, Knights 62
terrorism (in Mallorca)............258
theme parks
    Aqualand...................................85
    Hidropark...............................151
    Western Water Park...............82
Thomàs, Santa Catalina 111
time zones 40
tipping...................................36, 40
toad, Mallorcan midwife.........264
Torralba d'en Salord..................221
Torre d'Alcalfar Vell..................209
Torre d'en Gaumés 221
Torre d'en Penyat......................209
Torre de Sanitja 219
Torre Saura.................................238
Torrellafuda................................227
Torrenova......................................82
Torrent de Pareis............. 128, 129
Torrent, José Roberto...............234
Tossals Verds.............................128
tour operators.............................23
tourist information......................40
tourist offices...............................40
train contacts 24
trains
    from Palma 70
    from the UK 22
    in Mallorca 23
    to Sóller.............................91, 93
tram to Port de Sóller 91, 93
Tramuntana, Serra de 88, 124
Trapa, La.....................................119
travel agents................................23
travel insurance..........................38
travellers' cheques......................39
Trenc, Es.....................................188
tunnel to Sóller...........................93

V

Vall de Bóquer 141
Valldemossa.................. 108–112
Valldemossa 109
Vandals, the 245
vegan food...................................29
vegetarian food...........................29
Vicenç, Martí..............................134
Victòria, Ermita de la 147
Vikings, the 246

Villalonga, Llorenç....................159
Vin de la Terra 31
visas..37
vulture, black.......6, 141, 261, 262

W

Waldren, Jacqueline 105
Waldren, William.......................105
walking 33–34
    guidebooks, specialist............270
    guides 90
    maps...34
walks
    Alcúdia peninsula 148
    Alcúdia peninsula 149
    Barranc de Biniaraix 98
    Es Cornadors............................98
    Es Grau to Sa Torreta.....216–217
    Es Grau to Sa Torreta 215
    Es Migjorn Gran to the coast....224
    Es Migjorn Gran to the coast.. 225
    La Trapa 119
    Maó to Punta Prima.......208–209
    Maó to Punta Prima 210
    Port de Pollença to Cala Bóquer 141
    Port de Pollença to Cala Bóquer 139
    Serra de Tramuntana 90, 127
    Valldemossa to Puig d'es Teix 114–115
    Valldemossa to Puig d'es Teix 114
weather 36
Western Mallorca............86–121
Western Mallorca 90
Western Water Park...................82
windsurfing 34, 218
wine, Mallorcan 30
wine, Mallorcan (Binissalem) 160
wine, Spanish 29

X

Xoriguer gin distillery 201
Xoroi, Cova d'en 214
Xuroy beach 209

Y

Yannick i Ben Jakober, Fundació 147

Z

zebra crossings............................24
ziggurats............................ 192, 219

Map symbols

The symbols below are used on maps throughout the book

- ✈ Airport
- ★ Bus stop
- 🅿 Parking
- ✉ Post office
-)(Bridge
- ∩ Arch
- ⌒ Cave

- ♦ Place of interest
- ♛ Castle
- 🏛 Stately home
- ♦ Museum
- ⚲ Lighthouse
- ⚶ Viewpont
- ▲ Mountain peak

- Building
- Church
- ⚐ Church (regional)
- ⌂ Monastery
- Park

Listings key

- ■ Accommodation
- ● Café /restaurant/tapas bar
- ■ Late-night bar
- ● Shop

ROUGH GUIDES
A CHRONOLOGY

1982 The First *Rough Guide to Greece* – written and researched by Mark Ellingham, John Fisher and Nat Jansz – is published, shortly followed by Spain and Portugal **1983** *Amsterdam* – written by Martin Dunford – is published **1986** The first Rough Guides' offices set up in Kennington, South London **1987** Rough Guides set up as independent company **1989** BBC2 commission a Rough Guides TV series presented by Magenta Devine and Sankha Guha

1990 Rough Guides first published in the US under the name The Real Guides **1994** The first Reference titles – *World Music*, *Classical Music* and *The Internet* – are published • World Music Network starts selling Rough Guides compilation CDs **1995** roughguides.com is launched **1997** New York office set up

2001 First eBooks launched **2002** Rough Guides moves to Penguin headquarters at 80 Strand, London • Delhi office established • Rip-proof city maps series launched **2003** New colour sections added to the guides • First commissioned photographic shoots take place **2004** The *Rough Guide to a Better World* published in association with DFID **2006** First full-colour Rough Guide – *World Party* – is published • **2007** 25s series launched in honour of the 25th anniversary • *Make the Most of Your Time on Earth* becomes best-selling RG and is nominated in Richard and Judy Book Club awards **2008** A new RG TV series is broadcast on Channel 5 **2009** The first hardback picture book – *Earthbound* – featuring our commissioned photography goes on sale

2010 All guides are printed on FCO approved paper **2011** The new full-colour Pocket Guides series is launched • The first city guide iPhone/iPad apps are released **2012** Rough Guides' travel books are relaunched in time for our 30th anniversary, using full colour throughout • The first Rough Guide eBooks made specifically for the iPad go on sale **2013** roughguides.com is relaunched

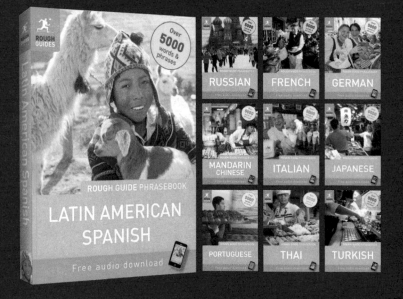